The Infamous
Dakota War Trials
of 1862

# The Infamous Dakota War Trials of 1862

*Revenge, Military Law and the Judgment of History*

JOHN A. HAYMOND

McFarland & Company, Inc., Publishers
*Jefferson, North Carolina*

LIBRARY OF CONGRESS CATALOGUING-IN-PUBLICATION DATA

Names: Haymond, John A., 1967– author.
Title: The infamous Dakota War Trials of 1862 : revenge, military law and the judgment of history / John A. Haymond.
Description: Jefferson, North Carolina : McFarland & Company, Inc., 2016. | Includes bibliographical references and index.
Identifiers: LCCN 2016019074 | ISBN 9781476665108 (softcover : acid free paper) ∞
Subjects: LCSH: Trials (Military offenses)—Minnesota. | Trials (Military offenses)—United States. | Courts-martial and courts of inquiry—Minnesota. | Dakota Indians—Wars, 1862–1865. | Judicial error—Minnesota. | Military law—United States—History. | Military law—Minnesota—History. | Indians, Treatment of—United States. | Dakota Indians—History.
Classification: LCC KF7641 .H39 2016 | DDC 345.73/025230899752430776—dc23
LC record available at https://lccn.loc.gov/2016019074

BRITISH LIBRARY CATALOGUING DATA ARE AVAILABLE

ISBN (print) 978-1-4766-6510-8
ISBN (ebook) 978-1-4766-2507-2

© 2016 John A. Haymond. All rights reserved

*No part of this book may be reproduced or transmitted in any form or by any means, electronic or mechanical, including photocopying or recording, or by any information storage and retrieval system, without permission in writing from the publisher.*

Front cover: illustration of the execution of the 38 Sioux Indians at Mankato, Minnesota, December 25, 1862 (Library of Congress)

Printed in the United States of America

*McFarland & Company, Inc., Publishers*
*Box 611, Jefferson, North Carolina 28640*
*www.mcfarlandpub.com*

For my father,
John F. Haymond,
who introduced me to history

# Table of Contents

*Acknowledgments* — ix
*Preface* — 1
*Introduction: Beginning at an End* — 3

## Part One: The War

1. A War and Its Language — 7
2. Spark, Fuel and Fire — 11
3. The Acton Murders — 19
4. "Over the earth I come" — 24
5. "My heart is hardened" — 39

## Part Two: The Trials

6. "Ferreting out and punishing the guilty" — 47
7. The Trials Begin — 52
8. Questions of Legality — 59
9. "A species of domestic rebellion" — 65
10. Due Process and the Lack Thereof — 69
11. The Rush to Judgment — 84
12. Violation of the Law: Sibley's Error — 89

## Part Three: The Reckoning

13. March to the Gallows — 99
14. Mass Punishment — 114
15. The Executions — 119
16. Concentration Camps and Ethnic Cleansing — 126
17. The Later Military Commission Trials — 132

## Part Four: The Controversies

18. Crimes or Culture? — 141
19. "The most horrible and nameless outrages" — 152
20. "A fair fight": Crimes That Were Not Crimes — 156
21. Exaggeration, Errors and Evidence: The Atrocity Debate — 165
22. The Power of the Self-Perpetuating Myth — 184

## Part Five: The Aftermath

23. Misspelled Names, Misplaced Records and Mistaken Identities — 191
24. Confusion and Contradictions — 198
25. Oral Histories — 207
26. Victims of Every Kind — 218
27. After the Storm — 222

*Conclusion* — 226
*Notes on Sources* — 231
*Appendix: The Creation of Military Commissions* — 237
*Chapter Notes* — 239
*Bibliography* — 254
*Index* — 261

# Acknowledgments

This book came about through the assistance of many people. Dr. Bill Miller of the College of St. Scholastica and Dr. Steve Matthews of the University of Minnesota Duluth were guiding voices at the beginning of this project and at various points along the way. Dr. Mark Kilen, MD—friend, mentor and fishing companion—resolved an early organizational problem when he suggested setting the text into the five distinct parts that it now has. He also did the world more of a favor than it will ever know when he steered me away from the career in medicine that I was considering when I left the Army in 2009. Dr. Pertti Ahonen and Dr. Felix Boecking of the University of Edinburgh read early drafts of certain chapters and gave me some valuable feedback. Four chapters of this book made up the bulk of my dissertation at Edinburgh, and the well-considered insights of my dissertation supervisor, Dr. David Silkenat, were a tremendous help as I refined my arguments.

Outside the world of academia, I am indeed fortunate in my friends. My father-in-law, Brad Ingersoll, read an entire early draft (if the redundancies remain, Brad, that's my fault, not yours). Andrew Harris read everything I shoved at him, for which I owe him more than a few pints. Sue Grove also slogged through the full-length, unrevised manuscript, and her editorial notes were helpful. John Isch and Walt Bachman, both well-established voices in the coterie of Dakota War researchers, were extremely generous with their time and their wealth of knowledge, and they shared the results of their own research with me, for which I cannot thank them enough. I am also indebted to John for his help with the maps that appear in this book. Carol Chomsky graciously agreed to meet with me and discuss her foundational legal study of the Dakota War trials. Professor Chomsky and I differ in some of our conclusions, but such is the nature of scholarly debate; her article holds a well-deserved position in the historiography, and she holds a high position in my esteem. Rhoda Gilman, renowned Minnesota historian and Henry H. Sibley's biographer, was kind enough to share her insights into Sibley with me in several informative email exchanges. The staff of the Gale Family Library at the Minnesota Historical Society were incredibly helpful all the long hours I that I worked with the papers of most of the principal characters in this history. In particular Jenny McElroy, Reference Librarian at MNHS, was indispensable to the process of sorting out the necessary publication permissions for some of the materials that went into this book.

Finally, but certainly not least, my family deserves my thanks. My parents, John and Elaine Haymond, fostered an environment of reading and exploration in my childhood which has stood me in good stead ever since. My wonderful wife, Elena, provided inspiration, motivation, support and a healthy dose of reality the many times that it was needed.

To everyone who played a part in this book's long journey to publication, my thanks and appreciation for your assistance, advice and guidance. This would have been a poorer, weaker text without your contributions to the process, and I am grateful for all the suggestions, corrections and ideas. Whatever shortcomings and errors remain in these pages are mine alone.

# Preface

In the century and a half since the U.S.–Dakota War of 1862, millions of words have been written about the conflict. Much of that writing has dealt with the military commission trials that took place immediately after the war; in fact, the trials are now considered one of the most controversial parts of this contentious history. In light of that extensive literature, what does this book contribute to the discussion that previous works have not?

To put it simply, this book is a detailed legal study of the Dakota War trials from the essential perspective of military law. The 1862 trials were conducted under military law, not the civilian legal system with which most historians are familiar, and the fact that this has not always been understood or recognized has led to some frequently repeated errors in the historiography. I was a soldier before I became a professional historian, and during the 21 years I served in the U.S. Army I acquired a close familiarity with the unique characteristics and features of military law, both from study and from participation in its practice.

This book began as a narrow research project that I expected to finish quickly and then move on to other things—I had no expectation that it would develop into anything else. To my surprise, when I finished that project I discovered that the story of the Dakota War trials had become something I did not want to set aside. The more I researched the events of 1862, the more compelling and consuming the topic became for me. Part of the reason for this was that I discovered early on in the process that my military background gave me some unique insights that lead me to conclusions that differed from many of those put forward by other scholars in the field. An informed perspective of military law has for the most part been missing from the published studies of the 1862 military commission trials—that gap in the historiography was one of the things that drew me deeper into this history.

I wrote this book with two main objectives. The first was to examine the Dakota War trials in their historical context and within the specialized framework of 19th century American military law. The second purpose was to examine how commentators have depicted this history since 1862 and evaluate the accuracy of those depictions. To that end, throughout this text I review the extensive historiography of this war and engage with it directly and, it must be said, sometimes bluntly. A great deal of confusion surrounds many of the most controversial events in 1862, and it is my hope that the reader will come away from this book with at least some of that confusion resolved and the history made a bit clearer.

At the same time, there are limitations to this book that should be clearly stated here at the outset. There are some aspects of this history, particularly the antecedents and aftermath of the conflict, which I have chosen to not examine in as great a detail as others. The history of the U.S.–Dakota War of 1862 encompasses more than just the months from when the war began in August to when the executions were carried out in Mankato in December. The full span of the history includes the years prior to the principal treaties between the Dakota people and the U.S. Government, comes forward through the war itself, and continues on for generations past that point. In the chapters ahead I will consider and discuss most of these wider factors in some measure, but there are parts of this story which deserve much more extensive treatment than I have given them here. In acknowledgement of that, at the end of the book I have listed some other works on this history that can help to fill in parts of the story I have omitted here.

Also, and this is critical to understanding both what this book does and does not try to accomplish, it should be understood that this is not a history of the Dakota War written from the perspective of the Dakota people. This text is a discussion of the historical controversies and legal arguments surrounding the 1862 trials and an examination of the broader historiography of the war—it is not a cultural or anthropological study of the Dakota experience. I consider the experiences of both white people and Dakota people during the war and afterward in this text, and I examine how both white and Dakota commentators perceive the war today, but I certainly do not claim to speak for the Dakota view of the war.

The research for this book took the better part of four years, most of which was spent working with documents held in the collections of the Minnesota Historical Society and the National Archives. Minnesota has a robust and dynamic network of County Historical Societies, and the archives of the Brown, Nicollet, Renville and Blue Earth County Historical Societies in particular are invaluable to researchers studying the Dakota War. I also spent a considerable amount of time reading through the vast trove of books, articles, essays and monographs that deal with the events of 1862. As I worked on this book I was fortunate to have the opportunity to engage with many scholars who have contributed to the literature of Dakota War history. That process of discussion, debate, advice, assistance, collegial disagreement and constructive criticism was an absolutely crucial part of the process—it has been said that no research occurs in a vacuum, and that was certainly true in this case. I am not blazing a trail here so much as I am following in the footsteps of others, shining a light on parts of the path that others may have overlooked.

As will become clear in the chapters ahead, I have chosen to confront the often controversial details of this history directly, and to cite my disagreements with other scholars' conclusions clearly and unambiguously when they arise. That means naming names, citing chapter and verse of the works where I maintain that errors exist, and presenting the evidence to support my countervailing conclusions. But I have tried to state my disagreements and refutations in a fair and professional manner—I have no interest in personal quarrels, and this history would be ill served by such sniping. A work of history must stand or fall on the strength of its own arguments, and so it will be for this text. At the turn of this book's final page its ultimate contribution to the contentious scholarship of the Dakota War will be determined by you, the reader, as you decide how thoroughly it has informed you, if you have learned anything from it that you did not know before, and whether or not it has convinced you.

# Introduction
## *Beginning at an End*

The morning of December 26, 1862, was warmer than usual for a mid-winter day in Minnesota. For the 38 men who were led from a makeshift jail in the riverside town of Mankato, the relatively mild weather must have been little comfort. They were Dakota Indians, some of mixed blood and some full, but they all had one thing in common— they were condemned to death, and the path they walked led to the largest single gallows ever erected in American history. In the aftermath of the short, bloody war that erupted in August earlier that year, a military commission of five U.S. Army officers tried 391 Dakota.[1] There were 303 men sentenced to hang, but after a review of the trial records, President Abraham Lincoln confirmed the sentences of only 39. One of those men received a last-minute reprieve; the other 38 went to the gallows. When the trap dropped them to their deaths they paid the ultimate price for the crimes for which they had been convicted.

But as the decades passed and the events of 1862 fell farther into the past, questions were asked about what happened in Minnesota that year, and why, and whether or not justice was really served. Historians began to ask if those men were, in fact, criminals, and if the trials that condemned them were even legal. In the years approaching the sesquicentennial observance of the war in 2012, an increasing number of commentators argued that the trials and the subsequent hangings were flagrant miscarriages of justice.

The scene at Mankato on that day in December closed one chapter of the most violent American Indian war of the 19th century. In the long and bloody history of American territorial expansion, the U.S.–Dakota War of 1862 was unique for several reasons. It saw the greatest loss of life of any of the Indian Wars, with American casualties exceeding Dakota losses by a ratio of nearly ten to one, and women and children made up a higher percentage of those deaths than in any other war of the period.[2] This was also the only one of the Indian Wars where the Indians made concentrated, sustained attacks on towns and population centers, as happened in the case of New Ulm, Milford, and Hutchinson. The fact that such a disproportionate number of the casualties were women and children had a profound impact on public reaction to the war, and it did much to stoke the fires of Minnesotans' enmity against the Dakota in the days that followed.

But if the hangings closed one chapter, they only opened other. The 1862 conflict marked the beginning of a long series of wars that would be fought between the United States and the various tribal groups of the Sioux over most of the following three decades. There were legendary battles still to come: the Fetterman Fight; the Wagon Box Fight; the Battle of the Little Big Horn, and others that would become famous in the history of the American West. First, though, there were the battles of Fort Ridgely, Birch Coulee, and Wood Lake, all in Minnesota. Indian names such as Sitting Bull, Red Cloud, Crazy Horse and Gall would become famous in American history, but before them there was a man named Little Crow, and others such as Shakopee, Wabasha and Big Eagle. The bloodshed would go on for years, but it began in Minnesota during the summer of 1862, when members of the Mdewakanton and Wahpekute bands of the Dakota broke out in open war.

Rather than diminishing with the passage of time, the controversies surrounding the 1862 trials and executions have grown, and they continue unabated. The guilt or innocence of the men hanged at Mankato is fiercely debated by the opposing sides in the argument, but the public consensus as of this writing holds that the trials that brought them to that end were marred by allegations of undue haste and procedural irregularities. And just as at least one of the men on the gallows that day was hanged for a murder he was later shown to have not committed, so was it also true that there were other men who by rights should have had a noose around their necks, who never stood on a scaffold at all and died peacefully years later in old age.

In the following chapters we will examine the trials in detail, and along the way consider how the history of this war has been portrayed through the years. But it is not enough to simply build a legal argument that crimes were committed and the accused perpetrators were tried by a legal court (as we will see, both of those points are disputed, as well). If there were no more to it than that, there would be far less debate surrounding the proceedings of the military commission. There are other questions that also need answers: Did the Dakota defendants receive anything even remotely resembling due process in the trials? Were they legally prisoners of war, or were they marauders and criminals? Were the right men brought to trial? Is there any truth to the allegations of widespread atrocities such as mutilations, and of acts of extreme violence—women raped, children murdered, entire families wiped out—or were these claims based on hysterical exaggeration? What about the human cost of the war, and the suffering on both sides of the conflict? How do the understandings and perceptions that modern Dakota people have of this war differ from the points of view expressed by conventional European-American history?

These, and many other questions about this controversial history, are what this book will try to answer.

# Part One

# The War

*[N]ature gives men a right to employ force, when it is necessary for their defense, and for the preservation of their rights. This principle is generally acknowledged: reason demonstrates it; and nature herself has engraved it on the heart of man.*
—Emmerich de Vattel

# 1

# A War and Its Language

*We can never fully understand the Sioux war of 1862 until the Indians tell their story.*
—Holcombe, "A Sioux History of the War"

More than a century and a half later, the war that wracked Minnesota during the summer of 1862, and its aftermath, are still highly sensitive topics for many people in that State. This makes the historian's task of engaging the subject that much more difficult, and words are part of the difficulty. In writing about history, as historian John Lukacs has observed, "The selection of every word is not merely a scientific or stylistic problem but also a moral one." Words are how our histories are transmitted, and therefore the words matter. So before undertaking an examination of this war, we are well advised to first consider the language used to describe it.

For the past 150 years, this war was most commonly known as "The Sioux Uprising." In histories written beginning in 1863, it also appears as "The Great Sioux Uprising," "The Sioux Outbreak," "The Minnesota Indian Massacre of 1862," "The Massacre in Minnesota," "The Dakota War," "The Sioux War," "The Minnesota Indian War," "The Dakota Conflict," "The United States–Dakota War," "The Great Massacre," "The Dakota Uprising," "The Sioux Campaign of 1862," "The 1862 Uprising," "The Little Crow Uprising," and even "The Other Civil War."[1] In the military history of the United States, probably only the American Civil War itself is known by more names.

Trying to decide what to call the war today means negotiating a minefield of shifting historical perspectives, cultural sensitivities, and the perpetually thin ice of political correctness. Part of the problem is that it depends upon whose perspective, whose culture, and whose politics are being championed or disregarded. To further complicate matters, the language used in the discussion has undergone a nearly continual evolution since the war ended.

The name "Sioux"—by which the Indian people of this story were once commonly known and how they are most often referred to in the older histories—has since fallen out of favor with most (but not all) in favor of the name "Dakota," a name which is both ethnically more specific, and has deeper cultural identity. (In an interesting comment on the cyclical nature of language and those labels that society deems to be acceptable, one observer noted in 1904 that these people were formerly called "Dakota," but that the name "Sioux" had since taken its place.) Minnesota historian Kenneth Carley offers a succinct distillation of the history of the two names in his work on the war. The name

"Dakota" means "friends" or "allies," while on the other hand, as Carley points out, "Sioux is a contraction of Nadouessioux (meaning 'snake' or 'snakelike enemy'), a name originally given them by their enemies, the Chippewa (or Ojibway)."[2]

Carley himself struggled to find the proper term for the war. His first book on the subject, in 1961, was titled *The Sioux Uprising of 1862*. In 1976, the revised edition of his work was published under the new title *The Dakota War of 1862: Minnesota's Other Civil War*. Royal B. Hassrick, a noted scholar of the American West, provides additional insight into the distinct divisions of the Sioux as a people. "In anthropological terminology," Hassrick says, "all three groups—the Dakotas, Nakotas, and Lakotas—properly may be called Sioux. However, in popular nomenclature, the word "Sioux" has become identified with the Tetons, the dashing buffalo hunters of the prairies."[3] The name "Dakota" is more accurately specific to the Sioux people who inhabited Minnesota in 1862. But using the term "Dakota" in a broad sense to apply to the war is also problematic, because as we will see, most of the Indian combatants came from the Mdewakanton and Wahpekute bands of Dakota from the Lower Agency, while the Sissetons and Wahpetons of the Upper Agency Dakota mostly opposed the war and did not engage in the fighting. With that caveat made clear, the general term "Dakota" will be the one most frequently used in this text to when speaking of active participants in the war, bearing in mind that one must always distinguish between the separate bands of Minnesota's Dakota people.

The conflict that erupted that year between the Dakota and the white settlers of southwestern Minnesota was a war by every definition of the term. It had characteristics of a war between two sovereign nations, and it was undoubtedly a war between opposing cultures. It contained some of the ugly elements of a race war. Its violence involved military and civilian elements of both societies, and for the Dakota themselves it was even close to becoming a civil war, at least on one level. Considering all of this, perhaps the most accurate term to describe this event is the U.S.–Dakota War of 1862, or simply, the Dakota War.

Aside from the name given to the war, some of the terms used to describe the events of the war can also indicate a particular interpretation of the history. As we will see, the use of the word "uprising" to describe the events of 1862 draws specific political limits around the conflict. "Massacre" is another highly volatile word, drawing fire from several commentators who refuse to accept the idea that anything like a massacre ever happened in 1862. The author of one recent book describes the killing of a group of settlers near Lake Shetek by saying, "the 1862 Lake Shetek attack—almost invariably called the Lake Shetek Massacre in white histories...."[4] This writer's implication, or at least the inference she expects the reader to take from her choice of words, is that the term "massacre" could only be applied to this particular incident if the observer were white, or came to the subject with some particular racial perspective.

On the contrary—"massacre" is precisely the correct word to use in referring to the killings at Lake Shetek, and racial perspectives have nothing whatever to do with it. The *Oxford English Dictionary* defines "massacre" as a noun meaning "a brutal slaughter of a large number of people," or as a verb meaning "to brutally kill a large number of people." There were at least 32 settlers in the group that was attacked at Lake Shetek; at least 15 of them were killed, and most of those victims were unarmed women and children. Scholars can quibble over how many lives must be lost before enough people have been killed to qualify as "a large number," but by most objective standards the killings at Lake Shetek were indeed a massacre.

There is, of course, another side to the argument surrounding this word. The historical evidence shows that "massacre" is precisely the correct term to describe *some* of the events that took place that August, but it would not be accurate to define the entire span of the war by the single term "massacre," as did many contemporary accounts written immediately after the war. This one particularly controversial word cannot be summarily dismissed, but neither can it be accepted without question. "Massacre," like the word "atrocity"—which will be considered in great detail later—is a completely valid word to use in this history, but only when the evidence supports its use. The record shows that there is ample evidence to justify its careful inclusion in the language of this war.[5]

The rancorous debate around the word "massacre" serves to illustrate a larger issue that one encounters when studying the Dakota War. For more than 150 years, different commentators have offered their interpretations of this history, and today conflicting points of view continue to struggle for the definitive understanding of the war. Each voice brings with it its own motivation, its own agenda, and its own understanding of a past that still inspires intense debate and sometimes acrimonious disagreement. A comprehensive reading of the literature of the Dakota War reveals a contentious situation similar to one that Lukacs has described as "a dialogue, or even a diatribe, among the deaf." Even today, so many years after the event, there is often little consensus as to what actually happened during the Dakota War and what meanings we should draw from it.

A French historian named Henri-Irenee Marrou once referred to the "massive intrusion of the historian's personality" as being a constant factor in historical writing. This intrusion is at work in every source on the Dakota War, and as those sources are examined in the chapters of this book, that dynamic will be apparent. In some works on this war, the commentator's view of the war is merely the lens through which the reader encounters these events. In other cases, the agenda-driven intrusion is so great as to render those writers' versions of events suspect. With that in mind, one of the objectives of this text is to consider the ways in which historians have dealt with the Dakota War, and to examine how different observers have understood it. Along the way, of course, my own thoughts, intentions and inclinations will inevitably be a part of the process, just as Marrou cautioned.

Another problem with the language of this war is that it involves two languages, English and Dakota (and at least two more if one counts the Norwegian and German in which some of the source documents were originally written). One area where a non–Dakota researcher is at a disadvantage in this history is in the matter of Dakota names. Many of the traditional Indian names that appear in the trial transcripts had never been written before that time, and each name was spelled out phonetically in an attempt to approximate as closely as possible how the name was pronounced. As a result, there are numerous variations on the spelling of certain names, and one has to be careful to ensure that the same person is being referred to when the spelling of a name changes slightly from source to source. Not speaking the Dakota language myself, I do not have the linguistic expertise to determine the most correct spelling or best translation of a name from amongst all the versions of it that are to be found in the record. Some complex Dakota names are particularly challenging (Toonnannakinyaoahatka is spelled at least four different ways in the sources), but even simpler names often have multiple variations—the name Wahehud, for instance, appears at least three different ways. With all of this in mind, and to try and avoid confusion as much as possible, when I render Dakota names in this text I will strive to be consistent and use the same spelling every time that a particular name is cited, and I apologize in advance if the variant I have chosen to use is not the best translation or the most linguistically correct one.

The Dakota War was no minor event, no brief frontier skirmish. No matter what name one might choose to call it, it absolutely *was* a war, and in the first days of the fighting, hundreds of women and children, not soldiers, were killed in Indian attacks that deliberately struck at civilian, rather than military, targets. The reckoning after the war was also severe. In an act of collective punishment, the U.S. Government exiled most of the people of the Dakota and Winnebago tribes from the remnants of their traditional territory.[6]

It would be a mistake (one frequently repeated in the historiography) to speak of this history in generalities, and thereby give the reader the impression that all white people were hostile to Native Americans, or that all white traders were exploitative cheats, or that all Dakota felt the same on the question of war, whether for or against it, and so on. One thing that quickly becomes apparent from an in-depth study of this history is that we cannot make overly broad statements about the events of 1862 and not distinguish between individuals. It would be indulging an egregious stereotype to declare "all Dakota did this" or "all white people believed that"; unfortunately, this is exactly the sort of language that permeates much of the commentary on the Dakota War.

Henry H. Sibley, the man who led the military expedition against the Dakota and who convened the military commission that tried and sentenced 303 of the Indians to death, wrote in a letter to his wife that in his view the Dakota War was "the greatest Indian tragedy of the age."[7] He did not specify for whom he thought it was a tragedy, Indians or white people, but the distinction would have been irrelevant, even had he made it. In the end, there was tragedy enough to go around, tragedy enough for everyone.

# 2

# Spark, Fuel and Fire

*Oppression is sometimes a plant of slow growth, but it is a dangerous one, and too long continued it ends in complete or attempted retribution.*
—Daniel Buck

To say that a war began with a "spark" is a familiar cliché of military history, and one that appears often in connection with the Dakota War of 1862. Cliché or not, the imagery still serves—there certainly was a spark that ignited this war. A spark by itself, however, burns out quickly and does no harm. There must be fuel or accelerant for the spark to become a conflagration. As it happened, the spark that set off the Dakota War was probably the least important detail in the whole tragic history of the conflict. There were other long-standing factors that actually caused the war, and those were the fuels that made the fire burn so hotly once it started. One early Minnesota historian described the causes of the war by saying, "underlying it all was the simple fact that the white man wanted to move in, the red man did not want to move out, and the two were so different that they could not live side by side."[1] There was, of course, more to it than just that, but that dynamic did indeed play a considerable role in the ultimate conflict.

The troubles that led to the Dakota War were years in the offing, and came to a head at the time of the annuity payment scheduled for the summer of that year. Over a quarter of a century, a series of treaties had been made between the U.S. Government and the Dakota, the most important of which was arguably the Treaty of 1851. In exchange for their signing of the Treaty of 1851 and the sale of their tribal lands east of the Mississippi, the Dakota of the Upper and Lower Agencies were guaranteed annual payments by the U.S. Government. The Mdewakanton and Wahpekute bands of Dakota were grouped around the Lower Agency, while the Sissetons and Wahpetons were located at the Upper Agency.[2]

The Treaty of Traverse des Sioux, as the 1851 treaty was also known, completely altered the traditional way of life of nearly 6,000 Dakota people. "No other single Indian treaty," one writer observed in 1904, "conveyed so vast and noble an estate. It involved fully one-half, and the best half at that, of the great state of Minnesota.... In brief, the treaty provided that the tribes sold and relinquished to the United States all of their lands in Minnesota and Iowa, east of the Big Sioux River and a line from Lake Kampeska to Lake Traverse and the Sioux Woods Rivers."[3] The Treaty of Traverse des Sioux has been the focus of criticism and condemnation ever since. The treaty, as Minnesota historian Rhoda Gilman puts it, "was a mask for naked conquest. If no treaty were signed, white men would swarm into the land anyway, and should the Dakota try to drive them out, some pretext would be found to send in the troops."[4] An earlier historian, writing in 1915, expressed the opinion that "the whole treaty and style of procedure was as farcical as the negro vote in Mississippi after the war."[5] Another commentator who considered the Treaty of Traverse des Sioux that same year wryly remarked, "The principle use of treaties ... is to start wars."[6] Considering the broad and shameful history of treaties between the U.S. Government and various Indian tribes, those statements are not at all inaccurate.

A subsequent treaty in 1858 saw the Dakota maneuvered into relinquishing their claims to the remaining lands north of the Minnesota River. In the fateful year of 1862, this was how the Dakota were geographically and politically situated, on a steadily shrinking peninsula of reservation land in a rising sea of white settlements that was hemming them on three sides.

The Dakota position was an untenable one even before the Treaty of Traverse des Sioux was ratified. Events happening far from Minnesota had already begun to exert pressures that would change everything. For years, the United States government had indulged itself in the chimera that a permanent "Indian Country" outside the territorial boundaries of the U.S. could be maintained for the resettlement of displaced Indian tribes. All that was necessary, so the fantasy ran, was to move Indians out into the vast western plains, where they could roam at will and where, more importantly, white men at that time had no desire to settle. It was another war, America's first extra-territorial war, which spelled the certain demise of that idea. "After the Mexican War and the Oregon settlement," Robert Weigley notes in his study of American military history, "the Indian Country no longer marked the effective western boundary of the United States, but divided two parts of the United States from each other. No such arrangement was likely to remain permanent."[7] The Dakota, though they might not have known it at the time, were caught in the steadily constricting vise of American territorial boundaries with the American east inexorably pushing westward, with them in the middle.

More immediate to the Dakota, the treaty provisions created problems almost from the beginning. One idea which has become enshrined in both the historiography and popular perception is the notion that the Bureau of Indian Affairs allowed white traders to exploit and steal from the Indians on a massive scale. According to this version of the story, traders would extend the Indians credit during the winter each year and then claim such a substantial portion of the summer annuity payments that much of the annuity monies were siphoned off before they ever reached the Indians. This image of grafting white traders has become so fixed in the history that the prevailing modern perception is that nearly every white man involved in trade with the Indians was a cheat and a crook. While it was absolutely true that corruption and exploitation were chronic problems in the trade system, some of the traders in fact had good relations with the Indians—one Dakota man in his narrative long after the war said, "I do not say that the traders always cheated and lied about these accounts. I know many of them were honest men and kind and accommodating."[8]

That said, many of the criticisms *do* have historical merit, particularly when that criticism is directed against the ways in which the U.S. government handled its post-treaty relations with Indian groups. In 1904, Daniel Buck, a judge of the Minnesota Supreme Court who was an eyewitness to the war as a young man, wrote,

> There always has been, and it seems as though there always will be, gross negligence on the part of our national Indian department. No matter what party has been in power, delay, willful or negligent, utter incompetency or gross mismanagement has been its history, and forever will be until all Indians die, or all politicians die, which can never be expected.

Buck concluded, "Very much of our Indian trouble can be laid at the door of our national Indian department, through its omission or commission of wrongs."[9]

The fiscal abuses and potential for fraud were certainly recognized at the time. Isaac V.D. Heard, who served as the Official Recorder for the military commission that conducted the trials of the Dakota after the war, was no particular friend of the Indians. In the book he wrote after the war, Heard categorized them as savages who were instinctively hostile and culturally inferior to white people; his general sentiments can be summed up in one phrase he used: "O treachery, thy name is Dakota."[10] In spite of this hostility, he still stated his belief that the main cause of the war was the U.S. government's duplicity in its dealings with the Indians. "[T]he treaties are born in fraud," Heard wrote, "and all their stipulations for the future are curtailed by iniquity."[11] Like other commentators, he went on to describe (in overly general terms) how the payment of treaty annuities owed to the Indians was attached by white traders, whose questionable business practices guaranteed that much of the Indians' money never reached them. In Heard's opinion, this was the government's fault. "The federal government," he wrote, "through the maladministration of the Indian Department, is largely responsible for the excitement of the Indians against the whites."[12]

In December 1862, just days before the 38 Dakota men were hanged in Mankato, the *St. Paul Daily Press* printed a letter from a man named Antoine Freniere, who had served as one of the principal translators during the military commission's trials of the Dakota Indians. He stated his belief that "it has been a habit with Sioux Agents and Superintendents to make rash and extensive promises to the Indians, which they never designed to keep and knew could not be kept."[13] This did not mean that Freniere was an advocate of mercy or compassion for the Indians; in the same article he expressed his opinion that almost all of the Indians condemned by the military commission were guilty as charged and ought to be hanged. And here again, it would be a mistake to assume that Indian Agents were all of a stripe. Thomas Galbraith, the Agent at the Lower Agency at the time of the war, did seem to have an adversarial relationship with the Dakota and more than once demonstrated a pronounced lack of understanding, but the same could not necessarily be said of Joseph Brown, one of his predecessors.

Moses Adams was a missionary who had spent years living and working with the Dakota people; he also was of two minds when he thought back on the causes of the war. "If the treaty stipulations had been honestly and faithfully carried out," he wrote, "the Sioux or Dakotas would have been satisfied for the time, and possibly the outbreak would have been forestalled...."[14] Once the war began, however, he believed there was "no justifiable cause" ... for the Indians to have committed "indiscriminate massacre of the innocent white settlers, men, women and children, without mercy." In Adams' eyes, the Indians were guilty of wholesale murder, but he still saw another side to the issue. "Yet we cannot afford to ignore the fact," he reflected, "that there was much at that time, as there had been for years before in the management of Indian affairs, that was exasperating to the Indians and increasingly provoking and vexatious to them."[15]

Dr. Asa Daniels, a Minnesota physician who lived through the war and its aftermath, also laid most of the blame for the Indian uprising on the U.S. Government. "The outbreak," he wrote, "was induced by long-continued violation of treaty obligations on the part of the government, inflicting upon these unfortunate wards [the Dakota] untold want and suffering...." He went on to say, "Like violent acts of mobs ... the massacre was a barbarous and unreasoning protest against injustice." "Had the government faithfully carried out the treaty obligations and dealt with the Sioux justly and humanely," Dr. Daniels concluded, "the outbreak would not have occurred."[16]

Even some of the hardliners on the American side of the conflict believed that the roots of the outbreak had non–Indian origins. Major General John Pope, sent out from Washington to take over Federal command of the war, consistently spouted off his opinions about exiling or exterminating every Dakota and Winnebago Indian in Minnesota, but even he saw the hands of white men in the events that had driven the Dakota to war. In a letter he wrote that fall, Pope said that in his view, "There will not long be trouble as soon as the government renders it impossible for white men to make money out of the Indians...."[17] Questions about causation were voiced at the highest levels of government—Gideon Welles, the Secretary of the Navy in 1862, was concerned with what he felt were one-sided reports coming from the field (particularly those dispatches coming from Major General John Pope). "What may have been the provocation," he wrote in his diary, "we are not told." He clearly had his suspicions, though—the Indian tribes, he noted, "have good land, which white men want and mean to have."[18] It was a perspective shared by later historians; writing in 1935 Theodore Christianson said, "The white man's determination to get all the Indians' land was the underlying cause of the Sioux Outbreak of 1862."[19]

Some white survivors of Indian attacks, including several who endured a harsh captivity in Dakota hands for weeks, also felt that the policies and practices of the U.S. Government were to blame for the outbreak of war. Minnie Buce Carrigan saw her parents and younger sisters murdered by the Indians; nonetheless, in her account of the war, she wrote, "The winter before the outbreak was a severe one and caused a great deal of suffering among the Indians.... The Indians' payment was due in June. August came and they had not received it. They were starving. All these were causes of the outbreak."[20] F.W. Boelter, who accused the Dakota of taking "brutish pleasure" in killing, conceded, "it cannot be concealed that the unfaithful, fraudulent government agents were the main fault of the raving fury manifested by these barbarous savages...."[21] Boelter seems to have held a genuine hatred for the Dakota, and he was not in the least bit sympathetic to their situation, but even he felt that at least some responsibility for the war lay with the U.S. government.

This was exactly how many of the Dakota saw the reasons for the war. Sam Brown, the son of former Indian Agent Joseph Brown, was captured along with his Dakota mother. An Indian named Dowanniye, he remembered later,

> would shout and yell at the top of his voice and say that the Indians would have a good time now, and that if they got killed it would be all right; that the whites were trying to starve them to death to get rid of them and were delaying the payment [of the annuity] for that purpose; that he preferred to be shot and to die as becomes a Sioux rather than be starved to death.[22]

In the waves of public hostility that were directed against the Indians in the months after the war, one of their staunchest advocates was the Episcopal Bishop of Minnesota,

Henry B. Whipple, who saw the situation in much the same light as did the Dakota themselves. "The system of trade," he wrote, "was ruinous to honest traders and pernicious to the Indian.... Every influence which could add to the degradation of this hapless race seems to be its inheritance.... The voice of this whole nation has declared that the Indian Department is the most corrupt in the Government."[23] On another occasion Whipple said, "our Indian system is an organized system of robbery, and has been for years a disgrace to the nation...."[24]

Henry H. Sibley, the commander of the military expeditionary force and the man who actually convened the military commission to conduct the trials, seemed to agree with this view, but in somewhat guarded terms—Sibley himself had started out in Minnesota as a fur trader working with the Indians, and he had certainly profited financially in his business dealings with them (although it would be incorrect to assume that he made a fortune off the Indians). In a letter to Bishop Whipple on December 7, 1862, shortly before the execution of the men at Mankato, Sibley wrote, "We do not disagree when you assess that these Indians have been unfairly dealt with by Government officials and others."[25] This was a view that he had held for years before the war, and as we will see, it adds even more complexity to any attempt to understand his decisions and actions during the war.

Finally, Little Crow—the Dakota chief who white Minnesotans at the time most associated with the Indian leadership of the war—made perhaps the most insightful comment on the factors that contributed to the war. In hindsight, his remarks have a poignantly prophetic ring to them. On August 15, three days before the outbreak of open war, Indian leaders demanded the release of provisions in the storehouses at the Lower Agency near Redwood Falls, provisions which had been sent by the government and which were intended for the Dakotas' use. The white traders who ran the Agency stores argued against it, insisting that the provisions not be released until the overdue annuity payment arrived, a stipulation predicated on business priorities rather than humanitarian concerns.

Witnesses reported that Little Crow said in response, "We have waited a long time. The money is ours, but we cannot get it. We have no food, but there are these stores, filled with food. We ask that you, the agent [Thomas Galbraith] make some arrangement by which we can get food from the stores, or else we may take our own way to keep ourselves from starving. When men are hungry they help themselves."[26] There was a clear warning underlying his words, but Galbraith missed it completely and chose to focus on the incident of the moment rather than the underlying cause. By some reports Galbraith was a man ill-equipped both for the position he held and the crisis that confronted him in it. "His excessive use of liquor had brought about a serious impairment of his mental faculties and he was really unfit to hold any official position," a friend later said of him. "Half the time he was out of his head. He had no diplomacy and treated the Indians arrogantly."[27]

As these accounts—narratives for the most part written immediately after the war—show, the dishonesty and corruption associated with the Indian treaty system were even then considered to be principal causes of the outbreak. Many commentators in 1862 and afterwards blamed the U.S. government itself for the outbreak of the war. The persistent mismanagement by the Bureau of Indian Affairs and its Agents, in particular, drew harsh criticism. The Reverend Stephen Riggs, a missionary who was to figure prominently in the military commission trials in the aftermath of the war, felt that there had been opportunities to avert the war, but they were missed repeatedly. "When President Lincoln's administration commenced," he remembered, "we were glad to welcome a change of Indian agents. But, after a little trial, we found that a Republican administration was quite as likely to make mistakes in the management of Indians as a Democratic one."[28]

The Dakotas' legitimate grievances were numerous, and when the moment came for a decision, there were those among them who argued that there was nothing left to lose by fighting. The matter had reached its limit; "the patience of the Indians had been overstrained by deceit and greed, neglect and stupid bungling."[29] Even in contemporary accounts of the war, written when anti–Indian sentiment was at its height, many white commentators accepted the idea that the Dakota started the war because they were driven to it by desperation. "The Indians did not lack grievances," Christianson said; "Civilized nations have gone to war on less provocation than the Sioux tribes had."[30] The Indians' decision to fight, therefore, was justified in the eyes of most well informed observers. The consensus broke apart on the question of whether or not that justification extended to the way in which the war was fought, and that debate continues unabated today. Did the *raisons de guerre* in 1862 justify the barbarity that marked the outbreak of the war? Or, regardless of legitimate grievances, was Dakota conduct in the war characterized by criminal acts of murder, rape and massacre for which no justification is possible?

There is another point about the Dakota War that is essential to understanding this history: this war was not a case of a traditionally peaceful and pacifistic native culture being forced to take up unfamiliar arms in an act of reluctant self-defense. Rather, the Dakota were, and had been throughout their long, proud history, a people for whom warfare was a near-constant activity and martial glory was the height of personal ambition.

The Dakota fought other Indian tribes long before Europeans arrived on the scene. In their own world, the Dakota were themselves a force of invasion and conquest. In 1750, the Dakota prosecuted a long, hard-fought war with the Iowas and Omahas in which they took control of premium territory by breaking those tribes as military powers in the region. Sometime around 1775, they drove the Kiowa out of the Black Hills region and seized that prime hunting ground. In 1792, they crushed the Arikaras and forced them north, thereby consolidating the Missouri Valley and the western part of modern South Dakota under their control. Expanding the reach of their territory west of the Black Hills, they defeated the Crows in 1822 and took the eastern half of modern day Wyoming. Even as late as the 1870s, they were still holding their own against other tribes, killing more than 200 Pawnee men, women and children in a fight over hunting grounds which the Dakota regarded as theirs and theirs alone.[31]

Within Native American culture, the Dakota were a warlike people well established as a military power. As one detailed ethnographic study of their culture says, "They made no concessions, few alliances, and many enemies. They were hated by many and feared by most, and they boasted of this reputation. They were proud of their superiority and were vigilant in defending it. They conquered relentlessly with a conviction of fortune. They were men among men and a nation among nations."[32] So much were they a nation among nations that, for a time, the northern plains were effectively a Sioux dominion.

## 2. Spark, Fuel and Fire

This perception of the Dakota was not unique to white observers; it was a view also held by their traditional Native American enemies. At a council convened by General George Crook to recruit Indian scouts for service with the Army against the Sioux, a Crow chief named Old Crow said:

> These are our lands by inheritance. The Great Spirit gave them to our fathers, but the Sioux stole them from us. They hunt upon our mountains. They fish in our streams. They have stolen our horses. They have murdered our squaws, our children.... Our war is with the Sioux and only with them. We want back our lands.... The Sioux have trampled upon our hearts. We shall spit upon their scalps.[33]

Old Crow's list of the injuries his tribe had suffered at the hands of the Sioux would be familiar to any student of the history of the American west, with one remarkable distinction: the same wrongs were inflicted on the Dakota and other native peoples by European-Americans during the American expansion of the 19th century. But in this case, both the injured parties and the oppressors were native peoples.

Warfare was such an integral element of native culture that when missionaries, Indian agents and the U.S. Army tried to prevent them from going to war with their neighbors, it provoked anger and resentment. A minor Dakota chief named Wamditanka, also known as Big Eagle, left an extensive narrative that is one of the most complete Indian sources in the historical record. Speaking years after the war he said, "There was great dissatisfaction among the Indians over many things the whites did." The first grievance he listed was, "The whites would not let them go to war against their enemies."[34]

Fiercely independent and intrinsically warlike, the Dakota lived in a continuous cycle of inter-tribal warfare characterized by raids and depredations on neighboring tribes, maintaining a constantly shifting array of alliances and enemies. As Vine Deloria Jr., the prominent American Indian scholar, pointed out, "The Sioux, my own people, have a great tradition of conflict.... During one twenty-four year period in the [19th] century the Sioux fought over an area from LaCrosse, Wisconsin, to Sheridan, Wyoming, against the Crow, Arapaho, Cheyenne, Mandan, Arikara, Hidatsa, Ponca, Iowa, Pawnee, Otoe, Omaha, Winnebago, Chippewa, Cree, Assiniboine, Sac and Fox, Potawatomi, Ute, and Gros Ventre."[35] This perpetual warfare was not just the motive of their survival as a people, though that was an important part of it. It was also a matter of individual ambition. "The pattern of heroics," Hassrick says, "was so institutionalized that reason, whether for individual well-being or group self-interest, was submerged by the obsession that war itself was the purpose of life."[36] For the Sioux, bellicosity was a well-established cultural norm.

Even after most of the Indian tribes had a common enemy in the form of the U.S. Army, this tradition of inter-tribal warfare continued, and the Indians continued to fight each other as much as they fought the Army, to their considerable detriment. Nearly 80 years after the Dakota War, General George C. Marshall made the observation, "It is always well to keep in mind that one fights to gain a definite end," he cautioned, "not simply to fight." For some Dakota, fighting was often enough simply for its own sake. "In the plains culture's last days of glory," one study notes, "individual fighting and raiding, no matter whom the opponent, continued to be the basis of a man's position in Indian society."[37]

The idea that the Native American peoples of the upper plains were wholly peaceful until they encountered white men is a fable not supported by history. Indian oral traditions and the records of the first Europeans to make contact with them both attest to this. The refutation of this misconception is nothing new, however—one of the most culturally sympathetic ethnographic studies of the Dakota people in the 19th century was written by Samuel W. Pond in 1870–1871. In his book, Pond pointed out that the Dakota were "far from being gentle, innocent, harmless creatures, pure until contaminated by whites."[38]

This does not mean, however, that in rejecting the myth of the "noble savage," Pond believed that Indians were inferior to white people. The Dakota, he wrote, "were by nature no worse than other men," and he consistently argued that the Dakota were simply culturally *different* from white men, not racially inferior.[39] On the question of inter-tribal warfare, Pond rejected the prevailing view of many white people of that era who believed that Indians were warlike because they were savages. "The Indians," Pond wrote, "did not make war on each other because they were Indians, but because they were men and like other men. Their wars were as necessary as wars generally are."[40] But even necessary wars can have disastrous outcomes, and in its aftermath this particular war proved to be an absolute disaster for the Dakota.

There is little doubt that the Dakota went to war in 1862 partly out of desperation—their own narratives are clear on this point. It is also true that they went to war because they were justifiably outraged and angry at their treatment at the hands of some white traders and government officials, and reacting to the loss of their traditional territory. But some among them welcomed the war as an opportunity for plunder, personal gain, and a chance to make individual reputations as warriors—motivations that also appear in their narratives, as we will see. "Retaliation, defense, conquest, and booty," it has been said, " were among the primary motivating causes of Sioux warfare."[41] With the sole exception of conquest, all of these issues factored into the Dakotas' *casus belli* in the summer of 1862. As Big Eagle remembered it, "It was also thought that a war with the whites would cause the Sioux to forget the troubles among themselves and enable many of them to pay off some old scores."[42]

Though there was debate and disagreement in Dakota councils as they made the decision to go to war against the whites, it was to some degree their familiar, traditional path. War—in their own manner and according to their own customs—was what they knew best. "The war that the Dakota fought was a war in which they held the advantage in terms of tactics, weapons, and determination," Minnesota historian John Isch says. "They knew how to fight in a raiding party or ambush, they were better armed than the clerks and farmers, and they fought for more than their land. They fought for their culture, their way of life, for their very existence."[43]

Provocation, desperation, culture and tradition—all of these factored into the Dakotas' calamitous decision to take up arms that summer. In the end, it spelled their ruin. When the war was over, there were almost no Dakota left in Minnesota. Some of the tribe fled, nearly 300 of their men were incarcerated in a military prison camp in Iowa, and most of the remnant—men, women and children—were banished into a dismal exile, an entire people dealing with the aftermath of a savagery wreaked by some of them in a war that many of them had never wanted in the first place.

# 3

# The Acton Murders

There were many reasons for the Dakota War of 1862, but the final catalyst for all of the war's tragic, bloody violence was one of the least important of them. Ironically, the war started as the result of an argument over some eggs, or so goes the most widely repeated version of the story. There are differing accounts of the incident, but what is certain is that, for whatever reason, four young Dakota men shot and killed five settlers—three men and two women—on August 17, 1862, in Acton Township, Meeker County.[1] The Indian men hurried back to their band's encampment and reported what they had done.

There was at least one group among the Dakota who could be expected to view war as a viable option. In Dakota society, as in several other tribes, like-minded men sometimes gathered together in a Soldiers' Lodge. This organization was usually militant in nature, though they also organized for protection of the community and often filled a civil policing role. And they occasionally operated outside the scope of the normal hierarchy of their bands—so much so that the discussions in their meetings were secretive, and on more than one occasion young men of the Soldiers' Lodge would head out on a raid without their local chief knowing anything of their intentions. A Soldiers' Lodge had organized in the Dakota camps some time before the night of August 17, and when the four young men came in with their story of the killings in Acton, it was the members of that group that first went into counsel to consider what was to be done.

The membership of the group largely ruled out any chance of moderation in their discussions. "Cut-hairs and Dakotas known to be friendly to the whites were excluded from the Soldiers' Lodge," one historian notes, "and thus it tended to be a group of militants who did not fully factor in the risks of waging war." This does not mean, however, that the Soldiers' Lodge was made up of discontents and marginal characters who mustered little influence in Dakota society. Many of its members had considerable influence, some of them holding positions of recognized leadership, and the group dynamic of the Soldiers' Lodge represented a force that no one in Dakota culture could ignore. On the night of August 17, these men discussed the matter for several hours, trending in only one direction—war. But if it was to be a war involving more than a few dozen men striking out on raids on their own initiative, the voices of conventional Dakota authority would have to be brought to bear.

One of the members of the Soldiers' Lodge was a man named Shakopee, also known as Shakopedan, or Little Six. He decided to take the matter to one of the most influential men among the Dakota. Shakopee's mind was already made up—he "was against the white men," another Dakota recalled later—but he needed the endorsement of leaders of more renown and wider influence if more than just his band of Dakota were to go to war.[2]

Little Crow, whose Dakota name was Taoyateduta, was a leader of just such influence. He was one of the signatories of the treaties between the Dakota and the United States government. By some appearances he was a man who had accepted many of the "civilizing" efforts of the white missionaries and Indian Agents—he occasionally wore white man's clothing, he sometimes attended the missionary church on the reservation, and he lived in a government-built house on the reservation rather than in a traditional teepee. In spite of all of that, Little Crow was Dakota to his core. Ironically, one of the most commonly reproduced photographs of Little Crow, that taken by A.Z. Shindler in 1858, almost makes him look like a white man's idea of what a Dakota Indian should look like. There is little sense of the man himself in the carefully accoutered, awkwardly posed photograph. On the other hand, in one photograph that depicts Little Crow dressed in a white man's black broadcloth suit and tie, his face looks every bit the strong, proud and influential leader that he was. In that portrait, he does not look like an Indian mimicking the white man, but rather an Indian deigning to don the white man's apparel for the moment, and looking all the more like a Dakota chief in spite of it. His face is open and calm, and one gets a sense from his expression that he could have been a man of deep thought and resolute decisions. Even so, some witnesses who knew him personally also described him as occasionally petulant and prone to bad temper. In other words, he was a rather normal man.

Little Crow's influence among his people had recently diminished somewhat when he stood for reelection to the position of speaker of the band and lost the election to another chief named Traveling Hail, and he was still smarting from the injury to his pride. But now, in this moment of crisis, the other chiefs sought his counsel.

There were opposing factions in the Dakota community, a reality that would cause them problems throughout their prosecution of the war. Some were "farmer Indians," who had taken up the plow, cut their hair and donned trousers, and who lived in brick houses built for them by the government, rather than in teepees. Derisively called "cut-hairs" by other Indians, they favored assimilation and argued for diplomacy with the whites. Some Dakota who still adhered to the traditional modes of dress and lifestyle also argued against open warfare with the whites. They may not have liked the whites, they may not have welcomed the proselytizing missionaries or the frequently corrupt Indian Agents, and they certainly resisted the U.S. government's pressure on them to abandon their culture and assimilate, but just as certainly they also feared the consequences of war with the Americans.

The strong war factions among the Dakota were undeterred by voices of caution and appeals for calm. They had endured enough insults at the hands of the whites, they argued, and their people were being systematically reduced to ruin. The traders at the Agency starved and cheated them while the Indian Agent did nothing on their behalf. They were losing everything that made them Dakota. The only recourse was to fight back, retake their ancestral lands, and reclaim their traditional life.

This was the dilemma presented to Little Crow. Woken from sleep in the middle of the night, his house crowded with men waiting to hear what he would say, Little Crow had the young men repeat over and again what had happened at Acton. There were basically two options open to the Dakota leadership at this point. They could hand the murderers over to the white authorities, who would soon be demanding them for punishment, or they could unite in opposition. Opposition, everyone understood, meant outright war.

A situation similar to this had confronted the Dakota a few years before. In 1857, a Dakota chief named Inkpaduta had led a series of raids on white settlements in the area of Spirit Lake, Iowa, killing 38 settlers and taking three women and a 14-year-old girl captive. Inkpaduta was the leader of a small band that had never signed the 1837 and 1851 treaties with the United States government, and he may not have felt himself bound by them. He was to some observers a renegade amongst his own people, and his actions did not represent the decisions of his tribe at large. "Inkpaduta and his band," Lincoln's secretary John Nicolay later wrote, "were outlaws, driven away by their own people for creating internal dissensions … it was not thought that the outrage had been countenanced by the rest of the [Dakota] nation."[3]

In the government's eyes, however, that did not matter. Though this was a unilateral action by one renegade group of Dakota, the government held the Dakota collectively responsible for the killings. Failing to bring Inkpaduta to justice themselves after he and his band easily escaped west into the Dakota Territory, the American authorities demanded that the annuity Dakota capture the raiders and hand them over. The tactic amounted to extortion: the Dakota's Indian Agent at the time, Charles E. Flandrau (a man who was to later figure prominently in the 1862 war) threatened to withhold that year's annuity payments as punishment for the Spirit Lake massacres unless the Indians captured Inkpaduta. Since the Dakota were increasingly dependent upon the annuity payments for survival, they were in a bind. Although Little Crow himself led the effort to bring Inkpaduta in, and even though several of the renegades were killed, Inkpaduta himself remained at large.

Matters had grown worse for the Dakota in the five years since the Spirit Lake incident. Already in the summer of 1862, the annuity payment had failed to be delivered as scheduled. There were two principle reasons for this: one was that Congress had taken longer than expected to appropriate the funds for that year's annuity payment, and the other was that the Treasury Department spent an entire month debating whether to make the payment in the usual form of gold coin, which was at a premium on account of the demands of the Civil War, or in paper currency, which the Indians were not willing to accept. (In a moment of supreme irony, $71,000 in gold arrived at Fort Ridgely, 12 miles from the Lower Agency, on the day the outbreak began. It was the Indians' long overdue annuity payment. Because of the war, it was never delivered.)

The summer of 1862 saw a bumper crop for the farming Indians, but the traditional Dakota, still clinging to the teepee and the hunt, were having a more difficult time of it. The previous winter had been hard; people were already hungry, and there was some worry a starvation winter was looming. Attitudes had grown more belligerent as the summer wore on, and now there were the killings at Acton. With that last incident, all of the considerable anger, resentment and desperation passed the point of critical mass.

In the heated debates that took place in Dakota councils on the night of August 17,

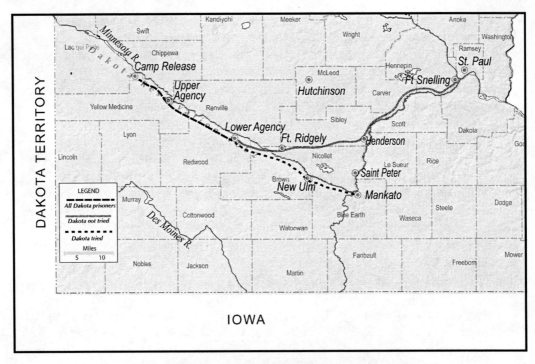

**Southwestern Minnesota, the area most affected by the Dakota War.**

the war factions among the Dakota advocated immediate attacks on the whites. There was nothing to lose, some of them argued—things were already so bad that war was the only option. Others who supported the idea of war said that they would never have a better opportunity to strike at the whites. For nearly a year the Dakota had noticed that the garrisons at Fort Ridgely, Fort Ripley and other army posts in Minnesota were being depleted as troops were sent east to answer the Federal government's call for troops to fight the Civil War. Recruiting parties were making the rounds of the frontier settlements, calling up men for the Union Army; some Indians wondered aloud if there were going to be any white soldiers left in the state at all. A year earlier the War Department had stipulated a requirement for almost 900 Army Regulars to garrison Minnesota's line of posts; now there were fewer than 300 troops on hand, and most of those were untried and inexperienced.[4] With the Army's presence thinner than ever, and with the spur of desperation goading them on, the militants among the Dakota pushed for war. They did so without truly understanding the odds that they faced.

"Few Indians," as one historian puts it, "understood the massive resources or the character of the United States and its citizens."[5] It was equally true that few Indians understood the sheer human numbers stacked against them. In 1862, the Dakota population of Minnesota was estimated to be approximately 6,000 people; by that time there already were more white people in the state capital of St. Paul alone. Big Eagle understood the odds better than most—he knew the "power of the whites, and that they would finally conquer us. We might succeed for a time, but we would be overpowered and defeated at last."[6] Little Crow also knew the full retaliatory power of the Americans. He had been to Washington, D.C. and had seen the sprawling might of the United States.

While some of the Dakota argued that there was nothing left to lose, Little Crow understood that the contrary was true—everything could be lost if his people went down this path. Besides, he pointed out to the Indians who sought his opinion: they had just rejected him as their speaker, so why come to him now, asking what he thought they should do?

No verbatim record exists of what Little Crow actually said that night, but words attributed to him in that discussion have long been a part of the story. What we have today is almost certainly *not* exactly what he said, which is unfortunate—he was apparently an articulate and charismatic speaker, and whatever he said was probably well worth hearing.[7]

His son, Wowinape, later gave an account of that night. "Braves, you are like little children; you know not what you are doing," Little Crow said. "See! The Whitemen [sic] are like locusts, when they fly so thick that the whole sky is a snowstorm. You may kill one, two, ten, yes, as many as the leaves in the forest yonder, and their brothers will not miss them. Kill one, two, ten, and ten times ten will come to kill you. Count your fingers all day long and Whitemen with guns in their hands will come faster than you can count."[8] Some of the Dakota still argued for peace, but the majority was going the other way. The hardliners were not dissuaded by Little Crow's warning. They were set on war, and Little Crow continued to argue against it, until, either out of frustration or by design, someone called him a coward.

That was more than Little Crow's pride could allow. "You will die like rabbits when the hungry wolves hunt them in the Hard Moon [January]," he is supposed to have retorted. The belligerent among the Dakota may not have been able to see the inevitable outcome clearly, but Little Crow knew exactly what the result of war would be. Even so, his wounded pride propelled him toward the same fate that he saw for them. "Taoyateduta is not a coward," the popular account has him saying; "he will die with you."[9] With that statement, the last barrier to war was removed from the Indians of the Lower Agency.[10]

Big Eagle was one of the men in Little Crow's house that night. In the narrative he dictated years after the war, he remembered that Little Crow said, "[W]ar was now declared. Blood had been shed, the [annuity] payment would be stopped, and the whites would take a dreadful vengeance because women had been killed."[11] The die was cast. "[S]oon the cry was 'Kill the whites and kill all these cut-hairs who will not join us,'" Big Eagle recalled. "A council was held and war was declared. Parties formed and dashed away in the darkness to kill settlers.... Little Crow gave orders to attack the agency early next morning and kill all the traders."[12] Little Crow, even though he had expressed some reluctance to commit to hostilities with the whites, was going all the way now that the decision was made. If the Spirit Lake incident was anything to go by, the Indians could expect that the white government would hold the Dakota collectively responsible—they were all going to be blamed for the crime committed by four men. If the Dakota were going to war, then Little Crow would lead them.[13]

# 4

# "Over the earth I come"

*There will be killing till the score is paid.* —Homer, the *Iliad*

*Flee, save your lives, and be like the heath in the wilderness.* —Jeremiah 48:6

The storm broke on Monday morning, August 18. The Lower Agency, 12 miles northwest from Fort Ridgely along the Minnesota River valley, was the first target for many of the Dakota war parties. The traders whom some of the Dakota blamed for cheating them out of their full share of annuity payments were located at the Agency, and they were the first targets. Indians attacked the stores, killing almost everyone they found there. At the same time other Indians, in large bands and small groups, began attacking settlers' homesteads across a wide swath of the Minnesota River valley.

Most of the white people in the area were caught completely unawares and defenseless when their homes and farms were attacked. As the smoke of burning buildings began to rise in the summer sky, word spread that the Lower Agency Indians had broken out in war. Panicked settlers loaded their families into wagons to flee, or struck out on foot across the prairie for the presumed safety of Fort Ridgely and the larger towns such as New Ulm. Many of them never made it.

Dakota warriors attacked settlers where they found them—some in their homes, still unaware of what was happening, others as they fled along roads or across open ground. At least 256 people were killed on the first day as the wave of killing spread out from the epicenter of the Lower Agency. Sex and age were no guarantors of survival; women and children were killed in some cases, captured alive in others. Most white men were killed outright or allowed to escape, depending on the whim of the moment—only one white man was taken captive.

As noted by other historians, the popular modern image of the ever-armed, ever-wary frontier settler apparently did not exist in southwestern Minnesota in 1862. Many in that area were German or Norwegian immigrants recently arrived from Europe. They came from countries where people did not openly carry guns, and where violence was not commonly encountered. "The population of Minnesota," John G. Nicolay observed, "was largely made up of foreign emigrants, German, French, Norwegians, and Swedes. They were unaccustomed to danger, and unused to arms."[1] From survivor narratives it is clear that what guns the settlers did have were predominantly shotguns, and the Indians were often better armed by comparison. "The majority of the settlers," one early history says, "were unaccustomed to firearms and had none. They were foreigners, Germans and

Scandinavians for the most part, and, except for those that had served in the European armies, had never owned a gun or fired one."[2] Even people long associated with the frontier seem to have been caught off guard by the maelstrom of killing, burning and pillaging that erupted around them.[3] Unarmed and untrained in war, "people had only one way to escape death, and that was to flee."[4]

Adding to the confusion, not all Indians the panicked settlers encountered were intent on harming them. There were cases where Dakota risked their own lives to save white people whom they regarded as friends, and other instances where some Indians saved whites who were total strangers to them. Some settlers were betrayed and murdered by Indians whom they had known for years, while other whites were saved by Indians whom they had never seen before. On the morning of the outbreak, Big Eagle rode to the Lower Agency along with the war parties. His intention, though, was not war. "I did not lead my band," he said, "and I took no part in the killing. I went to save the lives of two particular friends if I could. I think others went for the same reason, for nearly every Indian had a friend that he did not want killed; of course he did not care about anybody's else friend [sic]."[5] When the family of former Indian Agent Joseph E. Brown was attacked, one Dakota man recognized Brown's wife, who was a full-blooded Dakota herself. "This woman," he told the other Indians, "saved my life last winter, and I shall save her's now."[6] Brown's family was not killed, but was taken into captivity.

Even Little Crow's own half-brother, White Spider, tried to save someone in the midst of the killing. Mahpiyatowin, also known as Blue Sky Woman, was White Spider's wife. In her narrative of the war, she told how she had been unable to find her husband in the violent chaos of that Monday morning at the Lower Agency. She said that when he finally turned up, he told her "he had escorted two white women to a ravine and told them to follow it, traveling by night only to New Ulm." One of the women tried to give him her ring; White Spider told her, "No, no! I don't want your ring. Just look at my face and if anything happens, remember it."[7] In that moment he seemed to sense that someday there would be a bloody and vengeful reckoning, and he may have wanted to be remembered for an act of mercy rather than murder. One of the women that White Spider saved was Mrs. Nairn, the wife of the government carpenter at the Agency, and she later corroborated his story. She was the one who had offered White Spider her wedding ring as the only thing of value she had on her, but she said he would not take it. Mrs. Nairn and her family all safely reached Fort Ridgely.

When word of the violence at the Lower Agency reached nearby Fort Ridgely, the post commander, Captain John S. Marsh, reacted immediately. A sizeable portion of his garrison had left the fort the day before under the command of Lieutenant Timothy Sheehan. Marsh sent a fast rider after them with orders to return as quickly as possible. "It is absolutely necessary," Marsh wrote in his message to Sheehan, "that you return with your command immediately to this post. The Indians are raising hell at the Lower Agency."[8] Marsh then mustered 46 men of the Fifth Minnesota Volunteer Infantry and set off toward the Agency, leaving Fort Ridgely in the hands of 19-year-old Lieutenant Thomas Gere (who, improbably, was coming down with a case of the mumps that would incapacitate him for several days) and 29 men.[9]

In 1862, there was no bridge across the Minnesota River in the area where it separated Fort Ridgely from the Lower Agency. Redwood Ferry was the only crossing for miles. When Marsh and his detachment reached the ferry, the ferryman was nowhere to be seen. He was already dead, having stayed at his post ferrying panicked settlers to safety until the Indians reached the river and killed him.[10] The only person in sight was an Indian whom neither Captain Marsh nor the government interpreter, Peter Quinn, recognized. Marsh asked the Indian, whose name was Shoonkaska, or White Dog, what the trouble was. There was no trouble, White Dog replied. Or maybe, there had been some trouble, but things were okay now, and the soldiers should come across the river because the Indians were ready to talk.

As Marsh and White Dog were parlaying, Sergeant John Bishop noticed something amiss. There were a number of ponies hidden in the trees across the river; he could see their tails switching in the shadows. He immediately relayed this to Captain Marsh. Marsh, Bishop reported later, "then ordered Quinn to ask White Dog what the ponies were [doing] there, just above him, if the Indians were all up at the agency. The Indian, who had been talking to us, then raised his gun." Things happened quickly at that point. "Quinn exclaimed, 'Look out!' the Indians fired, and in an instant afterward a volley of shot came from the brush on the opposite side of the river; about one-half of our men dropped dead where they had been standing," Bishop wrote, "Quinn with about ten or twelve balls through him."[11]

The soldiers' ranks were decimated in the ambush. The survivors fragmented into several small groups and tried to fight their way clear of the Indians who had crossed the river to surround them. Captain Marsh drowned in the river, trying to lead his men out of the death trap; the Army lost 24 men killed in the first engagement of the war. That night the survivors of Marsh's command straggled back to Fort Ridgely, their story of the ambush at the ferry adding to the already considerable panic among the refugees. Lieutenant Gere scribbled a hasty note to the commander of Fort Snelling, the large military post near the state capitol of St. Paul, requesting that it be passed on to Governor Alexander Ramsey. "Capt Marsh left the post at [10:30] this morning to prevent Indian depredations at the Lower Agency," Gere wrote. "Some of the men have returned—from them I learn that Capt Marsh is killed and only thirteen of his company remaining. The Indians are killing the settlers and plundering the country. Send reinforcements without delay."[12]

Later that night, Gere wrote out a second message, this one to Lieutenant Sheehan, who was now in route back to Fort Ridgely after receiving Captain Marsh's earlier order to return. "Force your march returning," Gere wrote. "Captain Marsh and most of his command were killed yesterday at the Lower Agency." To underscore the urgency of his message, as if that were necessary, Gere concluded, "The Indians are killing men, women and children."[13] It was not an excited exaggeration.

Starting on that first day, a scourge of killing, arson and pillage swept across Brown, Renville, Nicollet and Redwood Counties. Gere's call for help made it through to St. Paul, where Governor Ramsey appointed Henry H. Sibley, a former fur trader who had served as the first governor of Minnesota, to the command of a military relief expedition. Sibley was granted a commission as a Colonel of Volunteers, but it would take time for a political appointment to translate into a viable military force on the ground. In the meantime the people in southwestern Minnesota were left to fend for themselves.

In those first days of the war, most of the settlers were utterly unprepared for the cataclysm that broke upon them. As noted earlier, one of the aspects of the Dakota War which makes it distinct in the history of the American West is the fact that the Indians made direct, concentrated attacks on towns and villages, not just once but on several occasions. No settlement suffered more, proportionally, than did the small German village of Milford in Brown County.

No one in Milford on the morning of August 18 had any idea of what was happening a few miles away at the Lower Agency, and when the Dakota arrived in the settlement there was initially no alarm. As would be their method in numerous other cases during the first days of the war, the Dakota feigned friendliness before suddenly attacking everyone in sight. At least 48 people were killed in Milford, 24 of whom were children.[14] No one was intentionally spared—the only survivors of the attack were people who managed to escape, not people who were captured, because the Indians took no captives in Milford.

At the same time that Milford was dying, the Dakota were striking other areas. Among the white settlers who were caught up in the outbreak of war, the list of victims is long. Most of them left no record of what happened to them—the dead could not tell how they died or what they suffered. Some members of burial parties later recounted the conditions in which they found the bodies of dead settlers, but they often did not know the names of the victims they were burying. Some of the survivors, however, left narratives that provide some insight into what the Dakota War was like for the women and children who were caught up in it.

Justina Boelter escaped the first attacks that killed her neighbors on August 18. Before they realized the Indians were killing settlers, her husband went to corral their cattle—she never saw him again. With her brother-in-law and her three young children she set out on foot for Fort Ridgley. Carrying her two older daughters, both of whom were younger than four years of age, she could not keep up with her brother-in-law, who was carrying her baby. She hid in the thick timber along the Minnesota River with her children. After five days, she ventured back to her brother-in-law's house, looking for food. "When I looked in the house," she later recalled, "I saw my mother-in-law dead on the floor, her head severed from her body, the premises plundered."[15] She fled back to her hiding place without realizing that the bodies of her brother-in-law's children, who had also been killed by the Indians, were lying in the door-yard. Hiding in the undergrowth, without shelter or food, Justina's situation quickly turned desperate as starvation set in. Five weeks into the ordeal, her older child died of malnutrition and exposure to the elements. By this time Justina herself was so weakened from hunger that she could not bury her child, yet she was still afraid to leave her hiding place. In a couple of days, as she recounted in her narrative, the dead child's corpse "became offensive" in the summer heat; nonetheless, she stayed there until the flies on the decomposing body forced her to drag herself and the surviving child some 50 yards away. When a party of soldiers on a burial detail finally found her, she was so malnourished that she was nearly blind. Justina had been out of doors, in all weather, for nine weeks. Her baby, carried safely to Fort Ridgley, survived. The burial party that rescued her buried the bodies of 47 settlers and saw 17 more, which they left uninterred.

Ernestina Broburg was the 16-year-old daughter of Norwegian immigrants who had a small farmstead in the vicinity of West Lake. The war reached their little community on Wednesday morning, August 20; remote as they were, they had heard nothing about the outbreak. Ernestina's family was at a religious meeting at a neighbor's house when the trouble began. Told that Indians were at their house, her father went to see what the matter was, accompanied by five neighbor men. Ernestina never saw any of them again. She was on her way home with her mother and eight-year-old sister a short time later when they were attacked by Dakota. An Indian grabbed her mother, who resisted. "My mother got away from him," Ernestina later wrote, "and was running across the prairie, when he shot her. She fell on the ground. He then ran after my sister, and caught her and struck her down with his gun, and then beat her to death, either with his gun or a hatchet." Her mother, she remembered, had been wounded but not killed by the shot that struck her; Ernestina saw her sit up. "The savage then went up to her," she recalled, "and beat her to death in the same manner."[16] Ernestina hid and eventually made her way to safety, traveling with a neighbor boy. She later learned that her parents, two brothers, sister, two uncles and an aunt had all been killed by the Dakota. Her uncle John Broburg had arrived in America from Norway just nine weeks earlier. Ernestina was the only survivor from her immediate family.

Lavina Eastlick's family was among a large group of settlers attacked near Lake Shetek in Murray County by Indians who first acted friendly toward them. When the killing started, the settler families tried to hide in the tall grass of a low-lying area that was afterward known as Slaughter Slough. Lavina's husband John was shot and killed there. As the Indians continued to fire into the settlers' hiding place, she repeatedly tried to crawl away from her young sons in an attempt to draw the Indians' fire away from them. "I tried several times to crawl away from the children, but could not," she recalled, "for, as soon as I moved away, they came after me. Frank and Fred seemed to think that mother could save them."[17] She could not. She saw her sons, Fred and Giles, beaten to death; exactly what happened to her son Frank was never certain. All three boys were younger than ten. Lavina herself was shot and left for dead. Later that night she searched through the corpses of her neighbors and friends, looking for her children and finding most of them dead.

Two of her children were not there. Merton, her oldest son, had escaped the massacre with his baby brother Johnny. The last thing Lavina had said to Merton was that he should carry his brother as far as he could. In an incredible feat of filial devotion, 11-year-old Merton carried his 15-month-old brother more than 50 miles, covering the distance in seven days as he tried to reach the safety of New Ulm. Lavina, seriously wounded, was eventually picked up by the area's mail carrier, who loaded her in his surrey. As they traveled down the road several days later they overtook Merton, carrying Johnny on his back. Merton was emaciated, his feet torn from walking barefoot, and he was so exhausted that he was unable to speak for days, but he had saved his baby brother.

Alomina Hurd lived on the shore of Lake Shetek. She was home alone with her children when a Dakota war party arrived at her farm. In one of the seemingly capricious acts that characterized much of the violence, the Indians killed the hired man, John Voight, but they allowed Alomina and her children to leave unharmed. Alomina later attributed this to the fact that she had always been friendly with the Indians, and she had made an effort to learn the Dakota language.

Out on the prairie, without food or shelter, carrying her baby and leading her barefoot, three year-old son William by the hand, Alomina set out for New Ulm, 60 miles away. Within a few days they were hungry, exhausted, and William was sick with a fever. She carried both children until her strength gave out. She then pressed on by carrying one child ahead a quarter mile, putting him down, and going back for the other. Repeating this process, she covered 12 grueling miles before reaching an abandoned house where she found a spoiled ham to feed herself and her children. Her husband, who was away from home when their farm was attacked, was already dead. Alomina knew this without having to be told—she had recognized her husband's horse among the Dakotas' mounts.

Exactly how many settlers were killed in the first days of the war has never been precisely determined and likely never can be, just as the question of how many people were killed in the course of the war will never be answered with certainty. Estimates at the time varied wildly and most were exaggerated to some degree. Edward D. Neill, who published a history of Minnesota in 1882, said that "in the short space of thirty-six hours, as nearly as could be computed, eight hundred whites were cruelly slain."[18] Both the number and the time-span that Neill offers are wrong—the number is too high and the time-span is too short. Charles Flandrau, who fought at New Ulm, claimed an even greater number when he declared that the Dakota "murdered in cold blood" no less than 1,000 settlers in the first two days of the war.[19] He was not the only one to peg the number that high; Dr. Damuel B. Sheardown, a surgeon with the military expeditionary force, claimed "not less than 1,000 murdered," although he applied his number to the course of the war entire.[20] The sad reality is that the cost in human life was bad enough without resorting to inflated estimates.

Compounding that cost was the fact that such a disproportionate number of the dead were women and children. At Lake Shetek in Murray County, where Lavina Eastlick and her neighbors were attacked on August 20, three women were killed. Of the children killed there, the victims included Sarah Ireland, age 5, Julianne Ireland, age 3, Freddy Eastlick, age 5, Giles Eastlick, age 8, William Duley Jr., age 10, Belle Duley, age 4, Willie Everett, age 5, and Charley Everett, age 2.[21]

Milford, the small German hamlet in Brown County, was nearly wiped out by the Dakota. The list of children who were killed there and elsewhere in Brown County is far too long: Henry Baumler, age 7; Edward Baumler, age 3; Charles Bluehm, age 6; Frank Harrington, 1 year old; Anton Henle, Jr., age 7; Martin Henle, age 11; Mary Henle, age 4; Paula Heydrich, age 5; Hedwig Heydrich, age 3; Frank Massopust, age 5; Bertha May, age 1; Henry May, age 4; Carl Merkle, age 2; Caezilia Zeller, age 5; Barbara Zeller, age 6; Conrad Zeller, age 3; John Martin Zeller, age 1; Monika Zeller, age 7; Anton Zeller, age 3; Elizabeth Zettel, age 8; Johann Zettel, age 1; Stephan Zettel, age 6; plus an infant girl of the Baumler family and a 3-year-old boy in the Rohner family, neither of whose first names are recorded. In addition to those 24 young victims, the Dakota killed at least 20 women in Milford.[22]

One of them was a young German woman named Theresa Engenhofer. She was 22 years old, and worked as a domestic servant at the Travelers Inn, a way station run by Anton Henle. The records indicate that she arrived in Minnesota with a trunk containing the bulk of her worldly possessions, including heavy winter clothing, which she did not live long enough to use. "The list of Theresa's lost property sort of hints at the dreams she had about coming to America," writes New Ulm historian John Isch.[23]

Theresa had only arrived in Minnesota in July, a few weeks before she was murdered. She herself had not dispossessed an Indian of anything; she was not engaged in defrauding the Dakota of their annuity or forcing them to change their way of life. But she was there, a white settler on traditional Dakota lands, even though she may have never known the local history of the Minnesota River valley or even understood that that land had belonged to the Dakota until recently, and in the eyes of at least one modern commentator that was reason enough to justify her murder.[24]

Such was the nature of this war, a war in which most of the killing occurred not in battles between soldiers, but in small villages and isolated homesteads and out on the open roads where Dakota war parties attacked settler families wherever they found them, killing many, taking others captive. Some settlers escaped the slaughter, some did not. Those who did carried stories of attack and massacre with them as they fled, and it was these reports that ignited the fires of fear, anger and hatred in white Minnesotans while the war was still being fought. The fact that so many of the dead were women and children did much to stoke public demands for vengeance once the war ended.

While all of this was happening, as the scattered homes and farms of settlers were being attacked across an area of several counties, the Dakota turned their attention to Fort Ridgely. The fort was only four hours' brisk walk from the Lower Agency. If the Dakota had attacked the fort on the evening of August 18, or even the next day, they almost certainly would have taken it. Ridgely was not built for defense, having no walls and being situated close to large ravines that permitted concealed avenues of approach. With the loss of 24 men of Captain Marsh's command in the ambush at Redwood Ferry, the garrison's combat strength was now less than 30 men. On Tuesday morning, August 19, a large body of Indians massed within sight of the fort, but the expected attack never came. One of the Indians' traditional methods of warfare was to prove their undoing—and the fort's salvation.

The Dakota usually sought the approval of influential men such as Little Crow, Shakopee and Mankato before going to war (although the members of the Soldiers' Lodges were notorious for acting on their own initiative). Once in the field, however, the chiefs exercised almost no degree of command and control over the warriors. Chiefs led by personal example and reputation, but their control over military operations was effectively nil compared to the authoritarian leadership practiced in the U.S. Army. As other historians have noted, the Dakotas' approach to waging war was more about tactical success than strategic planning; "In battle individual feats were of key importance, overriding the success of the group as a whole."[25] That morning near Fort Ridgely, this was the problem confronting the Indian leadership. The chiefs in council tried to convince their men that the fort should be attacked immediately, but the young warriors had a different idea. Ridgely was a military target, but not far away was the town of New Ulm, which promised more loot and female captives. Unable to reach a consensus for an assault on the fort, the Dakota force moved off to take New Ulm. While they were gone, the fort was reinforced with 180 defenders, and the Indians' best chance was lost.

New Ulm knew what was coming and had a day to organize its defenses—refugees by the hundreds had streamed in from the countryside, bringing with them tales of murder and mayhem. The town mustered more than 100 men into a citizens' militia, placed under the overall command of Judge Charles Flandrau. The former Indian Agent to the

Dakota, he was given the rank of Colonel of Volunteers and had just arrived at the head of more volunteer militia from the town of St. Peter.

The first attack fell on New Ulm on the afternoon of Tuesday, August 19. It was an ineffective assault lacking coordination or leadership, but it showed the townspeople that the danger was real. The heavy assault came on Saturday, August 23, when the Dakota returned in force and made a serious effort to take the town. The citizens had erected hasty barricades to create a defensible area encompassing the town's main street, and into this space were crowded more than 1,000 civilian refugees, many of them women and children. New Ulm held out, but only precariously. On August 24, with ammunition low and food running short, the decision was made to abandon the town and retreat to Mankato, about 30 miles away. Most of the town's buildings were destroyed, 34 of the defenders had been killed and 60 were wounded, leading Minnesota historian William Folwell to write, "This was no sham battle, no trivial affair, but an heroic defense of a beleaguered town against a much superior force."[26] The fighting at New Ulm constituted the largest Indian attack against a town in all the history of the American West. When the people of New Ulm retreated, they left the bodies of their dead, buried under the town's dirt streets.

In the meantime, the Dakota had decided Fort Ridgely had to be dealt with, after all. On the afternoon of August 20, they attacked the fort but were repulsed. In spite of its many shortcomings, Ridgely had one advantage: it was well supplied with cannon, fielding a six-pounder smoothbore, two 12 pounder mountain howitzers, a 12 pounder Napoleon, and a 24 pounder heavy howitzer. The Dakota had never before been on the

New Ulm came under sustained attack on two separate days. The fighting was often intense and occasionally at close range, but the defenders were able to hold the barricades. (courtesy Wellcome Library, London).

receiving end of artillery fire. When the first day's attack broke off unsuccessfully, the Indians returned to the Lower Agency for the night, talking about the big guns that fired the "rotten balls," as they called the explosive howitzer shells.

The main attack on the fort came on Friday, August 22, when as many as 800 warriors massed for a second assault. When that effort failed, the Indians regrouped and tried again. This time they succeeded in capturing several of the fort's out-buildings, from where they were able to fire on the defenders from covered positions. The soldiers' response was immediate—they turned their cannons on the buildings and blasted them with close-range fire until they were set ablaze.

Finally, the Dakota grouped in one of the nearby ravines for a direct frontal assault that might have overwhelmed the fort's defenses. Before they could launch the attack, however, the fort's big 24 pounder field piece was brought into action, blasting the Indian positions with its heavy shells while two other guns supported it with rounds of doublecharged canister. The Indian formation broke apart, and the concerted effort to take the fort was over. Surprisingly, for all of the heavy fire going back and forth, casualties among the defenders were few, and Dakota sources later claimed their losses to have been equally light (though witnesses later claimed to have found at least 21 Indian corpses that had been hastily buried in the ravines.) The cannon had made all the difference in Fort Ridgely's defense; Big Eagle was of the opinion that "but for the cannon I think we would have taken the fort."[27]

For the Indians the damage was already done. By failing to take the fort, they were stalled at the northwestern end of the Minnesota Valley. Had they captured the fort, the country would have lain open before them all the way to the state capitol of St. Paul. Big Eagle, whose account of the war is one of the most complete from the Indian side, later said, "We thought the fort was the door to the valley ... if we got through the door nothing could stop us this side of the Mississippi. But the defenders of the Fort were very brave and kept the door shut."[28]

Colonel Sibley, in the meantime, was moving slowly up the valley, gathering men as he went. The war at this point began to shift from Indian attacks on unsuspecting settlers and defended towns and forts, to engagements between Indians and organized units of soldiers and volunteer militia.[29] Sibley's slow, deliberate progress drew much criticism from the state's newspapers, which clamored for speed. His methodical advance was savaged in the press, with some commentators accusing him of sympathy for the Indians, with whom he had a prior cordial relationship. Editorials derisively called him the "State undertaker," since he seemed to spend more time burying the bodies of massacre victims than he did in fighting the Indians who had done the killing.

Yet Sibley had legitimate reasons for moving slowly: his force was made up of poorly trained volunteers, a hodge-podge of local militias and hastily enlisted troops, more civilian than military. In letters to his wife, Sibley repeatedly expressed his frustration with the undisciplined, unmartial character of his soldiers. He was also hampered by ordnance problems; much of the ammunition he had been issued was .68 caliber Minie balls, while his troops' obsolete muskets were bored for .51 caliber rounds. More than once in the field, Sibley's soldiers had to whittle down the oversized ammunition before loading. Another factor influencing his cautious movements was his fear that if he pressed the Indians too hard, the nearly 300 captives held by the Dakota would be killed before he could reach them.

Sibley tried to play for time, using the days to drill his green troops and toughening them to the demands of active campaigning. He also kept them busy fulfilling an unpleasant duty—burying the bodies of settlers killed in the first days of the war. Detachments of troops were sent out in different directions, finding corpses along roadways where they had been killed in their flight, or in the ruins of burned-out homesteads. Occasionally, they found survivors who had hidden in the woods for weeks. One of these burial parties almost became victims of the Dakotas' most decisive battlefield victory at the Battle of Birch Coulee.[30]

A force of about 150 men was sent out to find and bury the bodies of victims of the massacres in the vicinity of the Lower Agency. Sibley had specifically charged them with locating the bodies of the men killed when Captain Marsh's company was ambushed at Redwood Ferry—they had lain unburied since August 18. Dividing into separate groups, the burial party interred the corpses at Redwood Ferry, and also the bodies of other victims as they found them. Rendezvousing on the night of September 1, the separate burial parties bivouacked at Birch Coulee, a creek feeding into the Minnesota River. Captain Hiram Grant, commanding the military contingent of the force, chose the site for the encampment. Major Joseph Brown, the former Indian Agent whose Dakota wife and children were then being held captive by the Indians, had his doubts about the security of the position but did not insist on a different location.[31] The Indians, everyone believed, were miles away.

In fact, Dakota scouts had seen the movements of some of the force during the day and had trailed them back to the encampment. During the night, nearly 200 Indians moved into the area in preparation for an attack. The inexperienced soldiers had placed their pickets too close to their own perimeter to do them much good, and the Indians encircled the camp without being detected. In the grey light of early dawn, a soldier on guard duty finally saw Indians moving in front of his position and fired on them, raising the alarm. The surrounding Dakota warriors immediately took the encampment under a heavy and effective enfilade fire.

Most of the casualties inside the soldiers' lines were inflicted in the first hour of the engagement, until they managed to dig out shallow rifle pits with knives and bayonets. Nearly all of the expedition's horses were killed by Indian fire, their carcasses forming a makeshift rampart, from behind which the defenders fired. Caught off guard, and having made no preparation to occupy the site for long, the soldiers were in a dire predicament, especially as water began running low almost immediately.

The Indians kept the position surrounded and under heavy fire for nearly 31 hours, until Colonel Sibley brought up a relief column—slowly—from Fort Ridgely. The sounds of the battle at Birch Coulee had been audible from 16 miles away; if the battle had been fought farther away, it is likely that no rescue would have come, and the force at Birch Coulee would have been wiped out. When the Indians broke off the fight, most of the soldiers were down to just a few rounds of ammunition each. As it was, the butcher's bill was 13 dead, 47 wounded (four subsequently died of their wounds) and 90 horses killed. It had nearly been a disaster for the expeditionary force.

The same day the beleaguered unit at Birch Coulee was relieved, another detachment of about 57 men, under the command of Captain Richard Strout, fought a running skirmish near Acton with Indians who were led by either Little Crow or his half-brother,

White Spider. Fighting their way out of a converging encirclement of Dakota warriors, Strout's command managed to reach the town of Hutchinson, losing six dead and at least 15 wounded in the process. The next day bands of Indians attacked Hutchinson and the nearby town of Forest City, but the panic that had convulsed southwestern Minnesota since the outbreak on August 18 had prompted the citizens of both towns to build hasty stockades for defense. The attacks were successfully beaten off, but Strout later reported that the Indians had been remarkably well armed.

In the midst of all the maneuvering and fighting, a dialogue of sorts opened between Sibley and Little Crow. Before he left the battlefield at Birch Coulee, Sibley left a letter addressed to Little Crow on a stick where it was sure to be seen. As hoped, the letter was found by the Dakota, and the ensuing correspondence offers a remarkable insight into the last days of the Dakota War.

"If Little Crow has any proposition to make to me," Sibley wrote, "let him send a half-breed to me, and he shall be protected in and out of camp."[32] Little Crow could not read or write, but there were captives in his camp who could, and he selected a mixed-blood man named Campbell to act as his scribe. On September 7, he sent a reply to Sibley:

> For what reason we have commenced this war I will tell you, it is on account of Maj. Gilbrait [sic] we made a treaty with the Government a big for what little do we get and then cant [sic] get it till our children was dieing [sic] with hunger.... I have great many prisoner women and children it aint [sic] all our fault the winebagoes [sic] was in the engagement, two of them was killed I want you to give me answer by the barer [sic] all at present.
> 
> Yours truly, Friend Little Crow[33]

Sibley replied the next day. "Little Crow: You have murdered many of our people without any sufficient cause," he wrote. "Return me the prisoners, under a flag of truce, and I will talk with you then like a man."[34]

The correspondence went back and forth, carried by couriers. In his next letter, Little Crow said, "I want to know from you as a friend what way that il [sic] can make peace for my people...."[35]

Sibley took a hard line in his reply. "You have not done as I wished in giving up to me the prisoners taken by your people," he wrote. "It would be better for you to do so.... You have allowed your young men to commit nine murders since you wrote your first letter. This is not the way for you to make peace."[36]

In the meantime, other correspondents entered the exchange. Chief Wabasha was one of the Dakota who had opposed the idea of war, and he and another chief named Taopee wrote directly to Sibley. "You know that Little Crow has been opposed to me in everything that our people have had to do with the whites..." Wabasha wrote. "[H]e has now got himself into trouble that we know he can never get himself out of, and he is trying to involve those few of us what are still the friend of the american [sic] in the murder of the poor whites.... [I]f you will appoint a place for me to meet you, myself and the few friends that I have will get all the prisoners that we can, and with our family, go to whatever place you will appoint for us to meet.... We have not much time to spare."[37]

Sibley replied to them the same day that he answered a letter from Little Crow. "I have received your private message," he wrote to Wabasha. "I have come up here with a large force to punish the murderers of my people. It is not my purpose to injure any innocent person. If you and others who have not been concerned in the murders and expeditions [against the whites] will gather yourselves, with all the prisoners, on the prairie in full sight by you a white flag will be hoisted in my camp, and then you can come forward and place yourself under my protection...."[38] With this, Little Crow's already weakening influence among the Dakota was fatally undermined. Other chiefs were now treating with the Army without his knowledge, seeking a separate peace, and the remainder of the Dakota were increasingly in disagreement over what they ought to do.

The tide had definitely turned against the Dakota. They had never mounted anything like a united front against the whites. Several of the most influential chiefs, such as Standing Buffalo of the Upper Agency, actually threatened to fight Little Crow and his bands if they attempted to bring the war into their territory. Wabasha and Taopee were not the only ones advocating a peaceful resolution to the conflict, but the war party among the Dakota was still strong.

When the Dakota discussed their options in council, Wabasha's son-in-law, Rdainyanka, took a hard stance on the question. "I am for continuing the war," he is credited with saying, "and am opposed to the delivery of the prisoners. I have no confidence that the whites will stand by any agreement they make if we give them up." His reasons for this cynicism were based on well-established patterns. "Ever since we treated with them their agents and traders have robbed and cheated us," he said. "We may regret what has happened but the matter has gone too far to be remedied. We have got to die. Let us, then, kill as many of the whites as possible, and let the prisoners die with us."[39]

He was not the only one to argue for continuing the fight. A man named Mazzawamnuna reportedly told the gathered Dakota, "You men who are in favor of leaving us and delivering up the captives talk like children. You believe, if you do so, the whites ... will spare your lives." That was a pipe dream, he argued. "You say that the whites are too strong for us, and that we will all have to perish. By sticking together and fighting the whites, we will live, at all events, for a few days, when, by the course you propose, we would die at once." Mazzawamnuna pushed for keeping the prisoners to the bitter, bloody end, saying, "let them share our fate."[40]

Paul Mazakutemani, also called Shoots as He Walks and known to the whites as Little Paul, was a former speaker of the Upper Agency Dakota who was a Christian Indian. He had opposed the war from the start. He later said that when he addressed his fellow Dakota, he told them:

> Give me all these white captives. I will deliver them up to their friends. You Dakotas are numerous—you can afford to give these captives to me, and I will go with them to the white people. Then, if you want to fight, when you see the white soldiers coming to fight, fight with them, but don't fight with women and children. Or stop fighting. The Americans are a great people. They have much lead, powder, guns, and provisions. Stop fighting, and now gather up all the captives and give them to me. No one who fights with the white people ever becomes rich, or remains two days in one place, but is always fleeing and starving.[41]

Little Paul was right—there would be fleeing and starving in the months ahead. At that moment, however, no one seemed inclined to listen to him. Little Paul recorded in his narrative of the incident that, after his speech had been refuted, the warriors who rejected peace rode away singing a "warrior song": Over the earth I come/Over the earth I come/A soldier I come/Over the earth I am a ghost.[42] He remembered that he disliked the song very much.

In the meantime, Sibley had moved his force, now totaling at least 1,619 men, up to the area of the Upper Agency on the Yellow Medicine River. On the night of September 22 he established an overnight encampment on the shore of Lone Tree Lake. The expedition's guide mistook the site for Wood Lake, which was a little over three miles way, and thus the events of the next day went into history under the wrong name.

During the night hundreds of Dakota warriors, who knew all along the position and movements of Sibley's force, moved into the area and set up an ambush. The Indians knew their enemy well—a military encampment at dawn is usually alert and watchful, no easy mark. But a unit in the act of breaking camp and setting out on the march is distracted, strung out and out of its protective posture. The Indians intended to spring a linear ambush as the troops moved out into their line of march. Ironically, it was a lack of discipline on the part of a few of Silbey's soldiers that foiled this plan.

At about 7:00 a.m., several veteran soldiers of the Third Minnesota Infantry, apparently tired of their issued rations, decided to do a little extracurricular foraging. They loaded into wagons and set off to see if they could scrounge potatoes and pumpkins from the abandoned gardens around the Upper Agency. Their path took them directly into the unseen Indian ambush.

Big Eagle, remembering the event 30 years later, said, "They came on over the prairie right where our line was. Some wagons were not on the road, and if they had gone straight on would have driven right over our men as they lay in the grass."[43] The Indians rose up and fired, and the ambush was initiated without even a fraction of Sibley's force being anywhere near the kill zone.

Despite their momentary indiscipline, the foraging party from the Third Minnesota were experienced combat soldiers. The Third was a seasoned unit, recently paroled to their home state after being captured by Confederates at the Battle of Murfeesboro in Tennessee. The veterans knew how to react to enemy contact. Abandoning the wagons, they immediately formed a line of battle and returned fire. The sudden rattle of musketry alerted Sibley's camp, and other men of the Third formed up without waiting for orders and moved out to help their comrades.

The Indians, giving up on the failed ambush, fell back momentarily, but then threw an encircling attack at the small battalion of the Third Minnesota that had formed on the field, trying to take them from the flanks. Sibley, coming up from behind with the main body, saw the danger and ordered the Third to fall back on the security of the larger force. He had to give the order twice—the veteran infantrymen had their blood up and were in a toe-to-toe fight with a normally elusive enemy. Finally, after their commanding officer was wounded, they fell back into the main battle line.

For a couple of hours, it was a full-throated fight. Though Sibley was no soldier, and had no real training in tactics or maneuver, he apparently had a good eye for a developing engagement and reacted with clarity and decisiveness. On at least two occasions he saw threats developing on his flanks and quickly shifted companies of the Sixth Minnesota to beat them back before his lines were endangered, or used his mountain howitzers to break up developing Indian attacks.

The Indians broke contact after two hours of fighting. For them, it was a lost opportunity. Most of the large Indian force, spread out in anticipation of taking the soldiers unawares on the march, was too far away to get into the fight quickly. Chief Mankato was killed, and at least 14 other Dakota dead were on the field where they fell, their comrades unable to recover their bodies. Sibley's casualties were much lighter than they would have been had the ambush been sprung successfully—seven killed and 33 wounded.

The Indian war that erupted on the Minnesota frontier was largely unremarked upon in the eastern states, at least at first. There were larger, more immediate concerns to occupy the nation's attention in the second year of the Civil War. The battle of Second Manassas—another in a depressing series of Union defeats—was fought August 28–30; the battle of Antietam was fought on September 17, the bloodiest day in American military history; and the debacle of Fredericksburg played out on the Rappahannock River in mid–December. "Compared with the sacrifice in the South," Robert Jones says in his work on the concurrent wars, "the disaster in the Northwest was insignificant. It takes no imagination to see why the country's attention was focused on Virginia and Maryland, rather than Minnesota."[44] Weighed against developments in the Civil War, events in Minnesota hardly mattered to those in the East.

Once the scale of the outbreak became apparent, though, President Lincoln was confronted with the very real possibility that he might lose Minnesota's regiments in the Union Army unless the Indian crisis was quickly resolved. Governor Alexander Ramsey was not willing to settle for the short shrift his appeals first received from the War Department. In high agitation, he wrote directly to Lincoln. "Those Indian outrages continue," he wrote on September 6. "This is not our war; it is a national war.... I hope you will direct the purchase or send us 500 horses, or order the Minnesota companies of horse in Kentucky and Tennessee home." Then, abandoning all pretense of the respect normally accorded the office of the President, he demanded, "Answer me at once. More than 500 whites have been murdered by the Indians."[45] The national government finally responded.

Major General John Pope, who had just been relieved of his command after the fiasco at Manassas, was dispatched to Minnesota to take administrative charge of the war against the Indians. Never a humble man at the best of times, Pope was smarting under the perceived injustice of his dismissal. He arrived in Minnesota with all the grace of a man who felt himself unfairly exiled to the hinterlands, but his attitude changed quickly. He immediately began firing off salvos of telegrams back to the War Department, demanding more troops and newer arms. He got neither, at least not in the numbers he felt the crisis warranted, but that did not stop him pestering the General in Chief of the Army, Henry Halleck, and Secretary of War Edwin Stanton, with a laundry list of demands.

"When will the paroled troops begin to arrive?" he wrote to Secretary Stanton on September 25. "How many are coming? Preparations for them must be commenced at once certainly.... I fear the Sioux, being all mounted, have got into the rear of the expedition [Sibley's force] and are attacking the towns and settlements both north and south of the Minnesota River...." Pope never shied away from hyperbole in his language (as the western historian Robert Utley has remarked, Pope would never use a single word when ten would suffice), and he happily indulged his verbosity in his official correspondence.

"The money and supplies required ought to be sent at once or we must abandon our advanced positions…," he continued, "Everybody is green here. The service is inefficient, and the expenses will be enormous in consequence…. You will therefore see that my inquiries and applications should, if possible, be immediately attended to."[46]

As a matter of fact, this part of the war was already over, though no one seemed to have yet realized it. Pope's letter of dire warning to Stanton was written just two days after Sibley's forces fought the misnamed Battle of Wood Lake, which turned out to be the last full engagement of the war in Minnesota.

The same day that Pope dashed off his doom-and-gloom letter, Sibley finally arrived at the camp of friendly Indians, who handed over to him the white and mixed-race captives who had been taken during the war. It had been a long, excruciating wait for them, knowing that release was near but still under considerable uncertainty.[47] By then, though, many of the hardliners among the Dakota—particularly those who wanted to continue the fighting or who felt they had the most to lose by surrendering to the Army—had already fled west into Dakota Territory with Little Crow and the other holdouts. Sibley named his encampment at the site Camp Release, and it was there on September 27 that he formed the first version of the military commission, a three-man commission of inquiry. The next day he issued General Order No. 55, convening the five-man commission that was to conduct the trials over the next five weeks.

# 5

## "My heart is hardened"

*If I have the means and can catch them, I will sweep them with the besom of death.*
—Henry H. Sibley

As the principal American figure in the Dakota War, Henry Hastings Sibley merits close study. He commanded the hastily assembled expeditionary force that put down the outbreak that summer, and he led one arm of the punitive expedition against the holdout Dakota groups the following year. The decision to form a military commission to try Indians accused of criminal participation in the war was initially a matter of his sole initiative, contrary to what some historians have argued.[1] During the trials he exerted a considerable (and in some cases inappropriate) influence on the commission's proceedings. When the trials were concluded, he wrote numerous letters to state officials, military officers, the Departments of War and the Interior, and to President Lincoln himself, all urging that the death sentences which the commission handed down be carried out to the last man. In the vast scope of his professional and personal correspondence, he steadfastly defended his decision to convene the commission and never backed away from his belief that it was both correct and necessary. Throughout this book, I frequently refer to the military commission as "Sibley's commission," because that is exactly what it was, and as we will see, it largely functioned as he wanted.

By the time of the outbreak of war in 1862, Sibley was a man of considerable influence in Minnesota. He came out to the Minnesota Territory as a young man, looking for adventure and a chance to make his way in the world. His way turned out to be the fur trade; within a few years, he was well on his way to financial security. As he prospered, he built a reputation for respectability. A rather tall man, he was known to the Indians as "Wapetonhonska (The Long Trader)."[2] (At least one source claims another reason for this nickname: "The Dakota referred to Sibley as 'Long Trader' because he had profited unfairly from his dealings with the Indians," but Sibley's biographer disputes that allegation.[3]) Sibley went on to represent Minnesota in the U.S. Congress as a Territorial Delegate from 1850 to 1854, and was elected the state's first governor.

Sibley had a high regard for many of the Indians with whom he had contact in the decades before the war, and both his personal actions and the reports of others would seem to indicate that his positive relations with the Indians were consistent and genuine. In 1850, a young Swedish woman named Fredrika Bremer described her impressions of Sibley, whom she met while traveling into Minnesota on a steamboat. Sibley, she wrote, "has lived many years among the Sioux, participating in their hunting and their daily life, [he] has related to me many characteristics of this people's life and disposition. There is a certain grandeur about them.... Mr. Sibley is very fond of the Indians, and is said to be a very great favorite with them."[4]

Sibley expounded on his defense of Indian rights in numerous forums. In a paper that he presented at a meeting of the fledgling Minnesota Historical Society in February 1856, Sibley wrote, "The decay of the Dakotas in our midst may be dated from the time of their treaty in 1837, by which the U.S. Government acquired their lands on the East of the Mississippi River...." "Recourse to liquor, and other evil habits," he continued, "are but the natural consequences of that system which drives him from his home, interferes with his habits of life, and regards him as an outcast from the land of his fathers, without holding out to him any promise for the future."[5] From most reports of Sibley, and by his own statements, it seems that before the Dakota War he was as outspoken an advocate for the Indians of Minnesota as anyone was, and perhaps more so than many.

Henry Hastings Sibley as a Brigadier General, in an 1863 portrait. By this point in his life, Sibley had already been a successful fur trader, Justice of the Peace, Territorial Representative and the first Governor of Minnesota. Still, the only title he requested be engraved on his tombstone was the military rank that he acquired during the Dakota War (Minnesota Historical Society).

He was also personally acquainted with many of the Dakota men who came before the military commission as defendants. Sibley and Little Crow had spent considerable time together some years before the war—Sibley had organized a "Great Hunt" in southeastern Minnesota over the winter of 1841–42, and Little Crow was one of the Dakota men who participated in that hunt. Sibley was also closely connected with Henry Milord, a young mixed-blood man who was raised by white families but who sided with the Dakota during the war. There was some speculation that Sibley was in fact Milord's father, but no such relationship was ever proven. What was a matter of record, however, was that Sibley did take a personal interest in Milord's life, including setting up him in an apprenticeship, and looking out for him in other ways. Sibley might not have been Milord's biological father, but in some ways he certainly played the role of foster father to him, and at various times had a *loco parentis* relationship with him. For Sibley, many of the men who appeared in shackles before the military commission were not just names—they were people he knew personally.

Notwithstanding his overall positive relationships with the Dakota, Sibley still has his detractors where his dealings with Indians were concerned. He was, after all, a man of his time, and though his attitude toward the Indians was relatively progressive, he still expressed views that can be a bit jarring to a modern perspective. Some years before he married his wife Sarah, he fathered a daughter with a Dakota woman, a relationship he left behind as he settled into the life of a respectable man of business. He also apparently attempted to leave behind the paternity of his daughter, whose name was Helen Hastings Sibley. Though he acknowledged his relationship to her amongst his friends, he steadfastly refused to allow official recognition of that relationship in any state documents.

Sibley seems to have admired the Indians as a culture, and he may have genuinely counted some of them as personal friends, but at the same time he believed that the white man's culture and religion were inherently superior to those of the Indian. He accepted, apparently without much question, the common 19th century American view that civilization and Christianization could only do the Indians good, and were essential for their survival.

The supportable consensus seems to be that Sibley was, by and large, a principled man of good reputation who thought better of the Indians than did most of his fellow Minnesotans. Even some of his modern critics see him as a man of "integrity and humanity."[6] He was a shrewd businessman, and an experienced frontiersman, politician, and statesman. He had studied law and had the advantage of a good education. He was comfortable out on the prairie and was an accomplished hunter and tracker, and he also indulged an appreciation for refinement in his fine Mendota house. What he was not, however, was a soldier.

When Governor Alexander Ramsey placed him in command of the expedition against the Dakota in August 1862, Sibley was appointed a Colonel of Volunteers. With the stroke of a pen he was made a field grade officer, commanding the only military force available to respond to the Indian outbreak. He had no training in tactics or the military sciences, no practical experience as a soldier. It is true that in 1856 he was appointed a Major General of the Second Division in the state militia, but that was a grandiose title that came with a state political appointment. His strengths as a field commander were that he at least had an intimate knowledge of his enemy.

From Sibley's own words, it is clear that upon accepting command of the expedition against the Dakota, he experienced a sudden and pronounced change in his attitudes toward the Indians. In one of his first letters to his wife after accepting the commission, his language has a distinctly Old Testament tone to it. "My preparations," he wrote, "are nearly completed to begin my work upon them with fire and sword, and my heart is hardened against them beyond any touch of mercy."[7]

There are various explanations for this sudden harshness. One is that Sibley was adopting an exaggeratedly martial tone in light of his new charge as the military commander of the expedition against the Dakota. Another is that the outbreak of violence, and the shocking reports of marauding Indians, put Sibley in the position of feeling he had to distance himself from his well-known support for the same Indians who were now apparently intent on killing every white man they could find. There *is* a sense of personal emotion in Sibley's fire-breathing rhetoric in the early days of the campaign, but it was probably not merely a cover he was throwing up against public criticism. The full range of Sibley's personal correspondence over the course of the war suggests that the sentiment he expressed when he said "my heart is hardened against them" was an indication that to some degree, he felt personally betrayed by the Dakota uprising.

Another factor behind his reaction to the outbreak of violence may have been his long and intimate acquaintance with the Dakota, and his knowledge of their culture. The Dakota, as was true of many other tribes, lived by a code of life-for-a-life vengeance. In that societal norm, for the Americans to receive an attack as aggressive as the assaults on the settlements and do nothing would be to invite further attack. Viewed through the lens of Dakota culture, Sibley feared that restraint on the part of the U.S. government or the Army would not be interpreted as forbearance. It would be viewed as a weakness, and "the Dakotas would have no respect for any adversary who was so soft as to ignore that principle."[8] Sibley had known the Dakota in friendship, he had known them in trade, he had known them in diplomacy—now he was learning to know them in war, and it was because of all that background and long acquaintance, not in spite of it, that he spoke of severe punishment and reprisal.

There is also something in Sibley's tone at this point that indicates he felt that he had been wronged on a personal level. He had been a voice for Minnesota's Indian peoples in his time in government, and now his work on their behalf was apparently for naught. Many of the missionaries who had dedicated years of their lives to living and working with the Indians doubtlessly felt the same as Sibley, but his reactions were markedly different from theirs. Where they redoubled their efforts on the Indians' behalf, and argued that there were mitigating factors for the outbreak, Sibley initially reacted with outrage and anger. The fact that he himself had been instrumental in the machinations by which the money paid to the Indians as a result of the 1851 treaty was attached by some traders, and that he had personally profited from the arrangement, does not receive mention in the letters he wrote that summer. (At the same time, the frequently repeated claim that Sibley made a fortune from fleecing the Indians is almost certainly untrue. "One of the most persistent myths about Sibley is that he made a fortune in the fur trade," historian Rhoda Gilman points out. "The sums look large, but nearly every 'debt' he collected from the Dakota went toward paying his own debts to Chouteau and the American Fur Company."[9])

Once Sibley had called the Dakota "friends"; he now wrote that they were "fiends" and "devils in human shape."[10] Perhaps this is why in the weeks to come he sometimes threatened the Dakota with a retributive violence that would have been every bit as bad as the massacres of white settlers at the beginning of the war, had he actually carried it out. At one point after the fighting ended he wrote, "I repeated to them [the Dakota] what I had previously stated in my message to them, that if any more of their young men went off to war upon the whites I would fall upon their camp and cut them to pieces, without regard to age or sex."[11]

There is no suggestion in most of Sibley's letters from August through October 1862 that he relented from this new hostility toward the Dakota. If he had truly hardened his heart, it remained hardened, at least as long as he was in the field against them. This presents some problems when we consider Sibley's decision to impanel the military commission for trials, and his continued close influence over the commission. From the language of his correspondence, both official and private, it seems that he formed his opinions with regards to Indian guilt well before he created the commission, and he did not approach the matter with any degree of impartiality. He was determined to dispense a firm and rapid justice; all that remained was to lay his hands on the guilty. Finally, at the end of September, he could.

## 5. "My heart is hardened"

The citizens of Minnesota, in the majority, were not so interested in seeing justice dispensed under the law as they were in exacting an immediate and savage revenge against the Dakota. Newspapers across the state were calling for a punishment ten times worse than what the Dakota had done, and they wanted it meted out to all Dakota, not just the few who had committed acts of murder and massacre. This was the situation when the fighting ended—this was what confronted Sibley as he considered how to deal with the Indians at hand. When he convened the military commission, the fact was that the court of public opinion had already decided that almost every Dakota was a murderer, and the loudest voices in the public forum were demanding a harsh vengeance against an entire people, not simply justice against a few individuals.

On September 27, Sibley wrote to General Pope to report the recovery of almost all of the white and mixed-blood captives, whom the anti-war faction of friendly Indians had handed over to him. In the letter, Sibley repeated a request he had made several times before—that he be relieved of command in favor of a "strictly military commander"—and then, almost as an aside, he wrote:

> I have issued an order appointing a military commission, consisting of two field officers and the senior captain of the Sixth Regiment, Colonel Crooks, Lieutenant Colonel Marshall, and Captain Grant, for the examination of all the men, half-breeds as well as Indians, in the camp near us, with instructions to sift the antecedents of each, so that if there are guilty parties among them they can be arrested and properly dealt with. I have no doubt we shall find some such in the number. I will report the result in due time...[12]

With those few sentences, Henry H. Sibley set in motion a process that would end with the largest simultaneous hanging in American history.

# Part Two

# The Trials

*This Trial Record is not published to malign those concerned, their acts can be left to the Almighty, but to show that history is far from just to the Indian people, whose lands have been taken, by force, fraud and deceit, whose demoralization and destruction as a race is due to the advent of the white man. The record is a living picture of their treatment.*

—Marion Satterlee

# 6

# "Ferreting out and punishing the guilty"

*It is not my purpose to injure any innocent person.*—Henry H. Sibley

The historical records and the personal recollections of the participants both agree that the commission that Sibley first ordered to undertake the "examination of all the men, half-breeds as well as Indians," was *not* the commission which actually tried the accused in the following weeks. It was not the same in either intent or design. The three-man commission to which Sibley referred in his September 27 letter was essentially an investigatory body, fulfilling the function that the modern Uniform Code of Military Justice (UCMJ) would recognize as an Article 32 proceeding.[1] The purpose of this first incarnation of the commission, as Sibley explained it and as the participants understood it, was that it was a commission of inquiry, tasked with sifting the guilty from the innocent.

"Sifting," in fact, was exactly how the process was described at the time. Gabriel Renville, a half-Dakota man whose family had been captives of the Indians during the war, wrote in his account, "word came down that the Indians would be sifted as you would sift wheat, the good grain to be put into the bin, but the chaff and the bad seeds to be burned. This was done, and all those who by good evidence were proven to have done anything against the whites were put into irons."[2]

The Reverend Stephen R. Riggs, a missionary who had spent nearly 25 years living among the Dakota and who spoke their language (and who along with his family escaped the outbreak of war with the aid of friendly Indians), was attached to Sibley's command as the expedition's chaplain. Riggs wrote to his daughter the same day that Sibley wrote to Pope, and his letter makes this first version of the commission's mandate clear. "I was informed," Riggs wrote, "that I had to serve as interpreter to a military commission which was appointed to investigate the cases of the Indians so far as concerning their conduct in this uprising and also in regard to the captives."[3] The commission to which Riggs referred here was the three-man board of Colonel William Crooks, Lieutenant-Colonel William Marshall, and Captain Hiram Grant, with Riggs functioning as deposer of witnesses as well as translator.

"We have taken up and confined today eight men," Riggs continued, "seven Indians and one Negro. What will be done with them I don't know—probably it will go hard with them. They are charged with murder and rape." The "Negro" was Joseph Godfrey, the man whose case was the first to appear before the commission and who subsequently turned witness for the government. "The intention," Riggs explained to his daughter, "is to purge out the iniquity from the camp and thus save those who are good."[4] There was no way Riggs could have known it, at that point, but many of the good would suffer along with the bad. It was a fact that was to trouble him long after all was said and done.

The commission for which Riggs was interpreting was tasked with identifying those men against whom there was sufficient evidence to prefer charges upon which they might subsequently be arraigned and tried. That was Sibley's intent, and that was precisely what this first commission did, but not for long.

The day after informing Pope of the formation of the three-man commission, Sibley wrote to his superior again. "I have apprehended 16 Indians in the friendly camp adjoining," he said, "who are suspected of being participants in the late outrages, and I have appointed a military commission of five officers to try them." This is a crucial statement in the chronology of events, because this was Sibley's first reference to the military commission that was to be so controversial in the historiography. "If found guilty they will be immediately executed," he continued, and then he repeated his statement in his September 27 letter almost word for word: "although I am somewhat in doubt whether my authority extends quite so far. An example is, however, imperatively necessary, and I trust you will approve the act, should it happen that some real criminals have been seized and promptly disposed of...."[5]

Regardless of any doubts he may have had about the reach of his authority, Sibley drove ahead with the commission. What had begun as a commission of inquiry was replaced by a commission of judgment, empowered to convict and pass capital sentences. If there was any concern that this decision might incur official disapproval, it was put to rest with the arrival of a letter from Pope that had crossed Sibley's in transit. After taking a paragraph to petulantly chide Sibley for sending a dispatch to Governor Ramsey instead of directly to himself ("the Governor..." Pope wrote, "no longer has any control over military operations in this section.... I trust you will hereafter comply with the proper regulations on the subject"), Pope expressed sentiments that certainly seemed to legitimize Sibley's decision to put the Indians to trial by the commission. "It is idle and wicked, in view of the atrocious murders these Indians have committed..." he wrote, "[t]he horrible massacres of women and children and the outrageous abuse of female prisoners, still alive, call for punishment beyond human power to inflict." Whether Pope was expressing his personal feelings on the matter or was relaying official policy is a moot point—as Sibley's immediate superior, and as commander of the military district covering the area of operations, Pope's diatribe had the effect of a directive. "They are to be treated as maniacs or wild beasts," he concluded, "and by no means as people with whom treaties or compromises can be made."[6]

As the trials got underway, so did the records of the military commission's proceedings begin to accumulate. For researchers studying the Dakota War trials, the most important primary sources are probably the trial transcripts themselves. They are held in two locations—the originals are in the National Archives and a complete set of copies is held by the Minnesota Historical Society. As historical documents they are incredible. They are also not what a modern reader might envision when thinking of trial records.

For one thing, they are all hand-written (of course), and not all by the same person. In those cases where Isaac Heard functioned as the Official Recorder, the transcripts are written in a distinct and clear hand, easy to read. Some others, written by someone other than Heard, are written with a rougher penmanship and are a bit harder to decipher.

Another thing about them is that they are brief—*very* brief in some cases. Nor are they verbatim transcriptions of what was said in the courtroom during trial. Heard was not a stenographer, and the transcripts were not recorded in shorthand, capturing everything that the defendants or witnesses said. Some of the transcripts read like a summation of what went on in the trial; others are a bit more detailed, especially in those cases where there were multiple witnesses or when the defendants made statements of their own. But reading through all of the transcripts, it becomes quite clear that Heard and the other scribes were not attempting to capture a word-for-word record of the trials— it is doubtful that they could have, even had they wanted to. From a researcher's perspective, there is often a frustrating sense (or certainty) that more was said in the courtroom than was actually recorded.

The shift from a commission of investigation to one of judgment has sometimes been explained as the result of outside pressures. One commentator says that Sibley's plan for the commission "was innocuous enough at first, but pressure from public opinion forced a change in procedure."[7] Another historian believes that "in the face of mounting public pressure for vengeance, for retribution, the plan [to have a court of inquiry] had to be abandoned."[8]

Both scenarios seem unlikely when considered in the full context of the situation. From Sibley's correspondence over the duration of the campaign it is quite clear that he was sensitive to criticisms directed at him in the press, but it does not automatically follow that he was reacting to public opinion when he changed the commission from one of investigation to one of judgment. It is highly doubtful that such pressure could have come to bear upon him in such a short span of time. After all, the three-man investigatory commission was in effect for only one day, so it is doubtful that outside pressure forced the change to a trial commission. Sibley *was* coming under increasing pressure from his immediate superior, General Pope, but that was far more forceful and nefarious than the sort of broader public influence suggested above.

The distinction between the three-man investigatory commission and the five-man judgmental commission has not always been correctly understood in the historiography.[9] Oscar Malmros, the Adjutant General of Minnesota, contributed to the confusion the year after the war when he wrote in the Adjutant General's Report (AG Report): "The military commissions still prosecuted their labors, the one acting the part of a grand jury, by examining as to whether there were sufficient evidences of guilt against any particular Indian to justify his being put upon his trial before the other commission, and the other acting the part of a petit or trial jury, by trying all against whom charges had been found before the commission of inquiry."[10] This is a misrepresentation of the actual sequence of events. In fact, the first incarnation of the military commission existed for only one day before it was superseded by the five-man commission. There is no evidence in the record to support a conclusion that the two versions of the commission ever operated simultaneously or in concert with each other.

For clarity's sake, it may be helpful to consider the military explanation of a court of inquiry, an explanation that does much to distinguish it from a court martial or military commission. "The court of inquiry…" as the 19th century American legal scholar William Winthrop says, "is not really a court at all. No criminal issue is formed before it, it arraigns no prisoner, receives no plea, makes no finding of guilt or innocence, awards no punishments. Its proceedings are not a trial, nor is its opinion a judgement. It does not administer justice, and is not sworn to do so, but simply to 'examine and inquire.'"[11]

At any rate, once the five-man commission was convened it forged ahead, beginning the process of trying the Indians already in custody. Sibley continued to keep Pope informed as to his actions in that regard. On September 30 he wrote, "The work of the military commission still continues, and new developments take place daily incriminating parties in the friendly [Dakota] camp. Indians are arrested daily on charges duly preferred by me…."[12]

A week later, Sibley sent another dispatch to Pope, discussing another group of Indians whom he was expecting to surrender to him any day. "When they have all arrived I will surround their camp with my forces," he wrote, "and disarm, and take the men, except the older ones, prisoners, to be tried by a military commission…."[13] He was casting his net wider with each passing day—where at first he had identified fewer than 20 specific Indians for trial, by this point he was sweeping up all the fighting-aged Indian men that he could lay hands on. One of the mixed-race men who was present at Camp Release described the situation clearly by saying, "Any Indian could come into this camp but none ever got out."[14]

Sibley was looking for guilty men wherever they could be found, and he was even shaking up the Dakota bands whose chiefs had refused to join in the war against the whites. "The greater part of the last-mentioned bands," he wrote on October 5, "those of Standing Buffalo, Wanatua, and Red Feather, have been friendly throughout the outbreak … their decided refusal to receive or countenance Little Crow and his devilish crew is deserving of commendation and should insure them against injury by our troops." But after praising the constancy of these Indians, he concluded, "Still these bands require sifting and purging in order to discover the guilty individuals among them…."[15]

On October 7, Sibley reported that he now had 20 prisoners under sentence of death by hanging. "I have not yet examined the proceedings of the military commission," he wrote, "but although they may not be exactly in form in all of the details I shall probably approve them, and hang the villains as soon as I get hold of the others." What kept him from putting nooses around their necks immediately was not judicial forbearance, but rather a tactical consideration. Sibley had quite a few fish in his net, but he wanted more. "It would not do to precipitate matters now," he wrote, referring to his decision to postpone the hangings of the men already condemned, "for fear of alarming those who are coming forward to take their chances."[16]

If at this point Sibley would have decided to hang the Indians who were sentenced to death, he probably would not have encountered much official objection, at least not from his immediate superior. Pope was expressing similar sentiments in his own dispatches to Washington. On October 9, Pope reported to General Halleck, "Many are being tried by military commission for being connected in the late horrible outrages, and will be executed…."[17] The next day he wrote to Halleck again, telling him that Sibley was holding "about 1,500 prisoners," [this number included women and children who were not accused of any crimes] and expressed his belief that, "The example of hanging many of the perpetrators of the late outrages is necessary and will have a crushing effect...."[18] The Army's inclination at this stage of the process, at least as it was personified by Henry H. Sibley, was close to summary executions.

# 7

# The Trials Begin

*CHARGE—Participation in the murders, outrages and robberies committed by the Sioux Tribe of Indians, on the Minnesota frontier.*
—From the Military Commission's indictment

When the five officers of the military commission convened on September 28, the first case they considered was that of a mixed-race man named Joseph Godfrey, referred to in most of the records as a "mulatto" or "the negro Godfrey."[1] Godfrey's fate seemed sealed before the commission even opened his case. "As it was an easy matter to prove his apparent hostile acts, and impossible for him to prove his innocence or friendly intentions upon the common rules of evidence," the Adjutant General's Report says, "his conviction was certain."[2] That particular account of Godfrey's trial indirectly highlights some of the persistent faults of the military commission that we will consider at length—in particular the role of active prejudice in the commission's proceedings, and the presumption of guilt before trial. The AG Report went on to refer to "the prejudice existing against his race generally, and that excited against himself individually by comments in the public press...." Godfrey's guilt, the AG Report said, "might be considered as already proven."[3]

Godfrey's trial stands out from most of the other 391 cases presided over by the military commission in several ways. For one thing, the transcripts of his trial are altogether more complete, and of greater length and detail, than those of almost every subsequent trial. For all of their acknowledged initial bias against him, the officers on the commission seemed to come round to a much more sympathetic view of him in fairly short order. Charged with murder and participation in the "murders, robberies and outrages" during the late war, Godfrey protested that he had never killed anyone, and that he accompanied the war parties only out of duress. The Indians, he said, would have killed him if he had not gone along. His greatest contribution to the Dakota war effort was in transportation—Godfrey was a skilled teamster, and was pressed into service driving wagons for the war parties. He made an impression on the judges with his testimony about some of the most infamous events of the war, particularly the killings in the vicinity of Milford on August 18.

Unfortunately for Godfrey, in the first days of the war the Dakota had given him a nickname that cast his claims of innocence in a bad light. Otakle, they called him, which essentially translates to "Many Kills."[4] That name quickly became widely known after the war, leading many white observers to conclude that Godfrey was a murderer of the deepest dye who must have been complicit in the killing of untold numbers of settlers. The reality, however, was that this may have been one of the many areas of cultural misunderstanding, where traditional Dakota ways of war were utterly different from the European-American definitions. In Dakota warfare, a man could be credited with killing an enemy in situations where he himself had not actually delivered the fatal blow or fired the fatal shot. Touching an enemy could be as meritorious an action as killing him, so several Dakota might receive diminishing degrees of battle honors for one slain enemy—the first man to touch the body, then the second, and so on. Godfrey protested that he himself had never actually killed anyone, but that he had been present when settlers were killed by other Dakota, and that he received credit by proximity, as it were.[5]

The military commission seemed to actually recognize this distinction. After a trial that lasted longer than most of those that would follow, the commission acquitted Godfrey of the direct commission of any specific act of murder but convicted him of the more general charge of participating in murder and massacre. He was, essentially, convicted of felony murder.

There is a lingering misconception that Godfrey then became the government's star witness and that most of the men hanged at Mankato went to the gallows on the weight of his testimony alone. While Godfrey did testify against many of the 38 whose death sentences were confirmed by Lincoln, particularly those men who had participated in the killings at Milford on August 18, his was certainly not the only testimony against them. A close study of the trial transcripts leads to the conclusions that most of the executed men were convicted on the merit of their own self-incriminating statements, or on the basis of testimony provided by numerous witnesses of whom Godfrey was only one.[6] It is clear, though, that the military commission soon came to regard Godfrey's version of events with a great degree of confidence, especially as other defendants confirmed the accuracy of his account. Godfrey, it was later said, was "endowed with extraordinary perceptive qualities, and a memory for the retention of his perceptions such as is possessed by few, of any color or nationality."[7]

Godfrey's role in the Dakota trials remains the subject of some legitimate controversy. His input was not always limited to providing testimony, as we will see in a following chapter, but occasionally going so far as to act almost as if he were an adjunct prosecutor. The fact that he had a death sentence hanging over his own head, and that his motivation for acting as the government's witness could rightly have been suspect, was apparently never seen as a cause for concern. Nor did any member of the commission ever remark upon the fact that a legal question existed in American military law which could have cast some doubt on Godfrey as a witness. "The testimony of one who has been convicted of a felony or any other species of *crimen falsi*," military jurist Alexander Macomb noted in his 1841 commentary on military law, "is regarded by the law as of too doubtful a character to be admitted in a Court of Justice."[8] This does not mean, of course, that a witness is necessarily excluded from testifying because of culpability in the same crime as subsequent defendants, but this factor should at least be recognized and considered by the court. There is no indication that Sibley's military commission ever did this.

One factor seldom considered in depth by previous studies of the 1862 trials is the way in which military command influence imposed its will upon the court. Sibley, as we will soon see, exerted this type of interference with the commission, but so did General Pope. It has long been accepted that Pope approved of Sibley's actions and saw no reason to order him to cease with the military commission, but until recently no one had recognized the degree to which Pope directly interfered with the way the trials were conducted. This does not mean, however, as historian David Martinez asserts, that Pope "compelled former governor Henry H. Sibley to establish a military commission."[9] On the contrary—Sibley established the commission and began the trials on his own initiative; Pope's involvement came about after the trials were underway, but it was a far-reaching involvement and it had a serious effect on the trials.

Pope seemed eager to make his mark on the military commission process, perhaps in part to restore some of his reputation within the Army—he was still smarting under the perceived injustice of having been relieved of command after his defeat at the Second Battle of Bull Run. Whatever his reasons—sincere outrage at allegations of Indian brutality during the war, desire to enhance his public image, or sheer bellicosity—Pope took exception to what he considered to be Sibley's overly-lenient attitude toward the Dakota during the first 29 trials and ordered him to pick up the pace and produce more convictions. In a letter held in the National Archives, a letter which was largely unknown in the historiography of the war until legal historian Walt Bachman uncovered it, Pope blasted Sibley for what he termed his "unsatisfactory" handling of the trials.

Major General John Pope, from a portrait by Matthew Brady. Pope was supremely self-confident and given to a certain excess of language; transferred to Minnesota after his defeat at Second Manassas, he seemed determined to make his mark on the trials, and he frequently used words such as "exterminate" or "eliminate" when speaking of the Dakota (National Archives).

"The slightest effort that is made," Pope wrote, "to interfere with the well merited death of these Indians will be considered treason to the Govt., and treated accordingly." Sibley's personal connections with the Dakota in Minnesota went back many years to his fur trading days, and he knew many of the defendants personally; Pope used this to call his loyalties into question. "I cannot yet understand how you can consider any of the Indians whom you found in possession of the captives 'friendly Indians,'" Pope wrote, and he then reiterated his plans to "exterminate them all, if they furnish the least occasion for it."[10] Sibley was conducting the trials in the field, but Pope, from his temporary headquarters in St. Paul, was definitely setting the tone for the proceedings.[11]

Whether or not Sibley took Pope's

intimations of "treason" seriously or not is impossible to say. John Pope was a bombastic man at the best of times, and given to a certain careless excess of language—Robert Utley was not exaggerating when he described Pope as "a man who would never use one word when ten would suffice." Sibley might not have found the threats entirely credible, but he certainly took the chastisement to heart. He was an amateur soldier, and hardly secure in his position, while Pope was ostensibly the military professional and Sibley's superior senior officer. Bachman, considering Sibley's reaction to Pope's written diatribe, suggests that "the October 6 letter contained over-the-top threats that were essentially loud bells that no subsequent letter could ever unring. Even if Sibley had laughed off the prosecute-for-treason threat, he could not possibly have missed the underlying message that Pope wanted a draconian form of justice to be meted out."[12] If Sibley were a Regular Army officer, he might have known enough to protest the statutory irregularity of what Pope was doing, but he was not, and so he did not.

The reality of the mail service meant that letters were constantly crossing each other in transit, and more than once Pope or Sibley wrote letters to each other asking questions already answered by a letter as yet unreceived, or worrying about problems that were already resolved. So it was in this case. On October 7, the day after sending off his threat-laden missive, Pope wrote another letter to Sibley saying, "Your dispatch of the 3d just received renders unnecessary my letter of yesterday."[13] Pope might have toned down his language a bit, but the damage was already done, and the trials took a drastic turn as a result of his imprecations.

The evidence contained in the official correspondence, both published and unpublished, supports the conclusion that Pope's involvement in the trials process and his pressure on Sibley were directly responsible for the change in how the trials were conducted from October 15 onward. This has not been widely understood in the historiography, and some commentators have ascribed other reasons for the shift.

One such is historian Gary Clayton Anderson, who argues that the reason for the change in the trials was because of some nefarious scheming on Sibley's part. According to Dr. Anderson, Sibley first instructed the court to focus only on the crime of rape, and was then caught in a dilemma of his own creation when the testimony of the former captives only produced sufficient evidence to prosecute two Dakota for rape. "If he obeys the rules of law, he's only got enough evidence to convict two Indians!" Anderson declares. "And that's a problem. So what does he do? He begins to think about this for a while.... He begins to tell General Pope that he's going to figure out a way to do it."[14] Anderson's version of events, frankly, does not hold up in the face of the historical evidence.

It is certainly true that Sibley believed there would be far many more rape cases than there actually turned out to be; that much is apparent from his letters at the time. But rape was not the only crime the military commission was created to prosecute. From the first day of its proceedings, the court aggressively went after any Dakota who could be charged with the murder of specific people in cited incidents at known locations.

The first trial, Joseph Godfrey's case, never even considered a charge of rape at all. Contrary to Anderson's allegation, in the first ten trials all ten defendants were charged with murder or massacre, while only two of them, in Case No. 2 and Case No. 4, were arraigned on the additional charge of rape.[15] Case No. 2 (Tehehdoneche), was charged that he "killed the father, husband and nephew of Martha Clauson on or about the 19th day of August ... this at or near Beaver Creek, Minnesota"; the second charge against him was rape. Case No. 4 (Tazoo), was charged with murder with the specification that he did "on or about the 18th day of August, kill or by his presence or agency aid [and] abet in the killing of Francis Patoille and Mary Anderson, two white citizens of the United States, this between Fort Ridgley and New Ulm, Minnesota"; here again the second charge was rape. Thus, Anderson's contention that the commission at first only sought to prosecute on charges of rape and nothing else cannot be accepted as correct.

The claim that Sibley had to scramble to find some other means of convicting the Dakota defendants is inaccurate. The rule of law, to which Anderson refers, in fact provided all the legal grounds necessary for charging men with murder in the 1862 trials, if sufficient evidence was produced to support the charges. In at least 40 cases, such evidence was available and the court proceeded to charge, try and convict the defendants in capital murder trials that were considerably more thorough than the summary haste that marked the later trials. Contrary to what has sometimes been argued, that the Dakota "were convicted, not for the crime of murder, but for killings committed in warfare," the reality is that the military commission convicted dozens of men for acts of legally defined murder which happened to have been committed *during* a war.[16] There is a distinct legal difference between the two concepts.

In its first 13 days of operation, the commission worked its way through 21 cases, a tally verified by the trial transcripts. After October 15th, the pace accelerated, almost certainly as a result the direct pressure that General Pope applied in his letter of October 6. So much was this so that six days later, on October 21, the commission had tried a further 91 cases. By the time the trials concluded on November 3, 390 men and one woman had appeared before the court, with one man, Charles Crawford, being tried twice and acquitted both times. There were 69 acquittals, 20 prison sentences, and 303 sentences of death by hanging.

In 1862, the prevailing public sentiment among the white populace of Minnesota seemed to be that all 303 death sentences were justified and every man in that number should be hanged without delay. There were voices that appealed for varying degrees of clemency, but they were not as many, nor as loud, as those that called for execution. Sibley himself argued that it was necessary to hang all 303 condemned men for the deterrent value of the act, as an object lesson to other Indians. Even some people who advocated for clemency for the Indians felt that *some* of the death sentences needed to be carried out, a punitive example to prevent future outbreaks of violence.

The circumstances of the trials were not the same throughout the entire process, a reality that factored into the speed with which the commission worked. The situation at Camp Release suddenly changed on October 11. Sibley had apparently planned to execute the Indians who were already convicted and then launch his force in pursuit of the hostile Indians who had fled west into the Dakota Territory, but another dispatch from Pope changed all that. Pope ordered Sibley to move all the Indians in his charge, guilty and innocent alike, down to the Lower Agency near Fort Ridgley, where the Indian attacks on August 18 had begun the war. In his reply to Pope's directive, Sibley wrote, "I shall suspend the execution of the sentenced Indians, about 20 in number, and dispatch them with others whom I shall arrest in the neighboring camp this afternoon ... to be subject to your direction."[17]

By this time in the proceedings Sibley seems to have begun experiencing some conflicted feelings about the Indians. Perhaps his hardened heart was beginning to be troubled by stirrings of his former affection and sympathy for the Dakota, or maybe his sense of justice was disturbed by some of the details of the process that he had set in motion. In a dispatch to Pope on October 15, Sibley communicated "I have the prisoners in my camp, 101 in number, chained two and two together, preparatory to their removal to Fort Snelling.... There are doubtless some innocent men in the number I have secured in fetters, but there is no time to examine so large a number, and I have therefore thought it proper to place them beyond the hope of escape until their guilt or innocence is established by the tribunal to be appointed by you for their trial."[18]

There are several points worth noting in that statement. The first is that Sibley was allowing the pressures of military necessity (or direct pressure from Pope) to dictate choices he might not otherwise have made, even as he offered a rather half-hearted protest that innocent men were likely to suffer along with the guilty. Pope's scathing demand for harsh measures was apparently still much on Sibley's mind. The other important point is that it seems he expected some more formal court to be established to finish the judicial process that his field-expedient commission had begun. It was an expectation he would not hold long.

Later that day, Sibley sent a second letter to Pope—whether this was to address matters left out of the earlier communiqué or to reply to a dispatch received from Pope's headquarters in the hours since his first letter was drafted, is not clear. At any rate, its contents add to our understanding of Sibley's thinking. "[T]he plan adopted by you will work much better as an example than if the prisoners [were] taken to Fort Snelling to be tried," Sibley told Pope, "for the lack of evidence there might have enabled many of the guilty to escape punishment, which will not be the case here." "You need not fear," he concluded, "that any guilty Indian will escape punishment."[19] The plan to which Sibley referred here was Pope's directive that Sibley himself was to continue the trials by his military commission at the Lower Agency, rather than handing the process over to another authority.

Six days later, on October 21, Sibley reported, "The commission is proceeding with the trials of prisoners as rapidly as possible. More than 120 cases have been disposed of, the greater part of whom have been found guilty of murder and other atrocious crimes, and there remain still nearly 300 to be tried." The numbers given here are important, because the 420 Sibley refers to closely presage the final number of 392 cases the commission eventually tried. It is probable, then, that by this date Sibley had identified the men whom he regarded as fitting the broader scope of the military commission's altered focus—not just men who had committed murder or rape, but also men who had simply participated in battles. It was also around this time that he stepped back from his original and frequently repeated intention to hang the condemned Indians as soon as practicable. "I shall suspend the executions," he wrote, "until the pleasure of the President is known."[20]

This is the first mention in Sibley's correspondence of the legal requirement that capital sentences in military courts had to be reviewed by the President. It is possible (though unlikely) that Sibley was unaware of this legal stipulation until it was pointed out to him, but at Pope's headquarters, in the Minnesota state capitol, and in Washington D.C., the President's role in the matter had already been recognized. In July of that year, just one month before the Dakota war began, Congress passed legislation which mandated that no sentence of death passed by a military court could be carried out until it had been approved by the President himself.[21] In light of its direct bearing on the military commission trials, this legal requirement quickly became a subject of intense debate and argument in Minnesota, both in government and the press. Sibley, still in the field and dependent upon couriers for communication, was probably a few days behind most of the political wrangling over the matter. He was by this time fully aware that death sentences imposed by a military court required presidential approval, and he seems to have anticipated a quick decision on that question.

# 8

# Questions of Legality

*A disgraceful story of passion, partiality and cruelty is the trial of the Dakota Indians by a Commission from the military, at the close of the outbreak in 1862.*
—Marion Satterlee

Much of the current debate as to whether or not the military commission was a legally convened tribunal comes down to Sibley himself and his role as the court's convening officer. Several leading scholars in the study of the U.S.–Dakota War today have either suggested or explicitly stated that the military commission was an illegal court, since Article 65 of the Articles of War would have unequivocally prohibited Sibley from ever appointing such a court.[1] Two arguments in particular are usually marshaled to support this contention: first, that Article 65 would have prevented Sibley from forming the court because of a safeguard against prejudice contained in the Article's wording; and second, that Sibley had neither the rank nor the position required by Article 65 to convene such a court in the first place.

Since much of this debate depends upon how one interprets Article 65, we should consider the Article in its entirety:

> Article 65* Any general officer commanding an army, or Colonel commanding a separate department, may appoint general courts-martial whenever necessary. But no sentence of a court-martial shall be carried into execution until after the findings shall have been laid before the officer ordering the same, of the officer commanding the troops for the time being; neither shall any sentence of a general court-martial, in the time of peace, extending to the loss of life, or the dismissal of a commissioned officer, or which shall, either in time of peace or war, respect a general officer, be carried into execution, until after the whole proceedings shall have been transmitted to the Secretary of War, to be laid before the President of the United States for his confirmation or disapproval, and orders in the case. All other sentences may be confirmed and executed by the officer ordering the court to assemble, or the commanding officer for the time being, as the case may be.
>
> *Modification to Article 65 by the Act of May 29th, 1830:*
> Whenever a general officer commanding an army, or a colonel commanding a separate department, shall be the accuser or prosecutor of any officer in the Army of the United States under his command, the general court-martial for the trial of such officer shall be appointed by the President of the United States. The proceedings and sentences of said court shall be sent directly to the Secretary of War, to be by him laid before the President, for his confirmation or approval, or orders in the case.[2]

The first objection to Sibley convening the military commission—that command prejudice would have made it illegal for him to impanel the court—is an argument easily dealt with. Proponents of this view usually cite the second-to-last sentence in the amendment to the Article: "Whenever a general officer commanding an army, or a colonel commanding a separate department, shall be the accuser or prosecutor of any officer in the Army of the United States, under his command, the general court-martial for the trial of such officer shall be appointed by the President of the United States."[3] The wording of this sentence makes it clear that a military court could *not* legally be convened by a commanding officer in any case where he would be preferring charges against a defendant who was a subordinate officer of the U.S. Army under his direct command.[4]

But the Dakota were obviously not officers of the U.S. Army, and they were clearly not under Sibley's command as soldiers. Thus, it seems plain enough that the prejudicial safeguards of Article 65 cannot be applied to the Dakota War trials. Nonetheless, Article 65 continues to be widely misinterpreted to support various arguments that Sibley could not have legally impaneled the 1862 military commission.[5] Prejudice on the part of the officers who formed the military commission was certainly a legitimate concern, one that we will consider a bit later, but for an altogether different reason than the proscription laid out in Article 65.

It is also argued that, for reasons of rank and position, Sibley never had the necessary authority to convene a military commission. The author of Sibley's recent authoritative biography says "the military commission had no legal jurisdiction, and Sibley had no authority to create it."[6] Most commentators who take this view of the matter again cite Article 65 of the Articles of War, this time referring to the main paragraph of the Article. "Under the Articles of War," Carol Chomsky of the University of Minnesota School of Law says, "only a general officer commanding an army or a colonel commanding a separate department could convene a general court-martial, which alone had the power to conduct trials for capital offenses."[7] Her interpretation of the 1862 Articles of War is absolutely correct, on its face—Sibley, when he convened the military commission on September 28, did not have the full authority to do so. But a close study of the sequence of events in 1862 in the context of military regulations leads to a different, perhaps surprising conclusion.

There is no denying that when Sibley issued General Order 55, he was still only a Colonel of Volunteers, and he did not command a separate military department. But all that changed on September 29, when General Halleck, acting in his role as General in Chief of the United States Army, sent an official dispatch to Pope that read, "Col. Henry H. Sibley is made a brigadier general for his judicious fight at Yellow Medicine."[8] From that point on, Sibley, as a "general officer commanding an army in the field" had all the necessary authority to form a court in accordance with the Articles of War.

The force he commanded was certainly too small to be called an army in the conventional order-of-battle sense, but there are evidentiary reasons to conclude that this did not matter. Sibley's was the *only* operational force then waging the war against the Dakota, and it is clear from contemporary sources that his command was thought of and regarded as an army, both in Minnesota and at the national command level in the War Department. This is evident from his letter to Pope on October 13, in which Sibley described himself as "a general officer commanding an army in the field." Pope never

*Opposite:* General Order No. 55, convening the military commission, issued by Sibley on September 28, 1862. The day this order was issued, Sibley lacked the necessary authority to do so—but all that changed the next day (Minnesota Historical Society).

## 8. Questions of Legality

Proceedings of a military Commission convened at Camp Release opposite the mouth of Chippewa River by virtue of the following order viz –

Order no 55.

Head Quarters, Camp Release
September 28th, 1862

A Military Commission, composed of Colonel Wm Crooks of the 6th Regiment, Lt. Col. Marshall of the 7th Regiment, Captains Grant and Bailly of the 6th Regiment, and Lieutenant Olin of the 3d Regiment will convene at some convenient point in Camp at 10 o'clock this morning to try summarily the mulattoes and Indians, or mixed bloods, who may be brought before them by direction of the Colonel Commanding, if found guilty of murders, or other outrages upon the whites during the present state of hostilities of the Indians, the proceedings of the Commission to be returned to these Head Quarters, immediately after their conclusion for the consideration of the Col. Commanding.

The Commission will be governed in their proceedings by military law and usage –

(Signed) H. H. Sibley
Colonel Commanding
Military Expedition

objected to him styling himself that way, which is worth noting. If ever there was a man who was jealous of his prerogatives and a stickler for correct military usage, it was John Pope, and he would certainly have set Sibley straight on this point if he thought it necessary. The preponderance of evidence strongly suggests that as far as the U.S. Army itself was concerned, after September 29 Sibley had both the perceived and actual authority to convene military commissions and conventional courts-martial, even though he remained unaware of that himself until news of the promotion reached him on October 7.

At least one commentator has considered this question of convening authority and concluded that Sibley "lacked the authority to establish a military court-martial or commission, but it is clear that General John Pope, did have such authority and would have approved Sibley's action. Thus, the objection to Sibley's authority is a largely technical one."[9] That is not entirely accurate. Even though the assumption that Pope approved of Sibley's actions and urged him on is correct, the fact remains that it was Sibley, not Pope, who convened the commission, and under military law that is more than a mere technicality; such an action would have invalidated the entire trial process before it even began. In the Army some judicial and command authorities can be delegated down, others cannot, and one cannot simply convene a court by proxy just because the next senior officer in the chain of command would approve of it. Sibley's judicial authority came from his promotion to Brigadier General and his command of the expeditionary force in the field, not through a delegation of Pope's authority.

However, this still leaves us with the problem of the military commission's first day of operation, September 28, when Sibley was still a Colonel. In legal terms, this verifiable lack of sufficient rank and its accompanying authority is enough to show that the commission, on the first day of its existence, operated in violation of "military law and usage." Because of this, any case tried on September 28 ought to have been thrown out on review. But this technicality would *not* have invalidated the commission's proceedings on September 29 and afterwards.

For example, when the commission was conducting its business at the Lower Agency on October 15, one of its original members, Lieutenant Colonel William Marshall, was assigned to other duties and was replaced by Major George Bradley. The order convening the commission for that day, Order No. 65, was signed "By order of Gen. H. H. Sibley."[10] On this day, just as was true every day that the commission had worked since September 29, the commission was legally and duly constituted in accordance with Federal law and the Articles of War, and Sibley had all the necessary authority to act as both its convening and reviewing officer.

Although there are probably no definite answers to the question, it is worth asking why Sibley impaneled the military commission on that first day when he did not yet have sufficient authority. My impression is that he was not willfully flouting the law when he did so—if anything, his desire to dispense some form of justice before taking the field in pursuit of Little Crow and the other Dakota holdouts propelled him into a hasty decision, and his lack of familiarity with military law and regulation led him into error.

Nothing in his character or his correspondence indicates a lack of regard for the law. In fact, Sibley had studied law for a time and was a former Justice of the Peace, and he consistently respected the institution of American law. Considering his limited

## 8. Questions of Legality

**When Sibley relocated his base of operations to the Lower Agency in accordance with Pope's orders in mid–October, the latter half of the military commission trials were held in this building, a summer kitchen, one of the only structures left standing after the war. The contemporary caption was incorrect—the building was never used as a jail (photo by Adrian J. Ebell, Minnesota Historical Society).**

knowledge of military law, it is entirely possible that he did not know that he had overstepped his bounds when he impaneled the commission. His letter to Pope on September 28 makes it clear that he was somewhat in the dark as to what he actually could or could not do in that regard. Referring to his intention to execute Indians if they were found guilty in trial, he added, "although I am somewhat in doubt whether my authority extends quite so far. An example is, however, imperatively necessary, and I trust you will approve the act...."[11] The same day he wrote to Colonel Charles Flandrau, who had commanded the defense of New Ulm, saying much the same thing: "...perhaps it will be a stretch of my authority. If so, necessity must be my justification."[12]

These were not merely casual correspondents in whom Sibley was confiding. Pope was not only Sibley's superior in the military chain of command, he was a Regular Army officer of long service, well versed in the Articles of War and much more conversant than Sibley with the Army's judicial practices and regulations. Flandrau was a Justice of the Minnesota Supreme Court and thoroughly familiar with matters of judicial process. Neither man advised Sibley to pull in his horns; neither man suggested (in Flandrau's case) or ordered (in Pope's case) that he desist with the military commission. The reasons for this are debatable, but were probably different for each man—Flandrau did not know any more about military law than Sibley, and Pope at that time seemed more than willing to ignore the requirements of law when it came to prosecuting Indians.

It is also clear that Pope did not fear censure from his own superiors on this point, because in his communications with General Halleck and the War Department he was quite open about the fact that Sibley was conducting trials of Dakota prisoners. On October 9, Pope wrote to Halleck, saying, "The Sioux war may be considered at an end. We have about 1,500 prisoners—men, women, and children—and many are coming every day to deliver themselves up. Many are being tried by military commission for being connected in the late horrible outrages, and will be executed...."[13] There is no question that Sibley's actions were known, reported, and approved, through all levels of the military command structure.

Sibley actually sought guidance from Pope several times on questions of military law and the extent of his command authority. On October 13 he wrote, "Will you please inform me whether, under the 65th article of war, I have the right, as a general officer commanding an army in the field, to convene a general court-martial. There are men in arrest for desertion and other crimes who should be tried...."[14] Two days later he was writing again, with a sense of urgency: "I beg leave to remind you, lest it escape your recollection in the hurry of business, that it is quite necessary I should be informed whether I have the legal authority to order a general court-martial, as there are cases in the camp in which at least one officer and several privates are charged with grave offenses, which should be disposed of without delay."[15] Not waiting for a reply, a second letter that same day posed a technical question of law: "Can a member of my staff now occupying temporarily the position of acting assistant adjutant general under state authority serve as a member or as judge advocate of a court martial if you decide I have the power to appoint one...?"[16]

From the types of questions Sibley was asking and the persistency of his queries, it is clear that he knew very well that he was not conversant with all the intricacies of military law. Whatever his other shortcomings, he certainly was not afraid to ask for clarification. In light of this, it seems likely that when he convened the military commission without first asking if he was authorized to do so, it was because he believed that he already had that authority.

One thing lacking, however, was the authority to execute the Indians whom the commission had convicted and sentenced to death. It may well have been that Sibley, as one historian says, "labored under the misconception that he had the authority to order executions," at least for a time.[17] In any event, he learned soon enough that he did not hold the ultimate power of life and death in his own hands.

# 9

# "A species of domestic rebellion"

The issue of Indian sovereignty comes up frequently in the debate over whether or not Sibley's commission had any legal jurisdiction to subject the Dakota to trial. There are several basic questions in this regard: Were the Dakota an independent, sovereign nation, and therefore exempt from the laws and jurisdiction of the United States? If they were in fact sovereign, were there any contexts in which Sibley's commission would have had any legal authority to try them for crimes against American law? On the other hand, if they were a domestic entity rather than a sovereign nation, could they then be legally tried by a military tribunal rather than a civilian court?

In the United States today, Indian tribal groups are recognized as sovereign and the lands within their ceded reservations are independent of local government and law enforcement, though certain Federal agencies still reserve some authorities to themselves within tribal areas. In 1862, however, the relationship between the U.S. government and the various Indian tribes within its territorial boundaries was markedly different, not least of all because sporadic incidents of armed conflict were still part of the equation. This makes a historical discussion of the sovereignty issue a particularly muddy question to wade through, and there is no simple answer to it. There are logical and legal reasons to support the conclusion that the 1862 Dakota were entitled to recognition as a sovereign nation. On the other hand, there are historical realities which strongly suggest that they were not recognized as such in practice. To further complicate matters, the U.S. Government itself dealt with the Indians as both foreign and domestic peoples, and sometimes as both at the same time.

For more than 25 years, the most comprehensive examination of Sibley's military commission from the perspective of law and judicial process was an article by Carol Chomsky which appeared in the Stanford Law Review in 1990. Chomsky, a law professor at the University of Minnesota, spends a considerable portion of her essay making a case for the idea that the Dakota should *not* have been tried by the Army. Regardless of whether or not the commission was lawfully convened, or whether or not Sibley had the authority to impanel it, Chomsky concludes that the Dakota were not subject to American law in the first place. "It is questionable," she says, "whether a military commission had any lawful authority to try the Dakota."[1] In her view, the Dakota were a sovereign nation who were entitled to the status of legitimate belligerents and as such ought not to have been tried as criminals in a military court.

We will consider this argument in detail a bit later, but a point of clarification might be in order first. In recent discussions about her study of the military commission trials, Professor Chomsky has made it clear that she is *not* trying to argue that legitimate belligerency in war confers any kind of automatic immunity from criminal prosecution if it can be proven that crimes were committed during the period of hostilities. Legitimate belligerents can and do act outside the laws and rules of war—war crimes and common crimes committed by soldiers are both examples of this—and in such cases those same belligerents are liable to be regarded and treated as criminals who also happen to be soldiers. Chomsky recognizes that; her contention is a question of jurisdiction, not criminality.[2] Unfortunately, the wording in her article can give the impression that she is advocating sovereignty as a basis for immunity from prosecution, and for the past two decades that is the interpretation of the question most often made by commentators who cite her foundational work on the subject of the trials.

This matter of legitimate belligerency and national sovereignty brings us back to the discussion of what to call the war, this time for reasons of legal context. For many years after the war, historians most frequently referred to it as an "uprising." That particular word is imbued with connotations of domestic rebellion, and if the Dakota were rebelling then they most certainly were *not* a sovereign nation.[3] This is the view that Chomsky disagrees with when she says, "[T]he commission tried the Dakota for the wrong crimes. Based on the historical and legal views prevailing in 1862 ... the Dakota were a sovereign nation at war with the United States, and the men who fought the war were entitled to be treated as legitimate belligerents."[4] This is absolutely correct, to a point, but as is true of most historical debates, there are at least two sides to this discussion and each has some merit.

Through much of the 19th century, the U.S. government had an ostensibly consistent view of the Native Americans who shared the continent—Indian tribes were usually considered to be extra-territorial peoples. They were, in a word, foreign, and their territories were foreign lands, at least through the first half of the century. "By 1840 the boundary of the Indian Country was ... reasonably well fixed," as one military historian says, "and for the time being the strategic problem of the Army regarding the Indian nations became that of guarding a border which amounted almost to an international frontier."[5] Almost, but not completely or consistently so—in the full analysis, the relationship between the U.S. government and the various western Indian tribes was never a one-dimensional arrangement. Complicating the matter further was the fact that the U.S. government frequently seemed to take an ambiguous interpretation of Indian sovereignty.

The Judge Advocates General of the U.S. Army, during the period of the U.S.–Indian wars of the 19th century, issued a series of decisions that established the Army's official view on the question of Indian sovereignty, especially as it applied to war:

> Active hostilities with Indians do not constitute a state of foreign war, the Indian tribes, even where distinct political communities, being subject to the sovereignty of the United States. Warfare inaugurated by Indians is thus a species of domestic rebellion, but it is so far assimilated to foreign war that during its pendency and on its theatre the laws and usages which govern and apply to persons during the existence of a foreign war are to be recognized as in general prevailing and operative.[6]

A close reading of these two sentences reveals an oxymoronic conclusion: as far as the Army was concerned, Indian tribes were not sovereign or foreign, but during war they were to be thought of and fought against as if they were. As John Isch puts it in his excellent book, *The Dakota War Trials*, "The answer to whether the Indian is a citizen of an independent country or a rebel against the existing government is 'yes.'"[7]

No less an authority than the Constitution of the United States supports the conclusion that the Indian tribes were truly sovereign. After all, the ratification of treaties is an authority reserved to the U.S. Senate.[8] A fault with the Indian treaty process (one fault among many, it must be said) was the delay from the time when the treaties were signed on the frontier until the Indians could begin receiving the material benefits that the treaties promised. This lag resulted at least in part from the fact that all treaties had to be sent back to Washington for ratification, just as would be required of any international treaty. And treaties, to be clear, are signed with foreign nations, not domestic entities. Therefore, the Indian tribes with whom the U.S. government made treaties were recognized in legal form as being foreign and sovereign nations, even though theirs was a circumscribed sort of sovereignty.

Felix Cohen, an expert on the legal questions pertaining to issues of Native American identity in the 1940s, put forward three fundamental principles which still frame the concept of Indian sovereignty today:

1. An Indian tribe possesses all the powers of any sovereign state.
2. Conquest rendered the tribe subject to the legislative power of the United States and terminated the external powers of sovereignty (e.g., the power to enter into treaties with foreign nations), but did not by itself affect the internal sovereignty of the tribe (i.e., its powers of self-government).
3. These powers are subject to qualification by treaties and by express legislation of Congress, but unless explicitly qualified, full powers of internal sovereignty are vested in the Indian tribes and in their duly constituted organs of government.[9]

Cohen's second point neatly summarizes the principal countering view on the question of sovereignty : as soon as the various Indian tribes were allocated defined reservations within the territorial boundaries of the United States or its Territories, and especially once they began depending upon the Federal government for their support and livelihood (and thus became "annuity Indians," in the terminology of the time), then they were no longer completely independent and sovereign. There is a practical argument for this: if the Indians were truly sovereign (i.e., foreign), they would be engaged by the State Department of the U.S. Government, which they were not. Instead, their post-treaty dealings with the federal government were always with the Department of the Interior, in the form of the agency created specifically to deal with them, the Bureau of Indian Affairs. *Ergo*, in practice they were not sovereign in the fullest sense of the word. Both perspectives turn up in the contemporary accounts written by observers of the war in the 1800s, and both are part of the historical argument today.

There is also a third way of viewing the relationship that existed between the Indians and the United States in 1862, one that has its antecedents in ancient history. The Indian tribes, once they entered into treaties with the U.S. government—whether by choice, coercion, fair means or foul—remained sovereign peoples, but in much the same way that the Hasmonean kingdom of Judea was a sovereign nation under the sway of Rome

2,000 years ago. Judea was a sovereign kingdom to some degree, which could enter into agreements with an encroaching empire, and could break out in open warfare against its overlords if it chose, but it invariably suffered the bloody consequences for doing so. The Sioux (Dakota, Lakota, Teton, and other specific groups of the tribe) were sovereign, but only as far as they could enforce that sovereignty, and the dark, repetitious truth of U.S. history is that inevitably the day always came when the pressure of American expansion eventually overwhelmed them, as it did every other group of indigenous people.

The question of Indian sovereignty poses a thorny problem for all sides of the debate, and it defies simple answers. There are well established legal and bureaucratic precedents to support the idea that the Dakota were truly sovereign. Just as much evidentiary support exists, however, to uphold the view that as far as the U.S. government was concerned, by 1862 the Dakota in Minnesota had lost all meaningful claims to recognition as a sovereign nation. By U.S. law the Indians were sovereign, but in the 19th century that law was more sham than substance. Treaties between Indians and the U.S. Government were almost never respected or enforced when they conflicted with other American territorial aims or political imperatives. The reality on the ground was that the Indian peoples of the Dakota, Winnebago and other tribes were, at best, the unwilling vassal states of a pre-imperial American government that was steadily and irresistibly pushing its borders ever westward and swallowing up everything and everyone in its path. Treaties between the Americans and the Indians, it has been said before, were made to be broken, and inevitably were.

Does this mean, however, that the Dakota could not legally have been tried by the military commission in the aftermath of the war because they were entitled to a legal recognition of their sovereignty? It does not. The salient point which is often overlooked here is the other legal reality that applied to the Indians' situation. As established by General Winfield Scott in the Mexican War in 1847, and as has been the case with every subsequent incarnation of military commissions since then, military commissions have the specific latitude of having jurisdiction over foreign nationals as well as U.S. citizens, a scope which courts-martial do not properly have. This is one of the most important distinctions between military commissions and courts-martial.

If the Dakota were a sovereign people and engaged in legitimate warfare against the United States, then Sibley's military commission had the legal authority to try them for violations of the Articles of War (war crimes, in other words) in accordance with the precedents established in 1847 during the Mexican War. If they were not sovereign, but were instead some form of domestic population, then a military commission was still the appropriate court. In that scenario they would be legally exempt from trial by court-martial, and there was almost no chance at all that they could have received any form of fair trial in a civil court in the State of Minnesota in the autumn of 1862.

In the final analysis, the question of whether or not the Dakota were sovereign has little bearing on the legitimacy of the military commission that tried them, but William Folwell's comment on sovereignty is worth considering. "While keeping up the pretense that Indian tribes were independent nations," Folwell wrote, "by means of the agency and annuity systems we reduced them in fact to the status of dependents, not to say beggars."[10]

# 10

# Due Process and the Lack Thereof

> *[O]f nearly four hundred cases which came before the commission, only about fifty were cleared, twenty were sentenced to imprisonment, and more than three hundred were condemned to be hanged. The greater part of these were condemned on general principles, without any specific charges proved, such as under less exciting and excited conditions of society would have been demanded.*
>
> —The Reverend Stephen R. Riggs

Charles Flandrau, the former Indian Agent, Justice of the Minnesota Supreme Court and defender of New Ulm whom we encountered earlier in correspondence with Henry H. Sibley, delivered his opinion of the military commission trials after the war was over. He believed that the members of the commission were beyond reproach, and singled out Isaac Heard in particular as being "above prejudice and passion...." "I make these comments," Flandrau wrote, "because the trials took place at a period of intense excitement, and persons unacquainted with the exact facts may be led to believe that the court was 'organized to convict,' and unfair in its decisions."[1] The phrase "organized to convict" underscores a criticism of the military commission that has only grown in intensity since 1862.

Three of the most persistent questions in the debate concerning the judicial ethics of Sibley's military commission are these: did the commission adhere to the structures and requirements of law; did the defendants receive impartial justice and the due process of law; and were the convictions that resulted based on evidence that satisfied reasonable doubt? Stephen Riggs, who had first-hand knowledge of the commission's workings, sincerely believed that many of the accused were guilty, but still he had reservations about the way in which the verdicts were reached. "Many of those that are tried and condemned," he wrote, "are doubtless guilty of participation in the murders and outrages committed on the Minnesota frontiers—some of them as guilty as Satan himself, and richly deserving the punishment of death.... [Nonetheless, a] military commission, where the cases of forty men are passed upon in six or seven hours, is not the place for the clear bringing out of evidence and securing a fair trial to every one."[2]

What Riggs was referring to one is of the criticisms most frequently leveled against the commission; that it dealt with its cases so quickly as to give the question of each defendant's innocence or guilt only a cursory consideration, and sometimes not even that. This point is made by commentators from all sides of the discussion, and it is not in the least bit spurious. Isaac Heard acknowledged this view in his book after the war, saying, "Some people have thought that the haste with which the accused were tried must have prevented any accuracy as to the ascertainment of their complicity."[3] He argued that haste had no detrimental effect on accuracy, but the charge of unseemly speed in the commission's process is not so easily dismissed.

Before considering the reasons for this undue haste, however, it is appropriate to consider whether or not the members of the commission had the technical knowledge of military law that would have enabled them to recognize whether or not its proceedings even met the statutory standards. As one study of the history of military commissions points out, "military commissions must have a thorough knowledge of the laws of war. As trier of law and fact, commissions must determine whether offenses charged properly constitute punishable violations of the law of war."[4] The War Department itself, 20 years before the Dakota War, acknowledged that it was a matter of "the first importance in the administration of justice, that the Officers of the Army should be acquainted with the principles and rules governing Military Courts, and that they should also have a competent knowledge of the laws and usages of the service...."[5] Therefore, we must ask if Sibley's commission had this "thorough knowledge," as a modern historian has termed it, and "competent knowledge," as the War Department called it. The evidence suggests they did not. Beginning with the convening officer, Henry H. Sibley himself, most of the men involved were not professional soldiers with any experience in military law. The only exception was the president of the commission, Colonel William Crooks. A graduate of the United States Military Academy at West Point and a Regular Army officer, Crooks had certainly received instruction in military law. The other four members of the commission lacked this background.

This does not mean, however, that they were therefore entirely ignorant of law. Sibley was a former Justice of the Peace who had at one point studied law, while Heard, who served as the Recorder of the commission, had a reputation as being one of the best prosecutors in St. Paul with a considerable amount of trial experience. Major George Bradley, who replaced Lieutenant Colonel William Marshall on the commission in mid-October, was described as being "rated among the first lawyers in the state."[6]

They were undoubtedly familiar with civilian law—military law they did not know nearly as well. Sibley's repeated inquiries to Pope about courts-martial procedures and the scope of his authority clearly indicate that. An expertise in civil law would not automatically make a person conversant with military law—there are important differences between the two legal systems. Whether from ignorance or blatant disregard, Sibley's military commission repeatedly conducted its business in violation of many of the established protocols of military law, regulations and customs. For one clear example of this, we need look no further than the commission's Judge Advocate.

One of the most important positions on a court-martial or military commission was that of the officer appointed to act as the Judge Advocate of the court, a function which carried with it the expectation that the officer in question be familiar with both criminal and military law. In keeping with the sort of strange logic that military systems seem to delight in, a military Judge Advocate had a hand in both the prosecution and the defense.[7] (To be clear, a Judge Advocate was not a presiding judge; the position was more akin to that of prosecutor.) According to Article 69 of the Articles of War:

## 10. Due Process and the Lack Thereof

The judge advocate, or some person deputed by him, or by the general, or officer commanding the army, detachment or garrison, shall prosecute in the name of the United States, but shall so far consider himself as counsel for the prisoner, after the said prisoner shall have made his plea, as to object to any leading question, to any of the witnesses, or any question to the prisoner, the answer to which, might tend to criminate himself....[8]

In an 1846 study of military law as it was then practiced in the United States, a serving officer named John O'Brien pointed out that this peculiar role had existed in American military courts since their inception under the first codification of military law by the Continental Congress. The Judge Advocate, as O'Brien put it, was tasked with "the duty of being, to a certain extent, the protector of the prisoner from improper measures tending to convict him."[9] This responsibility would have been especially pertinent to the defendants before Sibley's military commission. "Particularly if the defendant is without counsel," as one study of military tribunals puts it, "should the Judge Advocate render him all proper and reasonable assistance."[10] Counterintuitive though it might be, the Judge Advocate was expected to protect the defendant from self-incrimination and leading questions, even while working to convict him.

This duality of purpose on the part of the court's prosecutor has never lacked for critics. As one commentator points out, "many authorities thought these duties unreasonable, objecting that 'the judge advocate, being both prosecutor and counsel for the prisoner, can, nine times out of ten, make the latter appear innocent or guilty at his pleasure: he is like a man playing chess with himself.'"[11] In the case of Sibley's commission, the Judge Advocate was Lieutenant Rollin C. Olin of the Third Minnesota, who was the most junior officer on the panel (although Lieutenant Heard also appears to have acted in that capacity during some trials). Readers will have to determine for themselves what effect that particular detail—Olin's lack of rank compared to the other members of the panel—might have had on his efficacy in the role to which he was appointed.

In 1927 a Minneapolis printer named Marion Satterlee published a book entitled *The Court Proceedings in the Trial of Dakota Indians Following the Massacre in Minnesota in August 1862*. In his preface he outlined a series of notes he wanted to call to readers' attention. The first item on his list was the inadequacy of the commission's Judge Advocate: "Note—In no case did the Judge Advocate interpose in behalf of the accused."[12] Satterlee's criticism is accurate. There is no record, in any case in any of the transcripts, of Lieutenant Olin acting or speaking on behalf of any defendant.

This is all the more egregious a failing because there *were* cases where the Judge Advocate's intervention would have been proper, and sometimes even necessary. In Case No. 96, the trial of Mahpeokanaje, better known as Cut Nose, there is an account of inappropriate behavior on the part of Colonel Crooks, the president of the commission. Thomas Watts, a soldier in Sibley's command, described the following incident:

> Cut Nose, through the interpreter, was asked a question, and he began babbling away in his native tongue until all were out of patience, then he was asked to answer the question by "yes" or "no." He commenced the same incoherent babble again, when Colonel Crooks said to Mr. Riggs, [who was interpreting] "Tell him to shut his mouth or I will split his head open with my sword." Crooks was second in command of the expedition and I write this to show that the private soldier was not the only one that harbored a grudge against the reds.[13]

There are some problems with the reliability of this account, the first of which is that Watts never makes it clear if he was present in the courtroom and personally witnessed this exchange, or if he got it secondhand from someone who told him about it. It is also worth pointing out that Antoine Freniere, not Steven Riggs, functioned as the courtroom interpreter during the trials. If this incident occurred as Watts remembered it (and it must be noted that he published his recollections of the war nearly 60 years after the fact), then it indicates a virulent hostility on the part of at least one member of the commission toward the accused. For a member of a judicial panel to offer physical violence in the courtroom to a defendant upon whose case he is sitting in judgment is such egregious behavior that it defies justification. When Watts wrote of the grudge factor, he was not accusing Crooks of holding a grudge; rather, he was offering anecdotal evidence to support his opinion that *everyone* in the 1862 military expedition had a grudge against the Indians, even the senior officers, a state of mind that he apparently felt was normal.

At any rate, this is one of the incidents in which the military commission's Judge Advocate was conspicuous by his silence. Lieutenant Olin never raised an objection on Cut Nose's behalf, nor did he react to what amounted to the president of the court attempting to force a specific answer from the defendant. In several other cases, Olin also failed to object when spontaneous comments from unsworn observers were allowed to enter the record as evidence against various Indian defendants.

Joseph Godfrey, the mixed-race man whose case was the first tried by the commission, became more than just a witness for the government after his own trial. On some occasions, according to Heard's account, Godfrey behaved as if he were a prosecutor for the commission, sometimes at the commission's behest, and other times apparently on his own initiative.

Heard described Godfrey acting almost as an adjunct prosecutor at times, engaging in direct cross-examinations of recalcitrant defendants. "[W]hen the court said, 'Godfrey, talk to him,'" Heard wrote, describing how Godfrey would interrogate other prisoners during their trials, "he would straighten up, his countenance become calm, and in a deliberate tone, would soon force the Indian, by a series of questions in his own language, into an admission of the truth."[14] From Heard's narrative, it also seems that Godfrey enjoyed interjecting his own reactions and rebuttals into the commission's official proceedings even when not invited to do so. In one case, Godfrey challenged a Dakota man who claimed innocence based on a lame arm and a defective gun, saying, "You say you could not fire, and had a bad gun. Why don't you tell the court the truth?"[15] Admittedly, the procedural protocols of military commissions were less rigid than those of conventional courts, but even so, this sort of independent questioning and examination by one condemned man of another defendant, with the results used by the commission to determine guilt, is well out of bounds.

In every one of these cases, Lieutenant Olin as Judge Advocate should have acted in the capacity of defense for prisoners when this extra-judicial questioning ensued. At the very least, he ought to have raised a formal objection on prisoners' behalf. The records show that he did neither the one thing nor the other. At no point in any of the trials did the Judge Advocate ever advocate for any one of the accused.

It is worth noting that this lack of active defense was by no means unique to the Dakota War trials—it was a regular feature of military courts at that time. Considering the broader context of U.S. Army courts-martial held during the Civil War, it becomes clear that Judge Advocates rarely expended much effort on the defendants' behalf in trial. Walt Bachman, himself an attorney of long experience who has thoroughly researched both the Dakota War trials and Civil War courts-martial, believes that "this principle was honored as much in the breach as in the observance. Judge Advocates typically served as prosecutors in practice, and in most cases there is little evidence that they helped out unsophisticated defendants by counsel."[16]

Beyond the inadequacies of the Judge Advocate, there is also the apparent problem of defense counsel. Numerous writers have commented on the fact that the Dakota defendants who were tried by Sibley's military commission did not have the benefit of counsel, which is correct—there was no defense for the accused, formal or otherwise—and the prevailing conclusion reached by recent commentators is that the trials were therefore invalid. Robert Norris, another legal commentator, expresses this view when he says, "Lincoln couldn't ignore the fundamental unfairness in the hastily convened trials without benefit of counsel. The Sixth Amendment mandates that an accused is entitled to a speedy trial with the assistance of counsel."[17] What is overlooked in this argument, however, is the fact that under the regulations applicable to the function of military courts in 1862, defense counsel was not a statutory requirement. There was much about the military commission trials that made them unfair, but the absence of defense counsel violated no law or judicial norm in 1862, so it would be a mistake to evaluate the trials by modern standards of judicial protections.

Using the Constitution of the United States as a line-by-line guide to understanding the Dakota War trials inevitably leads to some confusion and erroneous conclusions. American military law from its earliest inception has always had a few points about it which do not fall directly in line with the familiar civil protections delineated in the Bill of Rights. Counterintuitive though it may seem, the men and women who swear to "uphold and defend the Constitution of the United States of America" in the armed services must relinquish some of the civil rights guaranteed by the Constitution in order to do so, and so it has been since the beginning. To use the Sixth Amendment of the Constitution as a basis for arguing that the 1862 military commission was required by law to provide the Dakota defendants with defense counsel in the modern sense is to misunderstand both the structure and the practice of 19th century military law, which was the legal system under which the Dakota trials were conducted.

This particular point has been a stumbling block for modern historians when they try to explain the 1862 trials without fully understanding the ways in which military law differs from the civilian legal system. In his 2012 speech at Gustavus Adolphus College, Gary Clayton Anderson stated that the Articles of War required that a soldier tried before a military court "should be given counsel, and that counsel should have the right to object."[18] His implication is that military law stipulated counsel for defendants in the familiar form of defense attorneys, but he has misunderstood both the law and its historical context. In fact, Article 69 of the Articles of War, the only article to address the question of trial counsel, states what we have already read, that "the Judge Advocate General, or some person deputed by him, was to consider himself counsel for the prisoner."[19] A person does not need a degree in law to recognize the difference between the self-conflicted role of the Judge Advocate, whose primary purpose was to present the government's case against the defendant at the same time that he undertook to protect him against "leading questions" on the one hand, and a dedicated defense attorney whose sole purpose was to defend his client, on the other.

In 19th century military courts, "the accused is not entitled to counsel as a right but merely as a privilege...."[20] Under the military code extant 1862, a defendant could be charged, tried and convicted without ever having been advised or represented by a defense attorney, and the trial would still be legal and within the requirements of the law, modern misinterpretations to the contrary notwithstanding. At most, the accused in a military trial of that era was entitled to the presence of *amicus curiae* ("a friend in court") who was not permitted to address the court directly or take any overt part in the proceedings. It is important to note that this was exactly the same procedure followed in military courts in cases where the defendants were American soldiers, even when they were charged with capital crimes. The Articles of War made no requirement for separate, dedicated legal counsel for the defense.

As to whether or not the lack of defense counsel *should* have invalidated the commission's proceedings, that is a more nuanced question. A letter-of-the-law reading of the statutes in effect in 1862 makes it clear that the proceedings were legal in spite of the lack of defense counsel. All the same, such a state of affairs does seem completely contrary to modern ideas of judicial fairness and due process, and is certainly not the legal system familiar to Americans today. "Historians must be careful," as one scholar cautions, "to avoid the common trap of making anachronistic assumptions about legal standards in existence 150 years ago, particularly when common practices today make such claims plausible."[21]

Other criticisms of the 1862 military commission are that it was hopelessly prejudiced against the Indian defendants from the outset, and that the trials took place in circumstances that prevented any chance of the accused receiving impartial hearings. The principal points behind these views are, first, that the commission began working immediately after the cessation of active hostilities and that the venue was indelibly associated with the crimes of which the Indians were accused; and second, that the members of the commission were themselves too intimately involved in the war to allow for any hope of impartiality.

Contemporary observers noted these issues in their day, but their interpretation of them was not always negative. Harriet Bishop McConkey, whose account of the war will be considered at length in a later chapter, somehow managed to interpret this as proof that the military commission was displaying an admirable commitment to fair justice. When the continuing trials were relocated to Camp Sibley at the Lower Agency in accordance with Pope's order of October 11, the commission resumed its work at the site where the first attacks of the war had occurred nearly two months earlier. At the new setting for the trials, McConkey wrote, "a few steps away was the store of Nathan Myrick, where Lynde, the first victim, DeVill and Andrew Myrick were killed. With such reminders of their guilt before them, how could they [the Indians] hope for pardon?"[22] She did not express this as a criticism of the commission—McConkey's biases were clear. "We wonder," she continued, "that fair and impartial trials were given—we wonder at the staying hand which prevented their execution *en masse*—and we wonder at the patience of the commission in the long, tedious trial!"[23] McConkey is the only voice in all the secondary sources, contemporary or modern, who describes the military commission's processes as a "long, tedious trial."

Most modern commentators see the matter entirely differently, taking the view expressed so clearly by Carol Chomsky, who writes, "The trials began immediately after hostilities ceased; they were held near the scene of the fighting while passions were most inflamed and fears remained of renewed fighting by the Dakota who had fled. The Commission members had themselves fought in the battles and thus had been under attack by the very individuals on whom they now passed judgment. It is inconceivable," she concludes, "that they came to their task with open minds."[24] Bachman makes a similar point: "the knowledge that the defendants were among those who tried to kill the presiding judges in a recent military battle would cast a cloud of possible injustice over the proceedings."[25] These are all valid criticisms, as the language used by at least one participant of the commission clearly illustrates.

When Sibley relocated the commission and the prisoners from Camp Release to the Lower Agency, where the war had begun two months earlier, the signs of recent violence were everywhere. Heard, yielding to the allure of poetic language, described the scene by saying, "The avenging Nemesis had brought the guilty to an appropriate spot, and that on eagle wings, for here it was that the mad saturnalia first began. The fire had scarcely died out in the ruins of the goodly buildings which they destroyed, or the blood of their murdered, mangled victims sunk in the ground."[26] The commission was working through its caseload in the midst of what was nothing less than the scene of the crime. "All that was needed to complete the deep tragedy of the spot," Heard went on to say, "was the erection of a mighty gallows—one partaking of the gigantesque—and the culprits launched together from it into eternity, there to hang until the elements should scatter their dust to the winds."[27]

It should be kept in mind that Heard wrote this months after the event, and not while the trials were in session. Nonetheless, it cannot be denied that there is a tone in his language that reinforces the belief that the commission members did not come to the task with their impartiality intact. It would be going a step too far to claim with certainty that this passage describes how Heard felt while the commission was actually in session, but it certainly raises that ugly possibility. If that were so then he, for one, definitely allowed the setting to influence his feelings against the defendants. The argument that the judges were too personally involved in the late conflict to render impartial judgements is one that would be hard to refute.

As for the contention that the trials should be regarded as invalid because of where they were conducted, that is not so hard to dispute. A civilian court might be able to entertain motions requesting a change of venue for reasons of prejudice, but military tribunals do not necessarily enjoy that option. General Henry Halleck, the foremost legal mind in the U.S. Army during the Civil War, addressed precisely this matter when he pointed out that "courts-martial exist in peace and war, but military commissions are war courts and can exist only in time of war."[28] In time of war, and, it must be noted, by extension also in the field of war and close to the scene of active hostilities.

It is true that Sibley impaneled the military commission immediately after he had taken control of the captives released to him by the Indians at Camp Release, and it seems that his initial reason for doing this was that he did not expect to remain long at Camp Release. He had achieved the principal objectives of his campaign (putting down the outbreak and recovering the captives) but most of the main war leaders among the

Dakota, along with many of their bands, had fled west and were still at large. Sibley fully expected to resume his offensive operations, but orders from General Pope held him back. When he put the commission to work on September 28, he seems to have done so with the expectation that he would only be dealing with a few cases—his first dispatch to Pope on the subject cited 16 prisoners; the second number he mentioned was 20. Sibley's private letters to his wife support the idea that he originally had no intention of putting several hundred Indians on trial. Again, the accusatory finger of history points to Pope as the man who forced the broader scope and increased speed of the trials.

On October 11, Sibley wrote that he had been ordered to send all prisoners, "of whom I have more than fifteen hundred [the number included men, women and children]" to Fort Snelling. He told his wife, "I shall, at any rate, be saved the task of hanging a large number of the scoundrels, who richly deserve it, by turning them over to General Pope to be dealt with at Fort Snelling."[29] Up to this point in the process, some of the haste can be attributed to the fact that Sibley assumed he would be continuing his combat operations, and was prosecuting the first cases for their benefit as punitive examples, which he told Pope he felt was "imperatively necessary." Even with this desire for an expeditious process, though, the first cases that the commission tried at Camp Release were markedly more thorough and less precipitous than those that came later.

After Pope harshly criticized Sibley's relatively careful process in the first few trials, the investigative process was quickly altered by a shortcut, as Stephen Riggs later observed.[30] "Instead of taking individuals for trial, against whom some specific charge could be brought," Riggs wrote, "the plan was adopted to subject all grown men, with a few exceptions, to an investigation of the commission, trusting that the innocent could make their innocency appear."[31] This would seem to indicate that from that point on the commission was presupposing the guilt of all defendants. Isaac Heard as much as said that this was so: there was "nearly universal complicity..." among the defendants, he believed; "the inference was very logical and natural, that the defendant being an Indian, with the sentiments, inclinations, attachment and revengeful impulses of an Indian, did not fall within the exception, but acted as the vast majority of the other Indians did."[32] What Heard was describing was nothing less than a determination of guilt by association, and there is little doubt that it was at work in the commission's proceedings.

Innocent until proven guilty is one of the mantras of American law, and it applies to military commission trials just as much as to other trials. As legal scholar George Gordon Battle observes, "The familiar requirements that the accused is always presumed to be innocent and that his guilt must be established by the evidence beyond a reasonable doubt exist in these [military tribunals] as in other criminal courts."[33] In most instances, Sibley's commission neither assumed innocence, nor required in many cases that evidence prove guilt—it simply saw the majority of defendants as guilty before word one was ever uttered in court. This presumption of guilt is clearly one of the ways in which the 1862 commission operated contrary to the established protocols of American law. The burden of proof, as far as the commission was concerned, was not on the prosecution but on the defendants themselves.

Another problem with the military commission and Sibley's relation to it is the question of how the military chain of command may have affected the proceedings. In simple terms, the issue is this: Sibley was the commander of the expeditionary force in the field, the force from which the members of the military commission were drawn. Thus, he was the commanding officer of every member of the commission. Because of this, one might rightly wonder about the problem of undue influence at work in the commission's proceedings.

The terminology used here may need clarification. In the hierarchy of the American military there is a distinct difference between a "superior" officer and a "commanding" officer, and the two are not necessarily one and the same. An officer is superior by dint of rank in relation to another soldier, and thus has general authority, but that does not automatically confer the authority to impose non-judicial punishment in minor cases, or to convene a court-martial in more serious cases. A commanding officer is one who is in a soldier's direct chain of command and thus has judicial jurisdiction over that soldier. Sibley was both the superior officer and the commanding officer of every member of the commission.

If the commission operated with the sense that Sibley expected them to reach a certain decision in trial and they then delivered that decision to satisfy his expectation, then that would be a clear case of improper influence. A later example of this scenario would be the military trials of the Japanese generals Homma and Yamashita in the Philippines after the Second World War, where General Douglas MacArthur's interference with those trials was overt and egregious.

Edward Bates, who served as U.S. Attorney General in Lincoln's administration until resigning in 1864, recognized the presence of this risk in military justice. Bates was on record as faulting the military trial system because the courts were composed of people who "are selected by the military commander *from among his own subordinates*, [italics in the original] who are bound to obey him, and responsible to him; and therefore, they will, commonly, find the case as required or desired by the commander who selected them."[34] Bates went on to argue that military tribunals "exist only by the will of the commander, and that will is their only known will of proceeding"; regularly constituted courts-martial, on the other hand, having their origins in Congressional statute, imposed "*legal* [italics in the original] duties and rights" on their members.[35] His view, in essence, was that while courts-martial were bounded by law, military commissions were a law unto themselves and entirely too much under the influence of individuals, and they therefore posed a considerable danger to anyone unfortunate enough to appear before them.

There are cases in the trial transcripts that clearly show the 1862 commission reversing itself because Sibley *told* them to, as we will consider at length in a later chapter. There is no doubt that Sibley exerted undue and improper influence over the commission. To be sure, the direct way that he interfered with the proceedings was more overt than the subtly nefarious sort of indirect influence that Attorney General Bates was worried about; but Sibley's actions do serve to illustrate the worst-case scenario that some critics assume in military justice. Pope interfered with Sibley's handling of the commission, and Sibley in turn interfered with the commission's conduct of the trials. Inappropriate command interference was an undeniable aspect of the trials at least from the day that Sibley received Pope's threatening letter of October 6.

At the same time, misunderstandings of Sibley's actual role *viz.* the military commission persist in the historiography of the war. He was the commission's convening officer, but it would be an fundamental error to go further and claim, as Erling Jorstad does, that "He acted as prosecuting attorney...."[36] Sibley did no such thing, but his direct influence was still overtly exerted in other ways. Jorstad's confused understanding of the commission's proceedings is also further displayed when he attempts to place Sibley directly in the courtroom for the actual trials, saying that "Sibley read the formal charges and each Indian explained his deeds."[37] No contemporary account of the trials agrees with that version of events, and the sources indicate Sibley was never physically present at any trial.

There is also the matter of evidence. A court of law, whatever its configuration, must base its verdict on the dictates of evidence when it decides to convict, acquit, or dismiss. A military commission, just like a court-martial, was bound by this principle as much as a civilian court. It needs to be asked, then, if the evidence used by Sibley's military commission met the evidentiary standards necessary for a clear finding of guilt beyond reasonable doubt.

It seems clear that many of the Indian defendants who made statements in the course of the later trials, the participation-in-battle cases, did not intend them to be heard as confessions of guilt, did not understand that they were being interpreted as such, and almost certainly had no understanding of what the fatal consequences of such statements would be. There is another aspect to the issue of evidentiary testimony that is worth noting by its troubling absence. The only witnesses the commission ever called were those people who were already present at Camp Release, and who were present later at the Lower Agency. At no time did the commission ever request victims and survivors of Indian attacks who had *not* been held as captives to give their testimony in the trials. People who had survived the massacres at Milford and Lake Shetek, or who had witnessed the murder of their family members on isolated roadways, or who had lived through the attacks on Hutchison and New Ulm, were never given a chance to tell the court what they had seen and experienced. Had the commission included these kinds of testimony in its prosecution of the Dakota defendants, there would have been a much greater preponderance of evidence against individual men for specific crimes, rather than the more generalized specification of "participation in murders, robberies and outrages." As Bachman points out, "one of the salient and unusual features of Sibley's regime of military justice is that it was also unfair to the Dakotas' victims, most of whom were not even enumerated, let alone identified, in the trials."[38]

One other detail concerning the role of witnesses in the 1862 court needs to be considered. There is no indication in the trial transcripts that defendants were given an opportunity to call witnesses who could testify in support of *their* version of events. The Dakota were probably unaware that such an option even existed. All the witnesses available to the court were pooled by the prosecution. There were numerous cases where a witness, when questioned about the actions of a particular Dakota defendant, would reply that he knew nothing about the defendant's conduct during the war, but for the most part witnesses called by the military commission were there to incriminate, not exonerate.

Three separate sources support the idea that the military commission was predisposed to interpret all testimony to the detriment of the defendants: first, the observations of persons peripherally associated with the commission, such as the Reverend Stephen Riggs; second, the statements of some members of the commission, such as Isaac Heard; and third, the trial transcripts themselves. The importance of each might be discounted if considered individually; collectively, they support the criticism that the commission misused the evidence available to it.

Almost from the beginning, Riggs was troubled by many things about the military commission, even as he became more and more an active participant in its proceedings. He kept his concerns mostly to himself while the commission was in session, sharing them only in his private correspondence with family and close confidants. Three weeks after the commission began its work, in a letter to his wife Riggs wrote, "From my own knowledge of things here, I know that severe justice will be meted out to them. The outrages committed along the borders and to the prisoners [white captives held by the Indians] have steeled the hearts of men here, so my great fear is many will be punished on insufficient testimony."[39] He was not the only clergyman of long association with the Indians to feel this way.

On November 5, two days after the commission tried its last case, John Williamson, who like Riggs had spent years as a missionary among the Dakota, protested what he felt were injustices in the commission's process. Williamson wrote in the *Missionary Herald* that it was a travesty of justice that a single murder trial would normally last longer than these hundreds of trials did in the commission's hands. He went on to excoriate the commission for numerous failings: the Indians had no recourse to defense counsel (though we have seen that was not a statutory requirement of military courts at that time); most of the defendants did not know enough English to understand the proceedings; and the capital nature of the trials were never explained to them.[40] It seems clear, though, that he was directing these criticisms against the trials where men were convicted for admitting to having fought in battle; Williamson believed that Dakota who were found guilty of specific acts of murder deserved the punishment of law.

Some of the witnesses pooled by the commission also expressed dissatisfaction with the commission trials, but not because they felt the truth was being given short shrift. Nancy McClure had been held captive by the Indians during the war, and had personally witnessed more than one act of murder; she welcomed the trials of the Dakota, because, as she said, "Some of the Indians have been accused of taking part in that dreadful thing who are innocent; but a great many more are said to be innocent who are really guilty...."[41] The commission called her to testify, but she got no satisfaction from the experience. "I was a witness before the military commission that tried the Indians, and called several times," she wrote, "but I could not recognize any of the prisoners as those I saw taking part in the murders of the whites. I was sorry that the guilty wretches I had seen were not brought up."[42]

Having considered the issues of witness testimony and the impact of the defendants' own statements in the military commission trials, it is important to point out that in the full range of the 392 trials there are striking differences between the cases which were prosecuted on specific charges of murder, massacre or rape, and the later, more general participation-in-battle cases. In most of the murder trials (the bulk of which came earlier on in the process) the defendants did not make statements admitting guilt and were convicted on the basis of witnesses' testimony against them, rather than by unwitting self-incrimination. Gary Clayton Anderson makes another inaccurate statement with regards to this aspect of the trials when he claims, "There was no arraignment; there were no charges."[43] That is simply not true. The men who were tried on charges of specific, named murders *were* arraigned before the commission, as the trial transcripts clearly show. When the trials move to the participation-in-battle cases, it is at that point in the process that we find that the defendants were not formally arraigned, and they made statements admitting that they were in a battle, or fired a shot, etc., without realizing that doing so would put them in jeopardy. To describe all the cases in such general terms as Dr. Anderson does here is to add to the general confusion of misconception and misrepresentation that surrounds the military commission trials.

The evidentiary support for this refutation of Anderson's claim comes from the trial records of cases such as Case No. 6, the trial of Hinhanshoonkoyagmane. The defendant here was charged with murder, with a specification to the charge that he "did kill Alexander Hunter ... on or about the 19th day of August 1862...." The defendant's response to the charge was to say, "The charge is not true.... I don't remember killing a white man. That's all I have to say. I did not kill Mr. Hunter...." The prosecution's witness was the victim's wife, herself a mixed-blood Dakota woman, who testified, "I know this Indian. I have seen him before.... We were fleeing from the Indians towards the Fort walking. The Indian met us and shot my husband in the heart. He was within 3 feet of us. He took out his knife to cut my husband's throat, but I begged him to desist and he desisted.... I am sure the prisoner is this man." Another Dakota man gave testimony in the case that connected the defendant with the victim. Based on these testimonies, the commission returned a verdict of guilty.[44]

The record of this case shows that the defendant was clearly charged with the murder

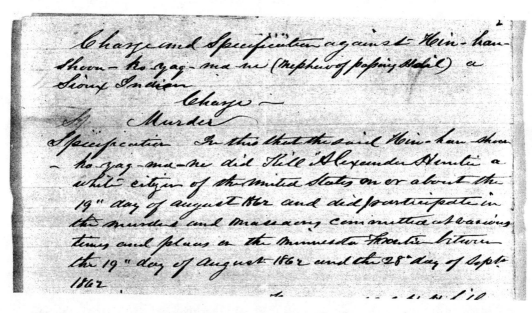

Page 2 from the transcripts of Case No. 6, the trial of Hinhanshoonkoyagmane, showing that the defendant was arraigned on a charge of murder with the specification that he "did kill Alexander Hunter ... on or about the 19th day of August 1862..."(Minnesota Historical Society).

of a specific, named victim; that he "was asked whether he was guilty or not guilty of the charge and specifications..." that he gave a direct response to the court in which he disputed the charge (he therefore clearly understood what he was being accused of); that the evidence against him was in the form of testimony from an eyewitness who was present at the scene of the alleged crime and who identified the defendant as the culprit.[45] For all its brevity, this case reads like a classic example of a capital trial, and it would not be accurate to lump it in with the wholly inadequate proceedings of the trials that came later in the process.

Another case that contradicts Anderson's claim of no arraignments and no charges is Case No. 9, the trial of Makatanajin, whom the court charged with murder on the specification that he "did on or about the 18th day of August 1862 participate in the murder of Francis Patoille...." The defendant admitted to being present at the scene of Patoille's murder and he further admitted to having been armed at the time, but he denied any direct culpability in the killing. A white woman, Mrs. Williams, who testified in the case, told the court, "Defendant was one of the party who killed Patville [Patoille]. I did not see much of him in the matter and don't know whether he took an active part."[46] The evidence was far from compelling in this case, and the testimony against the defendant was also inconclusive; the court acquitted Makatanajin on the charge.

In search of due process in the military commission's proceedings, it quickly becomes apparent that something else marks the trials—a lack of consistency. There is a widespread but mistaken impression that Sibley's commission treated all defendants the same and convicted all but a select few. A close examination of the records leads to a rather different conclusion.

In fact, dozens of men were convicted in trials which, although brief, assembled sufficient evidence of criminal conduct to justify the guilty verdicts the court handed down. But there were other cases, and many more of them, where convictions were determined on almost no recorded evidence, and still others where men were acquitted in cases that were practically identical to ones which produced convictions and death sentences. This fact has not always been recognized or acknowledged.

Gary Clayton Anderson insists that he has studied the trial transcripts thoroughly, and he is on record claiming that the transcripts of all the trials are all the same, from start to finish. "I sat down for three days and I went through every one of them," he said in his 2012 speech at Gustavus Adolphus College. "Three hundred ninety-two, and they're exactly 392 pages. In other words, every trial, one page long." At that point in his presentation, Anderson held up a single page from his lecture notes to impress upon his audience how meager one page of record would be.[47] The problem is that his description of the trial transcripts is absolutely and demonstrably wrong.

Considering just the first ten cases of the 392 total, the actual page count of the trial transcripts is as follows:

Case No. 1 (Joseph Godfrey)—ten pages, including the judges' recommendation for judicial clemency.
Case No. 2 (Tehehdoneche)—five pages.
Case No. 3 (Chaska)—six pages.
Case No. 4 (Tazoo)—five pages.
Case No. 5 (Wytehtowah)—three pages.
Case No. 6 (Hinhanshoonkoyagmane)—five pages.

Case No. 7 (Tahampuhicha)—two pages (acquitted).
Case No. 8 (Charles Crawford)—three pages (acquitted).
Case No. 9 (Makatanajin)—two pages (acquitted).
Case No. 10 (Mozzabomadu)—four pages.

The transcripts of the first ten cases on the commission's docket add up to 45 pages, and that is even if we do not bother to count the standard page containing the convening order, General Order No. 55, which prefaces each case record (adding those to the tally would bump the page count up to 55). Ten cases, three of which resulted in acquittals, totaling 45 pages of records—in other words, ten trials into the record, Anderson's claim that each trial transcript is only one page long is already proven to be so inaccurate that it seems unlikely that it was an inadvertent error. Rather than only 392 pages, the trial transcripts altogether amount to more than 1,000 pages. That kind of numeric difference is not the result of a simple miscount.

Anderson's depiction of the trial transcripts is also proven wrong when it is compared with the transcripts of trials that occurred later on in the process. As a representative sampling, the transcript of Case No. 42 (Winyanaketa), is four pages long; Case No. 115 (Henry Milord), is 12 pages long; Case No. 136 (the second trial of Charles Crawford), is six pages long; and Case No. 175 (Hypolite Auge), is five pages. In fact, there is not a single trial transcript that is only one page in length. Pick any case at random and examine the record of the trial, and even the sparsest, most insufficient transcript in the lot is several pages long. And Anderson's claim of having read all 392 trial transcripts is problematic for still another reason—the transcript for Case No. 105, the trial of Tomnawnakiwga, is missing from the archives, so no one can say how long or short it was.

If this disagreement over the actual page count of the trial transcripts seems like a bit of academic hair-splitting or a scholarly tempest in a teapot, then consider this: Dr. Anderson holds an endowed chair as a history professor at a university with an excellent reputation for scholarship and research, and he is considered one of the foremost authorities on the history of the U.S.–Dakota War, having contributed three major books to the canon. His misrepresentations of this history are therefore all the more troubling and far-reaching, and there are only so many conclusions one can draw from the verifiable inaccuracy of his statements.

The historical reality is that Sibley's commission did *not* handle every case with exactly the same rubber-stamped haste and disregard for individual factors. There were cases along the way—admittedly few—where there are glimpses of something that looks a bit more like judicial normalcy. Chotankamaza, Case No. 172, was charged the following way: "Charge 1, Murder of white persons near Beaver Creek; Specification, that he was one of four Sioux who killed several people near the house of J.N. Earle; Charge 2, standard charge (participation in the murders, outrages, etc.); Specification 1, standard specification; Specification 2, that he took a horse from the premises of J.N. Earle's house." The commission decided that neither the first charge nor its specification was proven, and that the second specification of the second charge was also not proven. Chotankamaza was convicted on the first specification of the second charge and of the second charge itself; in other words, the commission determined that none of the specific items against him could be proven, but found him guilty of all the standard, more general items.[48]

There are also occasional but rare instances where the commission was receptive to mitigating circumstances in a defendant's case. When Wechanhpeheyaya came before the court in Case No. 326, his statement was recorded: "At the battle of the fort, I was there and had a gun—did not fire—I was not at New Ulm. I was at Birch Coolie—my brother was killed by the Germans. The Indians threatened that they would kill my wife and children if I did not go—I had my gun loaded with balls, because the Indians threatened me if I didn't fire at the whites...." Another Dakota, called as a witness, said "I think the Indian tells the truth, because he told me he had been in all the fights—he did not tell me he had fired. I heard the Indians threatened the others before the battle at the fort."[49] In this case, the judges were willing to accept duress as a mitigating factor, and they found Wechanhpeheyaya innocent of all charges.

Rather than clarify the commission's position, however, this simply confuses things further, because in Case No. 316, the commission had convicted a man named Wakanna even though his defense was almost exactly the same as Wechanhpeheyaya's. Wakanna's statement to the court was "I was at the Fort but had no gun. I was not at New Ulm. I was at Wood Lake and Birch Coolie, had no gun, but had arrows. If I had been nearer I think I would have shot my arrows. I went to Wood Lake because I was threatened."[50] There was no testimony against him recorded in the transcript, and it is impossible to know what might have been omitted from the written record. The commission sentenced him to death, but he was fortunate enough to not be one of the men on the final death list.

It is not immediately clear why the commission was sympathetic to the one defendant but not the other—perhaps Wechanhpeheyaya's invocation of the threat to his family swayed them, or maybe Wakanna's indication that he might have shot his arrows if only he had been closer in the fight at Birch Coolie prejudiced his case in their eyes. Whatever the reasons, cases such as these make it difficult to find any logical or legal consistency in the commission's verdicts. It also underscores the maddening probability (maddening from a researcher's perspective, at least), that there was much more discussed in the court or known by the judges than was actually entered into the record.

In answer to the question of whether or not the military commission trials were conducted in accordance with due process, it is tempting to yield to the sort of "all or nothing" statements that litter the historiography of this war. In most of the trials, particularly the ones in which men were charged and convicted for nothing more than fighting in open battle as soldiers against other soldiers, due process was clearly lacking. In the murder cases, where the defendants were charged with murder, rape or massacre in specific, detailed incidents, there was a great deal more evidence, testimony and due process. All the same, it would be absolutely wrong to claim, as one historian did in 1882, that "a fair and impartial hearing was accorded to each...."[51] Reading through the records from the second phase of the trials, it is all too apparent that fairness and impartiality were rare commodities in most of the trials.

# 11

# The Rush to Judgment

*The court for the trial of the hostile Indians captured was set up at Camp Release and proceeded in its work with what seems to many with undue rapidity.*
—Doane Robinson

Without exception, every history of the Dakota War that considers the military commission trials remarks upon one fact: the panel of five officers rendered death sentences in hearings that in some cases lasted no more than five minutes. Five minutes to hear testimony, judge the merits of the case, reach a verdict of guilty, and pronounce a sentence of death or, much less often, imprisonment. No standard of legal proceeding, however lax, would regard this as due process of law.

In one illustrative instance, Case No. 350, the trial of a Dakota man named Wakanhdehota, the defendant was convicted after he said a total of seven words: "I fired two shots at the Fort."[1] Upon his statement, the courtroom was cleared, deliberation ensued that lasted less than 60 seconds, and a verdict of guilty was pronounced. This rush to convict, as John Isch describes it, was how the commission managed to get through 40 separate trials on November 2. These 40 trials in one day resulted in eight findings of innocent and 31 convictions. Of those convictions, all but one was sentenced to death. "For an eight hour day, with no breaks," as Isch observes, "that is a trial every 12 minutes."[2] By any standard, this was a travesty of judicial process.

It would be entirely wrong, however, to assume that all 392 trials were that hasty. Too often in the historiography, writers who have not studied the 1862 military commission trials in detail make overly broad statements about the speed of the process, such as: "Three hundred and three Dakota warriors, the vast majority of those tried, received the death sentence, after 'trials' that lasted little more than a few minutes."[3] Such statements tend to be accepted as accurate by readers, but this description is absolutely not true of all 392 trials. Here again, generalities lead us into trouble. What would be accurate is to say that *some* of the trials were conducted so hastily that they only lasted a few minutes, but there were others which occupied much more of the court's time.

This image of capital cases being decided in such short time was as controversial then as it is today. The Reverend Ezekial Gere, writing to Bishop Henry Whipple on December 19, 1862, said, "The expression 'five minutes,' in connexion [sic] with so serious a business, struck me as it did you, and from what I know of Mr. Sibley, I do not think he would have used it; though, in some of his official dispatches last fall or summer, he spoke of extirpating 'the virmin [sic].'"[4] Gere was correct in his guess that this figure of five minutes per case did not originate with Sibley. Rather, it comes from the commission itself.

When it was first convened at Camp Release, the commission worked through its case load steadily, but not exactly at a breakneck speed. For instance, there is every reason to believe that Godfrey's trial took up several days of the court's time. When Pope demanded that Sibley press the prosecution of the Dakota more aggressively at some point after Case No. 29, the judicial process underwent a drastic change. In an article for the journal *Minnesota Heritage,* Walt Bachman created a statistical rendering that clearly illustrates the differences between what he calls the Sibley Phase and the Pope Phase of the trials[5]:

|  | *Sibley Phase* (28 Sept–15 Oct: 18 days) | *Pope Phase* (16 Oct–5 Nov: 21 days) |
| --- | --- | --- |
| Total cases | 29 | 363 |
| Cases per day | 1.6 | 17.2 |
| Convictions per day | 1.1 | 14.4 |
| Murder or rape convictions | 12 (41%) | 28 (11%) |
| Battle convictions | 5 (17%) | 255 (70%) |
| Number acquitted | 9 (31%) | 60 (16.5%) |
| Defendants arraigned | 29 | 0 |

Isaac Heard was almost certainly not privy to the scathing letter Pope wrote to Sibley, which triggered the marked change in the scope and speed of the trials, so he ascribed the change to something else. As Heard described it, "The trials were elaborately conducted until the commission became acquainted with the details of the different outrages and battles, and then, only the point being the connection of the prisoner with them, five minutes would dispose of a case."[6] From this point forward, the majority of the trials lost any semblance of due process, though cases of defendants accused of specific acts of murder continued to be tried with greater detail and thoroughness than those accused of the general charge of participation in battle. By October 21st, when Sibley wrote to Pope saying "The commission is proceeding with the trials of prisoners as rapidly as possible," it was clear that things had sped up well past the point of due process.

One sign of this acceleration in the trials becomes apparent when we compare some of the first trial transcripts with those that came later. Case No. 1, Godfrey's trial, fills nine close-written pages of the record, several pages of that consisting of sworn testimony from witnesses. By the time the case numbers get up around 300, most of the trial transcripts only take up three pages, on average, and two pages of that is always taken up with the convening order and the standard charge and specification format. In the beginning the trials at least resembled conventional judicial proceedings—by the end almost all resemblance to regular trials was lost.

One thing which made it possible for the commission to process defendants at such a rapid pace was the use of a stereotyped charge sheet. Marion Satterlee, drawing on earlier work by the eminent Minnesota historian William Folwell, described this charge sheet in his annotated version of the military commission's trial transcripts. "After a few cases," Satterlee wrote, "the Charges and Specifications became a stereotyped form, as follows:"

CHARGE—Participation in the murders, outrages and robberies committed by the Sioux Tribe of Indians, on the Minnesota frontier.

SPECIFICATION—In this, that the said ——————— a Sioux Indian (or half-breed) did join with and participate in the murders, robberies and outrages committed by the Sioux Tribe, on the Minnesota frontier, between the 18th day of August, 1862, and the 28th day of September 1862, and particularly in the battles at the Fort [Ridgely], New Ulm, Birch Coulie and Wood Lake.

Signed, S.H.Fowler, S.M.A.A.A.G.

(Later signed: H.H.Sibley, Brig. Gen. Comdg.)[7]

With this method in place, the commission was able to drive ahead at staggering speed. The commission had dealt with 29 cases in the 19 days between September 27 and October 15, but by October 21, just six days later, it had tried and sentenced 91 additional prisoners. The commission was obviously not spending much time in the examination of each defendant. The charge sheet would in some cases list additional specifications unique to a particular defendant, as when the murder of a certain named person or the rape of a named woman could be ascertained, but for the most part the transcripts of the trials are notable for their repetitious lack of individual detail.

This paucity of detail was commented on by several people who were themselves directly involved with the military commission. Stephen Riggs, whose interviews of the released captives provided the details that enabled the arrest of the first 16 Dakota tried by the commission, was increasingly troubled by how things were proceeding. In a letter to his son, Riggs wrote that he had "told the members of the commission several times that I should be sorry to have my life placed in their hands. Oh they were trying Indians, was the answer."[8] The implication, as he understood it, was that there were different standards of justice depending of the race of the accused. If Riggs' version of the commission's response is accurate (and as a witness Riggs is usually dependable, especially about where he felt mistakes were made) then this might indicate some of the carelessness suggested earlier. It could also imply a pattern of racial bias, which could be even more nefarious than the general bias discussed in the previous chapter.

It is clear from the records that the members of the commission were aware that the defendants were not white men. This should not be taken to mean that there was an absolute racial bias that precluded any possible chance for the Dakota to receive a fair hearing, as has been argued by some observers. If the racial bias were absolute, then there would probably have been hardly any acquittals at all, and many more Dakota men would have been arrested and dragged into court. Here again, overly broad generalities will not serve. It is no exaggeration, though, to say that the historical evidence clearly shows that some active racial biases were in effect during the trial. Heard wrote that the defendants "were *Indians*, intensely hating the whites, and possessed of the inclinations and revengeful impulses of *Indians* ... [italics in the original]," making it clear that he, at least, thought that many of the men tried by the commission were guilty simply because they were Indians.[9]

Bachman, in his biography of Joseph Godfrey, points out another detail of the trials which could indicate a conscious bias on the part of the court. Not long before the relocation from Camp Release to the Lower Agency, the commission tried nine men who were identified as being mixed-blood Dakota. In these cases, as Bachman observes, "the court employed very different features when trying 'half-breeds.' The transcripts of those trials are longer and more detailed, and they record the testimony of more witnesses per case than do those of full Dakota defendants tried during the same period."[10] There were several possible reasons for this difference in how these cases were prosecuted: most of these defendants were relatives of white traders; the judges may have been receptive to the reports of coercive threats which forced many mixed-blooded men to participate on the Dakota side; and there may have been less need for extensive translation during the trials. It is also possible, though not absolutely certain, that a racial assessment also played a part in these particular cases.

Riggs, for his part, had no doubt that racial prejudices were a factor during the trials. Writing in the *St. Paul Daily Press* 12 days before the execution of the condemned Indians, Riggs expressed his differences with the commission's attitudes. "I have a very high regard for all the gentlemen who composed the military commission," he wrote. "I count them individually among my personal friends. But they were *trying Indians* [italics in the original]; and my sense of right would lead me to give Indians as fair and full a trial as white men. This was the difference between us...."[11] There is little argument with the conclusion that the members of the commission were generally so predisposed against the Dakota defendants that it was a lucky man indeed who walked out of the courtroom with an acquittal rather than a capital conviction.

Apart from the matter of obvious bias, the unseemly speed of the process disturbed some contemporary observers, just as it disturbs modern observers. Riggs was one who had no doubt that the commission's breakneck speed was making a mockery of the judicial process. "A military commission," Riggs wrote a month after the commission tried its last case, "where the cases of forty men are passed in six or seven hours, is not the place for the clear bringing out of evidence and securing a fair trial to every one [*sic*]."[12] The speed of the trials was, and remains, one of the most controversial aspects of Sibley's military commission. Working that fast, there was simply no possibility that each case was given the full consideration and deliberation that would satisfy the requirements of due process as it is understood in American law today. Here again, though, it must be noted that different legal norms existed in 1862. Military trials of American soldiers during the Civil War were also settled in such brief proceedings that they seem shocking to modern standards of legal process—the hard reality is that 19th century military justice was often a dangerous thing no matter who the defendants might be.

Even so, there were some observers who found this precipitous haste completely acceptable. "The court for the trial of the hostile Indians captured was set up at Camp Release and proceeded in its work with what seems to many with undue rapidity," the official state historian of South Dakota wrote 62 years after the war, "but military courts do not as a rule stand upon technicalities in testimony, nor is there the difficulty in obtaining testimony to convict Indians of murders that there would be to convict white men. They are given to boasting of their crimes, and very few of them were inclined to deny their guilt when charged."[13] The racial slant of this source is obvious. The feeling in some circles was that if the trials were hasty, it was only because there was no reason why they should have been more deliberate.

After the commission concluded its work, Sibley referred to the speed of its process in a letter that he wrote to Assistant Secretary of the Interior J. P. Usher on December 19, 1862, the date for when the executions had originally been scheduled. "The degree of guilt was not one of the objects to be obtained [in the trials]," Sibley wrote, "and indeed it would have been impossible to devote as much time in eliciting the details of so many hundred cases as would have been required while the expedition was in the field."[14] He seems to have been offering justifications for the speed with which the commission settled so many cases, but his excuse raises troubling questions.

Sibley's statement that "it would have been impossible to devote as much time ... as required while the expedition was in the field" prompts an obvious question: why, then, were the trials not postponed until the expedition was no longer in the field? After all, the accused Indians were already in custody, and by October 11 offensive military operations were suspended for the winter. The judicial process could conceivably have been transferred to more formal proceedings at Fort Snelling with no more difficulty than they were transferred to the Lower Agency for the commission's continued trials. It is possible to interpret Sibley's comments as an indication that he felt that the speed of the commission's work was acceptable simply because there was no compelling reason to take more time in the process. But men's lives were in the balance, and every option that might have ensured a more thorough, and therefore a fairer, process, should have been taken. Here again the evidence strongly suggests that Sibley was responding to direct pressure from Pope to expedite the pace of the trials.

Sibley, writing to his wife on October 17, said, "the Indian prisoners are being tried as fast as due regard for justice will permit."[15] One cannot help but wonder what he would have thought of a civilian court trying a capital case with the stereotyped haste that his military commission was using. As one commentator has noted, "The hasty trials and cursory treatment of evidence in most instances hardly added up to the modern view of 'due regard for justice.'"[16] The public perception at the time was a different matter altogether. Even though the commission was driving ahead with injudicious haste, haste to which Sibley saw no reason to object, the process was still too slow for many Minnesotans. The newspapers were urging more speed, all for the purpose of arriving at the conclusion most commentators had already agreed upon: guilty verdicts for every Indian and rapid execution of sentence.

Sibley took exception to that. "I see the press is very much concerned lest I should prove too tender-hearted," he wrote to his wife. "I shall do full justice, but no more. I do not propose to murder any man, even a savage, who is shown to be innocent...."[17] Unfortunately for many of the defendants, the military court as he established it and as Pope pressured it seemed more determined to prove guilt than to it was willing to consider innocence.

# 12

# Violation of the Law
## *Sibley's Error*

*I sent back many cases where men had been acquitted for lack of evidence for revision, and in several of these, additional testimony was adduced, and the Indians sentenced to be hung.*

—Henry H. Sibley

At some point, any discussion of due process in the military commission trials must come around to Henry H. Sibley himself. He convened the commission, he was the commanding officer of all its members, he was responsible for reviewing all of the commission's decisions, and he weighed in with his opinion when President Lincoln was reviewing the sentences. The military commission, according to one historian, was "one of the blackest pages in the history of white injustice to the Indian..."; part of that criticism naturally attaches to Sibley himself.[1]

It is perhaps remarkable that in the chaos of that summer in 1862, any form of court proceeding was undertaken at all. There was already a well-established military precedent for dealing with outbreaks of Indian violence, one that used the brutal method of retributive massacre rather than judicial process. In 1855, near Ash Hollow in present-day Nebraska, troops under the command of Brig. Gen. William Harney attacked a band of Brule Indians in retaliation for the killing of American soldiers the year before. The fact that the Indian attack seems to have been justified, and that the Brule in the earlier case did not start the fight but were fighting back when attacked, did not matter. The preponderance of Indians killed at Ash Hollow were women and children, so much so that one of the nicknames by which Harney was remembered by the Brule ever after was "Woman Killer." The indiscriminate, punitive violence that the Army employed at Ash Hollow was precisely what some people were calling for in Minnesota in 1862.

At least one commentator, Maeve Herbert, has pointed out that never before in American military history had the Army shown much inclination to apply the laws of war to the Indians it fought. In his 1818–1819 campaigns against the Seminole in Florida, Andrew Jackson employed summary executions rather than structured court proceedings. Against that historical backdrop, Sibley's choice to convene a military court is noteworthy. Even so, the court he created was flawed, and that is often the central focus of most examinations of the 1862 trials.

Some of the commission's observers and participants, men such as the Reverend

Stephen Riggs and Lieutenant Colonel William Marshall, later voiced their concerns with how the commission dealt with the cases of accused Indians. Marshall was on record as having said that for his part, "his mind was not in a condition to give the men a fair trial."[2]

Sibley himself never expressed any such doubt; he was consistently certain that the military commission was both judicially necessary and properly conducted, and for the rest of his life he stood by his decision to impanel the commission. In the tumult of that autumn in 1862 he continued to staunchly support the commission's verdicts. Writing to the Assistant Secretary of the Interior several days before the executions were carried out in Mankato, Sibley said, "no doubt exists in my mind that at least seven eighths of those sentenced to be hung have been guilty of the most flagrant outrages and many of them concerned in the violation of White [sic] women and the murder of children."[3] He was firm in his convictions.

A week earlier, in a remarkably candid letter to Bishop Henry Whipple, who was then earnestly working for clemency for the non-murderers among the condemned Indians, Sibley wrote, "The Mil. Commission was appointed by me, of, as I believed and still believe, fair and conscientious officers who were sworn and entered upon their duties with special instructions from me to ferret out the guilty, and to pass sentence upon every voluntary participant in any battle or massacre [underline in the original]."[4] On this point, Sibley only merits criticism for equating participation in battle with massacre, something which we will examine later in this text.

Two sentences later, however, he made a remarkable statement that admits to something worse. "I approved the proceedings," he wrote, "because I had no reason to doubt the criminality of every man that has been condemned. *On the contrary, I sent back many cases where men had been acquitted for lack of evidence for revision, and in several of these, additional testimony was adduced, and the Indians sentenced to be hung* [italics added]."[5] This is a staggering thing for him to have said, and it seems that he did not, then or subsequently, realize the full import of his words. With this one sentence Sibley incriminated himself in an admission of an outright violation of military law that ought to have subjected *him* to a court-martial, or at the least a relief-for-cause from his position as commander.

Under American military law, a commander with review authority of a military court has only three options with regards to that court's trial decision: to reduce the sentence, to let it stand as is, or to set it aside entirely and dismiss the case against the defendant. The one thing a reviewing officer is expressly forbidden from doing is altering the court's decision so as to increase the severity of the sentence. Likewise, the reviewing officer cannot force the court to render a guilty verdict where one was not already forthcoming. The Articles of War that were in effect in 1862 had exactly these same prohibitions in place, and a close review of the records proves that Sibley violated that law, not once but several times.

Case No. 301, the trial of a man named Echadooza, is a particular example. Echadooza's was a fairly typical case, with the stereotyped charges and specifications. The only testimony against him, such as it was, was the statement by a witness who said, "I know nothing about prisoner except that I saw him start down in a war party this way." Echadooza responded to that by saying, "They brought me down to Red Wood in a wagon and took me back again."[6] The commission apparently found Echadooza's

## 12. Violation of the Law

protestations of innocence convincing and recorded this judgment: "The Military Commission after due deliberation on the foregoing find the prisoner the said E-cha-doo-za, a Sioux Indian, as follows, Not Guilty of the specification, Not Guilty of the charge.'"

Up to this point all seemed to be going Echadooza's way. He had been exonerated when few others were. But at some point after—exactly when is impossible to say, but it was likely within a few days of the trial—someone altered the record. The words "Not" were crossed through with single lines, changing the verdict to read, "Guilty of the specification" and "Guilty of the charge." Below the verdict, and just above Colonel Crooks' signature, the words "and sentence him to be hanged by the neck until he is dead" were added to the page. This line is written in tiny script, apparently in order to make it fit into the available space.

Case No. 42 in the transcripts, the trial of Winyanaketa, is another example of the commission's initial finding being altered to produce a death sentence where one was not originally imposed. Winyanaketa was also charged under the stereotyped charge sheet, with the additional specification that he had participated in "the several attacks upon New Ulm, Fort Ridgely, and Birch Coulie and Wood Lake in all of which he was armed with a lance and exhibited a spirit of hostility to the whites." Testimony against him, such as it was, was given by David Faribault, Sr., a mixed-blood man who had been a captive of the Dakota. Sworn before the court, Faribault said, "I saw the defendant in the last battle [Wood Lake] but he was not armed except with a lance. He was encouraging the young men.... He said he was lame, or he would be with them." The trial transcript records that the only statement Winyanaketa made in his own defense was, "I was a good ways off at Wood Lake. Didn't say anything."[8]

Winyanaketa was found guilty of the charges against him, but he was one of the few convicted who was sentenced to a prison term rather than death. On the back of the last page of the record of his case, the sentence—"five years imprisonment"—is

The verdict and sentencing portion of the trial transcript of Case No. 301. The words "Not" in the verdict have been lined through, changing the verdict to "guilty of the specification," and "guilty of the charge." Below the verdict, the words "and sentence him to be hanged by the neck until he is dead" have been written in tiny script to make them fit in the available space (Minnesota Historical Society).

written in a hand which appears to be that of Lieutenant Heard, acting in his capacity as the commission's Recorder. That sentence did not stand for long. On the cover page of the transcripts a penciled note has been scribbled which reads "returned for further consideration of the mil comm." That handwriting is Sibley's—any doubt on that point is removed by the signature below it: "H.H. Sibley, Brig. Gen., Cmding." The commission's original sentence is then crossed out, and a different hand has written in ink beside it the words "be hung."[9] Winyanaketa was lucky enough to have that death sentence commuted by President Lincoln's review, but in the end it did him little good; he died of disease while incarcerated at Camp McClellan on November 7, 1864.

The verdict and sentence of Case No. 100, the trial of Washtayenapa, was altered in a similar way. Washtayenapa was also convicted and sentenced to five years imprisonment, and just as in Winyanaketa's case, that sentence was also crossed out sometime after the trial and changed to death. The cover page of that transcript also bears the penciled notation signed by Sibley, indicating that the case was returned to the military commission for "further consideration."

These cases, like all the others on which the commission ruled, went to Sibley for review after the commission issued its verdicts. Based on what he told Bishop Whipple, there is little doubt that these were some of the instances Sibley was referring to when he spoke of returning cases to the commission to produce death sentences that were not originally imposed. In light of this, there is no question that Sibley actively and directly interfered with the commission's decisions in some specific cases. Putting the matter in simplest terms, he broke the law.

At this point in our examination of Sibley's actions with regards to the commission's verdicts, another recent misrepresentation of the evidence needs to be noted. Referring to the trial transcripts in his 2012 presentation at Gustavus Adolphus College, Gary Clayton Anderson said,

> All there is at the bottom of the paper is 'guilty.' But if you look at the trial records next to it in pencil, is 'to be hung.' In fact, the commission never determined the degree of guilt. Sibley didn't want them to. Sibley looked at every trial record and he was the one who wrote 'to be hung' next to 'guilty.'"[10]

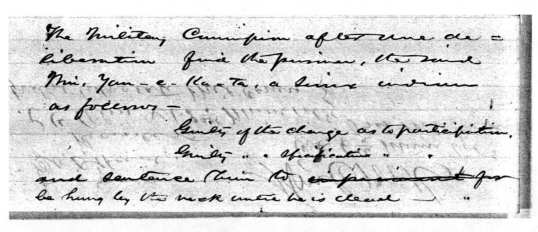

The verdict and sentencing portion of the trial transcript of Case No. 42. The original sentence, "imprisonment for five years," has been crossed out and the words "and sentence him to be hung by the neck until he is dead" have been added below (Minnesota Historical Society).

## 12. Violation of the Law

Actually, none of the trial transcripts bear the penciled death sentences which Dr. Anderson alleges Sibley wrote—in every case where a defendant was sentenced to death, the commission's Recorder wrote the sentence out at the same time the verdict was written, because the judges immediately determined sentence at the same time they reached a finding of guilt, and in each case the words "be hung" are written in ink, not pencil. Not a single transcript bears the penciled death sentence in Sibley's handwriting that Anderson claims are there—the penciled notations Sibley made on the transcripts are the ones we have already seen, when he indicated that he was sending particular cases back to the commission for further consideration. Dr. Anderson's erroneous assertions notwithstanding, a close review of the 391 available trial transcripts shows that Sibley himself never wrote a verdict or sentence on the transcript of any case.

It is not clear whether or not Sibley ever actually knew that his actions were in violation of law, when he returned cases to the commission. But in light of the position he held and the legal actions he was directing, he was responsible for knowing. At the least the senior officer on the commission, Colonel Crooks, certainly should have known and pointed it out the first time that Sibley returned an acquitted case to the commission with instructions to reach a finding of guilt or to impose a more severe sentence. And there is no doubt that Pope, Sibley's immediate superior, absolutely knew that this was a violation of regular military procedure.

In recent discussions of Sibley's actions vis-à-vis the military commission, there has been disagreement with this conclusion that he broke the law. Some historians at the Minnesota Historical Society have argued why, if Sibley actually violated established law, was he never censured by the Army or the War Department? If he broke the law, why was he

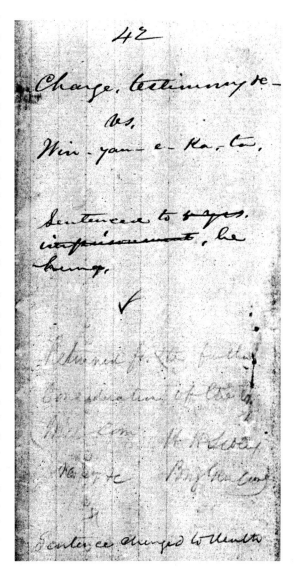

The cover page of the trial transcript of Case No. 42. The penciled notation on the lower half of the page, in Sibley's handwriting, reads "Returned for further consideration of the mil. comm. H.H. Sibley, Brig. Gen., Cmding." The original sentence of imprisonment has been crossed out and the words "be hung" have been added beside it, in a different hand. Below Sibley's penciled note the words "Sentence changed to death" have been written in ink, also by a different hand (Minnesota Historical Society).

never called to account for it? If he was so blatantly wrong, then why was there no official objection to his actions?[11] In fact, Sibley's actions *did* come in for official disapproval at a later time, though he himself was never directly criticized by his superiors. As we will see in a later chapter, in the 1863 military commission trial of Little Crow's son, Wowinape, the War Department found unacceptable what it was perfectly willing to accept in 1862. Even so, no one in the government or the Army seemed inclined to go back over the trial records and right the wrongs. As to the question of why Sibley was never called to account for his actions, the records provide no indisputable answers.

For my part, I think it most likely that in the white-hot intensity of anti–Indian feelings that were at their height in the fall of 1862, few members of the civil government or the military command were particularly concerned if the commission's reviewing officer broke the rules in his zeal to punish a few more Indians. There is also the issue that the tragedy unfolding in Minnesota that year was so removed from the immediate concerns of officials in Washington that many simply did not seem to care one way or the other what was happening on the frontier. To argue that Sibley did not break the law because he was never charged with a crime is to attempt to prove a negative. Sibley's interference with the commission's decisions *was* a verifiable breach of law—the fact that he was never held responsible for that breach is as much an indictment of the Army as an institution as it is of him as an individual. It also provides one more instance of Pope's culpability in irregular command influence and outright interference in the military commission trials—Pope's pressure on Sibley almost certainly contributed to the latter's actions, and Pope was the conduit by which the trial transcripts went to the President. Not only did Pope not object to Sibley's actions, he *demanded* them. Bachman is absolutely correct when he says, "Pope deserves far more responsibility for the course of postwar military justice than he has received, for Sibley was following Pope's orders."[12]

The legal guidelines that addressed this matter in 1862 were not obscure points of law; they were well established and widely disseminated. As early as 1809 it had been clearly stated that commanding officers "can no more interfere with the procedure of Courts-Martial, in the execution of their duty, than they can with any of the fixed courts of justice."[13] This restriction was applied to military commissions also, once those tribunals came into existence in the Mexican War. To put it another way, a commander "had the power to disapprove a charge, to remit cases back to the commission, to pardon, and to mitigate sentences, although he could not increase sentences or order an acquitted prisoner to be re-tried."[14] And 20 years before the Dakota War, the leading military jurist of the U.S. Army, Major General Alexander Macomb, echoed the earlier 1809 ruling when he stated that the convening officer of a military court "cannot interfere with its procedure, in the execution of its duty."[15] The law was clear on this subject, and Sibley clearly broke the law.

It might be helpful to clarify the wording used in the above quote. The phrase "remit cases back to the commission," does not mean that the reviewing officer could order the tribunal to reconsider a case on which it had already reached a verdict, whether that verdict was to convict or acquit, and if acquit, whether for lack of evidence or any other reason. Rather, it means that he (army officers in 1862 were exclusively male) could return a case upon which the tribunal was unable to reach a finding and require that they remain in session upon it until a decision was reached, whether for acquittal, dismissal, or conviction. By Sibley's admission, he returned cases which the commission had acquitted (cases that were therefore closed), and required them to reach a different finding. This created a situation of double jeopardy for the accused, and was unquestionably unlawful interference with the commission as a duly appointed court of law.

Unfortunately, this was not the only way in which Sibley violated military law and protocol in his handling of the commission's verdicts. When the list of capital convictions was telegraphed to Washington on November 8, Sibley included Joseph Godfrey's name among the condemned men as Case No. 1, but did not disclose the fact that the military commission judges had specifically recommended a reduction of sentence in Godfrey's case. In other words, Sibley petitioned the President to approve Godfrey's death sentence but said nothing about the fact that the judges had written an appeal for clemency. This omission, which seems to have been a deliberate decision on Sibley's part, is one more troubling mark against him.[16]

After all of this discussion of Sibley's actions in the trials, there is still one more crucial detail to the story, and it is an essential point on which to be clear if we are to really understand the ultimate results of his actions. Sibley sent at least 20 cases back to the military commission for "further consideration," and in almost every one of these cases, the same thing happen with regard to the original verdict—absolutely nothing.

Not a single case that Sibley returned to the commission resulted in an execution at Mankato. None of the 38 Dakota men who were hanged were there because Sibley returned their cases to the court, because Lincoln did not approve a single one of those altered sentences, so it would be erroneous to infer from this chapter that Sibley's violations of the law in these specific instances sent men to the rope. There can be little doubt, though, that such was clearly his intention. But just because Sibley sent cases back to the commission and tried to get them to produce death sentences in lieu of the original verdicts, it does not mean that the he always got his way. In a few case the commission's judges changed the sentences as their commander suggested they do; in most others, they declined to make any changes to their original findings.

This result, however (or lack of result), does not change the fact that Sibley's actions were violations of military law. It only means that his violations of the law were not, in and of themselves, the causation by which 38 men finally stood on the gallows. The post-trial alterations of the trial transcripts are evidence that the man who convened the commission, a man whom almost all commentators recognize as a man of integrity and strong moral character, in some cases attempted to manipulate the court's decision to reach the verdicts that he felt was appropriate. In doing so, he broke the law, and by rights should have been prosecuted in a military court himself. It is entirely possible that Sibley did not know that he had violated the same military law under which his commission was operating, but ignorance of the law is no excuse for breaking it.

# Part Three

# The Reckoning

# 13

## March to the Gallows

*If the people will be patient we will be able, I think, to dispose of those condemned, and will also succeed in removing the Sioux and Winnebago Indians from the state.*
—Senator Morton Wilkinson

President Lincoln was very much aware of the crisis in Minnesota from the beginning of the war, even if many other easterners were not. At first, his involvement consisted of little more than reassuring Governor Ramsey that Minnesota would be allowed to deal with its Indian war before having to send more men to the nation's war. When Minnesota had first petitioned the War Department to have the state's draft requirement postponed, Secretary of War Edwin Stanton refused. Ramsey then appealed directly to the President. "I have telegraphed the Secretary of War for an extension of one month of drafting, etc.," Ramsey wrote in a telegraph. "The Indian outbreak has come upon us suddenly. Half the population of the state are fugitives. It is absolutely impossible that we should proceed. The Secretary of War denies our request. I appeal to you, and ask for an immediate answer."[1] Lincoln replied immediately. "Attend to the Indians," the President wrote. "If the draft cannot proceed of course it will not proceed. Necessity knows no law."[2] A month later the Indians had been attended to by force of arms, and the question of how to deal with them after the shooting stopped became the bigger problem.

Sibley's military commission passed sentence on its last case on November 3, 1862. In the 37 days it was in session, it had tried 392 cases—323 men were convicted of the charges against them. Only 20 were given the relatively lenient sentence of imprisonment. The other 303 were sentenced to death by hanging. Sixty-nine defendants were acquitted, but in yet another miscarriage of justice, 61 of those exonerated by the commission remained in close confinement even after their cases had been decided in their favor. This was the situation when the death sentence cases went to the president for review—now Lincoln would have to attend to the Indians himself.

As soon as Sibley's military commission became a *de facto* court, the prospect of hanging condemned Indians caught the attention of people both in Minnesota and across the country. Lincoln's own administration was divided over the issue of the military commission trials; Secretary of the Navy Gideon Welles wrote that he was "disgusted with the whole thing; the tone and opinions of the dispatch [from Pope, listing the names of the condemned] are discreditable."[3] Lincoln was not sure if he ought to intervene, or whether he could properly delegate the final review of the death sentences to an officer in the field. He put the question to his Judge Advocate General, Joseph Holt.

Holt's reply was unambiguous. "I am quite sure," he wrote to Lincoln, "that the power cannot be delegated, and that the designation of the individuals, which its exercise involves, must necessarily be made by yourself."[4] One historian argues that "Lincoln wanted to be the final decision maker, not General Sibley," but there was much more to it than that explanation.[5] In fact, the law *required* that Lincoln as Commander in Chief make the ultimate decisions in the matter, and the President's personal preferences had nothing whatever to do with it. The dilemma was Lincoln's to resolve, and one of the questions he examined most carefully in his deliberations was whether or not any of the condemned men had actually committed crimes deserving of death.

The majority of the death sentences Sibley's military commission handed down resulted from guilty verdicts on the general specifications of "murders, robberies and outrages committed by the Sioux Tribe, on the Minnesota frontier, between the 18th day of August, 1862, and the 28th day of September 1862." These were the participation-in-battle cases. Lincoln was not inclined to assume that all of these convictions were equally justified. He gave the commission's trial transcripts to two legal advisors in his administration, George Whiting and Francis Ruggles, with instructions to specifically identify any men convicted of the specific crime of rape. Only two cases met that exact criteria.

If Lincoln was surprised by this, as has been suggested, it may well have had something to do with the fact that Pope had assured the President that the only real difference between most of the convicted men was a matter of which of them had raped more women. John Pope, per his habit, had exaggerated wildly. Lincoln directed Whiting and Ruggles to go back through the trial transcripts again, this time looking for cases where the convictions were based on specific charges of murder or massacre. That process produced an additional 38 names.

The loudest voices in the forum of public sentiment urged immediate execution of sentence on all the condemned Indians, but there were a few who protested against what they felt had been a precipitous rush to judgment, and urged clemency. Almost immediately the differing viewpoints took on connotations of geography as well as philosophy. Charles Bryant, writing the year after the war, saw the polarization of opinions as representing the physical divide between the Minnesota frontier and the sheltered lives back east. Bryant wrote,

> The idea of executing, capitally, three hundred Indians, murderers though they were, aroused the sympathies of those who were far removed from the scenes of their inhuman butcheries; and the President was importuned beyond all reasonable bounds by interested friends, for the release of these savages.

Eastern papers," he concluded, "in numerous instances, gave countenance to Indian sympathizers."[6] This idea that the clemency question broke along geographical lines lingered on in the history of the war. Writing 32 years later, J. Fletcher Williams, in his biographical monograph on Henry H. Sibley, wrote, "The execution of the condemned was prevented by the order of President Lincoln, at the earnest solicitation of some pseudo humanitarians at the East, much to the dissatisfaction of the people generally of this state."[7] Compared to Jacob Nix, the fire-breathing German militia officer from New Ulm, Bryant and Williams were relatively mild in their criticism of those calling for clemency. Nix railed against the "Quakers and other fanatics" in the nation's capital who he claimed had worked to prevent the execution of all 303 condemned men.[8] But as is so often the case, there was more to it than just an East-West divide.

It was true that many, if not most, Minnesotans were vehemently opposed to the mere suggestion of clemency for the Indians. More than 300 citizens of St. Paul signed a memorial which was sent to Senator Henry M. Rice for delivery to President Lincoln. The petition read,

> We ask that the same judgment should be passed and executed upon these deliberate murderers, these ravishers, these mutilators of their murdered victims, that would be passed upon white men guilty of the same offense. The blood of hundreds of our murdered and mangled fellow-citizens cries from the ground for vengeance.[9]

Newspapers across Minnesota also contributed to the impassioned rhetoric, most of them stoking the fires of public opinion rather than attempting to calm the growing storm. The *Mankato Independent* ran an editorial saying, "The final disposition to be made of the condemned Indians, is understood to depend upon the policy of the General Government, which, judging from repeated Washington telegrams, is averse to a wholesale execution." The writer of the editorial went on to suggest that if formal law did not produce the desired result, vigilante justice would. "That they will be finally executed, however, either by order of the President, or by the will of the People, who make Presidents, we do not harbor a doubt," the editorial continued. "Their guilt has been fully established upon careful and conscientious investigation by a competent court, and pay the penalty of their atrocious crimes they must and shall."[10] A few days later, the *Saint Paul Pioneer* echoed these sentiments, writing that it was hoped that the authorities would decide "that capital punishment shall be meted out to all the condemned...." If that should not happen, the paper hinted darkly, "we feel very confident that the people will take the matter into their own hands, and do substantial justice."[11]

Vengeance, not mercy, was what most people in Minnesota demanded. This was the public sentiment that Commissioner of Indian Affairs William P. Dole was reacting to when, during a visit to Minnesota that fall,

Reverend Stephen Return Riggs. A Presbyterian missionary who had lived among the Sioux for years before the war, Riggs and his family escaped the outbreak of violence with the help of friendly Indians. He then joined the expeditionary force as a chaplain, and served as a translator and deposer of witnesses for the military commission. His role in the trials is the subject of some controversy today, and was a source of much internal conflict for him later in life (Minnesota Historical Society).

he worried that the 303 death sentences had "more of the character of revenge than punishment."[12] In spite of this, there were some voices that called for restraint and clemency, though they were in the unpopular minority. Not surprisingly, the most vocal of these were many of the missionaries, such as John and Thomas Williamson and Stephen Riggs, who had worked for so many years among the Dakota and who knew some of the condemned men personally. Bishop Henry Whipple, who did not have as long and intimate a personal experience with the Dakota as did the Riggs and Williamson families, was nonetheless one of the most vocal and most active men advocating clemency, at the cost of considerable public opposition against him that quickly turned personal.

Whipple bombarded officials at every level of military and civil authority in the state with letters urging that the sentences be reduced. He published numerous articles in the newspapers of St. Paul, Mankato and St. Cloud, all arguing for clemency for the condemned Indians. Whipple also had personal connections in the Federal government that no other Minnesota clergyman had, and he took full advantage of them. His cousin was none other than Major General Henry Halleck, General in Chief of the U.S. Army, and Whipple used Halleck to gain access to everyone who might affect the outcome. The bishop even secured a meeting with President Lincoln, where he was able to personally present his appeal for clemency.[13] Whether or not that appeal affected the President's ultimate decision is impossible to say.

In November, sometime after he met with the President, Whipple wrote a letter to the *Republican Pioneer* newspaper in which he argued that at the least, there should be recognition that there were varying degrees of guilt between the men tried by the military commission. "[T]here is a broad distinction," he wrote, "between the guilt of men who went through the country committing fiendish violence massacreing [*sic*] women & babes with the spirit of demons & the guilt of timid men who received a share of the plunder or who under threat of death engaged in some one battle where hundreds were engaged."[14] Whipple was so adamant and outspoken in his appeals for clemency that he was roundly criticized in the public forum. "For openly asking this reform," he wrote, "I have been accused of sympathy with savage crimes."[15] Even some of his fellow clergymen cautioned him against his humanitarian efforts. "I embrace a moment before the mail closes this evening," one minister wrote to him, "to suggest you say nothing more on the subject of the Indian question in the papers."[16] The bishop was not dissuaded, and he continued to argue that the Indians were driven to war by desperation brought about by the greed of white men, and that justice had not been served in their trials. In a letter to General Pope, Whipple pointed out that the Indians had been provoked for years before the war broke out. "Of ninety-six thousand dollars due to the Lower Sioux not one cent has ever been received..." he wrote. "For two years the Indians had demanded to know what had become of their money, and had again and again threatened revenge unless they were satisfied...."[17] Pope's mind was already set against the Dakota, but Whipple did not relent in his advocacy.

Stephen Riggs did not have Whipple's connections in the Federal government, but that did not prevent him from using other channels to make his own petitions for clemency. Riggs presented his case in a personal appeal to President Lincoln in a letter he wrote on November 17. He made his argument obliquely, positing that the execution of some of the Indians would be necessary in order to save the remainder.

His long connections with the Dakota and his personal acquaintance with some of the condemned men, Riggs wrote, "would naturally lead me to desire that no greater punishment should be inflicted upon them than is required by justice." His concern, as he explained it to Lincoln, was that justice was absent from the process. He wrote,

> [K]nowing the excited state of this part of the country—the indignation which is felt against the whole Indian people in consequence of these murders and outrages—this indignation being often unreasonable and wicked, venting itself on the innocent as well as on the guilty—knowing this, I feel that a great necessity is upon us to execute the *great majority* of those who are condemned by the Military Commission.

His reasons for taking this harsh stance, he went on to say, were that the "demands of public justice" would be satisfied by nothing else; this was the only way, he believed, to guarantee the safety of "the [Indian] women and children and the few men who in this great uprising proved themselves loyal to our government and our people."[18] Having accepted the inevitability of some executions, he then put forward his argument for selective mercy.

"I may also say," Riggs wrote, "that I think there is room for the exercise of your *clemency*." There was a difference, he maintained, in "the grades of guilt from the man who butchered women and children to the man who simply followed with a party for the purpose of taking away spoils from the homes of settlers who had fled."[19] Not only were the condemned men not all equally guilty, Riggs argued, but there were mitigating circumstances that should be recognized in some of the Indians' favor. "There are, too, cases of men who in the beginning of the outbreak periled their lives to save white persons," he told the President, "and then by the force of the rebellion were drawn or forced into a somewhat criminal participation."[20] He went on to enumerate several specific cases by name where he felt clemency was particularly deserved, especially since hard evidence of criminal conduct was lacking against those individuals.

Riggs seemed to have accepted that not all of the condemned men could be saved—indeed, he did not *want* them all to be saved. He sincerely believed that some of them were guilty and deserved to hang. In his conclusion the missionary wrote, "This is all I have to say. Although it is unwise to think of executing so many men—yet I think with some exceptional cases—those I have mentioned among them—justice requires that it should be done."[21] It is also possible, though not certain, that Riggs' long and close association with the Dakota, and his knowledge of their traditional culture, factored into his thinking "that it should be done." As already noted, the Dakota followed a life-for-life code that invoked vengeance for illicit killings; Riggs may have believed that executing the men convicted of murder was necessary to forestall future conflicts.

Thomas S. Williamson, a missionary at the Lower Agency where the outbreak began, protested against the death sentences, and did so even before the military commission began its work. In a letter published in the *St. Paul Daily Press* in August, while the war was still going on and just days after he and his family had escaped from the scene of the Indian attacks, Williamson wrote, "Some say, exterminate them [Indians] all; but to do this will be both foolish and wicked. Some of them, I know, are as much opposed to this war as any of ourselves."[22]

On November 24, Williamson wrote a letter to Riggs. At that time the two missionaries did not see eye to eye on the military commission trials—Williamson was much more critical of them in 1862 than was Riggs, although they did come to a closer opinion the next year—but they were much more in agreement on the belief that innocent men had been condemned along with the truly guilty. "I am satisfied in my own mind," Williamson wrote, "from the slight evidence on which these are condemned that there are many others in that prison house who ought not to be there.... I doubt whether the whole state of Minnesota can furnish 12 men competent to sit as jurors in their trial."[23] Williamson was troubled by what he saw as a vengeance-minded bent on the part of everyone involved in the process. "From our Governor down to the lowest rabble there is a general belief that all the prisoners are guilty," he wrote, "and demand that whether guilty or not they be put to death as a sacrifice to the souls of our murdered fellow citizens."[24]

Although Riggs genuinely believed many of the convicted Indians were guilty to some degree—"as guilty as Satan," he said—he grew increasingly troubled by the way the commission had functioned in trial. In a letter published in the *St. Paul Daily Press* on December 14, Riggs said that the "testimony *as recorded* [italics in the original] was very meager in a good many cases, and I think this will be the opinion of President Lincoln.... This is one of the things that I regretted at the time, and I have not ceased to regret it."[25]

"My object in speaking of these cases," Riggs later wrote, "was to soften down, if possible, public opinion in regard to these Indians; there were good men among them still, and some of those who did evil were not *all evil* [italics in the original]."[26] He not only believed that there were innocent men who had been unjustly condemned along with the truly guilty, but also that not all of those who were guilty were guilty to the same degree. His wife Mary shared the same opinion. In a letter to her husband on October 13, while the military commission trials were still in progress, Mary wrote, "I clip a snip out of yesterday's Pioneer [the *St. Paul Pioneer*] about removing the Indians. I don't wonder people feel thus, but I think the Indians who have not participated in this rebellion should not suffer with the guilty...."[27]

Riggs' position on the Indian question came in for criticism from several quarters, not least of all from other people who also had close association with the commission. Antoine Freniere, who was the primary interpreter for the military commission, was one who took issue with the missionary's views. In the December 14 edition of the *St. Paul Daily Press*, the same day that Riggs' letter appeared, Freniere published a letter in which he said, "Reverend Mr. Riggs intimates that those condemned have not had a fair trial. This I deny. They are nearly all guilty of murdering men, women and children...."[28] Like Isaac Heard, Freniere was quite comfortable with the idea of levying collective guilt without distinguishing between individuals. It should be noted, however, that Freniere had a penchant for writing inflammatory letters to the newspapers, claiming much but proving little.

Years after the war, Riggs and Williamson were still being criticized for their advocacy on behalf of the Dakota. John Humphrey, who as a 12-year-old boy was the sole survivor of his family when the Indians killed his parents and sisters, later said, "These missionaries were overzealous in defense of the Indians subsequent to the awful massacre of 1862."[29]

As Christmas 1862 drew nearer the presses clattered all the louder in towns across

Minnesota, and people such as Freniere were not the only ones to mount the soapbox of public opinion in the newspapers. The perspectives, for the most part, were all of a type. The majority of opinions seemed not to distinguish at all between innocent Indians and guilty Indians. Most commentators did not even consider the possibility that there were any innocent Indians. As far as the majority of the public was concerned, all of the 303 men condemned by the military commission were damned to the same degree, and none less guilty than another. In the weeks after the trials concluded, and particularly while the President's review of the sentences was underway, most of the opinions expressed in the papers had no doubts at all about the legitimacy of the commission's verdicts. They also had no doubt as to what the course of action should be if Lincoln overturned the convictions. The people of Minnesota, the *Mankato Independent* wrote, "will never sanction or permit the exercise of a mistaken clemency by the Government, which will allow these rascals, whose hands are reddened with the blood of hundreds of our defenceless [*sic*] population, to escape the extreme penalty adjudged against them."[30]

As already indicated, recent contributions to the literature have ascribed this public animosity toward the Dakota to anti–Indian biases or outright racism on the part of white Minnesotans. It is certainly true that racial stereotypes were regularly invoked in editorials and petitions against the Indians that year, but there was another reason for the hatred so many people expressed toward the Dakota, and it is a reason too often overlooked in the historiography.

While some horrifying stories of gruesome atrocities were exaggerated and others were almost certainly fabricated (as we will see in a later chapter), there was no shortage of verifiable testimonies to show that some Dakota did truly terrible things in the early days of the war. And the fact that so many of the victims were identified by name makes it absolutely clear that public anger over the killing of women and children was not based on fabricated evidence or hysterical fictions, as some writers have claimed, but on real people who died terrible deaths. The dead children of Milford and Lake Shetek were real, and when Dakota murdered them and other children it provoked a reaction of an intensity that most Dakota probably did not expect, and may not have fully understood. There is no denying that racism was present in much of what Minnesotans said about Indians, both before and after the war, but the full depth of the vindictive anger against the Dakota was based on a great deal more than just racial bigotry and beliefs about the superiority of European-American civilization. Army surgeon Dr. Damuel Sheardown called the Dakota men hanged at Mankato "baby killers" in his letters after the war, and it was precisely that sort of sentiment that drove so much of the anger against the Dakota after the war.[31]

As November edged into a bleak, cold December, and Minnesotans became aware Lincoln might not allow the death sentences to stand, the public debate grew even more strident and rancorous. Where General Pope had originally expressed certainty that Lincoln would endorse all sentences, the outcome began to look more and more in doubt. Public outcry was immediate. Politically, the most aggressive voice to argue against any executive clemency was Minnesota Senator Morton S. Wilkinson. On December 5, he introduced a resolution in the U.S. Senate that called on the President to explain his decisions vis-à-vis the military commission's death sentences. Wilkinson took such a hard line in his opinion on the matter that he railed against the military commission trials as a waste of time that should never have been conducted in the first place. Sibley, he said, "ought to have killed every one of the Indians as he came to them."[32] The advocates for clemency had, in Wilkinson's view, "so wrought upon the President as to shake his purposes and reader him doubtful as to what he ought to do."[33]

Not everyone in the national government agreed with Wilkinson. Secretary of the Navy Gideon Welles, for one, believed that the Senator was leading a campaign of revenge, rather than justice. "The Members of Congress from Minnesota are urging the President vehemently to give his assent to the execution of three hundred Indian captives," Welles wrote on December 4, two days before the President actually wrote the execution order, "but they will not succeed."[34] Welles felt the attitude of the Minnesota delegation was hypocritical, on the one hand, and rebellious, on the other.

> When the intelligent Representatives of a State can deliberately besiege the Government to take the lives of these ignorant barbarians by wholesale, after they surrendered themselves prisoners, it would seem the sentiments of the Representatives were but slightly removed from the barbarians they would execute. The Minnesotians [sic] are greatly exasperated and threaten the Administration if it shows clemency.[35]

In early November Commissioner for Indian Affairs Dole wrote to Secretary of the Interior Caleb Blood Smith, asking Smith to convey to the President his view that executing so many Indians who had surrendered in good faith would be a miscarriage of justice. Dole had recently returned from Minnesota and had observed the direction of public opinion there for himself. The people of the state, he believed, were bent on revenge and nothing else.

Senator Wilkinson, undeterred by the arguments of men such as Welles and Dole, continued to advocate vigilantism and mob violence if the President decided on clemency rather than death. "The result will be this," he declared on the Senate floor, "either the Indians must be punished according to law, or they will be murdered without law."[36] Having raised the specter of mob violence—which he clearly felt was justified—Wilkinson then disingenuously attempted to wash his hands of complicity in that violence. "I could not stop it if I wished to do so," he claimed.[37] He never did go on the record as saying that he actually would wish to do so.

Even before this, Governor Ramsey had vehemently expressed his own feelings in a letter to Lincoln. "I hope the execution of every Sioux Indian condemned by the military court will be at once ordered," he wrote. "It would be wrong upon principle and policy to refuse this. Private revenge would on all this border take the place of official judgment on these Indians."[38] Ramsey's invocation of the specter of "private revenge" was a thinly veiled threat—if Lincoln attempted to commute the death sentence, the Governor implied, the people of Minnesota would take the matter into their own hands, regardless of the law. Ramsey went on to propose a solution, in case Lincoln found it distasteful to order the execution of the Indians. "If you prefer it turn them over to me and I will order their execution," he wrote. Lincoln was not inclined to take the Governor up on his offer.

General Pope wrote his own letter to the president the day after Ramsey dispatched his missive. Never a man to parse words, even when addressing the Commander in Chief, Pope gave free rein to his opinions, predicting chaos, violence and mobs in the streets of St. Paul if the President did not confirm the death sentences.

> The people of this state, most of whom had relations or connections thus barbarously murdered and brutally outraged are exasperated to the last degree, and if the guilty are not all executed I think it nearly impossible to prevent the indiscriminate massacre of all the Indians—old men, women, and children. The soldiers guarding them are from this state and equally connected and equally incensed with the citizens.[39]

Just two months earlier, Pope had written to Sibley that he intended to "utterly to exterminate the Sioux." Now he purported to express concern for the same people in his letter to Lincoln. "There are 1,500 women and children and innocent old men prisoners, besides those condemned," he wrote, "and I fear that so soon as it is known that the criminals are not at once to be executed that there will be an indiscriminate massacre of the whole."[40] Pope was describing a worst-case scenario to the President, trying to compel the decision he wanted to see.

The question is, why? It is entirely possible that Pope's primary concern was for the maintenance of law and order, which he felt would be jeopardized by public outrage if the condemned Indians were not hung. But Pope's earlier statements about exterminating the Indians cannot be discounted, and it is possible that he was expressing his personal feelings that the sentences should be carried out. He had assured Governor Ramsey just five days earlier that he knew what Lincoln would do. The executions were sure to be approved, Pope had written, adding "unless the President forbids it, which, from the tenor of his dispatches, I am sure he will not do."[41] Now the President seemed inclined to do just that, and Pope argued against it. "I do not suggest any procedure to you," he wrote in his letter to Lincoln, "but it is certain that the criminals condemned ought in every view to be at once executed without exception. The effect of letting them off from punishment will be exceedingly bad upon all other Indians upon the frontier, as they will attribute it to fear and not to mercy."[42]

On November 24 Pope wrote another letter directly to the President, this time saying that he had learned that groups of citizens were forming to carry out the vigilante justice of which he had earlier warned. "I apprehend serious trouble with the people of this state," Pope wrote, "who are much exasperated against the criminal Indians."[43] The threat of mob violence was real. On the night of December 4, a crowd of about 200 men, well fortified with liquid courage, made an attempt to seize the condemned Indians in the prison at Mankato. Colonel Stephen Miller, whom Sibley had placed in command of the prison, broke up the affair quickly and marched the civilians out of town before releasing them with a warning.

The incident was enough to show that mob actions were a real possibility. "Colonel Miller informs me," Sibley wrote in a letter to Brigadier General Elliot, the Commander of the Military District of Washington D.C., "that large numbers of citizens are assembling, and he fears a serious collision."[44] Sibley was deeply worried. "Please telegraph the facts to the President, and ask instructions," he concluded. "Any hour may witness a sad conflict, if it has not already occurred."[45]

Four days after the unsuccessful vigilante action at Mankato, Sibley wrote another letter to General Elliot, saying, "[S]hould the President pardon the condemned Indians, there will be a determined effort to get them in possession, which will be resented, and may cost the lives of thousands of our citizens. Ask the President to keep secret his decision, whatever it may be, until I have prepared myself as best I can."[46] The next day, word of Lincoln's decision reached Minnesota, and it was not what most Minnesotans had been hoping for.

Senator Wilkinson had relentlessly argued against any clemency for the Indians from the first. In letters to Lincoln and in speeches and editorials, he demanded that all the condemned men be hanged without exception. Lincoln's clemency decision came as a bitter disappointment to him. On December 9, Wilkinson wrote to Governor Ramsey, "I have done all in my power to induce our President to have the law executed in regard to your condemned Indians. We have made some impression upon him, and he has at last consented to order the execution of 39, but he will not permit the others to be discharged, but will order them held for the present." Wilkinson held out hope for an ultimate solution that would satisfy his view of justice. "I hope our people will not destroy these miscreants by violence," he wrote. "If the people will be patient we will be able, I think, to dispose of those condemned, and will also succeed in removing the Sioux and Winnebago Indians from the state."[47]

As Wilkinson reported, Lincoln's review of the trial transcripts did not approve most of the 303 death sentences. The instructions the President had given to Whiting and Ruggles that they identify specifically those Indians who could be proven to have participated in rapes, murders or massacres, had produced only 39 names whose capital sentences were allowed to stand. This did not mean, however, that this represented a commutation of those unapproved death sentences. Technically, every man left off the execution list was still under a sentence of death, awaiting an uncertain fate.

Lincoln may have delegated the review process to others, but the final approval of that review was his to make, and it is clear that his involvement was more personal than simply signing off on a list of names. The President wrote out the final order for execution himself in his own hand, listing each man's Dakota name, spelled phonetically, with its corresponding case number.

Addressed to Sibley, the list was dated December 6, 1862. It read, "Ordered that of the Indians and Half-breeds sentenced to be hanged by the Military Commission … you cause to be executed on Friday the 19th day of December, instant, the following…."[48] Thirty-nine Dakota names were then listed, each name followed by the notation of the number corresponding with the case in the trial transcripts. The final paragraph in the order, immediately following the names of the condemned, read: "The other condemned prisoners you will hold subject to further orders, taking care that they neither escape nor are subjected to any unlawful violence."[49] It was signed, "Abraham Lincoln, President of the United States."[50]

With the execution order in hand and the hangings set for just over a week away, Sibley moved to bring the matter to its close. Complications arose almost immediately. Colonel Stephen Miller, commanding the prison at Mankato, would be the officer in charge of the executions. Within a few days he notified Sibley that he needed more time to make the necessary preparations—among other things, he needed more rope.[51] He requested a postponement of the executions.

Sibley immediately passed the request on to Washington. As the final authority in the matter, only the President could sanction a change in the date he had set for the hangings. In the meantime, however, Sibley had another problem that needed to be dealt with, and urgently. In a short but remarkable letter dated December 15 he wrote to the

### 13. March of the Gallows

Reverend Stephen Riggs. He did not know exactly where Riggs was at that time, so the letter was addressed to Riggs at "Shakopee or Hutchinson." It reached Riggs on the road, as the missionary later recounted in his autobiography. "One day, as I was traveling in my one-horse buggy over the snow between Glencoe and Hutchinson," he wrote, "I was overtaken by a messenger from General Sibley, asking me to report to Colonel Miller, who was in command of the prison at Mankato, to be present and give assistance at the time of the executions."[52] At the top of the single page letter, Sibley had written "Confidential." The part of the letter that Riggs did not mention in his autobiography certainly warranted the cautionary heading.

"Your presence is very much needed here," Sibley wrote. "You had better go straight to Mankato, and report your arrival to Col. Miller as soon as may be." Then, almost as an aside, he asked, "Have you the list of condemned Indians? I supposed it was here but it cannot be found and you probably have it."[53] Incredibly, Sibley was saying that he had

Sibley's December 15 letter to Riggs, in which he said that the execution order was missing, and asked if it was in the missionary's possession. "Have you the list of condemned Indians? I supposed it was here but it cannot be found and you probably have it. I cannot say more for fear of miscarriage of this letter. Only speed your way, and above all say nothing of your having been summoned by me. Yours faithfully, H.H.S." (Minnesota Historical Society).

misplaced the all-important list of prisoners who were scheduled to die, a list personally drawn up by the President of the United States. Furthermore, he was asking Riggs, a civilian who was no longer associated with the military commission in an official capacity and whose only function with the expeditionary force was as a volunteer chaplain, if he had the list in his possession.

"I cannot say more for fear of miscarriage of this letter," Sibley concluded. "Only speed your way. And above all say nothing of your having been summoned by me."[54] Sibley may have been concerned about word getting out that the list was missing—it certainly would not have been a shining moment in his administration of the judicial process. Or, just as plausibly, he might have been trying to keep the execution date as closely guarded a secret as possible for fear of the vigilante unrest he had worried about earlier. Either way, his letter to Riggs was best kept within a close circle.

Riggs turned his horse around and started the long trip to Mankato. He did so, he said, "as a matter of duty."[55] Even so, it was a hard thing for him to do. Riggs had never been to a hanging before, and had absolutely no desire to see one. Now he was being asked to closely involve himself in one, and to be there at the drop. "From my youth up," he wrote later, "it had been a determination of mine never to go to see a fellow-being hanged. No curiosity could have taken me. Rather I would have gone the other way."[56] His responsibilities as a minister of the gospel, though, overrode that personal preference. Reluctantly or not, Riggs went to Mankato. "[I]f I could be of service to Indian or white man, in preventing mistakes and furthering the ends of justice and righteousness," he wrote, "my own feelings should be held in abeyance and made to work the line of duty."[57] He could not have known it, as he drove his buggy southward, but he would fail in part of his intended purpose. Tragic mistakes were about to be made, and he would be troubled by them for the rest of his life.

On December 16, just three days before the scheduled hangings, Lincoln telegraphed a reply to Sibley's request for a postponement. "As you suggest," the President wrote, "let the execution fixed for Friday, the 19th instant, be postponed to, and be done on, Friday, the 26th instant."[58] This was no run-of-the-mill telegram; it was literally a matter of life and death for the 39 men who had an appointment with the gallows, and Lincoln was mindful of that. In a postscript, he included a direct message for the telegraph operator: "Operator—Please send this very carefully and accurately."[59]

In the meantime, the missing execution list turned up. Riggs did not have it, had never had it, and upon receiving Sibley's letter he had immediately written to Colonel Miller asking about it. Miller replied to Riggs on December 19, the date the execution was originally scheduled to have taken place, while the missionary was still in route to Mankato. "The list to which you refer is in possession of Maj'r Brown [former Indian Agent Joseph Brown], who remains with me," Miller wrote. "I shall be gratified to have your presence and assistance until the great drama shall have passed."[60] And so it was that Riggs, who had been present at the beginning of the process when he was asked to interview the freed captives at Camp Release before the military commission trials began, was brought into the picture again and would be there at the end.

The condemned Indians had been granted a temporary reprieve of one week. In that time, they were allowed a final meeting with other Dakota, to hand over last mementos and messages. They also had an opportunity to make final statements on their cases.

"As the time of their death approached," Riggs remembered, "they manifested a desire, each one, to say some things to their Dakota friends, and also to the white people. I acceded to their request, and spent a whole day with them, writing down such things as they wished to say."[61] These final statements, which were subsequently published in the *Mankato Independent*, were later called "confessions" in the press, but the Indians probably did not think of them as such. Most of them repeated their earlier claims of their innocence—"Many of them, the most of them," Riggs recalled, "took occasion to affirm their innocence of the charges laid against them of killing individuals."[62] There was a cultural perspective at work, however, which Riggs noted. "[T]hey admitted," he wrote, "and said of their own accord, that so many white people had been killed by the Dakotas that public and general justice required the death of some in return. This admission was in the line of their education."[63] It is not exactly clear what Riggs meant by "the line of their education"; perhaps he was referring to the Dakota tradition of a life for a life, a rule of blood vengeance that characterized their age-old conflicts with their cultural enemies such as the Ojibwe. If this was the case, then it seems the condemned Dakota believed that their deaths would fulfill white Minnesotans' desire for revenge, even if the white people's peculiar concepts of justice eluded them.

One of the condemned men, Rdainyanka, the man who had urged the Dakota to fight to the bitter end and take the captives down with them, dictated a last letter that remains compelling reading 150 years later. Addressed to his father-in-law, the peace-advocating chief Wabasha, Rdainyanka's letter made it clear who he blamed for his circumstances. "You have deceived me," he said. "You told me that if we followed the advice of General Sibley, and give ourselves up to the whites, all would be well; no innocent man would be injured. I have not killed, wounded, or injured a white man, or any white persons...." "I have not participated in the plunder of their property"; he continued, "and yet to-day I am set apart for execution, and must die in a few days, while men who are guilty will remain in prison." "[W]hen my children are grown up," he concluded, "let them know that their father died because he followed the advice of his chief, and without having the blood of a white man to answer for to the Great Spirit."[64]

To the very end, Rdainyanka protested that he was not a murderer of women and children, but that he was a Dakota soldier and an innocent man. My sense of it is that he was right. Even so, he had taken a hard line during the war, advocating that his people fight to the bitter end, and that they ensure the deaths of all the women and children whom they were holding captive. He may not have murdered anyone himself, but his proposed course of action would have resulted in the deaths of many more people, white and Indian alike, and he called for the murder of the innocent and the helpless. In doing so he essentially urged his fellow Dakota to commit war crimes, and that must be taken into account when considering his case.

Lincoln's decision to confirm only 39 of the original 303 death sentences draws widely differing reactions from modern observers. One legal scholar argues, "Lincoln's distinction between those who committed massacres and those who participated in battles resulted in the commutation of the death sentences of 265 Dakota, an act of clemency unparalleled in our nation's history."[65] At the opposite end of the spectrum Arizona historian David Martinez declares "one can make the valid claim, as this author asserts, that Lincoln is unequivocally guilty of mass murder."[66] Martinez, in a 2013 article entitled "Remembering the Thirty-Eight," says that "anyone with the least amount of interest in the Dakota cannot fail to see the bitter irony in Lincoln using 'massacre' to determine the final sentencing of the Dakota prisoners.... What about the Dakota slaughtered, not to mention the mass slaughter that Governor Ramsey was calling for?"[67]

That is a false flag question. There never was a "slaughter" of Dakota people during the war, nor had there been at the time that Lincoln was deliberating over the trial records, and it is disingenuous to pose that question as if it were a fact. The historical evidence does not support such an allegation—in the recent historiography, this claim usually appears, as it does here, as a declarative statement that presupposes agreement without providing any reliable source of corroboration. It is an inflammatory exaggeration unaccompanied by any citation or documentation, and it contributes nothing of substance to scholarly discourse.

There is a distinct difference between the *language* of mass slaughter, which Ramsey and many other Minnesotans truly were using in the weeks after the war; and the *act* of mass slaughter, which some Dakota actually committed during the war. The Dakota murdered hundreds of unarmed men, women and children between August 18 and September 1, but there was never a similar act of mass murder carried out against Dakota people. The deaths of Dakota from disease during the confinement at the Fort Snelling prison camp are indisputable facts, as we will shortly see, but that was an altogether different sort of tragedy than what Martinez claims occurred in 1862.

Nor would it be an honest comparison to attempt to classify combat casualties of Dakota during the war as a slaughter, since the casualty rate ran about ten to one in the Indians' favor. One could justifiably say that some Dakota were *murdered*, because that absolutely was the case with the Dakota who died as a result of the mob violence in Henderson and New Ulm in November 1862, as the next chapter will show. But to claim or imply as Martinez does that there was a general slaughter of Dakota people is historically inaccurate. When dealing with a history as emotionally charged and controversial as this, the selection of every word is important—sensationalizing the issue with words that exaggerate the facts and distort the reality is at least irresponsible.

Over the years, Lincoln's decision to narrow the execution list to 39 names has been described as either an arbitrary choice or a politically motivated process.[68] These are not new arguments; similar views were being expressed just a few years after the war. Charles Flandrau, writing in 1900, expressed the unsubstantiated opinion that Lincoln's decision "was not because these thirty-nine were more guilty than the rest, but because we were engaged in a great civil war, and the eyes of the world were upon us."[69] Coming forward 153 years after the event, the most extreme distortions of this history can be found in the anything-goes-and-the-more-outlandish-the-better forum of the internet, which is hardly surprising. One website describes the execution at Mankato as "the 1862 Lincoln Massacre"; another makes the specious claim that Lincoln "offered the following compromise to the politicians of Minnesota: They would pare the list of those to be hung down to 39. In return, Lincoln promised to kill or remove every Indian from the state and provide Minnesota with 2 million dollars in federal funds."[70] There is no evidence in the record to support such an allegation, nor does the commentator making that statement offer any in support of his charge.

Gary Clayton Anderson is among those who believe that Lincoln's decision to confirm only 40 death sentences (counting Case No. 1, Godfrey, in that number) was politically motivated. Dr. Anderson has stated that Lincoln believed he could not be reelected to a second term as President unless he retained Minnesota's votes, and that this was the reason why he agreed to confirm any of the sentences.[71] In the same speech, Anderson claimed that Lincoln "decided, and there is absolutely no evidence that it was anything other than an arbitrary number, that forty would be enough."[72]

In order to make such an emphatic statement, Dr. Anderson has to be unaware of the evidence of Lincoln's own explanation of the matter, evidence which became an official part of the records of the Government of the United States in the form of the letter Lincoln sent to the Senate on December 11, 1862; either he is unaware of this, or he has chosen to disregard it. As Lincoln explained to the Senate, his process for determining which death sentences to confirm was based on his instructions to Whiting and Ruggles that they identify any defendants "who were proven to have participated in *massacres,* as distinguished from participation in *battles* [italics in the original]."[73] This indicates a clear recognition on Lincoln's part that the 303 death sentences were not equal in terms of proven guilt, or even in terms of the nature and severity of the crimes for which the defendants were convicted. Such an approach allowed for a case by case determination, which was anything but arbitrary. This is not Anderson's final word on the question, however; in the same speech he theorized that, when considering the death sentences, Lincoln thought "Thirty's not enough, fifty's too many," then concluded, "I think that's pretty much the way it was discussed in the White House."[74] To borrow a phrase from Dr. Anderson himself, there is absolutely no evidence to support such an allegation.

Rather, Lincoln's criteria for confirming the 39 death sentences were based on a close adherence to the rule of law. By establishing the guidelines he gave Whiting and Ruggles, Lincoln sought to eliminate from the gallows every man who was convicted of nothing more than fighting in open battle, and he thereby narrowed the focus onto men whose conduct during the war was criminal, not military. "Lincoln's ruling was consistent with the laws of war prevailing at that time," one legal scholar says. "Those who participated in battles should be treated as legitimate belligerents, while those who killed innocent civilians had violated the rules of warfare for which they were liable for the consequences."[75] If a statement such as this provokes an objection on the grounds that European-American rules of warfare ought not to have been applied to the Dakota, whose culture observed completely different rules of war, then hold that thought for just a little while. In the later chapter entitled "Crimes or Culture," we will consider that particular question in careful detail.

# 14

# Mass Punishment

*But woe to them that are with child, and to them that give suck in those days! And pray ye that your flight be not in the winter. For in those days shall be affliction, such as was not from the beginning of the creation …*

—Mark 13:17–19

As the short winter days moved closer to the new date of execution, the attention of most Minnesotans was focused on the men awaiting hanging in the Mankato prison. President Lincoln's review had confirmed the death sentences of 39 of them; the fate of the rest was only suspended. The confirmation of such a small percentage of the sentences did not, in any legal sense, commute the sentences of all the others. Most of the remaining 264 Dakota prisoners were effectively still under sentence of death, and the public expectation in the state was that each of them would also eventually wind up at the end of a rope. For the time being, though, they waited.

Nearly 1,700 other Dakota were also waiting. These were the people whom the military commission had not brought to trial—women, children, and older men, for the most part. They had either surrendered to the Army in the days immediately following the release of the white captives, or had been taken into custody by soldiers sent out to bring them in. In the eyes of the military, these people were the non-combatants among the Indians.

The decision to move all these people from the Lower Agency on the Minnesota River down to Fort Snelling at St. Paul was one of both design and necessity. The state was still on a war footing, even though active campaigning had halted for the winter. Some bands of the Dakota had fled west into the Dakota Territories or north into British Canada, and the Army was planning to take the field against them in the spring. But the Indian women, children and old people who came into Sibley's hands at the end of September and the beginning of October, from among whom he had "ferreted out" the fighting-aged men that were tried by the military commission, were still in his control when the weather began to turn cold and winter threatened.

Winter on the open Minnesota prairie is a malevolent, lethal force of nature, one not to be taken lightly. Public sentiment at the time might have been callous enough to let the Indians starve and freeze over the winter, but the troops necessary to keep them in place would have suffered just as much, and that was a different matter altogether. The Dakota would have to be moved.

Fort Snelling seemed the logical choice. Situated on the high bluffs of the Mississippi River close to St. Paul, it was the largest permanent army post in Minnesota. There was ample room on the river flats below the fort (ample in the military mind, at least) for a large winter confinement for the Indians, until a final decision was made on what to do with them. But this was not to be an open encampment to simply house the Dakota over the winter—this was a stockade enclosure that was nothing more or less than a prison camp. With this in mind, General Pope sent instructions to Sibley that he was to send the Indians under guard down to Fort Snelling.

Pope had been thinking about the Dakota for some time, ever since he was first posted out to Minnesota to assume Federal command of the war against them. He had been bellicose from the start, using words like "exterminate" in his correspondence with Sibley. Now that hostilities had stopped, at least for the moment, he was no longer advocating the wholesale killing of Indians, but neither was he planning to just let them be. In a letter to Governor Ramsey on November 6, Pope explained his thinking.

"I have proposed to the government," Pope wrote, "to disarm and remove entirely from the state all the annuity Indians, and all other Indians now within its boundaries, and to place them where they can no longer impede the progress of the settlements nor endanger the settlers."[1] What Pope was proposing was nothing less than an Indian-free Minnesota, and he was not distinguishing at all between Indians who had fought in the recent outbreak, and Indians of other tribes who had absolutely no part in it. It was necessary, Pope went on, "[t]o treat all Indians (as the late outrages and many previous outrages have demonstrated to be the only safe and humane method), as irresponsible persons—to occupy nearly the same relation to the government as lunatics do to the state authorities…."[2] In Pope's eyes, there were no innocent Indians; there were only Indians, and they were all guilty to some degree. "[T]his policy seems to me to be wise and conclusive of the whole question," he wrote, "and I shall spare no means to have it adopted by the government and carried out."[3]

In the meantime, the Indians not under immediate arrest by the military commission had to be moved before winter set in. The transfer was undertaken in November. The Dakota, mostly women and children, with a few men among them, were started south on the road to Fort Snelling under the command of Lieutenant Colonel William Marshall, who had been one of the original members of the commission. The area they traveled through had just weeks before been the scene of the outbreak, where hundreds of people were killed and property destroyed. Now, in the weeks immediately after the war, anti–Indian sentiment was at its peak.

Marshall was worried that white Minnesotans might see the Indians in his charge as targets of their vengeance, and he tried to forestall it. On November 8, the day after Marshall's column started down the road for Fort Snelling, the *St. Paul Daily Press* published an article that read:

> [Lt. Col. Marshall] earnestly deprecates any molestation, by inhabitants of the Minnesota Valley. Reports of threats to this effect have reached him, and we urge his appeal that no attempt will be made to execute them. Col. Marshall will have 300 troops under his command for the protection of his trains. On this subject, he adds: "I would risk my life for the protection of these helpless beings, and would feel everlastingly disgraced if any evil befell them while in my charge. Through the PRESS, I want the settlers in the valley, on the route we pass, to know that they are not the *guilty Indians* (some 300 of whom are to be executed at South Bend) but *friendly Indians, women and children*.' [italics in the original] The people of the Minnesota Valley had too distinct a recollection of Col. Marshall's service in the Indian campaign not to respect his wishes as above expressed.[4]

Tragically, Marshall's appeal fell on deaf ears.

As Marshall's column of Indian women, children and old men was escorted through the town of Henderson, a riot broke out. Townspeople set upon the Indians with just about any object that came to hand. Sam Brown, whose family had been among the captives held by the Dakota, was there, and he described the chaos in his journal.

> Men, women, and children, armed with guns, knives, clubs, and stones rushed upon the Indians as the train was passing by and, before the soldiers could interfere and stop them, succeeded in pulling many of the old men and women, and even children, from the wagons by the hair of the head and beating them, and otherwise inflicting injury upon the helpless and miserable creatures.

It was at this point that he witnessed one of the most infamous events of the Indian removal.

> I saw an enraged white woman rush up to one of the wagons and snatch a nursing baby from its mother's breast and dash it violently upon the ground. The soldiers' [sic] instantly seized her and led or rather dragged the woman away, and restored the papoose to its mother—limp and almost dead. Although the child was not killed outright, it died a few hours after.[5]

Brown had already seen some of the horrors of the war, and he had a perspective that led to comparisons. "[H]ere my thoughts reverted to the case of the Indian brave at the dance," he wrote in his journal, "who boasted in 'ghoulish glee' that he had roasted a babe in the oven, and I contrasted it with the case before me. An uncivilized heathen in the one case, and a *civilized christian* [sic, italics in the original] white woman in the other!"[6]

A Dakota woman named Good Star Woman made the trek as an eight year-old girl in 1862. The journey down to Fort Snelling was a terrible experience, as she recalled in the 1930s. "When they passed through towns the people brought poles, pitchforks and axes and hit some of the women and children in the wagons," she recounted. "Father was struck once and almost knocked down." The soldiers that were escorting them, she said, "tried to protect them but could not always do so." The mob assaults were so ferocious that "some Indians died from the beatings they received."[7] Precisely how many Indians died in the Henderson riot has never been accurately determined—there is no evidence to support claims of large scale loss of life, but it is certain that some Dakota lost their lives. Charles Flandrau, remembering the day that white Minnesotans evacuated New Ulm on August 25, described the settlers' movement by saying, "A more heartrending procession was never witnessed in America."[8] The Dakota who made the trek to Fort Snelling that November would probably have disagreed.

The day after Marshall set out with his column, a second contingent of Dakotas left the Lower Agency in route to Mankato, this time under the command of Sibley himself. This group included the prisoners who had been tried and convicted by the military commission. The column of wagons hauling the prisoners took them around the outskirts of the town of New Ulm, which had been the scene of the most concerted Indian attacks of the war. During the fighting, the residents of New Ulm had buried their dead in the dirt streets before they abandoned the town for the greater safety of St. Peter. They had only recently returned to their homes. It may have been ill-luck and bad timing that the column of Dakota prisoners reached New Ulm on the day that the townspeople were reinterring their dead. Or, it has been suggested, it might have been the deliberate machinations on the part of anti–Indian agitators in the town who hoped to incite the population against the prisoners that the dead were being reburied on that specific day. Either way, the situation could hardly have been worse for the Indians.

The hapless Dakota were shackled in the wagons two-by-two, unable to defend themselves. The residents of New Ulm attacked them with such ferocity that Sibley ordered his troops to drive them back with bayonets. Rocks, bricks, and timbers were hurled over the soldiers' heads at the Indians in the open wagons. "[T]hey were set upon," the Minnesota Adjutant General's Report says, "and many of them pelted and beaten with stones and sticks, in spite of the guard accompanying them."[9] A soldier in Sibley's column, John Nelson, kept a small pocket diary in which he scribbled a few notes each day. His entry for November 9, 1862, reads, "our marched [sic] reached New Ulm and there was a sight I shal [sic] remember the citizen men women and children gatherd [sic] determind [sic] to kill the Indians with stones axes and guns and knives myself and two other men was plased [sic] to guard an old dutch woman that had an axe determined to kill all the Indians...."[10] Before the howling townspeople were finally driven back, a number of Indians were seized by the mob and badly beaten.

Here again, exactly how many deaths resulted from this violence is unclear. Bachman, in his close analysis of the event, argues that only two Dakota can be proven to have died of wounds received at New Ulm.[11] New Ulm historians Darla Gebhard and John Isch believe that those men were Ohomni and Oyateicasna.[12] Regardless of the number of fatalities, though, there is no question that the mob was homicidal in its intent, and that the violence was of a lethal nature.

Sibley later described the scene at New Ulm in a letter to his wife. The column of prisoners, he wrote, "was set upon by a crowd of men, women and children, who showered brickbats and other missiles upon the shackled wretches, seriously injuring some fifteen of the latter and some of the guards...."[13] Sibley seemed shocked that most of the assailants were women. "I did not dare fire [into the crowd] for fear of killing women and children," he told his wife. "The Dutch she devils!? They were as fierce as tigresses."[14]

A cynical interpretation of Sibley's actions might conclude that he passed so close to New Ulm in broad daylight because he did not care about the safety of the Indian prisoners. That answer is unsatisfactory. Even if it were true, there was still the safety of his own troops to consider. Just as happened with Marshall's column in Henderson, some of the soldiers guarding the Indians were injured in the New Ulm melee. It is unlikely that Sibley would have jeopardized his soldiers simply because he did not care what happened to the Indians in his charge. It seems much more likely that he simply did not anticipate the degree of hostility that awaited at New Ulm, or the unrestrained violence the townspeople.

Jacob Nix, one of the leaders of the town's defense during the war, later took issue with Sibley's decision to bring the Indians past New Ulm. "That the bloodthirsty archenemies of New Ulm were transported to Mankato in bright daylight directly through the terribly afflicted town was an unjustifiable act of tactlessness of the military officials at the time," he wrote in his account of the war.[15] In Nix's view, the presence of the Indian prisoners was a direct insult to the residents of New Ulm, and he thought the resulting violence was completely justified. "Considering the circumstances," he wrote, "could one blame the poor people for laying their hands on their torturers, the destroyers of their happiness? Certainly not!"[16]

The reasons for this attack on the Indian prisoners by the mob at New Ulm have variously been attributed to racial hatred or a desire for revenge for the Dakota attacks on the town in August. There is probably a bit of truth in both of those reasons. The Adjutant General's Report of 1863 adds a third possibility which sounds plausible on its face but which is unlikely when examined in light of the evidence. The principal instigators of the violence, the AG Report says, were the women of the town, "impelled to the act, under the belief that the Indians were to be snatched from the punishment due their crimes, by the United States Government." That conclusion seems to owe more to the acuity of hindsight than it does to the reality of the time. After all, at this point in time (November) the results of President Lincoln's review were still pending, and were by no means a foregone conclusion.

The riots in Henderson and New Ulm did not meet with universal approval by all Minnesotans. "While we sympathize with the people of New Ulm in their sufferings," the *Mankato Semi-Weekly Record* said in an editorial, "we cannot but condemn as unjustifiable their conduct in thus attacking prisoners...."[17] There were other voices that echoed this censure, but for the most part, the overwhelming majority still called for the extermination or exile of every Dakota in Minnesota. In the court of public opinion, they were guilty of being Indians, and that was enough to damn them all.

# 15

# The Executions

*... till blood has answered for blood.*—Isaac Heard

If the presidential decision to confirm so few of the original 303 death sentences was not well received by most Minnesotans, Senator Morton Wilkinson was particularly incensed by it. Wilkinson introduced a resolution in Congress demanding that Lincoln to explain his decision. The President complied. "I caused a careful examination of the records of the trials to be made," Lincoln wrote in his reply, "in view of first ordering the execution of such as had been proved guilty of violating females. Contrary to my expectations, only two of this class were found." These two were Tehehdonecha and Tazoo, both of whom had admitted committing rape. "I then directed a further examination," Lincoln continued, "and a classification of all who were proven to have participated in massacres, as distinguished from participation in battles. This class numbered forty, and included the two convicted of female violation."[1]

One of the 40 was Joseph Godfrey, the man whose testimony had so impressed the officers of the military commission. Godfrey's sentence was immediately reduced, Lincoln told the Senate, to "ten years' imprisonment. I have ordered the other 39," he concluded, "to be executed...."[2] The day before the execution, word came of a last-minute reprieve for one of the Indians; Tatemina's death sentence was commuted by the President after several white settlers petitioned on his behalf, saying that he had aided them in their escape from Dakota war parties. That left 38 men to face the large single gallows that awaited them; as the names were spelled out phonetically on the execution order, they were:

1. Tipi-hdo-niche (Forbids His Dwelling)
2. Wyata-tonwan (His People)
3. Taju-xa (Red Otter)
4. Hin-han-shoon-koyag-mani (Walks Clothed with an Owl's Tail)
5. Maza-bomidu (Iron Blower)
6. Wapa-duta (Sacred Leaf)
7. Wa-hena (meaning unknown)
8. Sna-mani (Tinkling Walker)
9. Rda-inyanke (Rattling Runner)
10. Dowan-niye (The Singer)
11. Xunka-ska (White Dog)

There are no known photographs of the hangings on December 26, 1862, in Mankato. The Army brought in nearly 1,400 troops to ensure that there would be no civil unrest, and a tight security cordon was maintained around the scaffold. Illustrations such as this were made from eyewitness descriptions (Minnesota Historical Society).

12. Hepan (Second Son)
13. Tunkan-icha-ta-mani (Walks with his Grandfather)
14. Ite-duta (Scarlet Face)
15. Amdacha (Broken to Pieces)
16. Hepidan (Third Son)
17. Marpiya-te-najin (Stands on a Cloud) [Cut Nose]
18. Henry Milord
19. Chaska-dan (First Son, Little)
20. Baptiste Campbell
21. Tate-kage (Wind Maker)
22. Hapinkpa (Tip of the Horn)
23. Hypolite Auge
24. Nape-shuha (Does Not Flee)
25. Wakan-tanka (Great Spirit)
26. Tunkan-koyag-i-najin (Stands Clothed with his Grandfather)
27. Maka-te-najin (Stands upon Earth)
28. Pazi-kuta-mani (Walks Prepared to Shoot)
29. Tate-hdo-dan (Wind Comes Back)
30. Waxicun-na (Little Whiteman)
31. Aichaga (To Grow Upon)
32. Ho-tan-inku (Voice Heard in Returning)

33. Cetan-hunka (The Parent Hawk)
34. Hda-hin-had (To Make a Rattling Noise)
35. Chanka-hdo (Near the Woods)
36. Oyate-tonwan (The Coming People)
37. Mehu-we-mea (He Comes for Me)
38. Wakinyan-na (Little Thunder)

The week before Christmas, the Army began its final preparations for the executions. Anticipating a massive crowd, and mindful of the potential for civil unrest, the authorities were agreeable when the citizens of Mankato asked for the additional safeguard of martial law. With Colonel Miller's approval, the military Adjutant issued the following order:

Headquarters Indian Post, Mankato, Dec. 17, 1862.
The President of the United States having directed the execution of thirty-nine of the Sioux Indian and half-breed prisoners in my charge, on Friday, the 26th instant, he having postponed the time from the 19th instant, said execution will be carried into effect in front of the Indian prison at this place on that day at 10 o'clock a.m. The executive also enjoins that no others of the prisoners be allowed to escape, and that they be protected for the future disposition of the government; and these orders will be executed by the military force at my disposal with utmost fidelity.
The aid of all good citizens is invoked to maintain the law. The colonel commanding respectfully recommends that they assemble at Mankato the previous evening and adopt such measures as may contribute to the preservation of good order and strict propriety during the 26th instant.
By order of the colonel commanding.
J.K. Arnold
Post Adjutant[3]

Friday, December 26, was mild for mid-winter Minnesota, and a huge crowd was on hand for the hanging. Colonel Miller, commanding the prison at Mankato and overseeing the executions, had already dealt with threats of violence from vengeful-minded citizens, and he took no chances now. He prohibited the sale or consumption of alcohol leading up to the day of the hanging. To maintain order and deal with any demonstrations or unrest that might develop, he had 1,400 troops on hand. Mounted lines of cavalry kept the crowd back from the scaffold, while infantry formed up on three sides of the gallows, with two companies positioned as a corridor through which the condemned men would walk from the jail to the scaffold.

The hangings were scheduled for 10 a.m. The condemned men, housed separately from the rest of the prisoners since the final death list was announced, spent their last hours chanting their death songs. After their final breakfast, each prisoner was fitted with a white cap and their hands were tied in front of them. "Instead of any shrinking or resistance," a reporter from the *New York Times* wrote, "all were ready, and even seemed eager to meet their fate."[4] At the provost marshal's signal, the caps were pulled down like hoods over their faces, and then they were led out to the scaffold between a cordon of troops. Guided by pairs of guards, the condemned men mounted the gallows and were positioned under the ropes.

Nine soldiers placed the nooses around the hooded Dakota's necks. One of the men detailed for this duty was Emanuel Reyff, who four months earlier had watched from hiding as an Indian raiding party killed his brother, sister-in-law, niece and nephew. Reyff later said that he performed his task on the gallows "with pleasure."[5]

Hooded, noosed, and waiting the drop, the Indians began their death chant a final time, stomping and swaying on the gallows so that the scaffold began to shudder from the rhythm. There were three rolls of drumbeat to signal the drop. On the first beat of the drum, the Indians "made such frantic efforts to grasp each other's hands, that it was agony to behold them. Each one shouted out his name, that his comrades might know he was there."[6] On the third drumbeat a man named William Duley stepped forward. Duley had lost two children in the massacre at Slaughter Slough, near Lake Shetek, and his wife Laura and surviving children were taken captive by the Indians who had fled west. They had only recently been rescued by a group of young Dakota men known as the Fool Soldiers. As the final drumbeat fell away Duley cut the single rope that held the gallows traps in place.

The 38 men dropped simultaneously. A witness to the execution later described how "there was one, not loud, but prolonged cheer from the soldiery and citizens, and then all were quiet and earnest."[7] The execution did not go off flawlessly. One rope broke, and the man at the end of it, Rdainyanka, fell heavily to the ground beneath the gallows. He did not move—apparently he was already dead, the rope having broken his neck even as it snapped. Nonetheless, his body was hoisted back up and suspended from a new rope, and thirty-eight bodies hung in the morning sun.[8] It was, the *New York Times* correspondent reported, "an awful sight to behold. Thirty-eight human beings suspended in the air...."[9]

The general consensus among witnesses was that they died well—at least as well as men could die by hanging. Even Jacob Nix of New Ulm, who was absolutely unapologetic in his animosity toward the Indians, found their deportment on the gallows remarkable. Nix was the same man who had written, "Immediately after the capture of the red scoundrels, one should not have wasted any time in shooting or hanging every one [*sic*] who took part in the horrible crimes...."[10] Now, having witnessed the execution, he said, "I must admit they faced death courageously."[11]

After about an hour, the corpses were cut down and buried in a mass grave on the sandy banks of the Minnesota. They did not lie there long. Later that night, local doctors dug the bodies up and parceled them out for medical research. Nearly a century would pass before their bones—those that could still be identified—were repatriated to their people. Most of the remains, used as cadavers by medical schools, were never recovered.

The disinterment of the Indian dead remains a legitimate grievance for Dakota people today. To deny the dead men the decency of burial and to instead use them for medical dissection was an act of desecration, and one might assume that it provides just one more example of white Minnesotans' racial animus toward Indians at the time. However, in a wider historical context, the way in which the Dakota dead were treated was precisely the same way that the bodies of whites were treated in similar circumstances during the 19th century in general, and in Minnesota in particular, as indicated by something that happened a few years after the events of 1862, near to the same area.

On September 7, 1876, eight men attempted a daylight robbery of the First National Bank in Northfield, Minnesota. They were the James-Younger gang: Jesse and Frank James; Cole, Jim and Bob Younger; along with Clell Miller, Bill Chadwell, and Charlie Pitts. Miller and Chadwell were killed in the gunfight that erupted in the streets of Northfield when the townspeople fought back; Pitts was killed two weeks later when a citizen posse trapped him and the three Younger brothers in Watonwan County on September 21. The corpses of all three men were photographed in death and displayed for viewing by hundreds of people who flocked to the area. The bodies of Miller and Chadwell were buried on September 8; later that night they were exhumed by a medical student named Henry Wheeler, placed in barrels, and shipped off to the medical school at the University of Michigan. Clell Miller's family eventually managed to claim his remains; Chadwell's kin was never able to. After Pitts was killed, his corpse was dissected by a Dr. John Murphy before being reduced to its bones and preserved as an articulated skeleton for further use.[12]

There is another thread of similarity between the two distinctly separate incidents. For decades, the Minnesota Historical Society in St. Paul had in its collection (and sometimes displayed) part of Little Crow's scalp, taken after he was killed in 1863. That scalp, which was nothing less than part of the mortal remains of the Dakota leader, was finally returned to his people in 1971, along with part of his skull and an arm bone. The Northfield Historical Society, in its collection today, still has a piece of skin with an attached ear, taken from Charlie Pitts' corpse by Dr. Murphy. Pitts had a wife and children; his descendants never received his remains for burial and remembrance, just as the descendants of almost all the Dakota men hanged at Mankato were never able to recover their dead.

Anyone studying the often violent history of the American West will find ample evidence to support one conclusion about the corpses of outlaws and criminals: that public execution, exploitative displays of corpses, insensitive treatment of the dead, and souvenir-taking that extended to pieces of the bodies themselves, were all common occurrences. The racial identity of the dead did not necessarily play a part in it; what mattered more was how famous (or infamous) the dead were in life. In light of this, one could say that the Dakota dead at Mankato were treated quite the same as were white men who had also had a high degree of criminal notoriety. The frequent occurrence of this in American history does not provide a justification for what happened at Mankato—exploitation of the dead is objectionable to modern sensibilities no matter whose corpses are mistreated—but it does place the events of 1862 in a wider historical context.

This perspective does not, of course, lessen in any way the emotional impact of the fact that white men dug up the Dakota corpses and used them for their own purposes, but it does serve to establish a deeper understanding of that event. It almost certainly raises an entirely different point of controversy, however, to suggest that the Dakota dead were treated much the same as were the corpses of white criminals, because that means describing the men hanged at Mankato as criminals, and many members of the Dakota community today emphatically reject the idea that the 38 men who were executed in 1862 were guilty of any kind of crime.

It has been argued that the Dakota hanged at Mankato were scapegoats, executed in place of the truly guilty whom the American authorities were never able to bring to justice. There is no denying that some men who were guilty of committing massacre and murder escaped the noose and never stood trial for any crime. More than one white survivor of the war reported that the Indians whom they had witnessed committing crimes had escaped the Army's grasp and were never brought to trial. Red Middle Voice and Shakopee, the uncle-nephew chiefs who had so vigorously argued for war and who had participated in some of the worst of the violence, were not there. Little Crow, who had thrown his considerable influence behind the call for war in spite of his initial reluctance, was not there. (This is not to say that Little Crow was a war criminal, because he was not, but he was a war leader much more than were any of the 38 men who died on the gallows.) Also absent from the execution list were White Lodge, Medicine Bottle, Hapan, Sacred Rattle, and other men who had could honestly be said to have blood on their hands. And the four young men who had begun it all with the murders at Acton on August 17 were also long gone and out of reach. But these facts do *not* mean that most of the men on the gallows at Mankato did not deserve to be there on account of their own actions.

In recent books and articles, some commentators have characterized the 38 men executed at Mankato as being completely and collectively innocent of any kind of crimes. One writer, in a 2004 article in *American Indian Quarterly*, describes all 38 of them collectively as "warrior patriots" and categorically rejects the idea that any of these men were guilty of anything criminal.[13] This is also the perspective taken by David Martinez in his article "Remembering the Thirty-Eight." Martinez asks "how many men can a president allow to be unjustly executed before he is held accountable?"[14] He also rejects the idea that any of those men were actually guilty of the crimes of rape, murder or massacre.

No doubt some of the 38 men *were* patriots by every definition of the word—Wahehud, who was convicted of killing a soldier of the U.S. Army and of "making war against the U.S.," could certainly be described that way. I would also argue that White Dog, who had fought against soldiers in open battle and was not implicated in any crime against civilians, also fits that definition.[15] And it was tragically clear after the fact that at least one of the men hanged that day, Chaska, was there because he was mistaken for another man. But these exceptions do not apply to all 38 men. It is disingenuous to try to cloak all of them in the mantle of native patriotism without distinguishing between individuals. To label them all collectively as "the Glorious Thirty-Eight," as some do today, is to gloss over the historical record and ignore their individual actions.

Tazoo and Tehehdonecha were self-admitted rapists. Cut Nose was a murderer of women and children, a fact he boasted of until he was brought to an accounting for his actions. (Sam Brown later reported that Cut Nose had bragged to him of killing so many children with his knife that his arm was sore.) Napashue claimed to have killed 19 settlers, not soldiers; even if that number was an exaggeration, he had murdered enough people to justify the rope that hanged him. Several of the other Dakota men, such as Mazabomdoo, who admitted to the murders of an old woman and two children, were complicit in the killing of unarmed, defenseless people. These men's actions were not patriotic in any sense of the word. To assume that all 38 of them deserved the laudatory title of "warrior patriot" is to be just as wrong as Jacob Nix, who referred to them collectively as "the 38 Indian murderers."[16] They must be considered separately, not collectively, and most of the men on the Mankato gallows, had they been brought there by a less tainted judicial process, would properly be recognized as criminals solely by dint of their actions during the war.

Furthermore, most of the men hanged at Mankato were convicted in trials that were considerably more thorough than most of those whose death sentences the President did not approve. Charles Flandrau, the former Justice of the Minnesota Supreme Court who corresponded with Sibley during the trials, later expressed his opinion that the 39 men whose death sentences Lincoln confirmed were no guiltier than any of the other 303, but he was absolutely wrong about that.[17] There is no record or indication that Flandrau ever read the trial transcripts himself, so his was probably not an informed opinion. The murder trials, as distinguished from the participation-in-battle trials, "were conducted more slowly, with more safeguards, and held to a higher standard of proof than the subsequent cases. Moreover, many of the men on the list were convicted on the strength of eyewitness evidence."[18]

To be clear, the distinction here is not a matter of who won or lost the war, and who therefore had the right to claim the appellation of "patriot." A man is no less a patriot because he fights in a losing war—what matters more is the manner in which he fights. Measured by their conduct in the fight, and particularly their deliberate killing of children, many of the 38 men hanged in 1862 fell far short of the status of patriots, and their actions during the war fit the definition of war crimes.

# 16

# Concentration Camps and Ethnic Cleansing

Over the past 30 years, these two terms—concentration camps and ethnic cleansing—have appeared with increasing frequency in books and articles dealing with this war. Dakota activist and academic Waziyatawin, for one, uses both terms in an article she published in *American Indian Quarterly* in 2004. One could dismiss these terms as anachronistic—their use could be considered a superimposition of modern perceptions onto past events. Still, a case can be made for using them within certain contexts, and so it needs to be considered how these terms are used in relation to the Dakota War, and whether or not their use is appropriate.[1]

The term "concentration camp" is problematic because of its indelible association with the Holocaust of the Second World War. To describe something as a concentration camp today is to almost automatically invoke images of Dachau, Ravensbruk, Treblinka, Auschwitz, and the other notorious death camps set up by the Nazis. The association between concentration camps and Nazi Germany is so strong in that any writer attempting to use the term today in any other historical context needs to take great care to ensure that the intended, specific meaning is clear.[2]

Waziyatawin uses the term "concentration camp" with the deliberate intention of claiming a similarity between the internment camp in which the U.S. Army confined Dakota Indians over the winter of 1862–63, and the death camps run by the Nazis for the systematic extermination of Jews, Gypsies, communists, and other persons deemed undesirable by the German National Socialist state. As far as she is concerned, the two cases are inherently the same.

In fact, they are not, neither in shape, form or purpose. In order to argue that the Dakota internment at Fort Snelling was essentially the same as the Jewish experience in the concentration camps of WWII, one must willfully ignore the encyclopedia of established evidence which shows that the historical realities of the two situations were absolutely *not* the same. Dr. Stephan Malinowski, a German historian of the Holocaust, has pointed out that with regards to precisely this sort of attempt to draw parallels between the Holocaust and other unrelated events, "not all comparisons generate convincing results," and so it is in this case.[3]

Waziyatawin attempts to draw another inaccurate comparison with the imagery of concentration camps when she says "the condemned men were forcibly removed to the

## 16. Concentration Camps and Ethnic Cleansing

Nearly 1,700 Dakota people were confined over the winter of 1862–63 in this stockade on the Mississippi River flats below Fort Snelling. Debate continues as to whether or not this site can accurately be described as a "concentration camp." What is not disputed is that at least 150 people died here (Minnesota Historical Society).

concentration camp at Mankato where they continued to await execution orders."[4] The facility at Mankato was a conventional, albeit hastily established, prison and not a concentration camp by any accepted definition of the term, and the men who were held there were convicted prisoners. The fact that they were prisoners makes Waziyatawin's use of the word "forcibly" seem to be a case of sensationalizing the issue through exaggerated language—how else but forcibly is any prisoner removed from one place to another, no matter what penal or judicial system is doing the removing?

Once these points are established, however, there *is* a context in which the term "concentration camp" can accurately be used to describe the Dakota internment at Fort Snelling, though not the prison at Mankato. The concept and practice of concentration camps did not originate with the Nazis when they created a facility for the incarceration of political prisoners at Dachau in 1933. The first concentration camps to be so designated were probably those created by the British Army in 1900, during the Second Boer War. (The Spanish, fighting a colonial insurrection in Cuba, had created something similar five years earlier in 1895) The British, fighting an irregular enemy on its own ground, an enemy which relied on a civilian population for its commissariat, resorted to systematically rounding up Boer civilians, mostly women, children, and older men and "concentrating" them in internment camps.

The Dakota experience in 1862–63 closely resembles the later British concentration camps in two ways: first, the people who were interned were, for the most part, not the ones who had any role in the actual fighting of the war; second, there was a considerable rate of mortality among the interned population from disease. An undetermined number of Boer civilians died from disease and malnutrition during their incarceration; an estimated 200–300 Dakota people died from disease during the winter they were held at Fort Snelling.[5]

What is not helpful to an accurate portrayal of the event, however, is when a modern historian writes that the Dakota "remained imprisoned there in a disease-ridden enclosure throughout the winter, subsisting on rations of crackers, flour, and salt pork," and lets that statement stand alone without placing it within the full context. The fact is that the prevalence of those same diseases was equally high among the refugee settlers crowded into St. Paul that winter, and the rations which this writer implies were unfit or inadequate were exactly the same military-issue rations which soldiers in the U.S. Army subsisted on not for five months, but for the four years of the Civil War.[6] This matters because the broader historical context provides a more accurate assessment of the event.

Dr. Asa Daniels, in his narrative "Reminiscences of the Little Crow Uprising," referred to the "overcrowded conditions of the city [St. Paul] and the lack of sanitary conditions" resulting in widespread cases of "typhoid fever, diphtheria, measles and scarlet fever … cerebro-spinal meningitis … and smallpox," which ravaged the refugees and soldiers crammed into the city over the winter of 1862–63. These diseases, Dr. Daniels went on to say, "involved the whole city, resulting in many families being stricken, the cloud of disease and death hanging like a pall over many households."[7] Thus, the incident rate of disease among the interned Dakota, bad as it was, was comparable to the rate at which the same diseases effected the white population of St. Paul that winter. What we must remember is that between the two experiences, white and Dakota, the critical distinction is that for the Dakota their situation was exacerbated by the fact that they were confined against their will in a miserable stockade, facing an uncertain future at their conquerors' whim, a reality which made their experience all the more wretched, all the more dangerous, and on some levels, arguably more traumatic.

The Fort Snelling prison camp truly was a terrible situation for the Dakota—terrible, miserable, and frightening. Stephen Riggs, writing to a senior member of his mission board, described the confinement stockade in 1863: "It is a very sad place now. The crying hardly ever stops. From five to ten die daily. There are (or were) sixteen hundred worth women and children."[8] A disproportionate number of Dakota who died in confinement were children and the elderly. Despair and despondency settled into the wretched enclosure, especially after word of the December executions reached the camp. "The news then came of the hanging at Mankato," remembered Gabriel Renville. "Amid all this sickness and these great tribulations, it seemed doubtful at night whether a person would be alive in the morning. We had no land, no homes, no means of support and the outlook was most dreary and discouraging. How can we get back again?"[9]

With these factors in mind, the Dakota internment absolutely can be accurately described as a concentration camp in the sense of the *pre*–1933 model; even so, it has occasionally been suggested that worse options existed for them in 1862. As appalling as their internment was, how different might their experience have been had they simply been released by the Army after the trials ended in November, remaining out on the Minnesota prairie through the winter, with no provisions and many of their men in military custody, at the mercy of white vigilantes who were not inclined to distinguish between guilty and innocent Indians in the aftermath of war. For the Dakota people who were still in Minnesota that winter, the future was dark and forbidding, no matter which way they turned.

However one chooses to think of the Fort Snelling camp, the fact remains that the term "concentration camp" is now so inextricably connected with 20th century Nazism that a clear distinction *must* be made when the term is used in reference to the events of 1862. To claim, as one Dakota man did in a recent collection of oral histories compiled by the Minnesota Historical Society, that Fort Snelling was "kind of like Nazi Germany's oven house, Auschwitz," is to deliberately blur the lines between two things that were not at all similar in form, function, or fact.[10] It also has the effect of diminishing the absolute horror of Auschwitz, where according to the more conservative estimates at least 1.3 million people were murdered by the Nazis. Offered a comparison such as this, a skeptic might argue that if Fort Snelling was really like Auschwitz, then Auschwitz must not have been all that bad in either its purpose or its mortality rate. The historical evidence says otherwise. It cannot be accurately or honestly argued that the two were even remotely the same thing.

"Ethnic cleansing" as a concept existed in 1862, but was not in wide usage. It is mostly a modern expression, coming into the full blight of its existence as a military practice and political policy in the last century, but examples of it can be found throughout recorded history. The expulsion of Jews from Spain in 1492; that of the Huguenots from France after 1685; the Chios Massacre carried out in 1822 by the Ottomans during the Greek Revolution; and the expulsion of Muslims from Bulgaria and Greece in the 1800s: all these are examples of ethnic cleansings which have been the result of one people's homicidal animosity toward another.

As the term is understood today, the forced removal of the Cherokee and other tribes from the eastern United States that resulted in the Trail of Tears also qualifies as an example of 19th century ethnic cleansing, and by the same standard the Dakota people of Minnesota were the victims of an organized program of ethnic cleansing in the aftermath of the 1862 war. Frontier security was not the only impulse behind the Indian removal, although it was a frequently cited justification at the time; the old motivators of land and money were in play as well, and were remarked upon even shortly after the war. "The removal of the Indians from the borders of Minnesota," Charles Bryant wrote, "and the opening up for settlement of over a million acres of superior land, was a prospective benefit to the State of immense value, both in its domestic quiet and its rapid advancement in material wealth."[11]

The elimination or extermination of Minnesota's Dakota population was precisely what many people in the state were calling for in 1862. Some of those expressing this attitude were private citizens, as in the case of newspaper editors who called for the forced removal of all Indians from the state. They were the mild voices, comparatively. Others, such as the pioneering feminist editor Jane Grey Swisshelm, were not satisfied with what they saw as the half-measures of exile. "A Sioux has just as much right to life as a hyena, and he who would spare them is an enemy to his race," Swisshelm wrote, and she advocated the state-sanctioned murder of any Dakota found within Minnesota.[12]

This was similar to the pronouncements of some men holding official positions in civilian government and the military, positions that made their use of such language genuinely dangerous. General Pope, after all, more than once wrote that the Dakota should be "exiled" or "exterminated." Senator Morton Wilkinson, who was vociferously hostile to the Indians from the outset, expressed his view on the matter in a letter to Governor Ramsey, saying, "If the people will be patient we will be able, I think, to dispose of those condemned, and will also succeed in removing the Sioux and Winnebago Indians from the state."[13] Ramsey was in complete agreement, at least in his public statements. On this point, Waziyatawin is correct when she says, "Governor Ramsey's call for extermination or forced removal in September of 1862 was clearly a policy of ethnic cleansing...."[14] As the term is understood today, ethnic cleansing was exactly what Pope, Wilkinson, Ramsey and other officials with similar attitudes were calling for, and by the winter of 1862 the voices seeking to entirely eradicate the Dakota from the state were growing ever louder. It is important to make the distinction, though, that cases of ethnic cleansing do not automatically equate to actions of genocide. Gary Clayton Anderson expresses this clearly when he says, "Other actions such as removal or diminishment of ancestral lands require a different description because they are not genocide."[15]

In recognizing this as a historical fact, though, the discussion should not stop there. If the true meaning of ethnic cleansing is understood to apply to American actions against the Dakota in the aftermath of the war, then an unflinching application of the term would also consider whether or not the Dakotas' actions in the first weeks of the war were, for all intents and purposes, an attempt to conduct an ethnic cleansing of their own against white settlers.

In his narrative of the war, Big Eagle remembered that when the Dakota council on the night of August 17 made the decision to break out in open war, the call was "kill the whites."[16] Not "kill the white traders who have defrauded us"; not "kill the white men who have abused and debauched our women"; not "kill the white soldiers who enforce the fraudulent treaty stipulations," but instead a call to kill white people indiscriminately wherever they could be found, for no other reason than that they were there and they were white. That would seem to fit the established definition of ethnic cleansing.

Some commentators on the Dakota War have argued that one of the Dakotas' legitimate aims in the war was to drive white settlers off what had traditionally been Indian lands. Driving out invaders is indeed a legitimate recourse for any nation threatened with territorial incursion—nations have the right to protect the integrity of their borders, and force of arms is recognized as a justifiable means to that end. But it would be easier to defend the Dakota actions in 1862 if the brunt of their violence had been directed against the U.S. Army, rather than unarmed civilians. If the Turkish removal of its Armenian population or the American government's exile of Minnesota's Dakota population can accurately be cited as examples of ethnic cleansing, then so too can the Dakota campaign to kill or drive off white settlers be classified as an attempt at ethnic cleansing. Cries of indignation might greet this statement, but I believe that it merits some thought, nevertheless.

If ethnic cleansing is understood to be the effort of one group of people to eradicate, eliminate or remove another distinctly different group of people from amongst themselves, then the Dakotas' actions during the war fit that definition. One might object to this idea with the argument that the Dakota were only trying to drive invading white people from lands they were occupying illegally, lands to which the Dakota had legitimate prior claim. But even if we accept the fact that white settlers were occupying Indian land illegally in violation of the treaties (because this was certainly true in some situations), does that justify murder, rape and infanticide? It does not. Regardless of the motivations behind their actions, the methods which the Dakota used in targeting settler families in August 1862 amounted to ethnic cleansing. It is a historical fact that the Dakota were the victims of a deliberate program of ethnic cleansing initiated by the U.S. government—it is just as much a historical fact that they themselves perpetrated an earlier act of ethnic cleansing.

To be absolutely clear, this does *not* mean that the Indian act justified the American response. Not at all—some actions are morally indefensible regardless of the provocations or the justifications offered for them, and ethnic cleansing is a crime against humanity no matter who carries it out, no matter what rationale it is draped in. The fact that the Dakota had been swindled, cheated, and mistreated by white traders and corrupt Indian Agents did not justify their killing of white people who bore no personal responsibility for those injustices. The fact that some Dakota committed murder, rape and massacre did not in any way justify the U.S. Government's decision to hold the entire Dakota people responsible and drive them from their homes. There were members of both groups, Indians and whites alike, who acted out of a desire for revenge when they had the opportunity, but the ultimate, inevitable result of revenge was that people who had no share in the guilt suffered as much as those who did.

Both sides in the war employed the vitriolic philosophy and the consciously specific violence of ethnic cleansing in this war—the Indians during the fighting, and the whites afterwards. Especially after the war, official American policies adopted against the Dakota had all the hallmarks of ethnic cleansing. "With one voice," Lincoln's secretary John G. Nicolay wrote, "the people of that State demand the removal or threaten the extermination of their dangerous neighbors." Unlike many of the voices calling for exile or extermination, however, Nicolay could also see the human tragedy that would follow. "But whither shall they go?" he asked. "The swallowing tides of civilization encompass them on the east, the north, and the south; and the only other avenue, the west, is guarded by the gaunt wolf starvation."[17] In the end, they were forced to go west.

# 17

# The Later Military Commission Trials

*No white man, tried before a jury of his peers, would be executed upon the testimony thus produced ...*
—*The St. Paul Pioneer*, 1865

The military commission that Henry Sibley convened in September 1862 was conceived as a field-expedient measure, at least at first. From his official correspondence it seems clear that Sibley expected to launch his expeditionary force in pursuit of Little Crow and the other Dakota holdouts which had fled west into the Dakota Territory, a consideration which was very much at work when he convened the military commission trials on September 28. Once his punitive campaign was put on hold for the winter, though, there is good reason to believe that the military commission trials continued, and changed in their focus and tempo, because Sibley was under command pressure from Pope to do so.

None of these factors were at work the following year, when another military commission was convened to conduct the trial of Wowinape, the 16-year-old son of Little Crow. Wowinape had fallen into the Army's hands in August 1863. In September of 1863 Wowinape was put on trial on the same charges on which 303 men had been convicted the year before.

As had been the case with the commission a year earlier, Sibley was the convening officer for the military commission that was impaneled to decide Wowinape's fate. And as had so often been the case with the 1862 commission, the officers of the 1863 commission moved quickly to convict Wowinape of all the charges against him, and sentenced him to death by hanging. At that point in the proceedings, however, things took a different course.

When the sentence was pronounced by the commission, it went to Sibley for review. Sibley approved the verdict and the sentence, after which his superior, General Pope, passed it on up the chain of command to the Secretary of War and the Judge Advocate General. Pope expected the sentence to be reviewed at the national command level and either confirmed for execution or commuted. Surprisingly, neither possibility occurred.

Secretary of War Edwin Stanton and Judge Advocate General Joseph Holt declined to review Wowinape's case. Instead, they returned the whole matter to Pope along with a pointed reference to an 1861 statute that required "the General Commanding the Army in the Field (Pope, in this case) to confirm or disapprove the proceedings."[1] According to this new reading of a regulation that had been in full effect the year before, Pope's non-committal transmittal of the case from Sibley to the War Department was not acceptable. No one had required Pope to say "yes" or "no" on the 303 death sentences passed by the earlier military commission, but that was then and this was now.

Pope, as we have already seen, had been consistently outspoken in his animosity toward the Dakota during the war; liberally sprinkling his language with words such as "exterminate" and "eliminate." Now he suddenly back-pedaled from actually doing something of a concrete nature to eliminate even this one young Indian boy. Pope protested that he had no legal authority to confirm the sentence, saying he believed the military commission that tried Wowinape's case was "in violation of the spirit of the 65th Article of War," but hedging to the point of claiming that there was "a possible doubt."[2] He passed the matter right back to the Judge Advocate General, asking for an opinion on the Article of War question.

The Judge Advocate General replied that according to his reading of the law, while the 1862 military commission trials were in accordance with the letter of the law as far as Article 65 of the Articles of War was concerned, they had in fact violated the spirit of the law. Pope promptly disapproved the sentence of the Wowinape case.

When Sibley got word of this development, he reacted immediately. He had to, because Pope's actions in this single case could be interpreted as an official condemnation of Sibley's actions with regards to the 303 capital cases sentenced by the military commission the previous year. Pope had been all in favor of those proceedings at the time; now it seemed that he was taking a different tack. He had all but forced Sibley to take a hard line in the earlier trials, but now he was throwing Sibley to the bureaucratic wolves.

In a letter to Judge Advocate General Holt, Sibley wrote that "a precisely similar condition of things existed in 1862, when nearly four hundred Indian warriors, taken prisoner by the forces under my command, were tried and the greater number condemned to death by a Military Commission ordered by me upon charges and specifications preferred by myself."[3] Sibley's concerns were obvious. If this single trial was now thought to be improper and unacceptable, then every one of the 392 trials conducted the previous year could also come in for official censure. Sibley had never wavered from his defense of both the creation and the conduct of the 1862 military commission; he did not alter his position now. Just as he believed the earlier trials were legitimate, so he believed that this trial was legitimate.

The 65th Article of War, Sibley argued in his letter to the Judge Advocate General, pertained only to members of the United States Army, not to other persons who might also be subject to trial by military courts or commissions. Specifically, the wording of the article was designed to protect soldiers junior in rank from any overt prejudice that their commanding officers might exercise in preferring charges against them.

Sibley's letter raised some valid points, but in the end, nothing happened either way. Pope's disapproval of Wowinape's sentence was allowed to stand, and neither the War Department nor the Judge Advocate General's office weighed in on the question. Wowinape was incarcerated in Camp McClellan with the other Dakota prisoners, the shadow of a death sentence still hanging over him. He was left in a sort of legal limbo, his case remaining undecided until the President of the United States should decide to deal with him. Wowinape was eventually released from prison, pardoned in 1865. He later converted to Christianity and took the name Thomas Wakeman. He died of tuberculosis in 1886, having survived the war that killed his father and the noose that had once seemed his own fate.

General Pope's attitude certainly seems to have changed between the time that the first military commission trials were conducted, and when Wowinape's case was judged. At the least, he seems to have had second thoughts about appending his name and his approval to the later death sentence. He was not the only one to have experienced some change of perspective in the intervening months.

In December 1863, the former Recorder of Sibley's military commission, Lieutenant Isaac Heard, published his book about the Dakota War and the military commission trials. In response to the book's issuance, the Reverend Stephen Riggs published a letter in the December 17, 1863 issue of the *St. Paul Daily Press*. "I have since attended upon two Military Commissions," Riggs wrote, "the results of which show quite a change in the feelings of men towards Indians who were simply present in the battles." These altered feelings, he believed, would lead to very different outcomes to the trials. "These results," he said, "have led me to the conclusion that if the Indians who are condemned ... were to be tried now by any Military Commission appointed in this state, quite a number would be acquitted; a number more would only be condemned to imprisonment...."[4] This change in sentiment was enough to save Wowinape's life, which was justified—Wowinape was almost certainly guilty of nothing more than following his father and being present at several battles.

Sibley, for his part, never relented in his belief that the military commission was both proper and necessary, but some of his actions after the executions indicate that his attitudes toward certain of the Dakota defendants might have changed. In January 1863, exactly one month after the executions at Mankato, Sibley wrote to President Lincoln to endorse an appeal for the commutation of sentence on David Faribault, Jr. Faribault was one of the mixed-race Dakota men who had been sentenced to death by the military commission.

In his letter to the President, Sibley wrote, "I have no doubt that the young man referred to is among the least guilty of those condemned by the Military Commission," though he then qualified that by adding, "although enough was developed at his trial to warrant the finding of the tribunal."[5] Sibley added his official endorsement to the petition for the commutation of Faribault's sentence, telling Lincoln that a case could be made for the fact that the young man was "*forced* to participate in hostilities against the whites, and that he did not willingly act, nor, in fact was it proved against him, that he had anything to do with the massacres of women and children."[6] The appeal was successful; Lincoln issued Faribault a pardon on May 11, 1863.

The next year, on April 7, Riggs wrote another letter to the President asking for pardons on behalf of four Dakota men whom he said were innocent of any complicity in the fighting during the war. Sibley endorsed that request also, writing that there was "reasonable doubt of the guilt of the prisoners named from circumstances that have transpired since their trial by the Military Commission...." The prisoners, Sibley concluded, were "entitled to the benefit of that doubt."[7] Lincoln apparently required little argument

## 17. The Later Military Commission Trials

to exercise his clemency—he granted the four men full pardons a little over a week after he received Riggs' letter. Nor did he stop with that decision; 11 days later he pardoned 26 more Dakota at the request of missionary Thomas Williamson.

Meanwhile, the cases of other men condemned by the 1862 military commission had worked their way through the legal review process with greater deliberation than had occurred at the original trials. Lincoln's order which confirmed the death sentences of the men who were subsequently hanged at Mankato had concluded with the requirement that "[t]he other condemned prisoners you will hold subject to further orders, taking care that they neither escape nor are subjected to any unlawful violence." These men had been saved from the gallows, but in legal terms it was only a temporary reprieve—their death sentences were still in effect, and their lives were still in the balance.

Judge Advocate General Joseph Holt reviewed at least one representative case among the remaining 265 open death sentences and found it lacking. In the trial of Toonnannakinyaoa-hatka (whose name appears with at least four different spellings in the record), the military commission had found him guilty of the charge and guilty of the specification, and sentenced him to hang

Holt did not take long to make up his mind. On January 20, 1863, he wrote in Toonnannakinyaoahatka's case file, "This record is altogether too imperfect to justify the government in carrying the sentence into execution." At the bottom of the trial record, the words "Sentence disapproved" were written, along with the name "A. Lincoln," dated May 11, 1863.

One of the notable facts about the military commission that Sibley convened in 1862 was that none of the Indians put on trial were men who could be said to have fomented or led the outbreak. The 303 capital convictions that the military commission handed down were almost all on men who were basically rank-and-file Indians—soldiers, not leaders. There were some minor chiefs in the list, such as Big Eagle, but there was never much evidence that he or others like him had ever played a part in pushing for open war against the whites. The principle leaders of the outbreak—Little Crow, Red Middle Voice, Shakopee, Medicine Bottle, and others—had escaped west in the Dakota Territory or north across the international border into British Canada.

In 1864, however, Shakopee and Medicine Bottle were at last in American hands. They had been snatched from their sanctuary in Canada—kidnapped, to put it plainly. The two men were lulled into a false sense of security by men purporting to be friends, gotten drunk, and smuggled south across the border into the United States, concealed under a load of furs. They were taken to Fort Snelling and put on trial in front of a third version of the military commission.

By this time, nearly two years after the war, public sentiment was still running high against Indians. There were almost no Dakota left in Minnesota, and most of the white population, publicly at least, seemed quite all right with that. In spite of this, there was less acceptance of the sort of slip-shod, field-expedient justice that had characterized the 1862 trials. Shakopee and Medicine Bottle were both convicted and sentenced to death, but the public reaction to the verdicts was not quite what it had been in 1862.

The two Dakota chiefs were sentenced to be hanged on November 11, 1865, at Pilot Knob, just outside St. Paul. The day before their execution, an editorial in the *St. Paul Pioneer* considered their case. The writer stated that no "serious injustice will be done by the execution tomorrow, but it would have been more creditable if some tangible evidence of their guilt had been obtained...."[8] The editorial then revived one of the criticisms that missionary John Williamson had levied against the earlier military commission trials. "[N]o white man, tried before a jury of his peers, would be executed upon the testimony thus produced," the *Pioneer's* writer said. "The general supposition that they are guilty, is very likely correct, but their execution will, nevertheless, establish the precedent of hanging without proving...."[9] The editorial's point was well made. Shakopee, in particular, was widely known both to Indians and whites alike as one of the principle agitators in the outbreak, and he had been unapologetic about his hostility to the whites, but what was commonly known had still not yet been conclusively proven in a court of law.

The next morning, on November 11, Shakopee and Medicine Bottle went to the gallows. There is a story that as Shakopee was mounting the scaffold, he heard the loud

The execution of Shakopedan (Little Six) and Wakanozhanzhan (Medicine Bottle) at Fort Snelling on November 11, 1865. The two men were kidnapped from Canada and smuggled back across the border to be tried before a later incarnation of the military commission. Their open coffins lie on the ground in front of the gallows (Minnesota Historical Society).

steam whistle of a locomotive. Indicating the train, he supposedly said, "As the white man comes in the Indian goes out."[10] There was one other difference between the hanging of the 38 men at Mankato in 1862 and the hanging of the two chiefs in 1865. No photograph exists of the mass execution at Mankato, but there is a photo in the archives of the Minnesota Historical Society that shows the bodies of Shakopee and Medicine Bottle hanging from the gallows.

# Part Four

# The Controversies

*There have been many versions and interpretations of Dakota history and readers, like a hung jury, are persuaded first by one version and then another.*
—Dr. Elden Lawrence, *The Peace Seekers*

# 18

## Crimes or Culture?

*If [a white man] kills one of their people, the [Indians] kill him as an enemy not as a criminal. If an Indian kills one of us, we kill him as a criminal not as an enemy.*
—Judge Beverly Tucker

Perhaps the worst miscarriage of justice—worse even than an innocent being convicted of a crime which they did not commit—would be if a man were convicted of a crime which never occurred in the first place. There are two lines of thought that hold that this is precisely what happened to the Indians tried by Sibley's military commission. The first contends that the violence that characterized the Dakota War of 1862 was completely legitimate for the simple reason that it was in accordance with the Dakotas' traditional, established practice of warfare; therefore, there were no crimes, no matter how extreme the brutality. The other idea argues that everything the Dakota did, including any alleged incidents of rape and infanticide, was in the nature of national self-defense by legitimate combatants of a sovereign nation and was therefore justified and not criminal. The problem here, as in so many other aspects of the Dakota War's history, is that the view changes drastically depending upon the perspective of the observer.

History is not a static endeavor. The events of the past may themselves be fixed at a particular point in time, immovable and unalterable, but the men and women who are delving into the past are themselves constantly evolving. If it is true that history is not so much a matter of facts but rather of evidence and interpretation, then we must bear in mind that the interpretation derived from the evidence can change over time. This factor is certainly at work in the modern studies of the Dakota War and its aftermath.

The history of the Dakota War is one of violence, death, barbarity, inhumanity, and suffering, and all of these words apply to the universal human experience shared by everyone caught up in the war, Indians and white settlers alike. This commonality, however, does not mean that there is much agreement as to what that experience meant at the time, or what it means now. The debate continues as to what actually happened during the war, and to whom, and as to who owes who an apology for past wrongs. To stake any position in the debate is to draw fire from one group of partisans or the other.

Nevertheless, history that does not confront and examine its subject is not history at all, but is instead simply an accomplice in the perpetuation of myth. The reluctance to confront the more volatile aspects of this history has marred some modern scholarship in the study of the American West. As one historian observes, "The historical trend is to tread softly on events that might offend ethnic groups, but truth cannot be suppressed or history altered for the gratification of any group."[1] If the subject is important and the answers to the questions truly matter, then we do not have the luxury of remaining apart from the discussion, and we absolutely should not sugarcoat the truth just because it is unpleasant or unpalatable to a particular demographic or interest group.

The language used to discuss the Dakota War is, quite often, extremely emotionally charged. Emotion can be a valid part of the process—after all, emotional energy is what gives the historical past a real and immediate connection to the present. Unchecked emotion, however, obstructs the process and obscures the issue altogether. With this in mind, it may be helpful to clarify some of the terminology that provokes so much heated, antagonistic feeling, before wading into the historic fray. One word in particular—"atrocity"—draws barrages of indignant rebuttal from certain quarters. Much of the rancorous debate over the history of the Dakota War swirls around the use of this word, and before taking sides in the debate over whether or not atrocities occurred, we must be clear on what the word means.

Contemporary sources from the time of the war tended to use the word "atrocity" to cover a multitude of sins. Murders, rapes, infanticide, mutilations (both of the living and the dead), decapitations, torture, dismemberment, immolation, arson, pillaging and looting are all described at one time or another as "outrages," the 19th century equivalent of "atrocities."[2] (In almost every history of the Dakota War written in the last 75 years, the word "atrocity" has replaced "outrage," so I am focusing on the latter word rather than the former, but they are almost interchangeable in the literature.) In some accounts, even cases where the Dakota killed armed, uniformed soldiers of the U.S. Army in open battle are described as atrocities. But if we attempt to apply such a sprawling definition to the word, it loses its real meaning and we lose the ability to distinguish one thing from another. Skeptics would then be justified in protesting that atrocities occurred rarely if they ever occurred at all.

The English word "atrocity" derives from the Latin *atrox*, meaning "cruel"; the *Oxford English Dictionary* defines atrocity as "an extremely cruel or wicked act." At the risk of sounding cynical, it can be argued that there are atrocities, on the one hand, and then on the other hand there are *real* atrocities. Not everything that has been called an atrocity in the Dakota War was in fact an atrocity, and it is this distinction that we must parse out carefully, for it has a direct bearing on the military commission's views and perceptions, and ultimately on their decisions during the trials. In the commission's eyes, atrocities were crimes warranting punishment, so it is necessary to establish a baseline of what constitutes an atrocity. Having done that we can then ask, was the commission correct in its definition of the term? To do this it is necessary to first examine the perspectives that were prevalent in the U.S. Army in 1862, and consider the degree to which those perspectives might have influenced the thinking of the officers on Sibley's commission.

In 1758, a full century before the Dakota War, the Swiss philosopher and legal scholar Emmerich de Vattel published a book with the weighty French title of *Droit des gens; ou, Principes de la loi naturelle appliqués à la conduite et aux affaires des nations et des souverains.* Under its greatly truncated English title of *The Law of Nations,* de Vattel's book became a standard text of study for American diplomats and soldiers, as much for its groundbreaking ideas on the concept of lawful war as for its commentary on international relations. De Vattel drew on the work of a Dutch scholar of the previous century, Hugo Grotius, and advanced Grotius idea's to new levels.

Many of the 19th century's emergent ideas of lawful warfare had their antecedents in de Vattel's work. These ideas, in turn, had a tremendous influence on the codification of the Articles of War used by the U.S. military in the country's nascent years. American army officers who read *The Law of Nations,* or who were at least exposed to its influences, and for whom the War Department's Articles of War was the required manual for their profession as soldiers, would have found Indian ways of waging war to be starkly contrary to the principles set forth by those documents. It is clear that many of de Vattel's ideas directly informed the ways in which the officers of Sibley's military commission reacted to the violence of the Dakota War.

As we saw in Chapter Two, there were many American commentators after the war who believed that the Dakota were justified in going to war, and that the grievances which had driven them to war were legitimate. But almost every one of these observers also expressed the view that the way in which the Dakota actually *fought* the war was not justified, not legitimate, and not acceptable. In particular, they condemned the Dakota for what they characterized as barbaric excesses of violence. The killing of women and children was one of the principle reasons why so many voices in Minnesota in the fall of 1862 called for vengeance rather than justice.

De Vattel had anticipated precisely this sort of visceral reaction to wartime atrocities. In his study of how societies and nations conducted war, he theorized that excessive brutality in the prosecution of a war would inevitably lead to a fatal cycle of unending vengeance and perpetual hostility. "If you once open a door for continual accusation of outrageous excess in hostilities," he wrote, "you will only ... influence the minds of the contending parties with increasing animosity: fresh injuries will be perpetually springing up; and the sword will never be sheathed till one of the parties be utterly destroyed."[3] So it was in the Dakota War. But the question needs to be asked; were American observers correct in their condemnation of the ways in which the Dakota fought the war?

In studying the history of the American West, one sometimes encounters the view which argues that European-American observers are not qualified to criticize indigenous native cultures. Nothing in the traditional methods of warfare among the Dakota, this perspective would insist, can be described by so pejorative a word as "atrocities," and European-American conceptions of proper warfare should not be applied to Indian practices because the methods the Indians used were completely legitimate within their own culture. This is a well-established idea, so let us consider this question in detail: can European-American standards of legitimate warfare—i.e., the *Law of Nations*, the *Articles of War*, etc.—legitimately be applied to traditional Indian ways of waging war?

As Carol Chomsky rightly points out, "the Dakota, like other Indians, traditionally fought with methods substantially different from those of the Americans and Europeans. In particular, in intertribal wars almost all members of the enemy nation—including women and children—were legitimate targets of attack, and captives were rarely taken."[4] Chomsky has put her finger precisely on one of the most contentious issues in the modern debate, one that also generated intense reaction in 1862. This aspect of Indian warfare had an undeniable and strongly negative influence on the military commission's view of the defendants.

This matter of how the differing traditions of warfare should be perceived, and the terms in which they should be understood, have challenged historians for decades. The eminent Minnesota historian William Folwell, writing in 1927, described it this way:

> From the white man's point of view these operations amounted simply to a massacre, an atrocious and utterly unjustifiable butchery of unoffending citizens. The resources of invective were exhausted in the descriptions of the day. The Indian, however, saw himself engaged in war, the most honorable of all pursuits, against men who, as he believed, had robbed him of his country and his freedom, had fooled and cheated him with pretensions of friendship, and who wished to force upon him an alien language and religion. He was making war on the white man in the same fashion in which he would have gone against the Chippewa or the Foxes.[5]

The enemy that the Dakota were fighting in 1862, however, was not Chippewa or Fox; but rather an enemy whose understanding of legitimate warfare embraced completely different concepts. In *The Law of Nations*, de Vattel wrote: "Women, children, feeble old men, and sick persons, come under the description of enemies; and we have certain rights over them, inasmuch as they belong to the nation with whom we are at war.... But these are enemies who make no resistance; and consequently we have no right to maltreat their persons or use any violence against them, much less to take away their lives. This is so plain a maxim of justice and humanity," he concluded, "that at present every nation in the least degree civilized, acquiesces in it."[6] This was precisely how the members of Sibley's commission understood the matter.

De Vattel, writing in the Europe of 1758, had never seen a Dakota and had probably never even heard of them. His assessment of a nation's measure of civilization had nothing to do with a racially motivated condemnation of indigenous Native American cultures. It was, rather, the perspective of a man born and reared in central Europe, where the horrific ravages of the Thirty Years War a century earlier had laid waste to entire regions and killed hundreds of thousands of women, children, the aged and infirm; precisely the types of people whom the *Law of Nations* was envisioned to protect. It was this theory of lawful warfare, which attempted to impose limitations on killing and destruction, with which 19th century American soldiers were inculcated. The Dakota method of warfare was legitimate in its own tradition, but it was a tradition that the European-American military establishment did not recognize.

Within traditional Dakota society, a cultural norm existed which permitted the killing of precisely those people whom most Americans would have considered non-combatants. Years before the Dakota War, missionary Samuel W. Pond presented a paper to the Minnesota Historical Society in which he examined the Indian practice of war. One of his case studies looked at a series of reciprocal raids between the Dakota and their traditional enemies, the Chippewa (Ojibwe). Pond described a retaliatory attack by the Dakota on July 2, 1839, against a band of Chippewa from Mille Lacs, in which the Dakota waited until most of the Chippewa men separated from the main body to hunt, at which point:

> The Dakotas raised the war-whoop, but they said the Chippewas did not at first seem to realize their danger, they stood a while with their burdens on their backs gazing on their pursuers as though they did not know what to think of them. The Chippewas were thus taken by surprise, wholly unprepared, and about seventy of them were killed. The slain were most of them women and children. The few men who were present defended the women and children bravely, and sold their lives dearly.... The Dakotas lost more *men* [italics in the original] in that attack than they killed.[7]

Considering the era in which Pond was writing, it is remarkable the degree to which he considered the matter from the Indian perspective, trying for an empathetic reading of the event.[8] He leveled no accusations of atrocity for this massacre of women and children, an attack which came about as a revenge killing in retaliation for the death of a Dakota at the hands of Chippewas sometime earlier. Pond wrote that the Dakota chief "expressed some regret that the innocent should die for the guilty, but probably neither he nor any who went with him were less active or cruel in the work of destruction on account of any scruples of conscience. They were violating no rules of Indian warfare."[9] It is clear, then, that normal Indian practice of warfare made little or no distinction between men, women and children, or between the armed and the defenseless—almost any person was a legitimate target. There were no "civilians" in Indian warfare.

In that context and within those parameters, it may not be possible to legally define something as an atrocity in the European-American sense of a codified war crime when it takes place between two parties of the same cultural heritage, who share the same laws and standards of behavior, with the same concept of what constitutes "right," who share a societal norm, and both of whom accept the practice and participate in it. We can still describe it as a moral atrocity, one which violates the basic idea that every human life has value and all killings are reprehensible, but we could not in that particular situation apply modern conventions of lawful warfare to it in a formal prosecution.

That, however, is not the question before us. The question here is whether there are any circumstances under which the same act can legitimately be classified as an atrocity when it occurs in a conflict between two *different* cultures? Some modern observers think not. As Chomsky says, "the Commission should have at least considered these differences in culture and military methods in any attempt to determine whether 'military necessity' permitted killing noncombatants in the war."[10]

Cultural norms and military methodology have absolutely no bearing on the matter. It may have been Indian practice to kill women and children, but that does not mean that the American officers on the military commission were therefore required to accept that practice as legitimate in their deliberations during the trials.[11] It would be difficult, if not impossible, to find any historical precedent where one belligerent in a war, when confronted by enemy actions that it believed to be reprehensible and illegal, consequently subordinated its own laws, customs and military regulations in order to find some way of accepting the enemy's practices. To argue that the victors in war should examine the enemy's actions for mitigating circumstances in order to justify acts that the victor had *previously* and consistently considered to be unlawful might seem commendable, but is in fact completely unrealistic.[12] It is legitimate, though, to ask why the American side in the war had any right to expect that their value system should be the standard by which the conduct of the Dakota War was judged.

Numerous commentators have argued that what 19th century Americans called "atrocity" the Dakota and other Indian peoples called "normal." They contend, with good reason, that the one value system is every bit as legitimate as the other. Using this line of thought, it could rightly be said that the concept of *jus naturae*, or universal principles of nature, does not apply here since there is no consensus as to what is truly universal in human conduct, and certainly not in human conflict. One could argue that the only reason why American values are the ones by which conduct in the war was judged is because the Americans won the war and the Indians lost, and the victor makes the rules and writes the history. After all, *vae victis* is a brutal reality that has applied to wars across the entire spectrum of the human experience, and it certainly was at work in the bitter conflicts between white Americans and native peoples.[13] But there is much more to it than that simple answer.

American concepts of lawful warfare are the only ones which bear on the Dakota War because *all* parties involved—American soldiers, American civilians, and most importantly, the Dakota themselves—used those conceptions and definitions to frame their views of the war at the point of its conclusion.[14] The Dakota adopted American ideas of lawful warfare when it seemed in their best interest to do so in one particular, extremely important instance—at the point of their surrender to the U.S. Army, when they expected to be treated as prisoners of war (POWs). That required, logically and legally, that the entire scope of American rules of war also applied to them.

The question of POW status for the surrendered Indians became an immediate point of acrimonious debate in the aftermath of the Dakota War, and continues to be so today. Charles Bryant, who wrote one of the first histories of the war in 1863, expressed the attitudes of many white Minnesotans at the time when he said, "Had these dusky natives been engaged in open war, such as the law of races or nations tolerates, their advocates might have claimed for them the rights extended to prisoners of war." Bryant adamantly felt that the Indians were *not* entitled to the status of prisoners of war because they "had declared no open war...." Furthermore, he argued, "There is a wide difference between the killing of men in open war, and brutal massacre in time of peace."[15] He believed that the Dakota were without question guilty of the latter.

What Bryant failed to understand, or at least did not acknowledge, was that the use of the preemptive strike or surprise attack (which the Indians certainly used on August 18) had long been recognized as a legitimate tactic by European-American tacticians. Legitimate, yes, but it was one which came with certain risks. As the German tactician Herman Froetsch wrote in *The Art of Modern War*, "The impelling reason for a sudden attack ... is to strike at an adversary who is not yet fully prepared, and to catch him in a state of reduced ability to defend himself...."[16] The Dakota understood this principle as clearly as did European-Americans, and they used the tactic for precisely the same reason. The use of a surprise attack, in itself, was not sufficient reason to deny the Dakota the legal status of prisoners of war. However, this was not Froetsch's only word on the subject of sneak attacks. "The opening of hostilities through a sudden raid," he went on to say, "is politically a severe handicap which, while it may be lightly considered at the commencement of a war, is likely to have very unfortunate consequences should the war turn out badly."[17] So it was for the Dakota, and as the war turned out badly for them, so were the consequences very unfortunate, indeed. Compounding these consequences was the fact that the Dakota had made their surprise attacks not against purely military targets but rather against civilians, and in the eyes of many white Americans that utterly negated its legitimacy as a tactic.

This was the view expressed by Senator Morton S. Wilkinson and other members of Minnesota's congressional delegation in the letter they sent to President Lincoln protesting his consideration of clemency for the condemned Indians. "These Indians have been called by some, prisoners of war," they wrote. "There was no war about it. It was wholesale robbery, rape and murder."[18]

## 18. Crimes or Culture?

In 1862 the argument over POW status for the defeated Dakota went back and forth as the Minnesota autumn gave way to winter. "We cannot hang men by the hundreds," Bishop Henry Whipple wrote to Senator Henry Rice. "Upon our own premises we have no right to do so. We claim that they are an independent nation & as such they are prisoners of war."[19] Whipple was not the only commentator to take this position, but he was distinctly in the minority among white Minnesotans. Even Senator Rice, who would later express a perhaps disingenuous sympathy for "the poor Indians," was so initially shocked by lurid stories of Indian atrocities during the war that he wrote in his reply to Whipple, "I think you are in error in saying they are prisoners of war—in my opinion they are murderers of the deepest dye. The laws of war cannot be so far distorted as to reach this case in any respect."[20]

Big Eagle, the Dakota chief whose account of the war from the Indian perspective we have already considered, provides a view on the POW question from the Dakota side. Big Eagle was every bit a legitimate combatant. He did not favor the idea of war with the whites, but once the die was cast and war broke out, he was an active combatant. The point on which to be clear is one that Big Eagle repeatedly made himself: he fought in open battle, a fact he was clearly proud of in his narrative, and when the war was lost he expected that fact to be recognized. "I and others understood..." he said, "that Gen. Sibley would treat with all of us who had only been soldiers and would surrender as prisoners of war, and that only those who had murdered people in cold blood, the settlers and others, would be punished in any way...."[21] (In fact, Sibley initially felt that the Indians were not "entitled to be considered in the light of prisoners of war, but rather as outlaws and villains....")[22]

Big Eagle said that he, along with "many others who had taken part in the war, surrendered to Gen. Sibley." He had been promised, he said, "[T]hat if we would do this we would only be held as prisoners of war a short time, but as soon as I surrendered I was thrown into prison."[23] More than 30 years after the war, he was still understandably bitter about being treated like a common criminal, rather than as a surrendered combatant from a sovereign nation waging a legitimate war.

Wamditanka (Big Eagle), in a portrait made sometime while he was imprisoned after the war. Big Eagle was the hereditary chief of a small band of Dakota and fought in every major engagement of the war. The narrative he dictated in old age is the most complete account of the war from the perspective of a Dakota veteran (Minnesota Historical Society).

If I had known that I would be sent to the penitentiary I would not have surrendered.... I did not like the way I had been treated. I surrendered in good faith, knowing that many of the whites were acquainted with me and that I had not been a murderer, or present when a murder had been committed, and if I had killed or wounded a man it had been in a fair fight, open fight."[24]

Big Eagle's perspective is important to this discussion, coming as it does from a man who experienced the war first-hand and who had reason to be proud of his conduct in it. He objected to being treated as a murderer, when by rights he was a legitimate combatant. But the critical question is from where he got the terms "surrender," and "prisoner of war "? These were not Indian concepts, and they had no precedents in Dakota history or tradition. It is true that the Dakota sometimes took captives in war, but they did not voluntarily surrender themselves or accept the surrender of their enemies with some established expectation of protection and repatriation at the cessation of hostilities—the Dakota had no tradition of legally designated POW status defined by codified regulations. These are, instead, constructs of the European-American idea of lawful warfare.

Modern historians have weighed in at length on this question. Louis Roddis, author of *The Indian Wars of Minnesota*, agrees with the idea that the Dakota themselves recognized the European-American concept of prisoner of war status, saying that the Indians "believed they would be treated as prisoners of war...."[25] Erling Jorstad accepted the idea without caveat when he said, "Believing themselves to be prisoners of war, the Sioux pleaded guilty and were sentenced to hang."[26] Waziyatawin acknowledges that the Indians recognized the distinction between their traditional forms of warfare and that of the Americans, stating, "Dakota people began to surrender believing they would be treated as prisoners of war...."[27] And this is precisely the point where the argument of culture as legal justification starts to come apart under the countering evidence.

By claiming the official status of prisoners of war, the Dakota made themselves subject to the full catalogue of the U.S. Army's established rules of war. If the Dakota expected to receive the protection of American laws of land warfare after the fighting stopped, then by rights they also had to accept that American definitions of legitimate warfare applied to them while the war was still being fought, even after the fact. The argument that atrocities were simply the white man's definition of what was traditional Dakota warfare, and that those actions should thus be exempted from classification as war crimes, loses much of its traction when we realize that the Dakota attempted to avail themselves of American standards of legitimate belligerency once they believed the war was lost.

So what *was* the applicable definition of legitimate warfare in 1862? Then, as today, it was accepted that in open war between states, soldiers on each side were entitled to protection from the normal legal prohibitions against killing and destruction. Force of arms was (and is) a legitimate means of accomplishing a nation's goals. This does not mean, however, that all acts of violence in the course of war are automatically condoned. Even scholars who argue that the Indians were entitled to the protective status of prisoners of war still agree that acts such as "killing an enemy who had surrendered and killing unarmed civilians" were beyond the pale; "Such actions were considered punishable violations of the laws of war."[28] *The Law of Nations* addressed precisely this question when de Vattel wrote, "even he who had justice on his side may have transgressed the bounds of justifiable self-defense, and been guilty of improper excesses in the prosecution of a war whose object was originally lawful...."[29] This was exactly how most white Minnesotans, even the ones who were ostensibly sympathetic to the Dakota, viewed the methods with which the Indians fought the war.

The disputed legitimacy of these methods continues to foment confusion and argument as to what Sibley's commission should have done, what it had the brief to do, and what it actually did. "The only proper charge against a belligerent," Chomsky maintains, "is violation of the laws and customs of war. The Commission, instead, tried the Dakota on charges of murder, robbery, rape, and participation in the 'outrages' on the frontier."[30] Her first sentence is absolutely correct. The second sentence, though, gives the unfortunate impression that she supposes that murder, robbery and rape are not violations of the laws and customs of war.

Article 105 of the Articles of War *circa* 1862 refers to "robbery, burglary, arson, rape, assault with intent to commit rape, or of violations of the laws and customs of war...."[31] Chomsky could therefore be technically correct when she says that murder, robbery and rape are not violations of the laws of war, because the Articles of War lists these crimes separately from "the laws and customs of war." What has often been overlooked in this discussion of legal language, however, is the fact that these acts are specifically listed as capital crimes under military law, which in Article 105 are listed as concomitant with the laws of war, and the military commission therefore had legal grounds to try the Dakota for violations of that law.

Sixteen years before the Dakota War, John O'Brien addressed this issue in an 1846 comparative study of military law when he wrote that a military court "may and ought to refuse to try an accusation when the charge itself does not name any crime provided for, generally or specifically, by any of the articles of war."[32] Each of the specific charges that Chomsky lists—"murder, robbery, rape..."—do appear as particular crimes in the Articles of War. At the risk of stating the obvious, being a legitimate belligerent does not allow a combatant to commit illegal killings (such as the murder of prisoners or noncombatants), or perpetrate acts of rape. War is inherently violent, but that does not excuse excessive acts of violence, especially criminal violence.

There is one more answer to the objection that Dakota actions did not meet the statutory requirements of war crimes. This is one of those situations often encountered in discussions of military regulations, where debate arises over the differences between what is specifically authorized and what is specifically prohibited. Nineteenth century military law allowed for a greater degree of latitude in the construction of the charge against a defendant than was permitted by civilian criminal law. "The article has not specifically enumerated all the crimes which are thus made cognizable by a military tribunal," O'Brien noted, "because it is supposed, and with reason, that ... every one is able to judge what constitutes it; a crime within the meaning of the article being an offence against the person or property of another...."[33] Murder and rape certainly fall under the classification of offenses against persons; robbery is obviously an offence against property, thus, the military commission was correct to consider these as violations of the laws of war.

When de Vattel considered the legal status of prisoners of war, he contributed another point to this particular discussion. Prisoners of war, he argued, were entitled to humane treatment and protection, but he also allowed that they were still subject to the prosecution of law when it was appropriate. "As soon as your enemy has laid down his arms and surrendered his person," he wrote, "you have no longer any right over his life, unless he should give you such right by some new attempt, *or had before committed against you a crime deserving death* [italics added]."[34] This was precisely the principle that the military commission applied in its trials of the Dakota. The incidents of murder and rape with which some defendants were charged were crimes against military law, as well as violations of civilian criminal law. In light of this, even prisoners who were otherwise protected as prisoners of war could still be charged and tried for crimes they had committed during the late war. U.S. military courts have applied this legal principle in other wars besides the Dakota War. As far as clearly established legal precedence is concerned, this would seem to settle the question of whether or not the Dakota were accountable to the military commission after they had surrendered. However, as we will see in the next chapter, the military commission went beyond this point and classified some actions as crimes which were, in fact, completely legitimate military actions recognized by the laws of war.

A further perspective on the question comes from General Henry W. Halleck, whose influence in American military law in the latter half of the 19th century was probably unmatched. In early 1862, months before Sibley's commission was ever necessary, Halleck wrote that "Congress has recognized the lawfulness of these tribunals [military commissions], and, in a measure, regulated their proceedings, but it has not defined or limited their jurisdiction, which remains coextensive with the objects of their creation, that is, the trial of offenses under the common laws of war, not otherwise provided for."[35] That last phrase, "not otherwise provided for," would seem to indicate that military commissions were understood to have a broad and largely unspecified jurisdiction and application.

Culture is not, in and of itself, an adequate defense of crime, especially not when the culture in question subordinates itself to the victors' laws of war in an attempt to secure the protections of those laws once the war is over. And in this discussion of culture as opposed to crime, there is one more important thought to consider.

It continues to be argued today that the Dakota practice of killing women and children was simply an established feature of traditional Indian warfare, and that modern commentators are therefore wrong to condemn it as a reprehensible act. It is true that we must be careful when imposing modern sensibilities onto the past, or else we run the risk of creating anachronistic interpretations of the history. But this prompts a devil's advocate sort of question: if we are to tread carefully with regard to one side of the war, why do we not do so with both? If observers today should find it acceptable that Dakota culture in 1862 permitted the killing of children and unarmed women, why should they not also find it acceptable that 19th century American culture often regarded Indian peoples as savages, or believed that the advance of white civilization justified the displacement or killing of the indigenous peoples who already occupied the continent?

I do not accept the latter point of view, not in the least. But if one wishes to argue that traditional Dakota warfare must be held sacrosanct simply because it was legitimate at that time and in that culture, then logically one would also have to consider the view that 19th century white American ideas of racial superiority and continental domination were equally viable simply because they were also considered legitimate at that time. Such an idea is ethically repugnant. The reality is that both cultures have aspects of their history for which they can rightly be criticized. Just because an idea is legitimate in one era does not require that we must accept it as equally legitimate a century later. We are right to be appalled by the attitudes and actions of many white Americans in their treatment of native peoples in the century of westward expansion; it is equally appropriate to be appalled that Indian warfare involved the killing of children. The idea that two wrongs do not make a right is an old truism, and it applies with full force to the history of the Dakota War of 1862.

# 19

# "The most horrible and nameless outrages"

> *Today man is man's only foe, and homo homini lupus is as true as it was half a million years ago.*
> —J.F.C. Fuller

There is violence, and then there is criminal violence. There is lawful killing, philosophical objections notwithstanding, and then there is unlawful killing. Killing an armed enemy combatant in war is not a crime, regardless of the attendant violence of the act. To a limited degree, even nations that ascribe to the practice of ethical warfare still accept a certain amount of unavoidable "collateral damage," that rather awful 20th century military euphemism for civilian casualties. But no interpretation of modern military law, or of the Articles of War that defined 19th century American military law in 1862, permits the deliberate killing of children or the rape of women.

Some commentators on the Dakota War have suggested that Sibley's military commission sought to assign guilt for crimes which had not occurred. The reasons for taking that position vary depending on the writer. Roy Meyer, as we will see, dismisses almost all accounts of Indian atrocities as unconvincing, and therefore argues that no crimes are proven to have occurred. Waziyatawin, for her part, represents an extreme position on the spectrum.

Waziyatawin claims that every act of violence perpetrated in the war was ultimately, without exception, the fault of the white settlers, even when they were the victims of violence at Dakota hands. "[W]e as Dakota need to stand up most forcefully to call into question the innocence of whites in Minnesota in 1862," she says, "and to declare that the violence committed upon the whites in Minnesota during the war was not caused by the Dakota—it was caused by their own actions and the actions of their government."[1] Taken to its conclusion, *reductio ad absurdum*, Waziyatawin's view of the murder of women and children during the Dakota War is that it was the victims' own fault that they were shot, hacked, stabbed, bludgeoned or burned to death.

Murder is one thing; rape is something else altogether. Considering the difficulty of excusing that particular crime, it may be easier for the apologists to simply never mention it. To say that in the course of the war some Dakota men committed crimes of sexual violence requires one to also confront the fact that rape cannot be glossed over with the same veneer of cultural justification that is sometimes applied to every other sort of violence that Indians committed during the war. Waziyatawin and other commentators may believe that no rapes were committed in the course of the war and that reports of such were lies and fabrications, but the evidence leads to an altogether different conclusion.

Rapes did occur during the six weeks that most of the white and mixed-race women were held captive. Some women, such as Julia Wright and Laura Duley, were raped repeatedly, and both of them were pregnant by the time they were rescued. Gary Clayton Anderson claims that "the two women from Lake Shetek [Wright and Duley] said they were not raped," and that much later in old age ("around 1903," according to him) they changed their story.[2] That is a complete distortion of the evidence—their experience of sexual assault was widely known and reported after their release, and since Julia Wright disappeared from the historical record altogether a few years after the war, we frankly do not know what she did or did not say in old age.

At the same time, it is clear that sexual assault was not the experience of all the captive women. Thomas Robertson, a mixed-race man who carried messages back and forth from Little Crow and Sibley toward the end of the war, told *Harper's Weekly* correspondent Adrian J. Ebell that he had "seen no instances of cruelty toward them, and scarcely any of violation, and those by rowdies, unsanctioned and unapproved by the chief."[3] These contrasting realities—some women were sexually assaulted, many others were not—illustrate the divided perspectives found in the historiography. Some modern historians have expressed doubt as to whether or not incidents of rape ever occurred at all; some of the contemporary sources make it sound as if every white woman who fell into Dakota hands was raped repeatedly by red-skinned savages aflame with insatiable lusts. The reality, as is so often the case, falls somewhere between the two extremes.

In her book *The War in Words*, Kathryn Zabelle Derounian-Stodola maintains that rape was a relative rarity in the Dakota War. "Inflammatory claims of rape during the Dakota Conflict were widespread in the popular press," she writes, "and while a few may have been true, the vast majority were not."[4] She characterizes the preponderance of incidents of alleged rape as being the result of "the strong propagandist and prurient element of female sexual victimization" which she says appealed to 19th century readers.[5] It is true that rape was not as widespread during the captivity as many contemporary claims made it out to be, and people such as General Pope grossly exaggerated the frequency of the crime, but when Derounian-Stodola says "a few may have been true," she is hedging a bit with phrase "may have been." The historical record indicates that some cases of rape absolutely *were* true—the experiences of Julia Wright, Laura Duley, Mattie Williams and Margaret Cardinal, for example.[6]

Mary Schwandt was 14 years old in 1862 when the outbreak began. In the narrative of her experience that she wrote after the war, she described how on the day that she was captured by the Indians, "one of them laid his hands forcibly upon me, when I screamed, and one of the fiends struck me on my mouth with his hand, causing the blood to flow very freely. They then took me out by force, to an unoccupied tepee, near the house, and perpetrated the most horrible and nameless outrages upon my person."[7] To be sure, Schwandt needs to be considered carefully as a source, because of the variances between different accounts that she wrote over the years, but Derounian-Stodola, considering this statement, theorizes that Schwandt's claim of sexual assault is the result of "bias and editorialization," and doubts its truthfulness.[8]

Two other young women were captured along with Schwandt; Mattie Williams and Mary Anderson. Mary Anderson was shot and mortally wounded and died a short time later, a fact which did not prevent at least one Indian from attempting to force himself on her while she was dying. Mattie Williams, like Mary Schwandt, was repeatedly raped over the course of the six weeks that she was a prisoner of the Dakota. Stephen Riggs spoke with Mattie at length when he was tasked with interviewing the freed captives at Camp Release. In a letter to his daughter afterward, Riggs wrote, "Oh how glad I was that my girl was not among them. Poor Mattie Williams, she has been wonderfully abused. She grieves much over it. I am very sorry for her."[9] Riggs was a missionary and a clergyman, and the responsibility of interviewing sexually traumatized women for the purpose of assembling evidence for the criminal arraignment of their rapists clearly weighed heavily on him. "The work of today has not been pleasant to me," he wrote to his daughter. In the months that followed, he was to find that there would be other experiences that would trouble him even more.

The charge of rape as an atrocity of the war, while frequently leveled against the Indians in general in the press of 1862, is corroborated by more than simply secondhand accusations. As already established, there are statements in the record made by the victims themselves that attest to incidents of sexual assault. In 19th century American society the crime of rape had such a stigma attached to it that even the word itself was often avoided, being referred to obliquely as "ravish," or, in the case of women captured by Indians, "a fate worse than death." The fact that women such as Mary Schwandt, Mattie Williams, Margaret Cardinal and others would openly speak of having been raped while prisoners of the Indians, in spite of the societal prejudices attached to that admission, lends a considerable veracity to their accounts.

More importantly, accounts of rape are found in the trial transcripts, both in sworn testimony by victims and in statements made by defendants themselves. In Case no. 2, that of Tehehdonecha, and Case no. 4, that of Ptandootah, also known as Tazoo, both men confessed to raping women whom they had captured. Tehehdonecha was charged with murder with the attached specification of "in particular killing father, mother and nephew of Martha Clausen, Aug. 19, 1862, near Beaver Creek."[10] The second charge on which he was arraigned was the rape of Margaret Cardinal.

Tehehdonecha's statement before the commission is recorded in the trial transcript:

> Prisoner states: That he had not killed. Was compelled to go to the fort [Ridgely] and New Ulm. Came home from Birch Coulie without firing a gun. Was at Yellow Medicine, [Wood Lake] but did not fire a gun. I slept with this woman once. I did bad towards her once. I tell you the truth. Another Indian may have slept with her.[11]

Margaret Cardinal was then sworn in before the military commission. In her statement she said, "The prisoner has slept with me. He has raped me against my will when I was taken prisoner; the third night afterwards."[12] Tehehdonecha did not dispute her version of events; while he protested that he had not killed anyone as the first charge specified, he did not refute the charge of rape. Tehehdonecha was found guilty of all charges and sentenced to hang. His was one of the 39 death sentences confirmed by President Lincoln's review of the commission's transcripts. Interviewed by the Reverend

Stephen Riggs shortly before he was hanged in Mankato, Tehehdonecha never retracted his statement that he "did bad" towards Margaret Campbell.

In Case no. 4, that of Ptandoota, also known as Tazoo, the defendant was charged with murder on the specification that he aided and abetted in the killing of Francis Patoille and Mary Anderson on August 18.[13] The second charge on which Tazoo was arraigned was the rape of Mattie Williams. Tazoo protested that he was innocent of anyone's death—"Have sore eyes, am nearly blind; I didn't go any where's [sic]"—but he did admit to the charge of rape.[14] Tazoo claimed that he had saved Mattie William's life at the time of her capture when other Indians would have killed her, but then said, "I ravished her. She was not willing and I desisted. I tried to sleep with her twice, but she was too young."[15]

The next line in the trial transcript is, "Mattie Williams sworn: Prisoner raped her and repeated it...."[16] There is no record that Tazoo ever refuted Mattie William's testimony, and he never retracted his own statement. He was convicted and sentenced to death. He also did not retract his admission of guilt prior to being hanged at Mankato.

There are few absolutes in the history of the Dakota War, and any source that bandies about words such as "all" or "none" needs to be regarded with skepticism. Not every white woman captured by the Indians was raped, in fact, we could say that most were not and we would still be on the firm ground of historical evidence. Sarah Wakefield was not raped, almost certainly because of the active efforts of certain Indians to protect her. Sophia Huggins was sheltered and protected by a Dakota named Walking Spirit and his family after her husband was murdered. Other women also found protectors among the Dakota, quite often with Indian families. And it should also be noted that the Dakota practice of partially stripping the bodies of dead women was a traditional aspect of their intertribal warfare—half-naked female corpses did not automatically indicate that the victims were raped as well as murdered, but many white observers incorrectly assumed that it did. Some women *were* raped, though—Mary Schwandt, Mattie Williams, Margaret Cardinal, Laura Duley and Julia Wright, certainly. When it comes to the question of rape as a provable crime in the Dakota War, it can neither be dismissed altogether nor assumed to be commonplace. The historical record does not provide sufficient evidence to make absolute conclusions one way or the other.

One thing worth noting on this question is that while there was a widespread assumption during the war that the Dakota were perpetrating sexual assault on nearly every white woman they captured, a view that Sibley himself seemed to share for a time, the specific charge of rape as a crime was leveled against very few of the defendants who appeared before the military commission. When it came to prosecution under law, the commission only found two cases where the evidence was sufficient to support a charge of rape. On this point, then, the commission actually did distinguish between individuals, and connected certain men to specific actions.

This conclusion, however, does not only provide a justification for the commission's existence—it also highlights the undeniable fact that in many more cases the commission convicted men of crimes which were in fact not crimes at all. As we will see in the next chapter, Sibley's military commission failed to limit the definition of criminal conduct to the killing of non-combatants or the rape of captive women, and convicted men who were guilty of nothing more than fighting against soldiers in open battle.

# 20

## "A fair fight"
### Crimes That Were Not Crimes

The reality of war involves the deliberate effort to kill one's enemy. In the modern American military, the word "kill" fell somewhat out of favor during the 1990s, perhaps in an effort to sanitize the harsh reality of war. This resulted in the emergence of some rather absurd phrases such as "servicing multiple targets" in place of the more honest "shooting at people." Robert Grossman, a U.S. Army officer and psychologist and author of the important book *On Killing*, examined the difficulty that our modern society has with both the action and the description of killing as a necessary means to winning wars, and as a necessary and inevitable activity of soldiers. Simply put, while there may well be depths of moral and ethical complexity attached to the act of killing in war, societies and nations have accepted, even if reluctantly, the tenet that there is nothing criminal about killing when it occurs on the field of battle between legitimately recognized co-combatants.

Sibley's military commission in 1862 did not engage in any discussion of the philosophical or legal complexities of killing. In fact, they hardly used the word "kill" at all. The word that the commission applied to nearly every act of killing committed by the Dakota was "murder." As noted earlier, the commission made almost no distinction between the killing of unarmed women and children on the one hand, and the killing of armed soldiers in open battle on the other. In legal terms, murder and killing are absolutely *not* one and the same thing. Once the distinction between killing and murder is recognized, the two acts must be weighed in the balance separately. Sibley's commission never did this.

The stereotyped charge sheet that the court employed after the first 21 trials makes this problem clear. The universal charge, which was applied to all defendants after October 11, stated, with its accompanying specification:

CHARGE—Participation in the murders, outrages and robberies committed by the Sioux Tribe of Indians, on the Minnesota frontier.
SPECIFICATION—In this, that the said ———— a Sioux Indian (or half-breed) did join with and participate in the murders, robberies and outrages committed by the Sioux Tribe, on the Minnesota frontier, between the 18th day of August, 1862, and the 28th day of September 1862, and particularly in the battles at the Fort [Ridgely], New Ulm, Birch Coulie and Wood Lake.[1]

The problem with the wording in these two paragraphs is immediately apparent. According to the charge, every defendant was assumed to be guilty of participation in murder. The charge does not say "murders, outrages *or* robberies"; it says "murders, outrages *and* robberies." This allowed no distinction between the man who had helped himself to a few spoons and a barrel of molasses from a settler's abandoned homestead, and the man who had beaten a baby to death against a rock.

The specification paragraph is even more problematic, especially when considered in the context of legitimate belligerency between recognized combatants. The specification lists the battles of Fort Ridgely, New Ulm, Birch Coulee, and Wood Lake as part of the acts of "murders, robberies and outrages...." Thus, it is clear that the military commission drew no distinction at all between Indians who murdered women and children, and Indians who fought armed soldiers in open battle. There are two cases in the trial transcripts that clearly illustrate how the commission applied this skewed interpretation to their deliberations.

Case No. 12 in the record, the trial of a Dakota named Wahehud (a man whose name also appears as Wahehua), took place before the commission had adopted the technical shortcut of the stereotyped charge sheet. The transcript of Wahehud's trial indicate that he was arraigned on one charge of murder ("Specification—Killed Richardson, a soldier of the U.S. Army at New Ulm, or near Fort Ridgely Aug. 25, 1862"), and one charge of "Making war on the citizens of the United States" ("Specification—Participation in various onslaughts and murders").[2] One scarcely knows where to start delineating the legal fallacies in this case.

Wahehud's statement before the commission was that he "Was in three battles. Shot at White men but never took good aim. Don't remember killing any White men.... Had stolen horses. Fired at White men in battle...."[3] The testimony against him was simple; the witness, David Faribault, testified: "Heard prisoner say that they shot Richardson off his horse, and wounded him. After trying to get some news of him, they shot him dead, near the Fort or New Ulm. The prisoner shot him."[4]

By his own admission, Wahehud fought in at least three of the four major battles of the Dakota War. There was no reason, logically or legally, for him to deny it, and had he appeared before a different court in a different context nothing in his statement would probably have been held against him. He was a warrior of his nation, acknowledging that he had fought against an armed enemy in direct combat during a declared war. According to widely recognized traditions of war, and by the established protocols of the *Law of Nations* which the U.S. Army itself recognized, his statement implicated him of no crime. Unfortunately for Wahehud, Sibley's military commission did not see it that way.

The only person named as victim in the charge of murder in this case was "Richardson, a soldier of the U.S. Army." This referred to a man named Eliphalet Richardson. There are few details of his death other than the scant facts rendered in the trial transcript, but it is possible to parse out what most likely happened.[5]

The most damning scenario, as the commission would have seen it, would have been if Richardson was shot off his horse from ambush, before he knew the Indians were near. In the commission's eyes, as their interpretation of other cases makes clear, this would have been one more example of the treacherous, underhanded cunning of Indian warfare. The reality, which the commission disregarded, is that ambush is a completely legitimate military tactic.

There is no requirement in war today, and there was none in 1862, that a soldier must declare his presence to his enemy before taking him under fire. Sniping is a legal means of engaging the enemy, just as it is perfectly legal to set an ambush and take the enemy unawares. Richardson, if he was acting in a military capacity, was a legitimate target and the Indians committed no crime in shooting him, even if they shot him in the back from ambush.

Up to this point, there is no validity to the commission's charge of murder against Wahehud. Things become a bit more complicated, though, when we consider the testimony against him. The commission's witness said, "they [tried] to get some news of him [Richardson]...."[6] Trying to obtain actionable intelligence by interrogating a prisoner, even a wounded prisoner, is recognized as a belligerent's right in warfare, and it is important to note that there is absolutely no accusation in the record that the Indians ever tortured Richardson for information. Therefore, to this point, there was still no crime deserving of punishment.

Killing a wounded prisoner, though, is not within bounds. If this specific detail—"they shot him dead"—meant that Richardson was killed *after* he was wounded and captured, then the charge of murder was legitimate. However, the burden of proof in a criminal case is on the prosecution, a fact that applies to military commissions as much as it does to civilian courts, and nothing in the sparse records of the transcript indicates that the commission proved Wahehud's guilt beyond reasonable doubt.[7] He was, rather, convicted on the testimony of a single witness who reported that he had *heard* Wahehud make a statement implicating himself in Richardson's death, testimony that was apparently not corroborated by any other source.

The second charge against Wahehud, "making war on citizens of the United States," is harder to understand. It may have been because the specification on the first charge, that of murder, named a U.S. soldier as victim. (Richardson was technically a volunteer, akin to a militiaman, rather than a soldier of the Regular Army, but that is a technical distinction. He was armed, he was on a military mission, and he was a fully engaged combatant—in short, he was a legitimate target.) While many other cases used similar wording in the general specification, such as "go upon a war party against the white citizens of the United States...," Wahehud was one of the only defendants to be charged so specifically with it. At any rate, it is difficult to find any way to justify a charge of warring against the U.S. when the military commission had not first established a legal position on the question of the Dakotas' status as a sovereign nation. If the Dakota were a domestic entity of the United States, then their war was a rebellion and the charge might have had some validity (though in that scenario a charge of treason or armed insurrection would have been more technically correct). But if the Dakota were sovereign, then they had every right to declare and wage war against the United States and the charge was absolutely baseless.

Finally, the specification of the second charge –"Participation in various onslaughts and murders"—presents its own conundrum. This general accusation of complicity in murders where no instances are specified, no victims are named, and no specific details furnished, would never be allowed to stand in any normal court. The fact that the military commission applied it and tried the defendant under it is just one more black mark against their process. And one could read through reams of legal records and probably never encounter another case where a defendant was accused of such a general offense as "various onslaughts."

Both charges were allowed to stand, with their specifications intact. The commission at least took a little more time in judging Wahehud than they did many of the later defendants—his case was tried before the trial process accelerated to the infamous speed of five minutes per case. Even so, the evidence was still inadequate, the defendant's guilt was not established to a normal standard and expectation of law, and the case occupied less time on the commission's docket than a capital case in a civilian court ever would. In the end, none of that mattered. Wahehud was found guilty on both charges and sentenced to death. His was one of the sentences confirmed by Lincoln's review, possibly because of the fact that he was implicated in the death of a captured soldier, though it is impossible to say so with certainty. He was hanged at Mankato on December 26.

Another case which points out the difference between lawful warfare and criminal action is Case No. 35, that of Shoonkaska, also known as White Dog. He was accused of luring Captain Marsh into the ambush at Redwood Ferry on August 18, the first day of the outbreak. When Whiting and Ruggles reviewed White Dog's case, they came to the conclusion that he "was the leader of the party that attacked Captain Marsh's company, and was the man who detained Captain Marsh in conversation until the Indians crossed the river and surrounded his command, and then gave the signal to fire."[8] Their review upheld the commission's verdict of guilty and sentence of death. It is possible, though not certain, that they interpreted the ambush at Redwood Ferry as being a "massacre," which was one of the crimes the President had told them to identify in the transcripts.

Some of the same factors that were at work in Wahehud's case are also found here. Even if White Dog in fact led a war party, engaged Captain Marsh in a delaying tactic until the Indian warriors were fully deployed, and then gave the order to fire, not a single one of those actions represents a violation of lawful warfare. Once again, ambush is a completely acceptable (and even desirable) tactic. White Dog, if he lulled Captain Marsh into a false sense of security before springing the ambush at Redwood Ferry, did not commit either of the acts of deception which U.S. military law would have recognized as criminal—violating a flag of truce, showing a false flag, or wearing the uniform of the enemy with intent to deceive. Every tactic specified in the charge against White Dog would have been considered absolutely legitimate if they were employed by soldiers of the U.S. Army. It is possible that the commission interpreted White Dog's actions as being an attempt to portray himself as a noncombatant so as to deceive Marsh, but it is debatable whether or not that would specifically violate the Laws of War extant 1862.

It should also be noted that the evidence against White Dog was far from incontrovertible. Big Eagle said, "They [the Dakota] said that White Dog did not tell Mr. Quinn [the government interpreter] to come over, but told him to go back." The problem is that Big Eagle, as he himself makes clear, arrived at the ferry crossing after the ambush and was not a personal witness to this incident. "Of course I do not know what the truth is about this," Big Eagle concluded, and we are in much the same situation today. Both American and Indian sources disagree as to what White Dog's actual role was in the ferry ambush, and what he did or did not say there.

Here, as in the case of Wahehud, the commission was not inclined to consider mitigating factors. White Dog was found guilty and sentenced to death. The Reverend Stephen Riggs talked with him at length in the prison at Mankato, and wrote that White Dog "says that his position and conduct at the ferry was misunderstood and misrepresented.... He complains bitterly that he did not have a chance to tell things as they were; that he could not have an opportunity of rebutting the false testimony against him."[9] White Dog said that the Dakota had expected another trial; "they were promised it," he told Riggs. He felt "they have done great wrongs to the white people, and do not refuse to die," Riggs wrote, "but think it hard not to have a fairer trial. They want the President to know this."[10] When Riggs interviewed White Dog in prison, the execution order had already been issued and both men knew the result. White Dog was one of the 38 whose death sentences were confirmed by Lincoln's review. He went to the gallows insisting to the end that the testimony against him was false and the trial unfair. It was a view that others had of him as well; in 1908 Return I. Holcombe wrote, "White Dog bore a general good reputation in the country until the outbreak, and many yet assert that he has been misrepresented and unjustly accused."[11]

These two cases serve to illustrate the fact that the commission applied the charge of murder to Indians who admitted to or were implicated in nothing more than participation in open battle. Once the commission reached this interpretation of events early in the proceedings, they rarely backed away from it. There were a few exceptions, though, and they are not always easy to understand. A good example of this is Case No. 358, which involved a man named Wasoohdehayya. He admitted to being present at the attack on Fort Ridgely (his statement during his trial was that he "Was at Fort, to get a horse") and more seriously, he admitted to actually firing during the fight with Captain Strout's command near Acton on September 3.[12] Other Dakota were condemned to death on less damning statements than this, but inexplicably, for reasons that are not at all clear, Wasoohdehayya was found not guilty and acquitted.[13]

Isaac Heard, in his account of the commission's trials, felt that there was absolutely nothing wrong with the application of a criminal charge to every Indian who could be shown by testimony or self-admission to have fought in the war in almost any capacity. "I have already shown," Heard wrote, "that the point to be investigated being a very simple one, viz., presence and participation in battles and massacres which had before been proven, and many of the prisoners confessing the fact, each case need occupy only a few moments."[14] By Heard's account, the standard of guilt that the commission used was not proof of complicity in the murder of an identifiable victim, but rather any instance of hostile action against persons of the United States, whether civilians or soldiers. There does not, in his statement, seem to be any sense of the commission applying a distinction between degrees of participation, but Heard went on to insist that there *was* recognition of varying degrees of guilt.

"No one was sentenced to death for the mere robbery of goods," he wrote, "and not to exceed half a dozen for mere presence in a battle.... It was required that it should be proven by the testimony of witnesses, unless the prisoner admitted the fact, that he had fired in the battles, or brought ammunition, or acted as commissary in supplying provisions to the combatants, or committed some separate murder."[15] What Heard was saying here is that in the commission's eyes, there was no difference between the man who fought in battle, the man who provided ordnance, or the man who roasted corn to feed the warriors who were actually fighting. The accessory after the fact was considered to be just as guilty as the principal perpetrator.

The members of the military commission were not the only ones to consider those Indians who only rendered material aid as being equally guilty with those who were actual, active combatants. In a letter to Bishop Whipple after the commission had adjourned, the Reverend Ezekial Gere wrote, "I know not that I should differ materially with the writer [of an article in the *St. Paul Pioneer* newspaper] in putting the carrier of 'ammunition' in the same category with him who used it, unless it could be shown that he did it by compulsion."[16] In the immediate aftermath of the war, almost all Dakota were assumed to be equally guilty regardless of the degree of participation.

Many observers in 1862 thought that the Articles of War that governed the U.S. military through the first 60 years of the 19th century had already weighed in on this particular question. Article 56 of the Articles of War states, "whosoever shall relieve the enemy with money, victuals, or ammunition, or shall knowingly harbour or protect an enemy, shall suffer death or such other punishment as may be ordered...."[17] Taken in context, however, it is clear that Article 56 was written with American citizens in mind in order to prevent the domestic populace from rendering "aid and comfort" to a foreign enemy. This Article would not apply to the enemy's people, of whom it would naturally be expected that they would support their own forces. Therefore, Article 56 should not have been interpreted as applying to the Dakota, but many commentators in 1862 felt that it did.

There is one other detail in Heard's statement that requires comment. When he wrote that "not to exceed half a dozen" were condemned to death "for mere presence in a battle," the implication is clear—at least six men (he does not seem to have even been certain of the exact number), *were* convicted and sentenced to be hanged for nothing more than having been seen at, but not necessarily having fought in, one or other of the battles. It is unclear why these unnamed men were singled out for this severity of punishment when others were not, when they were all implicated in the same action. This is just one more aspect of the commission's process that is troubling. There was no universal standard applied to the question of guilt or punishment, just as there seems to have been no rhyme or reason to why a few men were acquitted on the same flimsy evidence that sent other men to the gallows on the same charge.

Even at the time of his writing Heard must have been aware that this point was a controversial one, because he addressed it directly. "If you think that participation in battles did not justify such a sentence [death]," Heard wrote, "please reflect that any judicial tribunal in the state would have been compelled to pass it, and that the retaliatory laws of war, as recognized by all civilized nations, and also the code of the Indian, which takes life for life, justified it."[18] He then went on to explain that in his view, the battles of Fort Ridgley and New Ulm were not ordinary battles because of the presence of civilians in both locations, and thus even in these situations the Indians were guilty of attacking noncombatants. This was a perspective which Sibley seemed to share.

As a legal position it is not without merit, though it does venture close to the "what if" conjecturing of the hypothetical. Minnesota historian John LaBatte has raised the valid question of what the likely outcome would have been had the Dakota broken through the defense of New Ulm and overwhelmed the town's armed defenders, and concludes that a massacre would almost certainly have ensued.

I do not disagree with that, in fact I think LaBatte is absolutely correct, but coming at the question from the military perspective of lawful warfare, I would suggest that another element should be added to any consideration of the battles of Fort Ridgely and New Ulm. It is true that both locations contained a large number of non-combatant civilians, but it is also true that both locations were actively defended by armed men of military age who were organized and led as combat units, even if the vast majority of them were not professional soldiers. Thus, I find the Dakota attacks on both locations acceptable, up to that point. After all, the Civil War saw civilian population centers such as Vicksburg, Petersburg and Richmond come under protracted siege and assault, and the legitimacy of those types of siege was accepted as lawful.

The crucial difference to this discussion, of course, is that if Grant's troops had taken Vicksburg by frontal assault there would have been no ensuing massacre of the defending troops and no slaughter of the women and children within the city. If the Dakota had managed to take Fort Ridgely and New Ulm there is little doubt that that is precisely what would have happened—the record of Milford, Sacred Heart, Beaver Creek and Lake Shetek indicate that all too clearly, so LaBatte's argument is on solid foundation. The tipping point would have come when the fighting transitioned from two armed forces opposing each other in battle, to an armed force committing massacre. If the Dakota had succeeded in overwhelming the defenses of New Ulm, they would not have accepted the surrender of the town's defenders, and based on their actions elsewhere in the war, they would have killed any children they did not choose to take as captives. That needs to be remembered when considering what could be classified as an act of lawful warfare, and what could not—what began as conventional battle would have degenerated to criminal massacre in short order.

At any rate, the commission's decision to make no distinction between those who participated in battles against the army and those who massacred unarmed settlers is referenced in a short, almost flippant sentence that Heard tossed off in the course of his narrative. Explaining the justification for charging participants of the battles at Fort Ridgely, New Ulm and Birch Coulee with murder, Heard wrote, "Besides, most of these Indians must also have been engaged in individual massacres and outrages."[19] If this was an idea that was at work in the commission's process, then it presents the troubling possibility that the commission assumed guilt for an unproven act based upon a defendant's admitted participation in a completely *separate* act. Furthermore, the phrase "most of these Indians," would seem to indicate that when the commission could not identify particular Indians as being guilty of a specific crime, it simply implicated all Indians in the act.

On this matter of the commission charging the Indians with crimes that should not have been classified as crimes, Carol Chomsky expresses it quite clearly. "The transcripts show," she writes, "that the Commission acted without recognition of the fact that most of the Dakota were guilty of nothing more than fighting in a war and that they were therefore guilty of no punishable offense."[20] She is correct—while some of the Indians, on basis of their actions, were no better than marauding criminals, most of the men hauled before the commission in shackles were guilty of nothing more than fighting in open battle. They were soldiers of their nation, just as the white men who faced them were soldiers of *their* nation. The Dakota men who fought the U.S. Army at Fort Ridgely, Birch Coulee and Wood Lake by rights should have been recognized and treated as legitimate combatants, not criminals.[21]

It has been questioned whether or not the irregular nature of American forces during this war added a measure of criminality to Dakota actions.[22] Most of the soldiers against whom the Dakota fought in the early weeks of the war were volunteer or militia troops—hastily organized, poorly trained, and haphazardly armed and equipped. They were not, in the main, Regular Army soldiers. I do not believe that this distinction matters. As I posited above, even though most of the men who fought at Redwood Ferry, Fort Ridgely, Birch Coulee and Wood Lake were not professional soldiers, they were still armed combatants, assembled into military units, and therefore the Indians violated no rule of war by fighting against them.

By assigning criminal culpability to legitimate combatants, the military commission failed to give full consideration to the real crimes which had been committed during the war. More than 100 children of settler families were killed by the Dakota; the commission heard evidence on fewer than 20 of those murders. "By spending much of their limited time on ordinary-soldier cases," Bachman argues, "Sibley's judges had failed to concentrate on the very sort of offenses—murder and rape—that the commission was initially created to handle."[23]

The bulk of contemporary opinions written on this question come, of course, from the American side of the war. But there are some accounts of the war from the Dakota side of the conflict, and those perspectives on the matter add an essential element to the discussion.

Big Eagle, whose narrative on the war we have already encountered several times, fought in the battles of Fort Ridgley, Birch Coulee and Wood Lake. He freely acknowledged it, but he resolutely denied any complicity in murder or massacre. Big Eagle was a man who fought other men, not a marauder preying on women and children, and he vehemently objected to being classified as a criminal during the commission's trials.

"On my trial a great number of the white prisoners, women and others, were called up," he said, "but not one of them could testify that I had murdered anyone or had done anything to deserve death, or else I would have been hanged."[24] No one could rightly accuse Big Eagle of murder, but on the sole basis of his admission that he fought in battle, he was sentenced to ten years imprisonment.

Another Dakota who left an account from the defendants' perspective was Wakandayamani, or The Spirit that Rattles as it Walks, a man whose white father had also given him the English name George Quinn. His bi-racial identity—he described himself by saying "I am half white man and half Indian.... I was raised among the Indians as one of them"—might have been held against him when his case came before the military commission.[25]

When the war began, Quinn sided with the people whom he knew best—the Dakota. Like many of the defendants brought before the commission, he was young, and his motivations were probably similar to those of other young Indian men. "I was nineteen years old and anxious to distinguish myself in the war," he recalled, "but I had no wish to murder anyone in cold blood, nor did I; nobody ever accused me of such a thing. I fought the white soldiers, but not the unarmed white settlers."²⁶ The distinction between soldiers and settlers did him little good, just as it proved to be of little help to other Indians who admitted to have been active combatants. "I was a prisoner for four years," Quinn wrote, "being sent to Rock Island. Nothing was proved against me except that I was in some of the battles against the whites. I took no part in killing the settlers and was opposed to such work"²⁷

There is one another detail of George Quinn's story worth relating. Some sources identify George Quinn as the son of Peter Quinn, an Irish immigrant from Dublin, who was the government translator at Fort Ridgely. It may not be possible to say with certainty that these two men were in fact related, but it is not altogether improbable. On the first day of the war, Peter Quinn was killed in the ambush of Captain Marsh's command at Redwood Ferry. According to at least one source, George Quinn may have been among the Dakota who fought at Redwood Ferry. Father and son were on opposite sides of the battle.²⁸ If the story is true, then it adds an even greater depth of tragedy to George Quinn's experiences in the war. Even if it is not, it still serves to illustrate the internecine nature of this war for the Dakota, with some of them fighting against the whites and some fighting with them, and others trying to stay out of the war altogether.

Big Eagle and George Quinn were not sent to prison because they murdered anyone, or because they were guilty of perpetrating massacres. They were incarcerated for the fact that they had fought the U.S. Army, as soldiers against soldiers. They were punished because they lost their war, and when the victors sought retribution they made no distinction made between the criminal and the soldier.

# 21

# Exaggerations, Errors and Evidence
## *The Atrocity Debate*

*The pure truth is for God alone; what is given to us is the pursuit of truth.*
—Søren Kierkegaard

In 1908, Return I. Holcombe, co-author of the three-volume history *Minnesota in Three Centuries*, expressed an opinion on the violence of the Dakota War which has been echoed many times before and since. "The details of the massacre occurring in the great Indian outbreak," Holcombe wrote, "are neither agreeable or profitable reading.... For the most part they constitute a record of sickening and horrifying atrocities, of unspeakable brutality, of loathsome crimes of every sort, murder being among the least."[1] This idea that the details of the war are too horrible to read is perhaps one reason why so many writers in the historiography have used generalities rather than the grim details that mark the narratives of eyewitnesses and survivors. And it *is* grim reading, no doubt about it.

The late Alan Woolworth, Research Fellow of the Minnesota Historical Society, was for many years the elder statesman of Minnesota historians. In a piece he wrote in 1994, Woolworth considered the issue of atrocity allegations during the Dakota War and said, "While recent histories downplay such accounts, this author believes that many 'atrocities' did take place. Published first-hand accounts and letters from captives and reputable individuals such as Stephen R. Riggs support this conclusion."[2] The trend of discounting or denying the veracity of accounts of atrocities to which Woolworth referred continues today—perhaps because of a reluctance to examine evidence which can often be genuinely unsettling, or, as is all too apparent in some cases, because to do so would be at odds with a particular agenda or a predetermined conclusion.

Accounts of the war written in 1862 and shortly afterward are thick with words like "massacre," "outrage," "atrocity," "ravish," and "murder." The view expressed by many newspaper accounts in 1862 was that the Dakota had risen up without any provocation, thereby displaying the innate treachery that was the natural trait of every Indian, and had fallen upon the hapless white settlers of the southwestern Minnesota counties with a vicious rapacity heretofore unknown on the American continent. There was much more to it than that, of course, but histrionics and hyperbole dominated much of the public discourse during and immediately after the war. Most newspaper accounts from the time of the war contain an undeniable degree of sensationalism and shrill invective, and in these stories one encounters the same lurid, bloody stories that tend to pop up over and over in various later sources. These stories are almost always unattributed and unsubstantiated.

These verifiable instances of exaggeration are at least part of the reason why some historians choose to summarily deny almost *all* accounts of Dakota atrocities, and why they reject atrocity allegations as having any foundation in historical fact. Kathryn Derounian-Stodola, in her recent book, dismisses charges of Indian depredations entirely, saying, "Historically considerable doubt exists about the extent of Indian violence during the [Dakota] Conflict, but it was useful for the military and the government to exaggerate the brutality and reinforce calls for Indian dispossession."[3] The implication there is that the preponderance of atrocity accounts—indeed, most of the reports of Indian violence of any kind—must have been the result of some vast military/governmental propaganda conspiracy. She does not, however, provide any immediate evidence to support that claim.

Carol Chomsky of the University of Minnesota, whose work I have cited repeatedly in this book, has written the best legal study to date on Sibley's military commission, but to some degree she also accepts this dismissive view of Indian atrocities. "Wild stories of mutilation by the Dakota in these encounters spread among the settlers," she writes, "but historians have concluded that these reports were probably exaggerations of isolated instances of atrocities."[4] Chomsky is a brilliant legal scholar, and I admire her outstanding work on the legal questions of the 1862 military commission, but I reach a very different conclusion on this point.

The work of two earlier historians, Kenneth Carley and Roy Meyer, is the support most often offered by commentators today for the argument that atrocity stories are hopelessly exaggerated. Carley, in his 1961 work on the war, says, "It seems probable that the condition of the bodies, which had lain in the hot sun for nearly two weeks, gave rise to some false charges of mutilation."[5] Carley's assumption notwithstanding, the truth of the matter is that a swollen, blackened corpse rotting in the sun for two weeks does not look the same as a corpse that has been cut, hacked, dismembered or decapitated, whether pre-mortem or post-mortem. From my own military experience, I can attest to the fact that the state of decomposition does not make it impossible to tell the difference, even when the corpse has swollen enough for the skin to split. Carley justifiably ranks as one of the canonical writers on the subject of the Dakota War, but he was assuming too much with his suggestion that stories of mutilations must have originated with observers who could not tell the difference between violent death and slow decay.

Roy Meyer, for his part, categorically dismisses accounts of widespread atrocities. "[T]he closer these stories are scrutinized," he writes, "the less foundation there seems to be for them.... Although the earth between Fort Ridgely and the lower agency was supposed to be virtually carpeted with mutilated bodies, Dr. Jared W. Daniels, who accompanied a burial party and who should have recognized cases of mutilation if anyone would, categorically denied that the corpses he saw had been mutilated." "[T]hese isolated instances," Meyer concludes, "were multiplied in the imagination of refugees and their details exaggerated to such a degree that the early accounts can no longer be accepted by sober scholarship."[6]

There are several problems with this particular argument, problems which illustrate some of the fallacies common to many of the atrocity denials. First of all, Meyer's statement that "the earth between Fort Ridgley and the lower agency was supposed to be virtually carpeted with mutilated bodies" is itself an exaggeration, an overstatement of the argument to make a point. There were plenty of lurid, sensational accounts in newspapers in the summer of 1862, all shrieking of slaughter and massacre and murder by marauding Indians, but research reveals no contemporary claim or belief that mutilated bodies carpeted the earth, however figuratively.

Secondly, Dr. Daniels, whose account is the only cited basis for both Carley and Meyer's assertions, accompanied *one* burial party, as far as can be ascertained from his journal, and a close analysis of his narrative of that experience leads to an altogether different conclusion than the one Meyer puts forward. Daniels wrote in his reminiscences that in route to the Birch Coulee encampment, "the burial party buried eleven bodies and the chared [sic] remains of two, and woman and a babe, and the burned Magner house about five miles from the Agency. These three found here were, Humphry [sic] wife and child, he was abliged [sic] to stop here in his flight owing to the severe illness of his wife. His boy of ten years secreted himself in the coolie back of the house when he saw the [Indians] coming and escaped." Daniels concluded his account of his personal observations by saying, "I saw every one that was buried and not one was scalped or mutilated in the least."[7]

Examining Daniels' statement, it seems that he witnessed the interment of perhaps 16 people (from his wording, it is not absolutely clear if the three members of the Humphrey family were included in the 13 first tallied, or if they were counted subsequently and separately). It is unfortunate that he did not specify what sort of wounds he thought qualified as mutilations, because his categorical denial, as Meyer describes it, is at odds with what is known about this situation from other sources. Dr. Humphrey's corpse, according to at least three other witnesses, was both scalped and decapitated. One of those eyewitnesses, Moses Adams, wrote that the Indians had "severed the head from the body, scalped it, and left it about fifty yards distant in the bushes. It was afterward found by us, on the expedition sent up from Fort Ridgely to reconnoiter and to bury the dead."[8] Decapitation would usually be accounted a form of mutilation, but Daniels may not have believed that it did.[9]

Daniels went on to say, a page later in his narrative, "Twenty-eight bodies were buried at the ferry where Capt. Marsh's command was ambushed the first day of the outbreak, one coming up the bottom, and four on the prairie near Beaver Creek. Mrs. Henderson and her two children were of the last number; they were put in a box and Mr. Gibbons of the mounted force made a prayer at their burial."[10] Daniels made no reference to any mutilations among this group, but neither did he claim to have personally seen each corpse, as he did in the earlier account, and he did not specifically state that there were no mutilations as he did in the former description. I do not infer from this omission that he was thereby obliquely indicating that this group of victims *were* mutilated, but as we will see shortly, when Moses Adams described this same group of victims in his account he reported seeing ghastly mutilations. Furthermore, S. D. Hinman, a survivor of the chaos at the ferry on August 18, reported that when he made his escape across the river he saw the ferryman's corpse and that the man had been "disemboweled; his head, hands and feet cut off and thrust into the cavity."[11]

Daniels did not take a position on the question of atrocities across the whole spectrum of the war, as Meyer suggests that he did.[12] Furthermore, a careful reading of Daniels' entire statement on the subject leads to the conclusion that he personally saw only a few of the corpses of the more than 600 settlers and soldiers who are known to have been killed in the conflict.

The claim that there were no verifiable atrocities is a house of cards. Jared Daniels' "categorical denial" that the corpses he encountered were not mutilated, which is the only citation Meyer used to support his "sober scholarship" claim, is the only primary source used to underpin the later advocacy of this idea. The chain of evidence in this argument is incomplete, and in the end it fails to support itself.

In the past 50 years, writers on the Dakota War have frequently approached the atrocity debate from the perspective that mutilations are the defining feature of atrocities. I take a different view of the matter. I draw a sharp distinction between mutilations and atrocities—the words are not synonymous, and the one act is not automatically the other. Mutilating a living victim (torture, in other words) is an atrocity; mutilating a corpse by dismemberment or decapitation, on the other hand, does not qualify as an atrocity to the same degree that hacking children to death or raping wounded women does. Even so, the sight of headless bodies and corpses cut into pieces horrified the white people who encountered them, as is readily apparent from eyewitness accounts.

Minnie Buce Carrigan was nine years old when the war broke out. Her parents and two sisters, one a just a baby, were killed by the Dakota; she and her brother and another sister were taken captive. In her narrative, Minnie said the Dakota then took them to a neighbor's house which the Indians had attacked earlier. "I started to go into the house," she wrote, "but my brother, who was standing at the door, stopped me. I waited a few minutes until he went away and then looked in. There lay Grandma Boelter on the floor with every joint in her body chopped to pieces. All winter after the outbreak I would dream about her and cry in my sleep over it. She was such a nice old lady and I thought so much of her."[13]

Emanuel Reyff saw the Indians murder his brother, sister-in-law, niece and nephew (the account of which is found later in this chapter), then he ran to the nearby house of the Smith family. "Here I saw one of the most horrible sights I ever witnessed in my life," he remembered. "Mrs. Smith's head was lying on the table with a knife and fork stuck in it. They had cut off one of her breasts and laid it on the table beside the head and put her baby nursing her other breast. The child was still alive, but the dog they had shot on the door step."[14]

These are graphic accounts, and the shock of witnessing these scenes had an obvious impact on both narrators, but according to the definition of atrocity that I am proposing in this discussion of the war, neither of these specific accounts rise to the level of atrocity. Modern laws of war classify mutilation of the dead as an atrocity and a criminal act, but no such legal distinction existed in 1862. The American public reacted with horror and outrage to reports of mutilation of their dead in this and other wars of the 19th century, but there was no codification of military law at the time that made those acts a martial crime—it was, rather, a societal perception. It would therefore be anachronistic to use a modern interpretation of military law to condemn post-mortem mutilations in the U.S.–Dakota War.

The Dakota practice of mutilating the dead was a cultural tradition, and on this point I agree that culture is a mitigating factor, *when specifically limited to acts of post-mortem mutilation.* "Acts of brutality committed by the Sioux included the mutilation of bodies, heads, and limbs," one historian has recently noted, "all of which were in keeping with traditional Sioux warfare. Dakota warriors believed their enemies should not be left intact because they would have to fight them again in the next world."[15] Chomsky also recognizes the difference between violent mutilation and deliberate acts of atrocity, pointing out that "some 'mutilation' would occur from the use of weapons like the hatchet, knife, and war club...."[16] It is necessary to understand, then, that mutilations did occur, which might accurately be characterized as brutality, but mutilations by themselves are not always indisputable evidence of outright atrocities. Just as importantly, the absence of mutilations does not automatically prove that no atrocities were committed.

Moses Adams lived among the Dakota for years before the outbreak of war, and he held a more favorable opinion of the Indians as a people than did many of his contemporaries—he does not seem to have been out to vilify them. According to Adams, most of the corpses that he saw *were* mutilated. As we have already seen, he reported that Dr. Philander Humphrey was both decapitated and scalped, an account which was corroborated by other witnesses. The bodies of Dr. Humphrey's wife and all their children but one were in the burned-out ruins of a cabin—it was unclear to Adams how they had been killed, and he did not offer an opinion. The bodies of the soldiers at Redwood Ferry, he wrote, "were dreadfully hacked and mutilated...."[17] Adams' impression was that those mutilations were the result of the methods by which those men were killed, or were deliberate injuries that had been inflicted post-mortem. "We found," he went on to say, "the remains of a murdered colored man. His body had been badly mutilated. An empty bandbox and the scattered contents were all that was left of his outfit, apparently that of a barber."[18]

In many eyewitness narratives where mutilations are mentioned, they are usually not described in detail. Hinman's account of the ferryman's corpse earlier in this chapter is one exception to that; another is the account of William J. Jones, one of several residents of Butter Nut Valley Township in Blue Earth County who left testimony of the Indian attacks on that community. Jones reported that when he and other men went out to bury the bodies of their neighbors, "John S. Jones' body was the only one mutilated. They had cut a cross on his face, and on his breast, and had scalped him."[19] Jones' testimony is worth noting for the fact that he avoids generalities—he specifies that only one of the corpses he saw was mutilated (unfortunately he does not give a total number of burials he conducted), and he describes what type of wounds the mutilations consisted of.

Another witness who was present at some of the same events as Moses Adams and Jared Daniels was Justina Krueger, who survived the attack in which her husband and neighbors were murdered near Sacred Heart in Renville County, and whose testimony appears later in this chapter. Left for dead after the Dakota attacked, she was found by the burial party that included Adams and Daniels. In route to the ill-fated bivouac at Birch Coulee, she recalled how "the train followed along the river bottom some distance, then took to the open prairie. Here we found a woman cut into four pieces, and two children by her cut in pieces also."[20] I would suggest that the fact that these three corpses were dismembered should not be counted as an atrocity, since there is no way to prove that the mutilations were inflicted before they were killed. What makes this incident a clear case of atrocity is that the dead were a woman and two children, unarmed and defenseless. It would have been just as much an atrocity if white settlers or soldiers had killed a Dakota woman and two Indian children. The crimes here were infanticide and murder, not mutilation.

C. M. Oehler considers the question of atrocities in some detail in his book, *The Great Sioux Uprising*. "The killing of numerous undefended women and children could not be denied," he writes, "nor could evidence of mutilation and some instances of torture. Mutilation after death was in the Sioux tradition but torture before death was not. Decapitation of victims had become almost a hallmark of Sioux killings in parts of the Great Lakes region...."[21] Harriet McConkey, whose writing on the subject we will encounter later in this chapter, claimed that torture was a standard practice among the Dakota, but her unsubstantiated allegation is refuted by every commentator who actually lived among the Dakota for any length of time.

By the time of the 1862 war, the traditional patterns of Indian warfare were well-established. "Northern plains warfare," as another historian notes, "did not usually include the torture of captives, although mistreating and beating prisoners and mutilating the dead were common."[22] Samuel W. Pond, who lived with the Dakota for nearly 30 years and studied their culture with considerable admiration, assumed that torture happened on rare, isolated occasions, but believed there was "no proof that any such practice was common among them."[23] Oehler, for his part, is careful to specify what he finds credible and what he does not. "Without question some of the outbreak's atrocity stories were false and others were greatly exaggerated," he writes. "Probably the torture accounts contained more inflation than the mutilation reports. Some mutilation may have been intended to horrify and terrorize the whites, speeding their departure, and some of the torture evidence may have had the same purpose."[24] Oehler does not try to claim that most of the atrocity stories were false, only that some of them probably were, which I believe is fair.

Atrocities happened during this war. The record provides compelling evidence that some Dakota committed terrible atrocities, and I maintain that there is more than sufficient evidence to conclude that while these atrocities were not universal, they *were* common and widespread. The attempt to deny this as a historical reality, as some commentators do and others accept to varying degrees, is inaccurate in the face of the countervailing evidence. Here, as in many other areas of American history, there is an unfortunate trend for historians to shy away from the subject of Indian atrocities.

Michael Kammen, in *Mystic Chords of Memory*, has suggested that "Americans have an inclination to depoliticize the past to minimize memories and causes of conflict. We try to remember only the aspects of history that will render it acceptable to as many people as possible."[25] In the modern scholarship on the U.S.–Dakota War, there is an increasing tendency to accept the claim that atrocity stories are overblown exaggerations with little foundation in fact. Some historians, perhaps reacting to modern patterns of cultural hypersensitivity and the dictates of political correctness, treat these accounts of Indian atrocities as an unpalatable subject and avoid the matter altogether. To do so is to fall short of the unflinching, direct engagement with the past that is required of legitimate history. As Arthur M. Schlesinger has observed, we should not "degrade history by allowing its contents to be dictated by pressure groups, whether political, economic, religious, or ethnic. The past may sometimes give offense to one or another minority; that is no reason for rewriting history."[26]

This struggle with the past is apparent in much of the recent writing on the Dakota War of 1862. Some commentators reject the unsavory aspects of the war out of hand; other scholars concede that there might be *some* truth underlying all of the hysteria of 1862, but this acknowledgement is often limited to the small print. "Some of the reports, then, were probably accurate," one writer allows in a footnote, "but wild rumors far exceeded the reality."[27] I would go a step further, and say that it is possible to winnow historical facts from the chaff of hysterical rumor. To do so, the process must begin with an examination of the sources themselves.

Newspaper stories from the period of the war are excellent examples of secondhand accounts of dubious accuracy. These are frequently the stories where the details are lurid, horrific, and almost always unspecific as to the victims or the witnesses involved. As historical sources, they are practically useless, other than to establish context. By the same token, some narratives written by white survivors of Indian attacks also must be handled with considerable caution—the historian is well advised to exercise a measure of skepticism when the source recounts stories that the narrator did not personally witness. "If only by definition," one recent writer observes, "a massacre must be considered an awful affair, but the superlatives various writers have attached to the Minnesota catastrophe are both excessive and inadequate."[28] The record of this war is full of superlatives, so much so that it can be difficult to separate fact from fiction. To make the distinction clear, we will first consider accounts of questionable authenticity.

Edward D. Neill wrote his account of the war 20 years after the fact, as part of his thick tome *History of Minnesota*. As was fairly common for conventional histories of that era, Neill's version is long on implication and sensational language that hints at grim and terrible things, without actually providing much in the way of detail or evidence. Describing the attacks on settler communities on the first day the outbreak, he writes, "The scenes of horror consequent upon the general assault can better be imagined than described. Fortunate, comparatively speaking, was the lot of those who were doomed to instant death, and thus spared the agonies of lingering tortures, and the superadded anguish of witnessing outrages upon the persons of those nearest and dearest to them." Having declined to describe the outrages to which he refers, Neill then continues, "The fiends of hell could not invent more fearful atrocities than were perpetrated by the savages upon their victims."[29]

Harriet Bishop McConkey wrote one of the first published depictions of the war, *Dakota War Whoop, or, Indian Massacres and War in Minnesota, of 1862–3*, in 1863. In the preface to her book, McConkey makes a declaration of the truthfulness of her account, saying, "In preparing this volume, the writer has been careful to present only reliable facts, in the plain unvarnished garb of truth.... The *worst* features of the subject remain unwritten; scarcely can they be told." [italics in the original][30] This statement is problematic right out of the gate—if the writer by her own admission regards some facts as untellable because of their nature, then her account is incomplete. McConkey actually sought Henry Sibley's endorsement of her book to help its sales, and wrote an effusive dedication to him in the book's second edition. Sibley declined to contribute a preface or attach his name to the book in any way, apparently on account of the extensive errors in her text. This did not stop McConkey from claiming that he had praised the "acute details" of her book.

What McConkey does commit to the page is often unsubstantiated, as when she claims, "Women were tortured in every imaginable manner. Some with infants in their arms had their breasts cut off; others their toes, and some were hamstrung and dragged over the prairie till torn and mangled; from that alone they died."[31] The problem with these general claims is that while she cites these atrocities as particular examples, she never supplies the sort of details that would permit the reader to know exactly who these victims were, or how these details were known to her. Reading McConkey's book, one quickly realizes that it is not a history, and that its author was neither a careful researcher nor a historian.

While any number of specific instances can illustrate the problem with McConkey as a historical source, the most lurid one is probably the oft-repeated story of the Indians killing babies by nailing them to trees. This particular atrocity story is so extreme, and so indelible in the literature of the war, that it should be examined in detail, and so we will consider this atrocity claim by itself in the next chapter. In the meantime, though, another of McConkey's stories can easily serve to demonstrate her lack of evidentiary support.

McConkey tells of one Indian, whom she does not name, who she says repeatedly boasted of having gone into a house where a white woman was baking bread with her baby beside her in a cradle. The Indian claimed, according to McConkey, that he tomahawked the woman to death and then "placed the babe in the hot oven, keeping it there till it was baked to death, when, not satisfied, he beat its brains out against the wall." "This is corroborated," she concluded, "by whites who have been at the house where it happened, and from the appearance of the bodies had no doubt but the 'boast' was literally true."[32] There are some glaring omissions here. McConkey does not name the perpetrator, the victims, or any of the witnesses whom she claims corroborated the Indian's story. Isaac Heard, in his 1863 book, also recounts this story, and his version is so similar to McConkey's (literally, almost word for word the same) that it is almost certain that he either borrowed it from her account, or took it from the same source she did and made no editorial alterations.

Even so, there might actually be some substance to this particular atrocity claim, but not because McConkey says that it was so. Sam Brown, one of the mixed-race men who were held captive by the Indians along with his family, made a passing reference in his journal to a story that could be the same one related by McConkey. In his account, Brown mentioned "the case of the Indian brave at the dance who boasted in 'ghoulish glee' that he had roasted a babe in the oven...."[33] We can extract no more identifying details from Brown's version of the event than we can from McConkey's, but earlier in his journal he wrote of an incident which is probably the same one. While still held in the Dakota camp, he witnessed a dance where the warriors took turns boasting of their exploits. Brown wrote that one Indian:

> [D]eclared that he had destroyed a whole family for which he deserved much honor. That he went into a stable and shot a white man in the back and then beat his brains out with the but[t] of his gun, then rushed into the house where he found the wife kneading bread and a babe in a cradle nearby. He

grabbed the shrieking woman by the hair of the head and threw her violently against the wall, then took the babe, put it into the bread pan, and shoved it into the hot oven, then turned and shot the woman as she was trying to get up, then set fire to the house and hurried away and joined his comrades.[34]

There are some details in Brown's account that give the story an element of authenticity—the Indian shooting the woman as she tried to get up, and the overall haste implied in his version of the story—but it is not possible to verify this particular atrocity story beyond all doubt. The incident of the baby in the oven remains apocryphal at best. Since Brown was an eyewitness to the war and spent six weeks in Indian captivity, and McConkey was a second-hand narrator, it is also entirely possible that McConkey drew on Brown as a source (McConkey almost never attributed her sources, except when she indulged in a bit of high-profile name-dropping).

In 1904 Daniel Buck also referred to this particular crime, but he attributed it to none other than Joseph Godfrey, the man who turned government's witness for the military commission after his own trial and conviction. According to Buck's version of the story, Godfrey in his old age was known to tell a tale similar to this one. "One feature of his narrative," Buck wrote, "is a statement to the effect that he killed a white man and woman and then took their infant child and placed it in a huge sheet iron pan and placed the pan in the oven of a stove and roasted it to death." "This story," Buck concluded, "he told at an Indian feast at Santee, about eleven years ago[circa 1893]."[35] From what other accounts tell us of Godfrey, it seems unlikely that Buck's story is true. Godfrey spent his years after the war living a life of quiet remove on a reservation in Nebraska where most of his Dakota neighbors never fully accepted his presence. He had steadfastly proclaimed his innocence at trial, and there was never any hard evidence to contradict his defense. Outright brutality and cruelty do not seem to have been part of his nature, so Buck's account seems rather suspect. At any rate, this particular atrocity story remains more hearsay than history.

There is one other factor that needs to be taken into account in any consideration of atrocity stories that are founded on Indian boasts. Dakota culture relied heavily on the telling and retelling of deeds of martial valor—men were expected to boast of their exploits. This does not mean that every boast was true. Several examples from the narratives of survivors of Indian captivity can illustrate this problem.

Minnie Buce Carrigan, who as a seven-year old girl was captured along with her brother and sister after her parents and two younger sisters were killed, was separated from her siblings shortly after arriving at the Indian camp. Another white captive, Wilhelmina Inefeldt (whose own story is recounted later in this chapter), asked Minnie how many of her family had been killed. "I answered that they were all dead but myself," Minnie later wrote, "as the Indians had told me they had cut the throats of my brother and sister because they cried." Fortunately, the Indians had lied to her. "The next day, however," she continued, "to my delight and surprise, I saw them both." The experience was the same for her brother, she said, because "the Indians had told him that they had killed me for trying to run away."[36]

In a similar situation, Helen Carrothers Tarble[37] related in her narrative that after she was taken captive an Indian boasted that he had killed a friend of hers, a Mrs. Hayden, by cutting off her head. Carrothers later learned that Mrs. Hayden was not only alive but had escaped from her Dakota captors. Carrothers also described how the same Indian had also told her that a woman named Mrs. Isenridge had been killed, when in fact she had been captured alive, along with her children. There are other cases in the record where Indians claimed to have killed this or that person, only to have the boast proven false.

Anthropologists have argued that since a man's place in Dakota society was so dependent on his deeds, deeds that were recounted through explicatory boasting, the culture required that the boasts be truthful; thus, great veracity can be given to those accounts. But there are too many cases in the record where Indian boasts were shown to be false or were later retracted, for them all to be assumed true without closer examination. It should not be assumed that Indian boasts rise to the level of historical fact unless they are corroborated by other evidence or testimony. However, the historiography of the war is replete with cases where the possibly fictitious is proclaimed to be factual, with little or no scrutiny of the claim. Harriet Bishop McConkey, for her part, accepted these apocryphal stories without vetting them or simply recycled stories of doubtful authenticity and proclaimed them to be true.

In contrast to the generalized claims and lack of specificity that characterize McConkey's account of atrocities, there is the testimony of particular witnesses whose narratives are limited to the events of which they had personal knowledge. Justina Krueger, Emanuel Reyff, Wilhelmina Inefeldt, and Lavina Eastlick each saw their families and neighbors murdered by Indians. Unlike McConkey's narrative, and unlike the allegations of Minnesota's Congressional delegation which will be considered a bit later, these narratives are specific, unstinting in their details, and exact in relating what they saw. The quotations I use here are lengthy; I have chosen to not use ellipses, so as to allow the narratives to stand on their own merit, without editing.

Justina Krueger's family learned of the outbreak and attempted to flee with a group of other settlers—a few men, mostly women and children. They were accosted by a party of Dakota who acted friendly at first, but the situation quickly deteriorated. The Indians first demanded their money and goods, and then attacked them. Just before the killings began, Krueger's husband handed her his pocketknife. When she asked him why, he told her that it was for her to remember him by, since he thought the Indians were going to kill all the men. The Indians killed more than just the men. In the attack that followed, Justina herself was so badly wounded that the Indians assumed she was dead. Hours after the massacre, she regained consciousness to find Indians scavenging among the bodies of the victims. In her narrative of the experience, she wrote:

> I saw one of these inhuman savages seize Wilhelmina Kitzman, my niece, yet alive, hold her up by the foot, her head downward, her clothes falling over her head; while holding her there by one hand, in the other he grasped a knife, with which he hastily cut the flesh around one of the legs, close to the body, and then, by twisting and wrenching, broke the ligaments and bone, until the limb was totally severed from the body, the child screaming frantically, "O God! O God!" When the limb was off, the child, thus mutilated, was thrown down on the ground, stripped of her clothing, and left to die.[38]

Emanuel Reyff was approaching his brother's homestead when a group of Indians appeared. None of the settlers were yet aware that the outbreak had begun. Reyff saw the attack as it began and hid in a tree. He later recounted what happened to his brother's family:

Just as I was coming to the cow yard the Indians were coming from the opposite direction to the house. My brother and his son, Ben, a boy [ten] years of age, were stacking hay near the house. One of the Indians shot at my brother with an arrow. It struck him under the jaw bone near the ear. As he fell from the load, the Indians grabbed him, cut off both his hands and scalped him before he was dead. Ben jumped off the stack and tried to escape, but there were about [forty] Indians and poor little Ben had no [chance]. One of the Indians grabbed him by the hair while the other Indians jumped off the hayrack, which was nearly empty, turned up the wagon tongue and tied Ben's feet together with a rope and hung him to the wagon tongue by his heels. Then they cut his pants off with a butcher knife and slashed up his body as only an Indian knows how. Then they poured [gun] powder over his body and set it on fire. He died quickly. I thanked God when he was dead. They scalped him, also. He was such a fat little fellow, and they seemed to like the job. My sister-in-law came out of the house and begged on her knees for her life. An Indian rudely seized her by the hair and held her while the other Indians drove four stakes into the ground and tied her to them; then they mutilated her body with butcher knives. After she was dead, they scalped her, too. Little Annie rushed out of the house screaming with fright. Two squaws grabbed her by the arms and cut her to pieces with butcher knives on the door step.[39]

Wilhelmina Inefeldt, whose husband was stabbed to death by the Dakota in the attack at Beaver Creek, was trying to escape with her children, her sister-in-law Mary, and several neighbors when they were attacked by a group of Indians. When the shooting started, the settlers attempted to scatter:

We jumped [from the wagon]. Mr. Houf grabbed his two little girls and ran down the bluff ahead, while Mary, my brother's wife, and I followed him. While we were running an Indian shot Mr. Houf and kicked his poor little girls to death. I could not stand this and said, "O, Mary, let us go back and die where the rest are dying." We turned and as we started an Indian raised his gun to shoot me. The cap snaped [sic] and the gun did not go off. He tried three different caps. Each one snapped. Then he put his gun down and took me by the hand and said, "Wash ta" (good). I did not want to go. There were three squaws in the crowd. One took me by each arm and the other pushed me from behind. The same Indian that tried to shoot me told Mary to sit down, while the squaws started off with me. I called back, "What is he doing with you, Mary?" She replied, "Nothing; he told me to sit down." The next moment I heard a shot fired. I asked the squaws what it meant. They told me the Indians had killed a dog. The next day I asked for Mary and they told me she was killed.[40]

Lavina Eastlick's family was among a group of settlers living in the area of Lake Shetek when the outbreak began. A Dakota whom they knew as Pawn, or Old Pawn, first acted friendly toward them and then, with a large group of Indians, precipitated an attack. The settlers, caught out on the open prairie, attempted to hide in a low-lying marsh of tall grasses that later became known as Slaughter Slough. The Indians ranged around the perimeter, firing into the slough wherever they saw the grass moving. After several people had been killed, the settlers were persuaded to come out. Their lives would be spared, they were told.

When the survivors emerged from the marsh they might have thought the worst was over. They were wrong; the killing continued, sporadically, and apparently almost by the whim of individual Indians. Lavina Eastlick, who had left her husband John dead behind her in the slough, described what happened next:

As it now began to rain, the Indians seemed to be in a great hurry. One Indian took Mrs. Koch and started. Some more of them took Mr. Ireland's two oldest girls. The largest, blackest Indian took Mrs. Duly [Duley] and myself by the hand, and started off, neither of us making any resistance. I looked back to see if the children were coming. Freddy started, when an old squaw run and struck him over the head with something, I did not know what, and pounded him on the back. She then left him to get up and come on after me, his face all streaming with blood. Not satisfied with her fiendish cruelty, she then ran after and knocked him down again, pounded him more, took him up in her hands, raised him as high as she could, and threw him down on the ground. Pawn told me to go on. I went a few steps, looked back, and saw Frank on his knees, with both hands raised, and calling "Mother!" the blood running out of his mouth in a stream.

Mrs. Smith and Mrs. Ireland were both shot on the spot where we first went to the Indians. Old Pawn told me again to go on. The Indian that was leading me went on and left me. I started again, and asked Pawn if he was going to kill me. He said he was not. I saw Mrs. Duly, with one child in her arms, and one at her side, holding on to her dress, and she was pleading for their lives. They told her the same as the rest, that they would not kill them. She had not gone three rods, when they shot her eldest son.[41] I saw Mrs. Everett running toward her husband, and an Indian just ready to take hold of her. Some Indian shot, and she fell. Pawn stopped, and loaded his gun. I trudged on, thinking how brutally my children had been murdered, and I could not help them. As I was hurrying along to overtake Mrs. Wright, Pawn shot me, the ball entering my back, and passing out at my side, just above my hip, and passing through my right arm.[42]

These narratives are each told in the first person, recounted by the people who experienced the events they were describing. Their accounts have a veracity lacking in the more histrionic tales found in most secondary sources. In *The War in Words*, Derounian-Stodola refers to "the unarguable moral status that the witness possesses merely by virtue of being a witness-participant," and that dynamic is certainly at work in these cases.[43] A statement in which a person can say, "this I saw and this I experienced," rather than "this I read or this I was told by another," has tremendous impact as testimony. Ironically, Derounian-Stodola in the same book criticizes "white histories," as she calls them, for describing the killings of defenseless women and children at Lake Shetek as a "massacre," a depiction she finds objectionable, and she includes survivor's narratives in that criticism. On the contrary—a massacre is exactly what it was, and the eyewitness testimony of the survivors makes the academic quibbling over semantics seem rather pointless when held up against the human suffering and enduring pathos of the event.

This does not mean, however, that eyewitness statements can always be accepted as truth without corroboration. Just as there is a need for critical analysis of the veracity of individual boasts (and of oral histories, as we will see in a later chapter), so there is also a need to closely examine the truthfulness of settler survivor accounts. As an example, one survivor's narrative describes in graphic detail the murder of a settler woman and her children. The narrator was herself a survivor of that attack, and she gives every indication that the events are related as she witnessed them. In reality, though, the narrator was at some distance from the killing, saw the burned remains of the bodies *after* the murders, and learned the details of how it happened from others who saw it themselves.

The account I refer to here is that of Helen Carrothers Tarble. In her narrative *The Story of My Capture and Escape*, she described how the Indians killed a woman named Mrs. Henderson by burning her alive with the corpses of her two children, who had been beaten or hacked to death; Tarble gave the impression that she saw the killing herself.[44] This is slightly at odds with an earlier statement she made about the incident. Tarble's first account appeared in Bryant's book, where her description of the incident was limited to, "We saw a fire where Mrs. Henderson had been last seen, and supposed they had burned her and her little children. This turned out to be true, as I afterward learned." There is no question that Mrs. Henderson and her children were murdered by the Dakota; Tarble's version of how they died was even substantively correct. The issue is only that Tarble did not have quite the firsthand knowledge of the killing that she implied in her later narrative. The murders were every bit as real as she said, and the details she gave seem to have been correct, but her initial implication that she was a primary witness to the crime was disingenuous.

The Tarble narratives demonstrate the necessity of examining all reports with a critical eye. With that as a condition, I maintain that the eyewitness testimonies of survivors are absolutely legitimate as historical sources. These eyewitness accounts are the same type of narratives that respected historians such as Roy Meyer have dismissed entirely with the statement "isolated instances were multiplied in the imagination of refugees and their details exaggerated to such a degree that the early accounts can no longer be accepted by sober scholarship."[45]

Meyer's point of view, which is widely shared in recent scholarship on this war, seems to hold to the idea that mutilation of bodies, whether pre- or post-mortem, is the only measurement by which atrocities can be judged, or that mutilation was the only manifestation of atrocity. By the same token, though at the opposite end of the spectrum, one might conclude from the survivor narratives I have cited above that I believe that most acts of atrocity involved the torture and murder of children. I do not; in fact, I draw the line far short of that extreme, as I will explain at the close of this chapter.

Meyer also apparently chose to not distinguish at all between first-hand accounts and second-hand reports. Had he done so, and based his claim only on the secondary sources (which would have left out most of the verifiable evidence), he would have found ample support for his argument. The secondary sources are incontrovertibly problematic, and unfortunately some of those accounts have been repeated so often as to become practically enshrined in popular histories of the war. Among these unreliable sources are the petitions that were sent to President Lincoln, protesting against any clemency for the Dakota men condemned by the military commission.

During the time that Lincoln was deliberating over the list of the 303 death sentences, he was barraged with petitions for clemency and also with demands for swift and vengeful justice. "It was, in part, a conflict between East and West," as one writer describes it, "between those living in such cities as Philadelphia and Boston, far from the threat of Indian depredations, and those in the plains, forests, and valleys of Minnesota, burying their dead, tending their wounded, and grieving for their losses."[46] Many of those who protested against clemency and who demanded that the President show no mercy to the Indians repeated, in their letters, the same litany of alleged atrocities that had recurred over and over in the popular press.

One such petitioner was a Dr. Thaddeus Williams, who in a letter to Lincoln claimed that he knew of "400 human beings butchered, their entrails torn out & their heads cut off & put between their lifeless thighs, or hoisted on a pole; their bodies gashed & cut to strips, & nailed or hung to trees; mothers with sharp fence rails passed through them & their unborn babes; children with hooks struck through their backs & hung to limbs of trees—these are the shadows which flit in the backgrounds of the picture, and cry, not only for justice, but for vengeance."[47] Dr. Williams provided no corroborating details in support of these listed outrages, and he named no victims, so his claims do not rise above the level of hearsay and are useless to the historian.

Unfortunately for the cause of justice at the time, impassioned citizens were not the only ones to fuel the hysteria over alleged Indian atrocities. Various government officials also employed unsubstantiated stories to make their case for severe punishment of the Indians, and one example of this illustrates some of the basic problems with unsubstantiated allegations of Indian atrocities.

Three members of Minnesota's Congressional delegation, headed by Senator Morton S. Wilkinson, submitted a letter to Lincoln protesting the President's consideration of clemency for some of the condemned Indians. "If this be your purpose...," they wrote, "we beg leave most respectfully to protest against it." They went on to enumerate "a few facts, which are well known to our people, but delicacy forbids that we should mention the names of the parties to whom we refer." The Congressmen described how:

> In one instance, some ten or twelve of these Indians visited the house of a worthy farmer, who was at the time engaged with his sons stacking wheat. They stealthily approached the place where the honest farmer was at work, and seizing the opportunity shot the father and two sons at the stack. They then went into the house, killed two little children in the presence of their mother, who was quite ill of consumption, and then took the sick mother and a beautiful little daughter, thirteen years of age, into captivity. But this is not all, nor is it the most appalling feature of this awful tragedy. Its horror is yet to be revealed....[48]
> 
> There is another instance of a girl eighteen years of age. We knew her well before and at the time of her capture. She was as refined and beautiful a girl as we had in the State. None had more or better friends; no one was more worthy of them than she. She was taken captive by these Indians, her arms were tied behind her and she was tied fast to the ground and ravished by some eight or ten of these convicts before the cords were unloosed from her limbs. The girl, fortunately, lived to testify against the wretches who had thus violated her. Without being more specific we will state that nearly all the women who were captured were violated in this way.[49]

There are numerous problems with these claims. First and foremost, by omitting identifying details with the excuse that "delicacy forbids that we should mention the names of the parties to whom we refer," the Congressional letter was just so much hearsay and allegation, providing no corroboration for any of its claims. Nineteenth century sensibilities might have prevented the naming of names, but historical accuracy requires it, and that accuracy is lacking here.

Another problem is the "girl eighteen years of age," whom the Congressional delegation alleged was gang raped by the Indians. Again, no name was provided, so if Lincoln had wished to verify this account for himself in the course of his review, he could not have. There *are* cases in the trial transcripts, as we have already seen, where Dakota were charged with rape, and where names were given of the women who were the victims because they personally testified against the accused. There is no case in the records of the commission, however, where an 18-year-old girl testified against "eight or ten" Indians who had raped her. (This unnamed girl may have been Mattie Williams, but if it was truly she then the Congressional petitioners embellished her testimony to a considerable degree.) Finally, the claim that "nearly all the women who were captured were violated in this way" makes an enormous general allegation, one the Congressmen made no effort to support with facts or evidence. For these reasons, these accusations would be inadmissible in a court of law, which was exactly the forum into which they were attempting to interject themselves by seeking to affect Lincoln's clemency decision.

If these are the only type of reports that historians consider when they argue that stories of Indian atrocities are exaggerated beyond the tolerance of scholarship, then they fail to include the full range of evidence. The eye-witness accounts of survivors cannot be dismissed out of hand. Atrocities *were* committed; most of these atrocities *were* violations of established law (both civil and military) and therefore were rightly classified as criminal acts. The perpetrators of these crimes absolutely should have been arraigned and prosecuted in a court of law. Sibley's military commission, in spite of its acknowledged shortcomings, was a legally convened court of law. It may have been military law, it may have been field-expedient and irregular, and there is no question that it committed some grievous judicial errors as well as ignoring the requirements of due process in most of the trials that were held after October 15. Most of its sentences were unjust, but it was legal in spite of all that—legal, unfortunately, does not always mean fair, and certainly not in this instance.

It is important to remember, though, that there are at least two sides in every quarrel, and the Dakota were not the only belligerents in 1862. The American side of the war also factors into this discussion of atrocities, and not only as victims. Atrocities occurred during the Dakota War, and it is a historical fact that the statistical majority of them were committed by Indians. It is also true that not *all* atrocities were the acts of Indians. The record shows beyond doubt that white men perpetrated atrocities as well, and these must also be acknowledged in any balanced assessment of the war. Two cases, in particular, serve to illustrate this fact.

When the fighting ended at the Battle of Wood Lake, leaving Sibley's troops in command of the field, the Dakota were unable to recover all their dead, as they usually tried to do. In the aftermath of the battle, soldiers scalped the Indian corpses they found, taking the hair as trophies. Sibley was outraged by this. The next day, he published an order that forbade any further incidents of scalp-taking or mutilation of dead Indians by troops in his command. Some historians, when considering this incident, have pointed out that the troops in question were members of the irregular Renville's Rangers. Most of these men were part Dakota themselves—"mixed bloods," in the parlance of that era—and so scalping the enemy was as much a cultural norm for them as it was for the Indians. That distinction is irrelevant. The fact is that troops under U.S. Army command engaged in the same sort of behavior that drew outraged protests when the victims were white and the perpetrators were Indians. Sibley felt that there was no excuse for it, no matter who was doing it, and he would not tolerate it. Unfortunately, he was in the minority.

What Sibley's men did as a spontaneous act at Wood Lake, the state of Minnesota had already sanctioned as official policy. In the *Annual Report of the Adjutant General for 1863*, the report that covered all military activity in the state for the previous year (and so dealt with the Dakota War), there is a rather mundane list which falls under the heading "Bills paid out from the military contingent fund." Most of the items on the list are just the sort of ordinary, work-a-day minutiae common to routine military operations: "Jan 3, stencil plates and paint, $23.00 paid to Williams Bros.; June 21, transporting arms from St. Peter to LeSeur, $4.70 paid to William Seeger; Aug 26, repairing and cleaning arms, $55.29 paid to P. Morison; Nov. 5, two copies of U.S. Military Laws, $10.00 paid to J.A. Callum, et cetera."[50] Basically, this was all the sort of humdrum, mundane matters of logistics, ordinance, transportation and administration that one finds in most military lists.

In the midst of all the monotonous accounting, however, there are several other items of a markedly different cast: "August 7, bounty for killing one Sioux warrior, $75.00

paid to W.M. Allen; August 31, tanning Indian scalp, $5.00 paid to Julius Schmidt; October 9, bounty for killing one Sioux warrior, $25.00 paid to J. C. Davis."[51] The Adjutant General's report makes it clear that the official policy of the state made killing Dakota Indians a matter of financial gain. As the entry for "tanning Indian scalp" shows, this particular atrocity, at least, was recognized, condoned and rewarded by the state government.[52] Some Indians committed worse acts of violence in the war than did the whites, but no one can claim that white men never carried out any acts of atrocities themselves.

Isaac Heard, in his book after the war, not only condoned Minnesota's official attitude toward an almost indiscriminate killing of Indians, he waxed eloquent on it. "Henceforth, for many a year on our borders," Heard wrote, "Indian hunters will be found who will emulate those of whom the early history of our country tells, bent on war to the death with the savage foe."[53] Heard used the phrase "hunters"—not "fighters" or "soldiers"—and there is a distinct and distasteful difference between the terms. He continued in the same vein, saying, "Men whose wives and children have been brutally murdered and hearthstones blasted forever, will never rest till blood has answered for blood. God's fierce avengers in the future! success [sic] to their unerring rifles."[54] What Heard was describing here was not justice of the judicial sort found in a court of law, but vigilantism that sought revenge more than judicial redress of wrong.

Heard's account also provides us with at least one more instance of white men committing an act that would, without question, have been called an atrocity if the perpetrators were Indians. Describing the battle of New Ulm, Heard quoted Charles E. Flandrau, who said that "a half-breed named Le Blanc lay in the grass as our men approached, and fired and wounded one of them." Attempting to escape, Le Blanc was shot on the run; not killed outright, but mortally wounded. "He was soon finished," Flandrau reported, "his head cut off and scalped."[55] From Flandrau's tone, there was nothing extraordinary about this event—he relayed the incident of decapitation and scalping almost as if one would expect nothing else in the situation.

The florid language that Heard used was not unique to him; in fact, his language on the subject was actually mild compared to others who were writing at the time. Jane Grey Swisshelm was a pioneering newspaper editor, feminist and abolitionist who had recently arrived in Minnesota from back east just before the war began. She was starry-eyed and idealistic at first, especially in her perceptions of the state's Indian population, but the realities of war shattered her naïve assumptions about life on the frontier. In the beginning she had "a highly romanticized image of the indigenous populations of the frontier, a benevolent attitude toward them, and boundless optimism in their ability to assimilate," but her dearly cherished ideas did not survive their first encounter with the harsh reality of Indian warfare.[56]

From being an idealistic admirer of the Indian, Swisshelm changed into one of the most ferociously anti–Indian voices at work in the public forum. She called for the forced removal of all Dakota from the lands ceded to them by the Federal Treaty of 1851, and advocated the legalized killing of any who would not go. She even pressed for a state law to this effect. "Let our present Legislature offer a bounty of $10 for every Sioux scalp, outlaw the tribe and so let the matter rest," she wrote in an editorial. "It will cost five times that much to exterminate them by regular modes of warfare and they should be got rid of in the cheapest and quickest manner."[57] Swisshelm called for an open hunting season on all Dakota people as if they were dangerous predatory animals. She "demanded that the state suspend the usual procedures for prosecuting and penalizing acts of murder and that it authorize settlers to proceed on their own to capture and execute any Native suspected of killing whites."[58] Revenge, vigilantism and war between races and cultures—war to the bloody end—were exactly what Swisshelm and other voices were calling for in the autumn of 1862. Swisshelm obviously never committed an actual atrocity herself, but she was stridently vocal in inciting others to commit them, and therefore a considerable amount of moral responsibility attaches to her.

Finally, in a careful examination of the debate over atrocities and the question of whether or not atrocities can be proven to have occurred during the war, it is possible to miss the forest while counting the trees. The evidence shows that atrocities are an undeniable part of the history of the Dakota War, and it also shows that atrocities were committed by both sides; the vast majority of them by Indians, but some were undeniably the work of Americans. This is where I strongly disagree with the interpretation used by Meyer and others: that atrocities can only be defined as those acts associated with the mutilation of bodies. There were things done in the war that were far worse than the mutilation of corpses, and the record includes far more cases of atrocity than just those characterized by mutilation.

Even if we concede the cultural differences in the way the war was fought, as when William Folwell noted that Dakota warfare was characterized by "hundreds of young braves to whom the eagle feather was the most precious thing in life; and that could be won by the murder of a baby as easily as by the killing of a foe in equal combat," we are not bound to accept those differences as sacrosanct and beyond condemnation.[59] To put it bluntly, the killing of every child was an atrocity. Every time the Indians killed an unarmed man or woman it was an act of murder rather than war, and thus an atrocity. Every rape was an atrocity. When the white residents of Henderson and New Ulm attacked defenseless Indian prisoners, those instances of mob violence were atrocities. The unnamed Dakota baby murdered by a white woman in the Henderson mob attack was just as much a victim of an atrocity as were the Buce, Eastlick and Reyff children who were murdered by Indians. The offering of bounties for killing Dakotas was an example of state-sanctioned atrocity.

Whatever provocation the Dakota had for the war, whatever legitimate grievances they had (and they had many, of that there is no doubt), none of that provides justification for massacre and the wholesale slaughter of random victims. Nothing justifies the murder of women and children and the rape of captive girls. No matter what excuses are offered, in the final analysis none of the rationalizations put forward in the historiography can justify wreaking that kind of destruction on fellow human beings. This is why a share of the collective burden of guilt belongs to some white residents of Minnesota in 1862. Just as the Dakota were not justified in venting their anger on the innocent, so were Americans not justified in committing atrocities in the spirit of vengeance.

A trend in New Western histories has been to dismiss or disregard the full range of Indian atrocities in this and other 19th century American frontier wars. When atrocities are reluctantly acknowledged as historical realities, it is often with the caveat that such acts by Native Americans were reactions to European-American provocations. That is little more than whitewash. As already established early in this book, the reality is that for the Indian cultures of the American Midwest, war was a way of life that existed long before Europeans ever appeared on the continent. Whatever the reasons for the outbreak of the Dakota War, once the war began many Dakota warriors seemed more interested in pillage and murder than they did in actually making a concerted military effort to drive settlers from the contested territory, or in eliminating the combat power of the U.S. Army which represented the ultimate threat to their security. Such an effort would have been doomed to failure in the face of the Americans' overwhelming advantages of population, technology and military force, but at least such an effort would have been morally unassailable.

It has also been argued that allegations of Indian atrocities, in this and other wars of the American West, are essentially expressions of an anti–Native bias on the part of white commentators. The use of the word "savages" to describe Indians in these incidents is particularly cited as evidence of nefarious racial prejudices at play in unfair depictions of Indian actions.[60] There is no denying that we encounter this word in the history of the Dakota War, and it is certainly true that there is an undeniable element of racial animosity in much of the American writings on the subject in the 19th century, but things are not always as simple as they seem. Bruce Tap, in his book *Over Lincoln's Shoulder*, discusses an incident that generated much the same sort of reaction and similar language.

Tap describes how Secretary of the Navy Gideon Welles, who was critical of much of the official language in the furor leading up to the executions at Mankato, was disinclined to believe everything he heard about stories of atrocities and mayhem. Referring to one particular incident, which took place far from Minnesota, Welles wrote in his diary, "There must be something in these terrible reports but I distrust Congressional committees. They exaggerate."[61] The situation to which he referred was one where horrible atrocities were being described in lurid detail in the newspapers and shouted about by politicians. Women and children were said to have been killed; prisoners burned alive, others buried alive; most men not taken prisoner at all but killed outright even as they tried to surrender. The public was outraged, and calls for blood vengeance filled the press. Welles did not agree. "The idea of retaliation—killing man for man—which is the popular noisy demand," he wrote, "is barbarous, and I cannot assent to or advise it."[62] He was in the dissenting minority. Public opinion demanded that the massacre—for a massacre it most certainly was—be punished by the most severe means possible.

A Congressional paper was published detailing the results of its committee's investigation into the outrage. "No cruelty which the most fiendish malignity could devise was omitted by these murderers," the report declared, going on to say that "no language we could use can adequately describe" the degree of atrocities.[63] What the official report claimed to be unable to describe, soldiers felt determined to avenge. One soldier from Iowa wrote that "We want revenge and we are bound to have it one way or another. They must pay for these deeds of cruelty."[64] The context in which he wrote this was to describe how he and his comrades had killed 23 prisoners to extract some measure of retaliation for the atrocities the enemy had committed. At the same time, while men were dying for no other reason than that they were scapegoats for the actual perpetrators of the massacre, some critics claimed that no massacre had ever happened and that reports of such were wildly exaggerated.

The debate continued unabated. These atrocities were so terrible, one official wrote, that they "could only be conceived of by *fiends* [italics in the original]. These devils are not fit to live on God's earth & would disgrace hell if they enter there."[65] More vitriolic language followed. "Retaliation," one Senator declared, "has in all ages of the world been a means of bringing inhuman and savage foes to a sense of their duty."[66]

Reading this vengeful hyperbole, the reader might assume the event described is another incident in the bloody history of U.S.–Indian conflict. In fact, it is not. All these quotations come from 1864, when Confederate troops under the command of Nathan Bedford Forrest massacred Union soldiers at Fort Pillow in Tennessee. In this case, both the perpetrators of the atrocities and the outraged voices demanding vengeance were white Americans. In the eyes of these Northern commentators, Southerners waging a war in the cause of secession were fighting with methods that were immoral, cruel, brutal and, yes, *savage*.

This is not to suggest that the language many white commentators used to describe Indians in the days after the outbreak of the Dakota War was not vitriolic, prejudicial and inciting others to violence, because it certainly was. I include this example of the public reaction to the Fort Pillow massacre only to show that denigrating language and bloody-minded vengeance were not directed solely against Indians, but were on occasion used against other whites as well. This one incident by itself certainly does not even begin to balance the equation and does not excuse the long record of racial hatred expressed against Native peoples—that is not my point. I am suggesting, rather, that when confronted with stories of atrocities committed against their own people, many Americans reacted in similar ways, with similar language, no matter who the offenders were. Atrocities elicited outrage, and the racial identity of the perpetrators was at times a minor detail.

# 22

# The Power of the Self-Perpetuating Myth

Perhaps the most persistent atrocity story of the Dakota War is that Indians murdered white babies by nailing them to trees. As alleged atrocities go, this one is more heinous and vile than almost all the others, and this is the one that seems to strike the deepest emotional chord with most readers. It is also one of the most frequently recurring atrocity stories in the literature of the war. But is it true?

In her book *Dakota War Whoop*, Harriet Bishop McConkey describes the murder of a party of settlers this way:

> In one instance, several families, not far away from home, had congregated in consultation as to their course, when they were overtaken by the Indians, at the head of whom was "Cut Nose," one of whom it might emphatically be said, "Ye are of your father the devil, and his works ye do." The first volley killed the few men, which the women and children seeing, in their defenseless state, huddled more closely together in the wagons, and bending low their heads, drew their shawls tightly over them. Two of the fiends held the horses while Cut Nose jumped into a wagon, containing eleven, and deliberately cleft the head of each, while, stupefied with horror, and powerless from fright, each awaited their turn, knowing the tomahawk would soon tear through their flesh and bones, in like manner. Then kicking these butchered victims from the wagon, they filled it with plunder from the burning houses, leaving them a prey to vultures and ravenous wolves.
>
> Forcing an infant from its mother's arms, with the bolt of a wagon they fastened it to a tree, and holding the mother before it, compelled her to witness its dying agonies. They then chopped off her legs and arms, and left her to bleed to death. And thus they butchered twenty-five, within as many rods.[1]

The account of the baby pinned to a tree with a wagon bolt and the mother dismembered first appeared in book form in McConkey, but she did not attribute it to any particular source. After McConkey, the account of this atrocity underwent several retellings that mirrored her language so closely that it seems highly likely that the subsequent authors were at least well-acquainted with her book, if they did not actually use it as their direct source. Isaac Heard recounted the same story almost word for word on page 261 in his book *History of the Sioux Wars and Massacres of 1862 and 1863:*

> A party of settlers were gathered together for flight when the savages approached; the defenseless, helpless women and children, huddled together in the wagons, bending down their heads, and drawing over them still closer their shawls. Cut-nose, while two others held the horses, leaped into a wagon that contained eleven, mostly children, and deliberately, in cold blood, tomahawked them all—cleft open the head of each, while the others, stupefied with horror, powerless with fright, as they heard the heavy, dull blows crash and tear through flesh and bones, awaited their turn. Taking an infant from its

mother's arms, before her eyes, with a bolt from one of the wagons they riveted it through its body to the fence, and left it there to die, writhing in agony. After holding for a while the mother before this agonizing spectacle, they chopped off her arms and legs, and left her to bleed to death.[2]

The similarities between Heard's version and McConkey's earlier account are obvious; nonetheless, Heard attributed the story to *Harper's Magazine* and not McConkey. More importantly, he did not cite any survivor's eyewitness account, nor any recorded testimony against any Indian defendant that had supported such a charge in trial.

The *Harper's Magazine* account was written by Adrian J. Ebell. Ebell's article was replete with sensational accounts of horrible scenes of massacre and mutilation, but he did not indicate the sources of most of the stories he relayed. His version of the baby-killing atrocity story is the earliest second-hand account found in the historical record, and a comparison of his language and that of later retellings makes it clear that his was probably the foundation upon which many subsequent versions were based. As Ebell told the story:

> Taking an infant from its mother's arms, before her eyes, with a bolt from one of the wagons, they riveted it through its body to the fence, and left it there to die, writhing in agony. After holding for a while the mother before this agonizing spectacle, they chopped off her arms and legs and left her to bleed to death. Thus they butchered twenty-five within a quarter of an acre.[3]

The chain of evidence is inadequate. It seems, however, that the story was first published in *Harper's* and was borrowed next by McConkey and then Heard. The story is not attributed to any particular person as an original source, which could help to verify it. In spite of this lack of detail, though, it is possible to say with a high degree of confidence that this story is a version of the massacre that took place near Beaver Creek on August 18. The trial of Cut Nose (Mahpeokanaje) was Case No. 96 in the transcripts, and there was an eyewitness to the event, Lewis Thiele, who identified Cut Nose as one of the perpetrators of the Beaver Creek massacre. Thiele's sworn testimony was that Cut Nose "shot one man off a wagon. I saw him strike the persons in the wagon with a knife. There were 4 women and 11 children. They were all killed."[4] Among the victims were Thiele's wife and four-year old daughter, so he is not likely to have forgotten what he saw. But nowhere in his testimony did Thiele make any mention of Cut Nose impaling a baby with a wagon bolt—Thiele had no reason to pull any punches in his statement against Cut Nose, so it is reasonable to assume that he made no mention of such an act because he did not see such a thing happen.

Even so, the story appears repeatedly in the literature of the Dakota War. Daniel Buck, the former judge of the Minnesota Supreme Court who in 1904 published a history of the outbreak, repeats the atrocity story of the baby nailed to a fence with a wagon bolt and uses almost exactly the same wording as McConkey:

> One of the most fiendish of the Indians was Cut-Nose, so called because in a fight with [John] Other-Day the latter bit out a piece of his nose. A party of settlers, mostly children, were gathered for flight, and got into a wagon, when Cut-Nose tomahawked them all, one at a time, striking each on its head, while the others, horror stricken and stupefied with fright and powerless to resist, heard the dull, heavy blows crash through the flesh and bone, awaiting their turn. Then taking another infant from its mother's arms, with an iron bolt from the wagon, he thrust it through its body and nailed it to the fence, and left it to die writhing in mortal agony, holding the mother for a while in full view of her dying child. He then chopped off her arms and legs and left her there to bleed to death.[5]

This particular atrocity story that McConkey tells, and Heard and Buck retell—the image of the baby nailed to a tree (or a door, or a wall, as it appears in other versions)—is almost *de rigueur* in popular histories of the Dakota War. It appears so frequently in any recounting of atrocities that after a while one almost expects to encounter it, but there are some good reasons to doubt its accuracy. As yet, no first-person eyewitness testimony that describes a single case of this specific atrocity has been located by researchers. The closest we are able to come to an eye-witness account of this atrocity, as we will see, is a second-hand attribution.

To be clear, this lack of first-person evidence does not conclusively prove that this particular atrocity *never* happened, but if it happened at all it was a much more isolated occurrence than the contemporary reports made it out to be. It is more likely that the horrific idea of babies nailed to trees (or doors or fences or any other object) captured the public imagination and became so indelibly associated with the war that it received constant repetition in spite of the fact that there seems to have been no hard evidence to support it. This is not to say that the Indians did not kill children, because they did, literally by the score. The records show conclusively that some settler children were shot; some were killed with hatchets or knives; others beaten to death; and in several cases, children were burned to death. The eye-witness accounts related in the preceding chapter, and numerous others which I have not cited, all attest to that. And in many cases, those children are identified by name and age. But there is absolutely no reliable evidence to support the accusation that the Dakota went around nailing babies to trees as a matter of course, habit, or custom.

In spite of this lack of evidentiary verification, McConkey's list of unsubstantiated atrocities shows up repeatedly in other, later accounts of the war, and the baby-nailed-to-a-tree story has been regenerated over and over. Taking the story at the point where it first appears in McConkey, the holes in the evidence are easily identified. McConkey named Cut Nose as the perpetrator of this crime, and that detail by itself casts some doubt on the accuracy of the story. If such information were known at large, it would be expected that these acts would have been incorporated into the specifications of the charges against Cut Nose when his case came before the commission for trial, as happened in other cases where details about the victims were known. Nothing like this incident is recounted in the transcripts of Cut Nose's trial before the military commission. Stephen R. Riggs, who spoke with Cut Nose at length more than once, never made reference to such an incident, as he almost certainly would have had he known of it. As historical evidence, then, McConkey's version of this incident is inadequate and is best consigned to the rubbish heap of sensational fiction.

There is at least one eyewitness testimony of an atrocity that is similar to but not precisely like the baby-killing story we are concerned with here. One of the settlers who escaped from the Lake Shetek community was a man named Aaron Myers, who with his wife and children and some wounded survivors set out by ox-drawn wagon in an attempt to reach New Ulm. When the oxen gave out, the group decided that Myers would try to get to New Ulm alone and bring back help. In a narrative he gave some 40 years after the war, Myers described how he "started and went straight across the country, passing several houses, and at one place I saw four dead bodies, the father, the mother, the son, and the 6 year old daughter, the latter having been nailed up to the side of the house, naked, arms and limbs extended, and large nails driven through hands and feet."⁶ The similarities are obvious, and what Myers described was absolutely an atrocity, but a somewhat different one than the specific allegation propagated by McConkey *et al.*

The closest that we can come to an eye-witness account is the second-hand testimony I referred to above. Mary Schwandt's brother August, who survived the attack on their family, said that he saw his pregnant sister Karollna Walz killed by Indians who then cut her open and nailed her unborn child to a tree, still moving. The problem, though, is that even this account comes into the record second-hand:

> The daughter of Mr. Schwandt, enceinte, was cut open (as was learned afterwards), the child taken alive from its mother and nailed to a tree. The son of Mr. Schwandt, aged thirteen years, who had been beaten by the Indians until dead, as was supposed, was present, and saw the entire tragedy. He saw the child taken alive from the body of his sister, Mrs. Waltz, and nailed to a tree in the yard. It struggled some time after the nails were driven through it. This occurred in the forenoon of Monday, 18th of August, 1862.⁷

August Schwandt did not leave a personal narrative of his own, and the story as quoted above is relayed through Justina Krueger's narrative. Because of this remove from the incident, I do not ascribe the same level of authenticity to this report that I do to ones which are delivered first-hand by people who actually witnessed the events they described.

As a general allegation, this particular atrocity is usually included in lists along with other acts of brutality of which the Indians were accused. John G. Nicolay, one of President Lincoln's secretaries, published two reports of his western travels during the time of the Dakota War. In one of them, he reproduced an address that Minnesota Governor Alexander Ramsey made to the Minnesota legislature. As oratory, it is a set-piece example of 19th century verbosity, heavy on color and emotionality. Ramsey said that the war had involved:

> Infants hewn into bloody chips of flesh, or nailed alive to door posts to linger out their little life in mortal agony, or torn untimely from the womb of the murdered mother, and in cruel mockery cast in fragments on her pulseless and bleeding breast; rape joined to murder in one awful tragedy; young girls, even children of tender years, outraged by their brutal ravishers, till death ended their shame and suffering; women held in captivity to undergo the horrors of a living death; whole families burned alive; and as if their devilish fury could not glut itself with outrages on the living, its last efforts exhausted in mutilating the bodies of the dead; such are the spectacles, and a thousand nameless horrors besides, which their first experience of Indian war has burned into the brains and hearts of our frontier people....⁸

Isaac Heard, whose knowledge of the war and the resulting military commission trials was much closer and more personal than Ramsey's (but who still repeated McConkey's account almost verbatim, as we have already seen), cited almost the same list of atrocities in his book:

> Children were nailed living to tables and doors, and knives and tomahawks thrown at them until they perished from fright and physical pain. The womb of the pregnant mother was ripped open, the palpitating infant torn forth, cut into bits, and thrown into the face of the dying woman. The hands and heads of the victims were cut off, their hearts ripped out, and other disgusting mutilations inflicted. Whole families were burned alive in their homes.⁹

In spite of all the reasonable doubts as to this story's accuracy, it has become a standard part of the literature of the Dakota War, most often repeated in general terms. In 1959, C. M. Oehler published *The Great Sioux Uprising*, a text which has become part of the canon and is frequently and deservedly cited in later works. Oehler seems to have accepted this particular atrocity story at face value. "Children were nailed to doors," he wrote, "spikes through their arms and legs...."[10] Nearly 50 years later, Hank Cox, in his 2005 book *Lincoln and the Sioux Uprising of 1862*, repeats the story of a child being nailed to a tree at least three times (twice on page 51 and again on page 75 of his text), and does so without attribution or citation of any kind. Most of the atrocities that Cox lists seem to be drawn directly from McConkey, and he apparently accepts her version of events without question or qualification.

In the case of this particular story, when we try to trace it back to its original source, the results are inconclusive and unsatisfactory. This provides a clear example of the consequence of writers simply repeating unvetted stories from earlier sources—this is the insidious process by which unsubstantiated hearsay is introduced into the canon as historical fact. From a historian's perspective, therefore, this story must be classified with other reports of dubious authenticity; but this has not prevented the self-perpetuating cycle of wild claims from continuing through new rounds of books that accept and repeat the most lurid of the atrocity stories, without any effort to examine the sources or validate the evidence. This is doubly injurious to the accurate history of the war, because it reinforces fiction at the expense of fact. It is precisely this sort of unsubstantiated allegation which is cited by commentators past and present who would deny all atrocity stories out of hand. Until some corroborating evidence can be found, the shocking story of the baby nailed to a fence/tree/wall/door must be regarded as lurid allegation rather than an actual and verifiable historical incident. It may have happened, but there is no incontrovertible proof that it ever did, and that is where we must leave it.

# Part Five

# The Aftermath

*Why must the innocent thus suffer and sorrow and die?*—Daniel Buck

# 23

# Misspelled Names, Misplaced Records and Mistaken Identities

In researching the trials that followed the Dakota War, a historian is sooner or later faced with the inescapable conclusion that the military commission not only played fast and loose with judicial due process in many of the trials; it also was disturbingly lax in its handling of some of the basic administrative details. It would be an overstatement to say that the record is rife with examples of shoddy clerical work, but there are enough examples of it to be problematic. Three particular issues come up in the history of the military commission: misplaced records, misspelled names, and mistaken identities.

The trial transcripts themselves, the single most important primary source related to the military commission, actually were missing for decades. Until 1927, when Minneapolis printer Marion Satterlee published his small book *The Court Proceedings in the Trial of Dakota Indians Following the Massacre in Minnesota in August 1862*, the case-by-case details of the trial had been all but lost. Before Satterlee's book, the trial transcripts of the military commission had never been available for public review; in fact, the transcripts were buried in the black hole of government bureaucracy for more than 60 years.

In 1862, General Pope sent the original transcripts of the trials to President Lincoln for his review. After narrowing the list to 40 names, Lincoln sent the transcripts on to the Senate, along with his report on his clemency decisions, as called for by the resolution sponsored by Minnesota Senator Morton Wilkinson. Once in the hands of the Senate, the transcripts dropped out of sight. The Minnesota Historical Society asked for copies of the transcripts in 1881, but to no avail; the War Department said that the transcripts were not on file in their archives and never had been. The Adjutant General's Office, the Department of the Interior and the Bureau of Indian Affairs likewise denied any knowledge of the transcripts' whereabouts. Lawyers for the Sisseton and Wapeton Bands of Sioux Indians requested the transcripts in 1901 in support of a civil case then being heard by the U.S. Court of Claims, but were again told that the transcripts could not be located.

The transcripts were finally turned up by William Folwell in the early 1920s. Folwell was a professional and thorough historian who, in the words of John Isch, "never did suffer fools gladly."[1] Apparently, the records had been archived by the Senate after the Congressional review of the trials, and there they were promptly forgotten. Another historian, Dr. Newton D. Mereness, arranged for photostatic copies of the transcripts to be made for the Minnesota Historical Society in 1927, and those were the source of Satterlee's book. Copies of the original court transcripts are now filed as P1423, U.S. Army Military Commissions, Sioux Trial Commissions, 1–392, Boxes 1–3, in the Minnesota Historical Society archival collection.

In Gary Clayton Anderson's 2012 speech at Gustavus Adolphus College, a presentation we have already considered several times for its misrepresentations of the history, Anderson incredibly claimed that it was he, with the help of an archivist, who located the misplaced transcripts in the Senate files of the National Archives sometime in the 1980s. "I found all those records then," he said, "and had them copied; they're now in the Minnesota Historical Society."[2] If Dr. Anderson is really trying to say that he was the person responsible for returning the trial transcripts to Minnesota, then he is claiming a credit that rightly belongs to other men—Folwell and Mereness beat him to it by about 60 years.

While the misplaced trial transcripts were a problem for historians more than anyone else, their inaccessibility was scarcely a matter of life or death. Another document was misplaced, however, which was nothing less than a matter of life and death. As we saw in a previous chapter, someone in the military chain of command, either Sibley himself or a member of his staff, lost track of the all-important list of names the president himself had written out on December 6.

This was no off-hand laundry list, and it was not an arbitrary list of hard to pronounce Indian names. It was nothing less than life to the 264 men whose names were left off it, and it was a hanging death to the 39 men whose names were on it. In spite of the gravity of the president's list, the military managed to misplace it. This was the reason that Sibley wrote his hasty, "confidential" letter to Stephen Riggs, asking the missionary if by any chance he happened to have the list in his possession.

More than 150 years later, the why and how of the execution order's misplacement remains a mystery. The document was hardly the sort of thing one might casually misplace—almost everyone in Minnesota had been waiting for the president's review decision for weeks, and the death list had an immediate importance attached to it.

In the matter of names, the trial records and subsequent histories created their own fog of confusion about how certain names should be spelled. That this would happen when the court was transcribing Indian names is hardly surprising—as several historians have pointed out, many of the Indians tried before the commission had never before had their names written down in any language, so accurate transcription presented its own particular challenge.

Right from the outset, the commission's recorder recognized the challenge of trying to accurately render Indian names in a language not geared to their transcription. For this reason, almost all of the Dakota names in the trial transcripts were written out phonetically. In an attempt to clarify who was who in the records, the recorder also identified each defendant by a case number. The thought was that this would keep the confusion to a minimum.

Difficulties with spelling Dakota names was perhaps to be expected, but the records

### 23. Misspelled Names, Misplaced Records and Mistaken Identities 193

also show that the commission did not bother to ensure that they spelled names of white people correctly, either. Mary Schwandt, one of the young German settler women who were captured by the Dakota, and who was the victim of repeated sexual assaults, was several times sworn in by the commission to give testimony in trials. In spite of the fact that several recorders, including Stephen Riggs, spelled her name correctly in their interviews with her, the commission itself recorded her name as "Mary Swan," and never corrected the mistake.

Sometimes the misspelled names crept into the histories of the war and resisted most attempts at correction. Where this provides a problem for historians is that when a principal figure shows up with multiple spellings of the same name, it becomes necessary to ensure that one is dealing with the same person and not several different people. In an illustrative case, Laura Duley, one of the survivors of the massacre at Slaughter Slough, and her husband William Duley, the man who sprang the gallows trap at the executions in Mankato, appears in some accounts with the last name "Duly"; Harriet McConkey renders the name as "Dooley." The family name of Minnie Buce Carrigan appears in the Renville County records as "Busse." Wilhelmina Inefeldt, whose husband was killed in the outbreak and whose narrative I cited earlier, is in some sources listed as "Eindenfeldt." A man named Max Haack, killed in Renville County, shows up in some records as "Heck," or "Hack." Justina Krueger, whose narrative we read earlier, appears in some source as "Kreuger," and most often as "Krieger."

The most serious mistakes in the records of the commission and its trials, though, are in the documented cases of mistaken identity that resulted in the deaths of innocent men. When President Lincoln wrote out the list of the 40 Dakota whose death sentences he confirmed, he spelled each name phonetically, differentiated by hyphens. To ensure that there was no doubt as to which man was associated with which name, the president also identified each prisoner by the individual case number used by the commission in the trials.

Acting as the principle interpreter for the Dakota, Stephen Riggs was closely involved in this part of the process at the prison in Mankato. Remembering how the authorities separated the condemned men from the rest of the prisoners a few days before the executions, Riggs said that the case numbers were the principle method used to correctly identify the men on the death list. "In the findings of the commission they were all numbered," he wrote in his autobiography, "and the order for the executions was given in accordance with these numbers."[3] It was at this point that the fatal problem arose. "[N]o one could remember which number attached to which person," Riggs recalled. "The only way of avoiding mistakes was by examining closely the individual charges."[4] In the end, it devolved to one person to make the final selection. "To Joseph R. Brown [the former Indian Agent], who better than any other man knew all the condemned men—and he did not recognize all perfectly—was mainly committed the work of selecting those who were to be hanged."[5] Brown, with Riggs assisting, called out the names of those condemned. As the Dakota came forward in response to their names, they were segregated in a different area of the prison.

The safeguard did not prevent at least two errors. "Extraordinary care was meant to be used," Riggs wrote in his autobiography, "but after it was all over, when we came to compare their own stories and confessions, made a day or two before their death, with the papers of condemnation, the conviction was forced upon us that two mistakes had occurred."[6] Much has been made of this in writings on the 1862 executions, and numerous misconceptions have arisen from it. It is true that at least one man, Chaska, was hanged for a crime he did not commit, but that is not the same at all as saying that he was completely innocent of any crime, as we will see in a moment.

The other man whose execution Riggs referred to as a mistake has sometimes been assumed to be Tatagaga, who was one of the youngest Dakota tried and convicted by the military commission. Like most of the others, he was charged under the stereotyped charge sheet, with the additional specification that he had murdered Amos Huggins, a missionary whose wife's narrative was included in Chapter 2. The South Dakota historian Doane Robinson, writing in 1904, claimed that soon after Tatagaga was hanged with the other 37 Indians, evidence was produced that "reasonably well established that he was not guilty. He was a boy and present when Amos was killed but the act was undoubtedly performed by a Lower [Agency] Indian...."[7] The case may not be as simple as all that, however.

It was clearly established that Tatagaga admitted to being armed when he entered Amos Huggins' house; he said as much in his trial. This made him complicit in an act of felony-murder, even if he did not himself shoot Huggins, a standard of guilt which is a well-established precept of American law. If a man carrying a weapon, in the company of an accomplice, enters another man's house and the resident is killed by the accomplice, the first man would have a hard time arguing that he was completely innocent of complicity, even if he himself did not fire the fatal shot or strike the killing blow.

That being said, it is also true that there were mitigating details in Tatagaga's case, such as the fact that he was apparently (and widely) known to be feeble-minded, in the parlance of the time. This might not have shielded him from the murder charge, but it was a factor that today would almost certainly be taken into account during trial. In 1862, however, the judicial standards on mental illness were altogether different, and that was true whether the accused was a Indian or white.

Chaska, for his part, has frequently been seen as one of the truly tragic cases in the whole affair. It seems quite clear that he was not only hanged for a crime that he never committed, but what was even worse, he was hanged for a crime for which he was not even *convicted*. He was truly the victim of mistaken identity. This is not to say, however, that he was absolutely innocent of complicity in any crimes. In fact, Chaska had been tried and convicted for participation in the murder of a man named George Gleason; by his own admission he was present at the killing, but he maintained that he had never actually fired at the victim and had only "snapped" his gun in Gleason's direction. At the least, he also could be said to be guilty of being an accomplice in the commission of a murder. But the important point here is that Chaska's case was not one that Lincoln had approved for execution, and his name was not on the final death list of 39 names. His death really was a tragic case of being mistaken for someone who was guilty of a far worse crime.

Chaska was already a figure of some controversy when the military commission concluded its business in November. He had come to the public's attention because of the determined and vocal efforts that Sarah Wakefield, who had been captured and held by the Dakota, made to clear his name. Mrs. Wakefield had been sheltered and protected

## 23. Misspelled Names, Misplaced Records and Mistaken Identities 195

by Chaska and his mother, and when the captives were handed over to the troops at Camp Release she had been passionate in his defense. In retrospect, she was perhaps a bit too passionate.

In a letter to his wife the day after securing the captives, Sibley wrote, "The woman I wrote you of yesterday threatens that if *her* Indian, who is among those who have been seized, should be hung, she will shoot those of us who have been instrumental in bringing him to the scaffold...."[8] While he did not identify her by name, all indications are that this woman was Sarah Wakefield.

Most white Minnesotans reacted negatively to the idea of a white woman taking up this kind of energetic defense of the very Indian who had held her captive. Even Mrs. Wakefield's husband did not understand her behavior on Chaska's behalf. "He cannot realize," she wrote, speaking of her husband, "how a woman could try to save an Indian who had her a Captive ... he little knows a Mother [*sic*] feelings that Indian saved my Children and what Mother could forget it and not only my Children lives were spared but I was saved from dishoner [*sic*]...." In hindsight, Wakefield seemed to understand how she might have prejudiced her case in the realm of public opinion. "I was so afraid that people would think I was abused," she wrote, "that I overexerted myself giving them reason to believe what I was trying to the contrary."[9]

As the date of the execution drew nearer, Sarah Wakefield felt sure that her efforts on Chaska's behalf had saved him from the rope. After all, his name and case number were not on the final list of names approved for execution by the President. She was horrified, days after the hanging on December 26, to read the account of the hanging in the newspaper and see that Chaska was listed among those executed. She immediately wrote to Stephen Riggs.

"I would be pleased to learn," she demanded in her letter, "the particulars also in what way and by whom the mistake was made whereby an innocent man was Hanged [*sic*]."[10] In a subsequent letter she explained her feelings. "Death I could have borne," she wrote of her time in Dakota captivity, "but their [*sic*] are many evils worse than Death and from all I was saved by his intervention."[11] As the war drew to a close, Chaska had apparently considered fleeing west with Little Crow and his hold-outs, but Wakefield persuaded him to stay and surrender. He was innocent of any crime, she assured him, and she would vouch for his protection of her. Surely that would save him. It did not, and when his role in Gleason's murder was mad revealed, he was arrested, charged, tried and convicted. Writing in the spring of 1863, after the tragedy had played out and Chaska was hung, Mrs. Wakefield said, "I over persuaded him to remain and I feel as if I was his Murderer."[12] Now she wanted answers as to how this terrible mistake had come about, and she demanded an answer from Riggs.

Riggs replied to the first, angry letter she wrote in March. "In regard to the mistake by which Chaska was hung instead of another," he answered Mrs. Wakefield, "I doubt whether I can satisfactorily explain it.... We had forgotten that he was condemned under the name We-chan-hpe-wash-tay-do-pe. We knew he was called Chaska in prison.... [W]hen the name Chaska was called in the prison on that fatal morning, your protector answered to it and walked out."[13]

Part of the confusion over names may have come from the fact that the name "Chaska" was one of the most common informal names to be found among Dakota men.

Literally, the name simply means "oldest child if a son"; hundreds of Dakota men would have been known by this nickname nearly as much as by their longer, phonetically rendered proper names. As best as can be determined, the man who was actually intended for the gallows was named Chaskadon. Chaska answered when "Chaskadon" was called out, and went to his death for another man's crime. The safeguards employed to prevent precisely this sort of confusion failed completely. Even the use of the matching case numbers on the execution list failed to catch this fatal error. Chaska, who was tried under his full name Wechankwashtadonpee, was Case No. 3; Chaskadon was Case No. 121. No one, that morning in the prison, caught the mistake. No one became aware of it during the several days that passed between the segregation and the hanging. Chaska himself apparently never protested that the name by which they were calling him was not actually his name, or at least there is no record that he did. He was hanged the day after Christmas.

The theory has also been put forward that Chaska's execution was in fact not the result of a mistake over similar-sounding names, but was instead a deliberate act on the part of the military authorities who controlled the process. The notion that a white woman may have taken a romantic interest in an Indian man, this position argues, so offended public sensibilities that Chaska was singled out in spite of the fact that his name was not on Lincoln's execution order. That scenario is certainly not impossible, but neither is there any conclusive proof to support the contention as factual.

Sarah Wakefield was justifiably outraged when she learned that Chaska was hanged. To some degree, she also blamed herself. "[M]y anxiety to save him just cursed me and killed the Man," she said.[14] Earlier, in another letter to Riggs, she wrote "I wish when you see Chaska's Mother that you would explain to her how her Son was executed...."[15] Riggs, already deeply troubled by the hangings and the mistakes that he knew had been made, had no explanation that would suffice for Chaska's mother, for Sarah Wakefield, or for himself.

Chaska's story has become widely known, even to the point of a recent movement to urge the Governor of Minnesota to grant him a posthumous pardon. But there was one other case where the wrong man might have been executed at Mankato, and that story is not as widely known. The other case of mistaken identity to which Riggs referred might actually have been a man named Waschechoona.

Waschechoona's record appears in the trial transcripts as Case No. 332. There is a real possibility that he may have been mistaken for a man named Waschechoon, Case No. 318. Part of the evidence in support of this conclusion comes from a list of all the Dakota prisoners that was compiled by the missionaries Stephen Riggs, Thomas Williamson and a few others. On this list the missionaries marked the names of every man hanged at Mankato with a "+"; two names that were not on the original execution order, Chaska and Waschechoona, were marked this way. The same "+" appears in front of the names of Chaskadon and Waschechoon, but the additional notation "supposed to be hung but not" was written after their names. From this, it seems that the missionaries knew that mistakes were made in the final selection of condemned men, and that in two cases there were discrepancies between those who should have been hanged, and those who actually were.[16]

From what can be parsed out of the sources, Waschechoona was a mentally-challenged young white man who was orphaned as an infant and adopted by a Dakota woman. He was raised among the Indians as one of them and would have spoken Dakota better than English, if he knew any English at all. At least four sources agree that Waschechoona was hanged in error, with general agreement as to his mental impairment.[17]

# 24

# Confusion and Contradictions

Years ago, Minnesota historian Kenneth Carley noted that "the literature of the Sioux Uprising and its aftermath is extensive and frequently contradictory." He was right on both counts—there are shelves worth of books, articles and pamphlets published on the war, and much of it disagrees with all the rest of it. This is particularly problematic when the primary sources themselves do not agree on some of the most basic details. A careful reading is necessary to parse out those details that can be established beyond doubt, and even then there are still many things about the war that are open to debate, argument, and speculative interpretation.

Anyone reading through the primary sources of the Dakota War will quickly note the profusion of mutually-contradicting versions of events. There are widely differing accounts of the same incident, or outright disagreements over the facts. Writing in 1916, Marion Satterlee expressed some of the historian's frustration with this when he said, "Stories of the massacre in Renville County are very deficient in details, and badly mixed as to localities, names are omitted or misspelled, several people reported killed, really escaped, while many of the victims are unnamed in any account."[1] Coming forward from 1862, many of these differences and disagreements are repeated and recycled through later books on the war, and the task of separating fact from fiction is a perpetual challenge.

Some of the errors in the contemporary sources are minor, the sort of inaccuracies that do not have much impact on the history of the war other than to confuse some of the less important details. Some, however, are serious mistakes which can distort the history altogether. This is true of the very first incident of the war, and much that follows after.

The event that precipitated the outbreak of the war, the killing of five settlers by several Dakota men at Acton on August 17, has been presented in markedly different ways. The consensus of most sources and most historians is that four Indians carried out the murders as an unpremeditated act. In at least two accounts these perpetrators are named, but even then there is a lack of agreement. Were the four men named Sungigidan (Brown Wing), Kaomdeiyeyedan (Breaking Up), Nagiwicakte (Killing Ghost) and Pazoiyopa (Runs against Something when Crawling), or were they Nagiwicakte (Ghost Killer), Kaomdeniyeyedan (One Who Scatters), Sungigidan (Yellow Wing Feathers), and Hepan (Second Born Male Child)? They are usually described as young men, but at the coroner's inquest held on August 18, Mrs. Baker, whose husband was one of the victims of the crime, said that all four Dakota were middle-aged men. Return I. Holcombe, writing in 1908, said, "None of them were more than thirty years of age, but each seemed older," but does not indicate how he knew this.[2] Most accounts mention a dispute over eggs, or accusations of cowardice; others make no mention of either issue. Whiskey is a factor in some versions; not in others. Some sources say that the provocation for the killings was an insult, some do not.

Dakota War historian John LaBatte has identified at least 26 separate versions of the Acton incident. Harriet McConkey, in her book *Dakota War Whoop*, claimed that "six or seven reckless young warriors from the Lower Agency ... had gone out the previous day on a Chippawa [sic] 'scalp hunt,' but meeting no success in that line, and imbibing largely of 'fire water,' they entered that isolated settlement, intent on carrying out whatever promptings their evil hearts might devise."[3] McConkey's particular bias is clear in her word choice. A few other sources such as Adrian J. Ebell have also suggested that the killings at Acton were the result of whiskey, but the white survivors of the attack adamantly maintained that the Indians were not drunk. Edward Neill, in his 1882 history of Minnesota, also posited that the Dakota at Acton were returning from an unsuccessful raid against the Ojibwe, and that they had "obtained whiskey, and drank freely."[4]

At the far end of the scale from McConkey, at least one recent Native American commentator has claimed that the entire story of the killings at Acton is a fabricated myth, and that no such incident ever took place. The historical evidence indicates otherwise—for one thing, a coroner's inquest was held into the killings at Acton, a legal proceeding that went into the county records. Since one does not hold an inquest to determine cause of death in a case where no one has been killed, it is hard to see how one could seriously argue that the Acton murders did not occur. Whatever the exact events of that day actually were, about the only thing that seems absolutely certain is that five settlers were killed by Dakota men. LaBatte's conclusion on the issue is probably the most insightful in the historiography: "There are many versions of the events in Acton Township," he writes. "To give one version and allow it to stand as the only version is incorrect."[5]

President Lincoln's secretary, John G. Nicolay, wrote a report of his journey through Minnesota during the time of the war. His account contains at least one fairly inconsequential mistake. According to Nicolay's version of the events immediately prior to the outbreak of the war, "The coin, $71,000 in silver (Indians understand silver coin, and will scarcely take any other), was finally shipped by express from the sub-treasury in New York city [sic], on the 12th of August...."[6] Most sources, except perhaps for Daniel Buck, agrees that the payment was in gold, which is also what the records of the U.S. government indicate; Return I. Holcombe described the annuity payment as "$72,000 in gold and silver."[7]

Most accounts of the war report that of the nearly 300 white and mixed-race captives held by the Dakota during the war, there was only one white man among them, a man named George Spencer, who was a clerk in one of the traders' stores. Spencer was wounded in the initial attack on the Lower Agency on August 18, but he was saved by an Indian who claimed him as a friend and protected him. Sam Brown, whose eyewitness narrative we have already encountered in earlier chapters, gave a different version. According to Brown, "The names of the four white men who were kept captives by

Little Crow were as follows: "George Spencer, Peter Romsseau, Louis La Belle and Peter Rouillard. I mention this," Brown said, "to correct the impression that there was but one white man (Spencer) made prisoner by the Indians."[8]

Whether George Spencer was the only white man to be taken alive by the Dakota or not, the controversy over his experience has another element to it. At least two Indians have been named as his rescuer. Big Eagle, in his personal narrative, claimed that *he* was the man who had saved Spencer's life, but if he did, he was probably a late-comer to the scene. Spencer himself, who might logically be expected to know better than anyone, named one of Little Crow's principle warriors, Wakinyatawa, as the man who protected him. When the other Indians threatened to finish Spencer off after he was wounded, Spencer said in his account that Wakinyatawa grabbed a hatchet and said, "If you had killed him before I saw him, it would have been all right, but we have been friends and comrades for years, and now that I have seen him I will protect him or die with him."

The ambush at Redwood Ferry, where Captain Marsh and 23 other men were killed on the first day of the outbreak, is also a subject of disagreement in some contemporary sources. The military commission charged the Dakota man named White Dog with leading the ambush, and sentenced him to death for it. When the Reverend Riggs recorded the last statements of the condemned men just before their executions, he reported that White Dog had said "his position and conduct at the ferry was misunderstood and misrepresented...."[9] Whether or not White Dog was in fact responsible for the ambush was never established beyond reasonable doubt (although as explained in earlier chapter, ambush is a completely legitimate tactic of war and I contend that White Dog should never have been charged with a crime for participating in that fight). At least one source, though, also implicates Little Crow in the fight at Redwood Ferry.

Isaac Heard maintained that it was Little Crow, not White Dog, who was the actual Indian leader at the ferry. "As soon as it became manifest that the idea of crossing [by the soldiers] was abandoned," Heard wrote, "Little Crow gave the signal to White Dog to fire. White Dog passed it to others...."[10] Heard is one of the only sources to put Little Crow at the Redwood Ferry ambush, and to make him the principle figure of command in the incident.

Heard's book also contains a few of the factual errors that researchers encounter in the story of the massacre of the settler families at Lake Shetek. After Lavina Eastlick's husband and three of her children were killed by the Indians and she herself was shot, she told her oldest boy Merton to take his baby brother Johnny and carry him as far as he could. The story of an 11-year old boy walking more than 50 miles, carrying his brother, became an instant *cause célèbre* among Minnesotans. It was easily one of the most recognizable and familiar stories to emerge from the war. That, however, did not prevent it from becoming the subject of numerous errors and misrepresentations.

Heard got several details of the story—the names, the ages, and the distance—wrong when he wrote his book. "Mrs. Eastlick's son Burton," he wrote, "not ten years of age [meaning that he was younger], and his little brother, age five years, having become separated from their mother, arrived safely at the settlements days after the attack. Burton alternately led and carried the little fellow a distance of eighty miles."[11]

In Heard's defense, it can at least be said that he did not attempt to add any fictive elements to his version of the story—he simply got some of the basic details wrong, but a reader familiar with the story would still recognize the factual incident under the errors in his telling. This is not the case with Harriet McConkey, who handled the Lake Shetek story with an enthusiastic carelessness that was a regular feature of her writing.

Reading McConkey's book, one quickly gets the idea that while she made claims of being a historian, her real ambition was to be a novelist. Her narrative is highly sentimental and melodramatic, her language is florid and effusive, and she never allows the unadorned facts to stand in the way of a wildly imaginative telling of events. When she did not have the details, she filled in the blanks with creative conjecture; as she herself said in her book, she employed a "certain fertility of imagination."[12] That was exactly how she handled Merton Eastlick's story.

"Beside his dying brother [Freddy, Frank, or Giles; McConkey does not specify which brother because she wrote the scene as she imagined that it happened] he watched until the angels bore his spirit above," she emoted, then creatively described how Merton "placed the dear little form beside his idolized father...."[13] McConkey focused more on the emotional floridity of her prose rather than rendering a factual account of the event. She got her protagonist's name wrong, calling him "Burton," put his age at 12, and went on to gushingly describe how "[n]inety miles, thick with dangers, lay before him, but our little hero, Burton, faltered not."[14] Kathryn Zabelle Derounian-Stodola, who has undertaken a comparative study of many of the narratives emerging from the Dakota War, uses McConkey's version of the Merton Eastlick story to underscore how untrustworthy *Dakota War Whoop* is as a source. "[T]he fact that McConkey repeatedly misnames the boy Burton indicates her haste and carelessness..." Derounian-Stodola writes. "The wrong name is just one indicator of essentially fictive elements she uses throughout her work."[15]

When the captives were finally released on September 27, the efforts of Sarah Wakefield to protect the Dakota man who had protected her, We-chan-hpe-wash-tay-do-pe, or Chaska, gave rise to a series of assumptions and outright misconceptions.

Shortly after securing the captives, Sibley wrote to his wife that "One rather handsome woman among them had become so infatuated with the redskin who had taken her for a wife that, although her white husband was still living at some point below and had been in search of her, she declared that were it not for her children, she would not leave her dusky paramour." Sibley did not identify this woman by name in his letter, nor did he the next day in a second letter to his wife, when he wrote, "The woman I wrote you of yesterday threatens that if *her* Indian, who is among those who have been seized, should be hung, she will shoot those of us who have been instrumental in bringing him to the scaffold, and then go back to the Indians"[16] Sibley never named this woman, but others have theorized as to her identity.

Derounian-Stodola wrote an article in 2005 in which she examined the correspondence between Sarah Wakefield and the Reverend Stephen Riggs in the months after Chaska was hanged at Mankato. Derounian-Stodola refers to Sibley's letter, and posits, "Since we know of no other woman publicly defending an accused Dakota Indian, this fact alone proves that Sibley must be referring to Sarah Wakefield."[17] While this is certainly suggestive that Sibley was referring to Sarah Wakefield, it does not conclusively prove it. But in the absence of a better candidate for this unidentified woman, it is certainly likely that Wakefield *was* indeed the woman referred to in Sibley's letters.

Derounian-Stodola's considerable strengths as a researcher of literature notwithstanding, as a historical commentator she is problematic because of her propensity for reaching or accepting unsupported conclusions. In *The War in Words* she repeats a claim that she made in her earlier article, to the effect that "Riggs was in the prison to oversee the executions," which implies that he, a civilian missionary, was in charge of the military proceedings. That assertion is absolutely wrong—Riggs was not in charge of any part of the matter in any capacity. Rather, Sibley had asked him to "be present and give assistance at the time of the executions," as we saw earlier. Riggs was there (reluctantly, it should be noted) at Sibley's request and with Colonel Miller's approval, and his primary function was as a translator. Riggs did not control the execution list, and he was not responsible for selecting the men to be hanged from among the 303 prisoners. Riggs probably knew several of the condemned Dakota personally, by sight, but Joseph Brown was the man actually tasked with identifying the men on the death list.

Returning to the Sarah Wakefield story, though, an even-more unlikely interpretation comes from a contemporary source. The connection between Wakefield and Chaska is well established as a historical reality; Wakefield herself wrote of it at length both in her own book and her personal correspondence. In Jacob Nix's book of his experiences during the war, however, he claimed that a romantic liaison existed between a white woman captive and White Dog. Though Nix does not name the woman in question any more than Sibley did in his letters, the basic details closely match those of Wakefield's experience.

Nix offered no evidentiary support and no explanation for how he came by his information. "That he [White Dog], who was otherwise a sly Indian," Nix wrote, "should be caught in the trap at Camp Release and give himself up to General Sibley in the hope of receiving a pardon can only be attributed to the fact that he had a love affair with a white woman who had been taken captive by the Indians."[18] Nix's next lines, to a point, most closely match the Sarah Wakefield/Chaska story. "She had assured him that her influence and her testimony would certainly free him," Nix claimed. "But the lady was mistaken. The shameful atrocities of the red scoundrel were so definitely proved to him that all the pleading, wringing of hands, and the tears of this white woman could not save him from the gallows."[19] In the entire pantheon of contemporary literature on the Dakota War, Nix is the only source who claims that White Dog was involved with a white woman who attempted to save him from execution.

Coming forward to the execution itself, the record is replete with contradictions. The construction of the gallows itself is a subject of disagreement between several sources. Most sources describe it as a square in shape. Daniel Buck, who was present at the hangings, described it as a diamond, which may have simply been the result of his physical location in reference to the scaffold. At least one source said that the gallows were oval-shaped. Jacob Nix said the gallows were built as a circle. Isaac Heard did not describe the gallows specifically, but said that the troops who were assembled at the execution "formed a large square, with the scaffold in the centre."[20]

One detail that Heard got completely, inexplicably wrong in his book was the date of the execution, but it is unclear why or how the error came about. Heard wrote that "thirty-eight were ordered to be executed at Mankato on the 26th day of February, 1863."[21] Heard was closely connected with the process that brought these men to the gallows at Mankato, and it is hard to understand how he could have put the date of the execution not just in the wrong month, but also the wrong year. What confuses the issue further is that four pages later in his book he reproduced the order appointing citizen marshals for the hanging, and in that instance gave the correct date that the order was issued, December 22, 1862. Consequently, it is unclear whether the erroneous execution date was a mistake on Heard's part, or his editor's.

Daniel Buck indicates in his 1904 book *Indian Outbreaks* that William Duley (whose name he spells as "Duly," as several other sources so) needed two strokes to cut the rope that held the gallows trap. "His first blow failed to cut it, but at the second stroke the platform dropped with a thud, intensified by the dancing motion of the prisoners…" Buck wrote. "It is said that the first blow failed to cut the rope because of the excitement under which he labored, but the second blow was successful, and speedily sent the thirty-eight murderers to the happy hunting grounds—if such characters are there admissible."[22] Buck is one of a few sources who describe Duley as nearly bungling the task.

Contrary to most eyewitness reports from the hanging, including Jacob Nix's testimony and that of the *New York Times* correspondent, Buck asserts that the Indians did *not* die well. "To those near the gallows, evidences of fear and nervousness under this trying ordeal were manifest," he wrote. "One Indian managed to work the noose to the back of his neck, and when the drop fell he struggled terribly; others tried to clutch the blankets of those next to them…."[23] Contrary to Buck's version of events, Jacob Nix, who was unapologetic in his hatred of the Indians, conceded in his book, "I must admit they faced death courageously."[24] Isaac Heard said that the Indians went to the gallows "eagerly and cheerfully, even crowding and jostling each other to be ahead…."[25]

Almost every source, contemporary and later, names Rdainyanka as the Indian who fell when the rope broke. Buck, however, claims that the Indian who fell from the broken rope was Cut Nose, saying, "A physician from an adjoining town secured the body of Cut Nose, one of the most brutal of the Indians, and the one who fell from the rope at the time of the execution."[26] He also adds one other detail that is not found in other sources. "As he fell," Buck wrote, "a tremendous shout went up from the crowd, 'Put him up!' 'Put him up!'"[27] Most other versions of this incident simply say that the dead man was hung up with a new rope, and make no reference to shouts from the crowd.

As for the number of men executed at Mankato, a 1915 history of Minnesota claims, "One of those who were to have been executed died before the day of doom arrived. The other thirty-eight were hanged…."[28] This writer seems to have been unaware that one of the 39 men actually received a last-minute reprieve, rather than died in prison. Charles Bryant wrote two books about the Dakota War; in one of them, he confused both the circumstances and the identities of the executed men. "The number condemned was forty," he wrote, "but one died before the day fixed for the execution, and one, Henry Milord, a half-breed, had his sentence commuted…."[29] Here again, it was Joseph Godfrey whose sentence was commuted, and Tatemina who received a last-minute reprieve. Henry Milord was hanged.

Many of the most authoritative works on the Dakota War contain an error or two, and by and large these minor mistakes do not in any way detract from the overall veracity of these books. There is a feeling among some modern Dakota people that the preponderance of history dealing with the war is written by white commentators, and that it is therefore wildly inaccurate, but that is not an fair assessment of the entire spectrum of the extant histories. Yes, there are mistakes in the historiography, but a few mistakes do not render the entire past unrecognizable or change it altogether, especially not for a critical, well-informed reader. And many of the extant mistakes are errors about the white side of the history, made by white commentators, as when Erling Jorstad utterly confuses the protocols of military law when he says that Sibley "reserved the right of review over each case."[30] In fact, Sibley as the convening officer was *obligated* by military regulation to function as reviewing officer for the verdicts of the commission he had impaneled.

Minor errors aside, however, there are some books on the war that are completely problematic. Harriet Bishop McConkey's *Dakota War Whoop*, as we have seen, is a highly imaginative, sensationalized account—more a work of fiction than in any way a serious history. But it is possible to find a heavy dose of factual errors in modern works, as well. Most books that focus solely on the Dakota War tend to get their facts straight. It is in books that deal with the Dakota War in general terms, where the war is just one event considered in a broad sweep of history, that the mistakes seem to be most often found, and in greater numbers.

Peter Maguire's *Law and War: An American Story*, published in 2000, is one such book. Maguire is an eminent scholar and researcher in the field of war crimes trials, and his book is a wide study of the conduct of war crimes trials by the United States; the events of 1862 in Minnesota come in for just 11 pages of his overall study. Yet even in so brief an account, his handling of the Dakota War is remarkable for the number of factual errors it contains. In 11 pages Maguire makes 11 major mistakes in his facts, mistakes which suggest that he has a considerable amount of confusion with the history.

Maguire claims that General Pope "ordered [Sibley] to carry out reprisals before any surrender was accepted or any settlement was made."[31] No such order was ever given—Pope's bellicose statements about exterminating and eliminating the Dakota, and his directives to Sibley to "destroy everything belonging to them and force them out to the plains..." were instructions on waging total war, not orders to conduct systematic reprisals prior to allowing the cessation of hostilities. Further along, Maguire claims that "Little Crow succeeded in drawing the soldiers into his trap..." at the battle of Wood Lake/Yellow Medicine.[32] As already established, the intended ambush set by the Dakota at Wood Lake in fact *failed* because a foraging party from the 7th Minnesota Infantry inadvertently forced the Indians to spring the ambush prematurely. Indian and white witnesses alike described the intended Indian plan as a failure.

Maguire also confuses some of the principal characters. He identifies Rdainyanka as Little Crow's son-in-law, when in fact Rdainyanka was the son-in-law of the peace-advocating chief Wabasha. In the same paragraph Maguire quotes Little Crow as saying, "We may regret what has happened, but the matter has gone too far to be remedied. We have got to die. Let us, then, kill as many of the whites as possible, and let the prisoners die with us." Every single primary source, most importantly the Dakota sources themselves, make it clear that it was Rdainyanka, not Little Crow, who made that particular statement.

Maguire also confuses the three-man court of inquiry, which was formed on September 27 and operated for only one day, with the five-man military commission which was convened on 28 September and subsequently conducted all of the 392 trials. Maguire gets the sequence of events completely wrong, makes the inaccurate statement that "the chairman of the Court of Inquiry was a missionary named Stephen Riggs," and goes on to say that "the Court of Inquiry would try as many as forty-two Santee [Dakota] in a single day!"[33] On the contrary—Riggs was associated with but not a member of the short-lived investigatory body, and was certainly *not* its chairman (a position which existed only in Maguire's muddled misunderstanding of matters). Sibley's letter to Pope on September 27, 1862 named Colonel Crooks, Lieutenant Colonel Marshall, and Captain Grant as members of the commission of inquiry—Riggs was not mentioned at all. Furthermore, the "Court of Inquiry" to which Maguire refers here never tried a single case—that was the role of the five-man military commission, and Riggs' only function in the five-man military commission itself was as an occasional translator. By naming Riggs as the "chairman" of the "Court of Inquiry," and then going on to state that this body "tried as many as forty-two" cases a day, Maguire arrives at the completely erroneous conclusion that the Reverend Riggs was the senior member of the military tribunal that sentenced 303 Dakota prisoners to death. This is a complete mishmash of the history.

Beyond these problems, Maguire clutters his text with half a dozen inaccurate assumptions that seem to stem from a lack of familiarity with the sources. His account of the Dakota War and the military commission trials is valuable, but only for its cautionary value on the dangers of insufficient research. Maguire apparently conducted no primary source research into this history himself, and he bases all of his conclusions on the Dakota War from a reading of secondary sources, which is a perfectly acceptable approach when done carefully. But even that is problematic in this case—Maguire cites Chomsky's excellent article several times, for example, but he distills many of her complex and well-reasoned arguments into a grossly oversimplified misrepresentation of her work.

Published histories of the war are not the only accounts to contain errors—the narratives and reminiscences of participants in the events can also be hampered by inaccuracies. This is particularly the case with accounts written years or decades after the fact. The further out from the event the witness statement, the more inconsistencies creep into the story.

One such narrative was written in 1903 by Richard Mott Jackson, who had been a soldier in the 1862 expedition against the Dakota. The list of details he misremembers is lengthy. He ascribes the rescue of the white captives to a pre-dawn raid on the Indians' camp, rather than a peaceful handover after the battle of Wood Lake. Jackson also has the trials taking place in Mankato after the mob attacks on the prisoners at New Ulm, rather than weeks earlier at Camp Release and the Lower Agency. By his account, the soldiers themselves were in the process of erecting a gallows to hang the convicted prisoners when they were stopped "by the arrival of the General commanding, who upon become acquainted with our summary actions, ordered the proceedings and finds of the court martial to be forwarded to Washington for approval." He then goes on to claim that two of the condemned men on the final execution list were killed in prison prior to the scheduled hanging—"It was proposed to put in 2 substitutes, as there was plenty of material, but on the morning of the execution only 38 Indians reported for business."[34]

These are just a representative sampling of the inconsistencies that one encounters reading through the literature of the Dakota War. Some of the contradictions are minor, and only of importance to a researcher; others are extremely important details that can entirely alter the public perception of certain events. Some of the verifiable inaccuracies are limited to early accounts, where the error was noted and remarked upon in subsequent texts, but other mistakes have become part of the established literature on the subject and are now part in the canon, resisting all attempts at excision.

# 25

# Oral Histories

*We can't create history in our own image, according to how we would like it to be. The truth in history is for those who are willing to spend the time and make the effort to find it.*

—Dr. Elden Lawrence, Ehanna Wicohan Oyake

What many of us think of as history is probably less a matter of what we know about the past, than what we *think* we know about the past; and what we think we know often does not agree with what actually was. The broad strokes of history are usually there, to be sure, at least enough of them make the event recognizable. But the details are where the train of memory comes off the rails for most of us. Some of the details that we know best are not the facts that we assume them to be, but are instead just familiar fictions to which we have grown accustomed through long acquaintance. Once it reaches that point, human nature tends to resist any information that contradicts what it has already accepted as "history." The poet Garnett Weston once observed that "hell hath no fury like an old-timer corrected in his memories," and so it is with most of us when we are confronted with historical realities that do not agree with our cherished ideas of what we think the history was. We want our histories, especially those that involve our own people and our personal antecedents, to support the perceptions and understandings that we already have of ourselves. Divergence is seldom welcomed.

This is why the historian's role can sometimes feel rather like that of a man tiptoeing past a sleeping bear. Nothing stirs up indignation and anger quicker than challenging someone's long-held beliefs about their own past, and by "someone" I mean nearly everyone. It is just too intensely personal a matter. This is especially true when one contradicts two particular types of histories—family histories and oral histories, which are often one and the same thing. When the accuracy of their forebears' oral histories is questioned, there is an understandable tendency for people to feel as if their cultural values and personal identities are being attacked.

Those of us who explore the oral histories in our own families sooner or later encounter the inescapable fact that not every story that has come down through the generations can be relied on as truth incarnate. But this does not mean that these stories are lies—not in the least. It is just important to keep in mind that stories take on lives of their own, and as the events of which they tell us fall farther and farther behind in the mists of time, details are lost, anecdotes alter, and the tales change; sometimes in subtle ways, and sometimes in important ways. Eventually, our oral histories begin to incorporate as much myth as fact.

The word "myth" is often used to mean something inherently false. That is one definition of the word, but in the historical sense, myths can also be understood as stories that we tell about ourselves as a means of acquiring an understanding of who we were on the way to becoming who we *are*. Myths keep us connected to our personal and cultural pasts. And as often as not, myths are grounded on foundations of historical fact. The facts may cloud over and grow dim as years pass, but the stories carry on, and the myths with their faint outlines of historical fact and their newer fictional accoutrements become enshrined in our personal canons.

Oral histories have a vital place in the broader context of historical study, and it is important to note their undeniable strengths. Oral histories are valuable for their ability to connect the present to the past in an immediate, human way. They usually possess a human element that strictly scholarly history can never hope to achieve. Conventional history might have an intellectual power to it, but oral histories have spirit and soul.

At the same time, however, we must be mindful of the inherent weaknesses of this type of source. Oral histories should not be regarded as the last arbiter of fact and truth. *All* sources need to be challenged and examined for accuracy, and if we regard oral histories (especially our own oral histories) as being somehow sacrosanct and untouchable then we fall short of the mark. In any scholarly work of history, sources must be examined and details must be scrutinized to ensure that they are factual. Our personal histories should be vetted just as stringently, especially if we intend to use them to define our sense of self, or if we try to construct our identities and understandings of our pasts on them. A personal example may help to illustrate my point.

My maternal grandfather once told me a story about my great-great-grandfather, who served as a surgeon with a Texas regiment in the Confederate Army during the Civil War. It was a funny story, one which suggested that my ancestor had both a keen wit and a real sense of humor, and at the same time it also said a great deal about the deprivation and hardships of fighting on the losing side in a war. It happened to be one of the last family stories my grandfather told me before I left home for the Army. He died while I was overseas, and there were no more stories. So that story is extremely important to me for several reasons. It gave me a picture of an ancestor that made me feel a real connection with a pivotal moment in the history of both my family and my country, and it is a story given to me by my grandfather. I love that story. I also realize that it is completely anecdotal, and there is no way to verify it as historically accurate or factual. It is more legend than history, and that does not lessen its value to me one iota. I treasure it as part of my family lore, though I know that it cannot rise to the level of concrete history in the academic sense.

These are the inherent problems of oral histories. Sometimes, in spite of the color and context and emotional immediacy which they impart to past events, oral histories simply cannot be corroborated or independently verified. When mistakes creep into the stories, as they so often do, the errors eventually become accepted as facts without being recognized for what they are. Thus enshrined, they come to be revered with a devotion that will brook no questioning and accept no inquiry. It is absolutely legitimate and correct to honor the elders who pass on our oral histories to us, but that does not mean that we should therefore suspend all our faculties of critical thinking. It also does not mean that we should assume that any questions about the accuracy of our historical traditions constitute an attack on our elders or ourselves. History, if it is to serve all of us, must favor none of us. This idea is what brings us back to our examination of the Dakota War.

Throughout this book, I have looked at the ways in which the Dakota War has been portrayed by commentators in books and narratives from 1862 to the present day. Most of this, inevitably, has come from books of conventional history. But there is another element that must be considered in any thorough study of this war, and it is the one not found in most of the extant historiography. These are the oral histories about the events of 1862, and we find them among the descendants of both Indian and white people who lived through the war.

In the 1971 fall edition of *Minnesota History,* the journal of the Minnesota Historical Society (MNHS), the Editor's Page column considered the historian's role in dealing with the emotionally-charged subject of Native American history. "The historian writing about Indians now must have more than sympathy," the editorial said. "He must be aware that though Indian culture may have changed, it has not vanished."[1] That point is well-made. The Indian peoples of Minnesota may have been persecuted and scattered to the west and north in a great diaspora, but they have endured. More importantly, many of them have returned to the state from which they were once forced out. Minnesota is once again home to Dakota people, for whom it was home long before the events of 1862.

Those events, the MNHS editorial went on to say, "must be told in terms of the clash of cultures and what this did to the men and the land—for it shaped both victor and vanquished."[2] Again, the observation is valid. The Dakota War might be as forgotten as ancient history by many non–Native people in Minnesota—indeed, until the sesquicentennial observances in 2012 a depressing number of young people seemed to have no idea at all that anything significant happened in the state in 1862—but the older generations on both sides have a greater awareness of it, and for the Dakota people today the war has an immediacy and importance that has hardly diminished with the passage of time. This is why any serious examination of the war must include what the British military historian B.H. Liddell-Hart called "the other side of the hill"; that is, an attempt to understand how the other side experienced the war.

As we have already seen in our close examination of the 19th century primary sources, a great deal of caution and careful fact-checking is essential. The fact that this has not always been done, and is still not consistently done, means that later secondary sources must be handled with the same scrutiny before their version of events is taken as true. And still, after all that, there remain some things in the history of the Dakota War that simply are not verifiable beyond all doubt, that cannot be conclusively proven or categorically denied—there are some questions to which we just do not have adequate answers.

I make all of these points with conventional (i.e., white-written) histories in mind. I hope by now the reader is well versed in the shortcomings of some of these sources, even those that are otherwise strong, dependable works. But what of the history as it is understood by the Dakota themselves? It has been observed before that there are as many versions of a story as there are witnesses to it, and this truism includes commentators who come to the subject years after the event. This is one reason why the war is remembered differently in the white communities of Minnesota (where, until the sesquicentennial observances in 2012, many people seem to barely remember it if they knew of it at all) and in Dakota communities (where everyone seems to know of it even if they are not particularly well informed as to the historical details).

Over a period of months leading up to the 150-year anniversary of the war, the Minnesota Historical Society conducted a series of interviews to collect oral histories from both white and Native American people, partially with regards to their perceptions and thoughts on the war. The results are instructive, especially from the point of view of a historian who is trying to separate fact from fiction and distill the history from the myth. It is with that objective in mind that I now turn to these interviews, recognizing that doing so is a process fraught with peril. Questioning the veracity of oral histories, especially the oral histories of a group of which I am not a member, could be perceived as a philippic exercise. That is not my intention in any way—I do not wish to engage in a polemic of any sort here. But if the history of this war and its aftermath really matters, and I absolutely believe that it does, then it is incumbent on us to ensure that the history we accept and the history we believe is the history that truly was, as much as we can ascertain it.

As noted in the preface, I am a conflict historian, not a scholar of Native American Studies, and I approach the matter of oral histories from the perspective of conventional history, a discipline which requires certain standards of evidentiary support which are not part of the oral tradition. My intent in this chapter is to evaluate the way in which recent oral histories have portrayed the Dakota War, and to assess the accuracy of those histories against the evidence of the historical record, not to impugn the narrators or denigrate the value of the process.

One Dakota man interviewed by the MNHS made a comment that provides an appropriate starting point in this discussion. "The greater population," he said, "all they know is their side of the history. It's written by white folks. None of it is ever written by Dakota. And so therefore, they have free gratis in regards to how they want to write it."[3] This narrator is absolutely right in his observation about who is producing the histories of the war. It is a tired maxim of warfare that the victors write the histories, and that has certainly been the case with the history of the Dakota War of 1862. To date there is not a single book-length, comprehensive study of this war that has been written by an enrolled member of the Dakota tribe. The conflict has been rendered almost exclusively through the lens of white historians—some of them have been sympathetic to the Dakota and critical of American actions during the war, but nonetheless they are still white, and therefore of the victors' camp, at least in terms of their racial and cultural identity. As one historian phrases it, European-American writers of history, who were "travelers, traders, colonial administrators, military officers, missionaries, Indian agents—represented a cultural tradition very different from that of the Sioux. Even when these observers were sympathetic to Indians, they usually failed to understand enough of native culture to empathize with Sioux perspectives."[4] That is always the difficulty—trying to empathize with a perspective that is not one's own.

The oral history narrator quoted above goes somewhat awry, however, when he delivers his judgment of white-written history in the next sentence in the transcript. "And so therefore," he concludes, "90% of it is inaccurate."[5] I disagree, and not simply because I myself am a white historian. I disagree because a long and careful study of the Dakota War and its sources leads me to a different conclusion. Yes, there absolutely *are* inaccuracies in the extant histories on the war, and some of those inaccuracies are so deeply imbedded in the canon that they are nearly ineradicable. There are errors in almost every source on the war; a few in some, page after page of them in others. Some of what might be construed as "errors" are actually differences of interpretation—those details on which there is much debate and no consensus among historians, and for which there is not enough conclusive evidence to allow us to say definitively one way or another.

But if a particular source has a couple of factual errors in its text that does not necessarily mean that it is 90 percent inaccurate, nor that the cumulative effect is to render the overall body of history inaccurate to that percentage. The sources must be considered individually rather than being dismissed with an all-encompassing generality, and especially an unsubstantiated generality, at that. To make such a claim legitimately, one would have to tally the sources systematically. I would accept a claim that there are *many* inaccuracies in the history of the Dakota War, but after studying the resources at length, I dispute the claim of a 90 percent inaccuracy rate as itself being inaccurate.

This is one of the several instances where there is a wide gulf of difference between what Dakota people believe about the war and what their non–Native neighbors believe. The majority of the Dakota oral histories are at odds with the conventional history of the war, as we will see, but it would be just as fair to turn that around and say that the conventional histories are at odds with the oral histories. To better understand the disparity between perspectives, it might be useful to consider how the oral histories view specific topics such as the causes of the war, the hangings at Mankato, the removal of the Dakota to Mankato and Fort Snelling, the internment at Fort Snelling, the exile of the Dakota from Minnesota, and the narrators' perceptions of the other group's views on the same subjects. We begin with a long quotation from an interview with an elderly Dakota man:

> I don't know what the story really is, but in my storybooks with my auntie, she says it was an Indian Agent that started the whole war in Minneapolis. That Indian Agent was supposed to give out all this money and cattle and farming implements and everything that was supposed to be for the Dakota Indians, farming, and he didn't do that. Instead he gave all that stuff to his friends and family, and so the Sioux were starving. And they went to the Indian Agent and said, give us something, we need food. And the Indian Agent said, No, you're dogs, so you go out there and you eat grass.[6]

This is an excellent example of an oral history that incorporates the essential elements of the history but is a bit hazy on the details. The Indian Agent at the Lower Sioux Agency was Thomas Galbraith, a man who exacerbated the Indians' desperate circumstances that summer through his incompetence and stubbornness. But there is no validity to the allegation that Galbraith "gave all that stuff to his friends and family"; rather, he refused to release the Dakotas' allotted supplies in the government warehouses until the arrival of the much delayed annuity payment. When the narrator claims that the Indian Agent then told the Dakota to "eat grass" he is confusing Galbraith with the trader Andrew Myrick, who supposedly made the insulting remark. The crucial point to this interview is the opening sentence, "I don't know what the story really is...." That is often the case with oral histories, especially those that come down to us through a family line. But this does not mean that the oral history is useless for that reason,—on the contrary; it can still serve as an excellent starting point for research and inquiry that can open up new angles on the story.

A white narrator in this oral history series, when asked, "What do you think was the cause of the war?" answered, "According to what I know [again, one of the key signal phrases in oral histories], the Dakota were starving." She went on to say, "I suppose that's one of the things. But you hear so many sides of things. I think sometimes we probably started it too, you know, making trouble. Who knows? It's so long ago."[7] When she said, "we probably started it too," the "we" she was referring to were German immigrants who made up the majority of settlers in and around New Ulm at the time of the war; the narrator, herself of German ancestry, is echoing contemporary reports that the German settlers did not have as friendly relations with the Dakota as did many of the Norwegian or Swedish settlers.

One Dakota woman was asked by the MNHS interviewer, "What is your opinion of the war?" "I don't know what to think of it," the narrator replied, "because I don't know much about it." Several questions later in the transcript, the interviewer asked, "Is it a good idea to commemorate the events of the mid 1800s?" The narrator replied "Yes… . So people will know what went on a long time ago among the Sioux. A lot of them don't know nothing, the white people, you tell them and they're really surprised."[8] The observation that "a lot of them" ("them" in this case being white Minnesotans) do not know about the war is fair and accurate, in my estimation, at least when applied to the years leading up to the sesquicentenary of the war in 2012. It is worth noting, though, how the narrator transitions from not giving an opinion on the war because she herself does not know much about it, to a few sentences later criticizing the other group for their lack of detailed knowledge on the same subject.

This critique of the other side's knowledge of events, or its version of those events, is not limited to only one side of the issue. John LaBatte, a historian with both Dakota and white ancestry, said in the interviews, "There's an interesting aspect. A Dakota Indian person can claim, 'that's my oral history. I know there were a lot of deaths [on the march to Fort Snelling] because I was told by my ancestors….'" LaBatte objects to the idea that oral histories are unassailable, concluding, "Maybe they actually believe what they are saying…."[9]

On the other side of the equation, one Dakota narrator declared, "The white man lies a lot. Excuse the impression, but they do. When it comes to greed, they go beyond the limits to lie."[10] Another Dakota interviewee said, "I see untruthfulness on the part of the non–Native people that were in the war. You know, we are a peaceful people, we are a very spiritual people…."[11] These two perspectives are important for what they get right, what they get wrong, and what they have in common with most oral histories.

Both narrators refer to the perceived untruthfulness of white, or non–Native people. One could attack these statements as thinly veiled claims that all Native commentators are by contrast truthful and that no Indian person ever lies. I do not see it that way. If the narrators' comments are directed against specific white people whose untruthfulness was demonstrated by their conduct during the treaty period leading up to the war, or by their one-sided, skewed depiction of events after the war, then the accusations certainly have some foundation. As argued in the chapter discussing allegations of atrocities, there are undeniable problems with many of the contemporary (i.e., white) accounts of the war. It is also established that there was a general consensus at the time of the war, among white observers as well as Indians, that the outbreak was caused in no small part by the dishonesty and corruption of the U.S. government's dealings with the Dakota.

Up to this point, we can accept the narrators' comments as having some valid support. But on the other hand, if the accusation of inherent dishonesty is being levied against *all* white people, past and present, then it is fair to ask if the narrators are harboring precisely the same sort of racial bias that lends itself to broad generalizations and the stereotyping of an entire people without due regard for individuals. Native Americans have been on the receiving end of that sort of attitude for generations, but that does not make the attitude any less reprehensible if it is expressed by them.

It is also worth remarking on the comment made by the second narrator, who said "we [Dakota] are a peaceful people...." The context in which that statement was made in the transcripts is that the Dakota were effectively driven to war in 1862, which I do not dispute. But the wording of the statement illustrates one of the areas where oral histories can lead us astray. By saying "we are a peaceful people," the narrator here is claiming an identity, one encompassing the past as well as present, which is simply not supported by historical evidence. As discussed in Chapter Two, the Dakota had a long, well-documented history of nearly constant warfare with their Indian neighbors, warfare in which they themselves were frequently the aggressors. This narrator might like to think of her ancestors as being benignly peaceful souls, but in truth the Dakota were a warring culture *par excellence*. This oral history tries to claim an historical identity that simply did not exist in reality.

Contrast this with another Dakota narrator, who described his understanding of his personal history by saying, "One side of my family for the most part was a warrior side.... The other side was actually peaceful at that time, trying to find a peaceful resolution. So even in my family there were differences."[12] This is an accurate reflection of the situation that confronted many of the Dakota in August 1862. More importantly, it avoids sweeping stereotypes and allows for the fact that there were individual distinctions between the Dakota of 1862, just as there were among white Minnesotans at the time.

When the interviews move to the subject of the removal of the Indians noncombatants to Fort Snelling, the oral histories are again at odds with the evidence. Many Dakota view the march in November 1862 as a "death march," a horrific experience in which Dakota people supposedly died on a massive scale. One particularly influential voice lending itself to that portrayal of the event is that of the Dakota academic and activist Waziyatawin.

The title of Waziyatawin's 2004 article, "Deconstructing the 1862 Death Marches," comes from her claim that the experience of the Dakota people as they were moved from Camp Release to Fort Snelling was essentially the same as that of American and Filipino POWs who suffered through the Bataan Death March in the Philippines in 1942. To support her allegation that the Dakota were subjected to a "death march" she quotes the narrative of a family member who lived through the experience in 1862, a woman who described how the Dakota "went through some [towns] where the people were real hostile to them. They would throw rocks, cans, sticks, and everything they could think of: potatoes, even rotten tomatoes and eggs…. Then when they would pass through the town they would be all right."[13] The oral history cited here certainly describes a humiliating, frightening and even dangerous situation, but it falls far short of anything that would justify the use of the term "death march."

In contrast with that depiction, Bataan was a hellish ordeal. More than 70,000 American and Filipino soldiers, most of whom had been subsisting on starvation rations for weeks before their surrender, were marched up the dusty miles of Rural Highway 5 in scorching tropical heat without food or water while Japanese soldiers beat, shot, bayonetted and beheaded men who broke ranks for water, or who fell out from exhaustion or sickness. Some of the Japanese brutality might be ascribed to the martial code of *bushido,* but much of it seemed utterly capricious. Survivors of the march reported seeing men who collapsed in the road being deliberately driven over by Japanese trucks until their corpses were unrecognizable. Filipino civilians who tried to give food or water to the prisoners along the route did so at great peril—witnesses reported seeing some bayonetted or burned to death for trying to do so.

There is no question that the Dakota people underwent a miserable experience as they were marched to Fort Snelling and Mankato, and we have already seen how they were attacked by mobs of white people in New Ulm and Henderson. Independent observers of the march, such as missionary John P. Williamson, were clear on the fact that the Dakota experienced some real danger to life and limb along the way. The Indians, Williamson wrote, "performed the march with much fear, and notwithstanding the guard of soldiers, they received sundry salutations in the form of stones & sticks, to say nothing of the curses which were heaped upon them from the doorways & hillsides."[14] It is also true that some Dakota (one of whom was just a baby) died on the march as a result of direct violence at the hands of white Minnesotans. But as the narrative cited by Waziyatawin herself makes clear, and as the historical evidence supports, the incidents of sporadic violence that marked the Dakota march were the exception rather than the norm during the movement. Bataan, on the other hand, was a case of nearly unremitting brutality and casual murder from start to finish, and Japanese soldiers killed hundreds of American and thousands of Filipino prisoners during the march.

This is not to suggest that the any of the deaths from the one incident were more heinous than those from the other—all lives have value. But I maintain that the march in Minnesota in 1862 and the march in Bataan in 1942 were not in any way similar to each other, other than that in each case a group of people were moved from one place to another. Waziyatawin's assertion that the two events were essentially the same thing is an outright distortion of the history. As Mary H. Bakeman and the late, eminent Minnesota historian Alan Woolworth put it, in their study of the march to Fort Snelling, "there is no evidence of either intent or outcome to support Wilson's [Waziyatawin's] characterization of these journeys as 'death marches' similar to the military treatment of prisoners on Bataan during World War II."[15] If Waziyatawin sincerely believes such a comparison is legitimate, then perhaps she does not understand the historical realities of the Bataan Death March. Her attempt to describe these separate histories as similar represents a gross disservice to the people who suffered in both events.

A countering perspective on the 1862 march comes from the MNHS oral history interview with John LaBatte. "The Indians taken to Fort Snelling were not forced marched," he argues. "It took about seven days to travel that, maybe a hundred and forty miles, twenty miles a day. That's not a great distance to travel and there was food along the way."[16] Most of the Dakota oral histories disagree with this view of the march, but there is some evidence to support LaBatte's argument. Sibley, he correctly points out, "sent only three companies to Fort Snelling [as escorts for the Dakota; the rest of the command took the condemned prisoners to Mankato]. They weren't forced marched.... They had wagons, if you look at the inventory of wagons at Fort Snelling." This is disputed by some Dakota today, but personal accounts from Indians who made the journey themselves in 1862 support the view that it was *not* a forced march.[17]

One such Dakota narrative comes from Good Star Woman, who made the march as an eight-year old girl and described the attacks on the column commanded by Lieutenant Colonel Marshall by saying, "When they passed through towns the people brought poles, pitchforks and axes and hit some of the women and children in the wagons...."[18] Sam Brown, the half-Dakota man whose family had been held captive during the war, was also there. "Men, women, and children, armed with guns, knives, clubs, and stones," he wrote, "rushed upon the Indians as the train was passing by and, before the soldiers could interfere and stop them, succeeded in pulling many of the old men and women, and even children, from the wagons by the hair of the head and beating them, and otherwise inflicting injury upon the helpless and miserable creatures." These eye-witness accounts agree that the Dakota did encounter violence on the march, violence from which the military failed to adequately protect them, but it also supports the argument that many of the women and children rode rather than walked.

Waziyatawin is not the only commentator to exaggerate the severity of the Dakota experience during the movement to Fort Snelling, and she is certainly not the only one to believe the idea that the march to Fort Snelling was a death march. One of the Dakota narrators in the MNHS interviews said, "That whole march, that road, there must be bones laying all over."[19] This is a moving image, one that elicits an understandable emotional response from people whose ancestors, frightened and bereft, made that march to a miserable confinement at Fort Snelling. The problem is that it is simply wrong. The idea that the march route is littered with the forgotten bones of Dakota dead is not historically accurate. This narrator may believe that Dakota people died in droves along the way, but no evidence, whether provided by white witnesses and government reports (both of which might naturally be considered unreliable by a Dakota skeptic) nor those from contemporary Indian narratives (which might be more acceptable to a Dakota reader), support such an idea. This version of the event is a vivid part of some traditions and oral histories, but it is not historical reality.

Exaggerations of death rates are not limited to Dakota oral histories, however; they also appear in the oral histories of white narrators. One elderly white woman, talking about the Indian attacks on New Ulm (which her grandfather experienced as a very young child) claims "about a hundred people were killed at that time."[20] The reality is that 34 settlers died in the fighting at New Ulm, and approximately 60 were wounded. This narrator might have confused the overall casualty count of nearly 100 dead and wounded at New Ulm, but there is a considerable difference between 34 dead and 100.

The hangings at Mankato are one of the most sensitive topics touched upon in the MNHS interviews. This is hardly surprising, since the mass execution continues to be one of the most controversial issues pertaining to the war, among white and Indian commentators alike. As in other cases, the perceptions derived from the oral histories can sometimes take a wide departure from the historical evidence.

One Dakota man, when asked what his feelings were when he visited the execution site in Mankato, replied, "I felt anger. Anger that the president would one day free the slaves and on the next day hang 38 of our chiefs."[21] This narrator believes that all of the men hanged at Mankato were leaders of the Dakota people, but such was not the case. One of the valid criticisms leveled against the executions is that none of the men hanged on December 26 could be said to have been a prominent war leader or authority figure of the Indians—the Army hanged men who were almost exclusively rank-and-file followers.

White Dog was remembered by Big Eagle as being "the Indian head farmer who was replaced by Taopi..." but that hardly made him an influential man in the war counsels.[22] Tatagaga was hardly more than a boy, and reportedly feeble-minded at that; Henry Milord was a mixed-race man of no great standing among the Dakota. Chaska, hanged because he was mistaken for another man with a similar name, was by most accounts a man of no particular political influence among his people. The narrator of this oral history has every right to be angry that 38 of his people were put to death, but his oral history embraces a misunderstanding of the event when he posthumously promotes all of the executed men to the position of chiefs.

Another Dakota man described the executions as an atrocity. "All the guys were doing, all the people that were hanged," he said, "defended what was rightfully theirs. That's all they were doing. And they were condemned."[23] The trial records dispute that characterization of the condemned men. Tazoo and Tehehdonecha were self-confessed rapists. Cut Nose murdered women and children, and others among the men hanged at Mankato were guilty of the crimes of massacre and murder. I use the word "crimes" deliberately, because as I stated earlier, I do not see how rape and infanticide can be excused as acceptable methods of self-defense. On the other hand, if the narrator had specified men such as Wahehud or White Dog, I believe the assertion would be valid.

To conclude this examination of the oral histories of the Dakota War, we should consider Waziyatawin's perspective again. Waziyatawin has a view of the historian's purpose which is best explained by an article she wrote in 1998, when she was publishing under the name Angela Cavender. "Our role as historians," she writes, "should be to examine as many of the perspectives of the past as possible—not to become the validators or verifiers of stories, but instead to put forth as many perspectives as possible." According to her, historians should simply recycle as many versions of the past as possible without regard to accuracy, provenance, or corroboration. In her view the telling of the tale is the only thing to value, and the truthfulness of the tale matters not at all; thus, a completely fictitious story would be as legitimate for historical purposes as a factual one. What Waziyatawin is advocating, though, is more properly a function of anthropology than history. An essential part of a historian's task is to winnow the facts from the fiction, Waziytawin's assertion to the contrary notwithstanding. If it is not, then we as historians become little more than peddlers of legends and fables.

It is perhaps worth noting that the article in which Waziyatawin made her statement about the historian's role was entitled, "Grandmother to Granddaughter: Generations of Oral History in a Dakota Family." Family histories are important parts of our individual identities, but as we have already seen, the family stories that come down through the generations are not always accurate in their details. It might not be inappropriate to ask, then, if Waziyatawin's argument that historians should not be "validators or verifiers of stories" stems from a reluctance to examine too closely the historical accuracy of the oral traditions that she extolls in her article.

Oral histories are important, valid and essential to understanding the things omitted from the conventional histories. They absolutely have a place at the table of historical discourse. But oral histories cannot claim an unchallengeable veracity simply because they come down through generations of family traditions. As this chapter has tried to show, there are problems of historical inaccuracy in many oral histories, just as there are inaccuracies in many of the conventional histories. If we are to sift fact from fiction, we must examine *all* the sources we encounter with the same rigorous standards of analysis and corroboration. But at the end of the process, no matter what arguments are made or what evidence is produced, it still comes down to the individual's choice of what is believed and what is denied.

In fairness, perhaps an oral history should itself be allowed the last word in this chapter on oral histories. In one of the MNHS interviews, the interviewer asked, "What did you learn about Dakota history while you growing up?" The narrator, himself a Dakota, replied, "That there are very, very many viewpoints on Dakota history."[24]

# 26

# Victims of Every Kind

*Who shall tell the fate of the innocent sufferer?*—Justina Krueger

Any place can be a battlefield—cities, towns, villages, and all the inhabited countryside between. War lays waste to crops, burns houses, displaces entire populations, and destroys lives. The ugly reality of war is that soldiers are not the only people who die in war; civilians suffer also, and sometimes more. Sometimes civilians are killed for no reason—crossfire does not discriminate. But often war is deliberately and directly waged against them. This was precisely what happened in 1862.

There were hundreds of victims of the Dakota War—thousands, if we include the survivors with the dead. But two groups should not be thought of as victims in any sense of the word. The men of the U.S. Army, whether they were regular troops or hastily enlisted volunteers, were soldiers, organized, armed and led. And if they were killed while fighting the Indians, it was nothing more than the soldier's lot in all wars. The men of Captain Marsh's command who were killed in the Indian ambush at Redwood Ferry were legitimate military targets and casualties of war, not victims of murder. In the same way, the Dakota men who were killed in the fighting were also not victims. They were soldiers, men of war from a warring culture, who took up arms against the Americans either for the martial glory that their traditions extolled or for the lure of plunder. Many of them, beyond question, fought for their people and their embattled way of life. Whatever their individual motivations, when Dakota men were killed in battle, they were not victims of any more than were the men of the U.S. Army.

Aside from soldiers and warriors, though, victims abounded in the Dakota War. Waziyatawin tries to argue that there were no innocent white people in Minnesota in 1862—settlers and soldiers alike; men, women and children as young as infants—she claims they all deserved death for having invaded the Dakota's traditional territory.[1] She is wrong, as wrong as any white writer would be who would suggest that Indians deserved to die for impeding the westward advance of Euro-American progress and civilization. If she were to be consistent in her argument, she should perhaps also posit that the Dakota deserved to die for having taken the lands of the Iowa, the Omaha, the Crow, the Arikara, and other tribes, but she does not.

Waziyatawin's version of the matter is countered by contemporary Dakota sources that actually experienced the war, sources which she does not to cite in her text. Cecilia Campbell Stay, the Dakota woman whose testimony we have already heard regarding the anti–Indian riot in Henderson and who witnessed the outbreak of the war before that, said, "Even if some sinner deserved the death it was yet slaughter...." "Too many innocents," Stay went on to say, suffered for the sins of the ones who were actually guilty of offenses against the Indians.[2] The reality was that people on both sides of the conflict, white and Indian alike, suffered terribly in the war—white settlers more in the first weeks of the war, and Indians for long afterwards.

If the belligerent factions among the Dakota hoped that the war would reverse the tide of white encroachment onto their lands, it was a catastrophic failure. Within months of the war's end, the U.S. government vacated all treaty rights previously granted to the Dakota, confiscated their remaining lands, and exiled the Lower Agency Dakota from Minnesota under the Forfeiture Act of February, 1863. More than just the Lower Agency Dakota suffered, though; the government permitted the Upper Agency Dakota to stay on their land, but anti–Indian sentiment in the state was running so high that for their own safety most of them opted to leave Minnesota as well. "As few as 50 Dakota," one historian calculates, "remained in Minnesota in 1867 from a population estimated at 4,370 in 1805 and 6,000 in 1850."[3] Only a relatively small percentage of the Dakota in Minnesota had actively participated in the war, but almost all of them suffered in the aftermath, even the ones who had vigorously opposed it. And the Dakota were not the only ones punished—on February 21, 1863, the U.S. Government passed an act forcing "the removal of the Winnebago Indians, and the sale of their reservation in Minnesota...."[4]

Among the white settlers who made up most of the victims murdered during the early days of the war, the majority were family groups. In some cases entire families were wiped out; in others, only a few members survived the maelstrom. Brown County, home of communities such as Milford and New Ulm, was particularly hard hit. Of the Bluehm family, only a small boy was left alive. The Zeller family were all killed. The Massopust family lost two daughters and a son; the father and one child escaped. Anton Manderfeld, a German settler whose life was saved by a Dakota man, reported finding "the body of a woman, and, by her, three children, all dead" in a house he came across during his flight.[5] Their identities were unknown to him, and are lost to history. All of the children in the Henle family were killed, but the parents survived. Three children of the May family lived to recover from their wounds, but their parents and two siblings were murdered. Adolph Schilling and his daughter were killed while his wife and son escaped the massacre. The Heuer and Zettle families were both entirely wiped out, all 11 of them. John Meyer survived the war, but his wife and children were all murdered by the Indians. Ole Sampson was murdered along with two of his children; his wife escaped with their baby. Philander Humphrey's family was all killed except for the oldest child, 12-year-old John.

John Humphrey later wrote an account of his childhood in Minnesota and described his experience of the Dakota War. In his narrative, he made a point well worth considering: "They [the Dakota] were quite intelligent enough," he wrote, "to discriminate between white men who had misused them and helpless women and children, who were physically and mentally incapable of doing so...."[6] He was absolutely correct—the only offense that could be laid to the charge of most of the settlers in the war-ravaged part of Minnesota was that they were there. They were not the members of the U.S. Congress who had delayed that year's annuity payment. They were not traders who profited from the corrupt system that siphoned off so much of the Dakotas' treaty benefits.[7] They were not even the American soldiers who represented the military arm of the invading power. They were nothing more than targets of opportunity in an orgy of killing and destruction that had some measure of self-defense in its motives, but which in the long run was an expression of wanton criminality more than anything else.

By the same standard of measurement, the Indian women and children who were confined on the river flats below Fort Snelling over the hard winter of 1862–1863, and who were attacked by mobs of white people before they ever got there, were guilty of nothing criminal. Some Indian women, it is true, had accompanied war parties that committed murder, and a few white survivors—such as Emanuel Reyff and Lavina Eastlick—specifically described how Dakota women had participated in killing settlers' children. But the guilt of a few unnamed women in no way implicated the hundreds of Indian women who had taken no part in any act of violence.

In fact, several of the white women held captive by the Indians later described how they were protected and sheltered by Dakota women. Minnie Buce Carrigan, Mary Schwandt, Sophia Huggins and Sarah Wakefield, in particular, all wrote with admiration and affection of the Indian women who had helped them survive their ordeal. In the immediate aftermath of the war, though, their benefactors were treated the same as the worst of the Indians. Just as there was no justification for the Dakota to have murdered settler women and children, so there was no justification for Minnesotans to vent their anger against defenseless Indian women and children. Dakota women and children simply represented an easy target of opportunity for angry whites when the true objects of their wrath were out of reach.

Lavina Eastlick with her surviving children, Merton, 11, and Johnny, 15 months. Eastlick lost her husband, John, and her three sons, Freddy, Frank and Giles, at Slaughter Slough in the Lake Shetek Massacre. Merton carried his baby brother to safety, 50 miles across the prairie, alone and on foot, before being reunited with his mother. This portrait was made at the request of Governor Alexander Ramsey in the fall of 1862 (Minnesota Historical Society).

Women and children, as a group, suffered more than almost any other people during the war. White women and children were murdered, or saw their husbands, fathers, brothers and sons murdered. Many of them were held as captives of the Dakota and suffered abuse for the six weeks of their ordeal. Indian women and children, for their part, lost everything in the aftermath of the war. Not a single

Dakota child could be said to have committed an atrocity or murdered anyone, yet nearly 1,700 Indian women and children were hemmed into the stockade below Fort Snelling, where hundreds of them died of disease before they were finally transported out of the state to a miserable exile at the wretched Crow Creek Reservation in modern-day South Dakota.

Even Henry H. Sibley, so ardent in his support of the military commission and the death sentences it handed down, was able to see the human tragedy that befell Dakota women and children. When he separated the convicted and condemned men from the main group of Indians prior to sending them down to Fort Snelling in October, he wrote to his wife that "the poor women and children ... were the very picture of distress when they learned that they were to proceed ... without their natural protectors. Poor wretches, they are objects of pity, notwithstanding the enormities perpetrated by their fathers, husbands, and brothers."[8] Even so, he proceeded as he felt that duty required him to, and compassion apparently played no part in his decisions.

The children of Justina Krueger, Lavina Eastlick and Justina Boelter were victims of the war. The Dakota children who were injured by white mobs at Henderson were also victims, and the fact that very few of their names are known to history in no way lessens the reality of their suffering. The Indian baby killed by the white woman at Henderson was no doubt loved by his mother every bit as much as Lavina Eastlick loved her children. That child's mother knew his name, even if we do not, and I believe she felt his loss every bit as deeply as every white woman who lost a child in the war.[9]

White settlers suffered for injustices that other people, in the main, had inflicted on the Indians; Dakota women and children suffered for the fact that they were Indians when the people of Minnesota sought vengeance on *all* Indians, even the innocent. The Dakota War, as most wars are, was indiscriminate in its victims.

# 27

# After the Storm

Within a year of the war's beginning, Little Crow was dead. He had returned to Minnesota with his son Wowinape on a horse-stealing raid in the summer of 1863. Wowinape later said, "When we were coming back, he [Little Crow] said he could not fight the white men, but would go below and steal horses from them...."[1] There are different versions of Little Crow's death, but the essential facts are these: late on the afternoon of July 3, 1863, Little Crow and Wowinape were spotted in a wild raspberry patch by two white farmers, Nathan and Chauncey Lamson. In the minds of most white Minnesotans in the tense months after the war, any Indian in the southwestern part of the state was hostile and dangerous. It did not matter to the Lamsons that the Indians they saw were not in a hostile stance; it did not matter that they had no idea who these particular Indians were. They shot first, with no thought of asking any questions later.

Little Crow was wounded in the first fire. He immediately shot back, and for a few moments the men tried to maneuver for advantage in the thick undergrowth. When it was all over, Nathan Lamson was wounded and Little Crow was dead, shot twice. Wowinape escaped.

As far as the people of Hutchison knew, the dead Indian was just another dead Indian. The corpse represented a certain monetary value to the Lamsons, since the State of Minnesota had a standing bounty on the scalps of dead Dakota, but beyond that no one really cared who the dead man was.[2] The body was laid in the town's dirt street for all to see, where boys amused themselves by sticking firecrackers in the dead man's nostrils and ears.[3] Little Crow's unidentified corpse was eventually dumped in the town's refuse pit. It was nearly a month later, after Wowinape's capture, before the desecrated, rotting body was finally identified as that of the man who, when his fellow Dakota refused to listen to his warnings against starting a war, had prophetically said, "I, Taoyateduta, am not a coward: I will die with you."

Henry H. Sibley, Little Crow's one-time acquaintance and eventual adversary, remained in the Army well after the 1862 war was over. Appointed to the command of the Military District of Minnesota, in 1863 he and Brigadier General Alfred Sully mounted a two-pronged punitive expedition into the Dakota Territory in pursuit of the hostile Indians who had fled Minnesota the year before. It was a campaign of mixed results, but it ensured that the fighting between the Sioux peoples and the United States would henceforth be waged west of Minnesota.

Sibley was brevetted a Major General of Volunteers in 1865, and left the Army the following year. He remained an influential figure in Minnesota and beyond, serving as the president of the board of regents for the University of Minnesota, as well as involvement in several railroads and banks. He was appointed president of the Board of Indian Commissioners in 1875, and was on the board of visitors to the U.S. Military Academy at West Point. A founding member of the Minnesota Historical Society, he remained an active member the rest of his life.

His command of the expedition against the Dakota in 1862 remained the capstone of his career, overshadowing his other accomplishments, even his tenure as the first governor of Minnesota. Sibley never seemed to waver in his conviction that the military commission had been both necessary and proper, and that it was conducted correctly. There is no indication that he ever knew or acknowledged that his own actions in trying to change some of the commission's sentences were violations of the law. He died at the age of 79 in 1891. His decision to convene the military commission after the Dakota War, and the results of that commission, colored his posthumous reputation as the commission increasingly came in for criticism from various sources.

Colonel Stephen Miller commanded the prison at Mankato and was in charge of the mass execution on December 26, 1862. On the strength of his performance in the Dakota War, and with Governor Ramsey's endorsement, he successfully ran for governor of Minnesota in 1863. He served one term as governor, and chose to not stand for reelection. He was an advocate of education and social progressivism, going so far as to argue (unsuccessfully) for the extension of the voting franchise to black people in Minnesota. He died in 1881, alone and impoverished, a decent man left behind by the advance of time.

Lieutenant Colonel William Marshall, like Colonel Miller, had enlisted in the Army as a private in 1861. In August 1862 he was appointed to the command of the Seventh Minnesota Volunteers, which was the position he held through the Dakota War. Many supporters of the Dakota, particularly missionaries such as Stephen Riggs, regarded Marshall as a consistently fair and decent man. He served briefly as one of the five officers on Sibley's military commission when it was first convened, but this does not seem to have harmed his reputation in any circle. In 1865 he succeeded Stephen Miller to the governorship of Minnesota, and served for two terms. He was able to pass into law the black suffrage amendment that Miller had wanted but was unable to complete. Like Sibley, Marshall was involved in banking and railroads in the years after the war. He died in California in 1896.

Joseph Godfrey, the mixed-race former slave who was the "negro" or "mulatto" whose case was the first one tried by the military commission in 1862, escaped the noose in spite of Sibley's conscious choice to ignore the court's recommendation for clemency. Incarcerated along with the other convicted Dakota, Godfrey was always a step away from a violent end—many of his fellow prisoners had reasons to hold a grudge against him for his testimony on the government's behalf. He was not the monster that many white commentators made him out to be immediately after the war, but neither was he the complete turncoat that some Dakota thought he was. He was a man caught up in the most violent event of his time, and though he was unable to keep out of the fray as he seems to have wanted to do, he was not a murderer. He settled on the Santee

Reservation in Nebraska, where he was at least safe from vengeance-minded white men, and for the rest of his life he remained among the Dakota with whom he had taken refuge when he escaped from bondage as a young man, even though he was never fully accepted by them after the war. It was the best choice of a bad lot available to him—there were plenty of white men who would have readily murdered him if he left the refuge of the reservation. Godfrey was an industrious man, and he lived out his days farming his allotment, keeping largely to himself. He died of natural causes in July, 1909.

The Reverend Stephen Return Riggs spent 40 years working among the Dakota as a missionary, continuing his work even after his wife Mary died shortly after the war. In 1871 he produced the first New Testament in the Dakota language, *Dakota wowapi wakan kin*. For the rest of his life he was troubled by what he felt were the injustices of the military commission trials. Writing in 1863 after the publication of Isaac Heard's book, Riggs wrote, "Mr. Heard has linked me with the Military Commission.... I accept this linking, not to criminate or blame any one [sic], but to act as confessor—to acknowledge that we belonged to a common erring humanity." He went on to say that "the pressure and means often brought to bear upon the prisoners to make them convict themselves were not in accordance with Military Regulations and the spirit of Christianity.... Many were more guilty than they appeared to be, while many were condemned to death on insufficient evidence." There was a reckoning owed for how the commission had dealt with the Indians, he believed, and that reckoning was one no man could avoid. "These acts of ours are passing into history," he said, "and we are individually passing on to appear before the military Commission that sits on the Great White Throne."[4] He died in Beloit, Wisconsin, in August 1883. His feelings on the military commission trials can best be understood through his own words: "We all did as nearly right then as we knew how," he wrote, "But we will not now, in looking back upon it, defend the wrong whatever it be; but rather confess it and ask God's forgiveness."[5]

Big Eagle, the Dakota chief whose narrative provides one of the most complete accounts of the war from the Indian side, was sentenced to ten years' imprisonment by the military commission. He was incarcerated until he received a presidential pardon in 1864. After several years in exile with the other Dakota, he voluntarily moved his family back to Minnesota in 1869, settling near the site of one his old battles, Birch Coulee. Big Eagle was adamant that he had fought the whites as a warrior, man to man, in "open fight, a fair fight," as he said in his narrative. He was not a criminal, no matter what the military commission thought, and he resisted that characterization all his life. His version of events did not sit well with all of his Dakota neighbors; at least one later called him "a very big liar." Big Eagle became a Roman Catholic, and died an old man in January 1906 near Granite Falls, Minnesota.

Justina Krueger was 27 years old at the time of the massacre that nearly killed her. Her husband was murdered as she watched, then she herself was wounded so seriously that the Indians believed she was dead. She was rescued by a unit of soldiers on burial detail just in time to live through the harrowing experience of the battle of Birch Coulee. All of her children and stepchildren survived the war, except for her youngest, a baby, who was lost in the chaos of the children's escape. She was never able to learn what happened to her child. After the war, she married another German settler named John Jacob Meyer, who had lost his entire family in the violence. In what can only be described as an enormous understatement, she concluded her narrative of the war by saying, "My experience is a sad one thus far. I hope never to witness another Indian massacre."[6]

The women who survived the Lake Shetek massacre did not find it easy to rebuild their lives. Lavina Eastlick lost her husband, John, and saw her young sons Freddy, Frank and Giles murdered. In what must have caused her enormous heartache, Frank's body was never found, and years after the war there were rumors that he was still alive, somewhere in the Dakota Territory. She was never able to confirm that. She herself was shot repeatedly and left for dead but was eventually rescued and recovered from her wounds. Her son Merton, who had carried his baby brother Johnny 50 miles to safety, died young at the age of 24 from a pulmonary illness, but Johnny lived until 1942. Lavina remarried, only to be divorced by her new husband. She married a third time, but that man disappeared a few months later, leaving her pregnant. She died in Alberta, Canada in 1923, at the age of 90.[7]

Julia Wright and Laura Duley were both taken captive by the Dakota after the massacre at Lake Shetek. Julia was raped repeatedly while in the Indians' hands, and became pregnant. When the baby was born after her release and her husband saw that the child was part Indian, he left her. He reportedly said that she should have died rather than allow herself to be raped by an Indian. Julia took the child and relocated to Nebraska, where she disappeared into history. Laura saw her ten year-old son William killed while she begged the Indians to spare his life. Like Julia, she was raped numerous times in captivity; she also became pregnant as a result of the rapes, but miscarried after her release. Three weeks after being reunited with her surviving family, the cumulative physical and mental trauma she had experienced caused her to become completely deranged. She reportedly later regained some measure of her mental faculties, but she was never again the same person.[8] In one of the iconic images from the war, there is a photograph in the collection of the South Dakota State Historical Society that shows Julia Wright and Laura Duley with the surviving children who were taken captive with them after the Lake Shetek massacre. In the photograph, Laura stares at the camera with an empty-eyed, emotionless expression. She looks haunted. By all accounts she was, for the rest of her life.

As for the Dakota people, perpetrators and bystanders alike, guilty and innocent, hostile and friendly, their old way of life was gone forever. And for a long time, so were most of them, gone from Minnesota. Samuel Pond, the missionary who wrote so eloquently of the Dakota people he had lived among all those decades past, wrote a letter to Sibley not long before he died. "From Lake Pepin to Lac Traverse, from Rock to Frenier, they are gone—all gone—gone to oblivion: for who knows that they were ever here?" Pond lamented. "They have not been succeeded by their children, but supplanted by strangers, some of them strangers from beyond the sea."[9]

# Conclusion

The events set in motion by the outbreak of the Dakota War on August 18, 1862, did not end with the battle of Wood Lake, nor even with the hangings at Mankato that December. By the following summer, nearly all of the Dakota in Minnesota were gone, forced out of the state. What followed was nearly 30 years of intermittent warfare between the United States and the Sioux tribes—the Dakota, Lakota, Nakota and Teton. There would be periods of truce and occasional pauses in the hostilities, but war was the new reality for the next three decades.

The fighting that began that Monday morning in Minnesota erupted at least in some part because the Dakota were striking back against wrongs long endured and threats perceived. Twenty-eight years later, Siouxan independence came to its final, tragic end on a cold day in December, 1890, in the massacre at Wounded Knee, South Dakota.

Little Crow had been dead 27 years by then, but had he lived to see the end he probably would not have been surprised. That August night in 1862 he purportedly told his fellow Dakota, "The Whitemen [sic] are like locusts, when they fly so thick that the whole sky is a snowstorm.... Kill one, two, ten, and ten times ten will come to kill you. Count your fingers all day long and Whitemen with guns in their hands will come faster than you can count." Little Crow had foreseen the bloody result before the fighting ever began. "You will die like rabbits when the hungry wolves hunt them in the Hard Moon [January]," he is supposed to have told the men in his house that night.[1] In the fullness of time, his prediction came true in the blood-stained snow of Wounded Knee.

But as 1862 ended, all of those events still lay decades in the future. When the snows melted in the spring after the war, the search for the bodies of dead settlers was an ongoing process—many were never identified and so were buried without even their names to mark their graves; the remains of others were never found. Settlers' homesteads were in ashes, or broken open to plunder, and in many cases taken over by squatters (who were always other white people, not Indians). Thousands of people were dislocated from their homes—many of the settlers eventually returned, or voluntarily relocated to other areas, but the Dakota were banished to a dismal exile. There they endured three years at the wretched Crow Creek reservation; three terrible years of near starvation and epidemics of disease before they were finally moved again to a different area. The war was over, but their suffering had only just begun, and it continued for long after. The wounds were slow to heal. More than 150 years later, some of those wounds are still not healed.

So if this is the legacy of the Dakota War—suffering, sorrows and scars—who owes whom an apology for it all? The question of responsibility and blame always follows close on to any discussion of the war, with advocates for both sides pointing accusing fingers at each other. This is natural enough, and by itself it need not prevent constructive dialogue from taking place. Where the problem arises is that there are those on both sides of the debate who refuse to countenance any portion of the other side's point of view. Some Dakota people today, as we have seen, claim that the conventional histories are nearly all fabrications of European-American bias. Some white commentators point to the allegations of horrible atrocities committed by the Dakota during the war and base their entire perception of the war on that and nothing else.

Considered against the greater arc of history, the factors that led to the Dakota War, and indeed the war itself, are neither unique nor singular. The displacement of Native American people by European-Americans is, unfortunately, not a historical anomaly. Human history is one long sequence of societies emerging and growing, often by absorbing or invading and conquering societies that were there before them, and just as often eventually being absorbed or conquered by newer, more powerful societies in their turn. Wave after wave of human migration has encroached upon the pre-established territories of people who have fought back—sometimes successfully, sometimes not—against tides of foreign outlanders who threatened their culture, their independence, and sometimes their very existence. Defeat in a war in one place has frequently driven people from their ancestral homes to new lands where they have subsequently assumed the roles of aggressors and conquerors themselves. Some of the settlers in Minnesota in 1862 had precisely that sort of experience.

As I have tried to show in this book, the war between the United States and the Dakota in 1862 has produced conflicting accounts and differing interpretations. The war's history continues to be fiercely debated today. Even so, I believe that it is possible to state the following facts with certainty: After years of mounting grievances caused in some part by the maladministration of the U.S. Government, the Dakota started the war on August 18, 1862 by attacking the Lower Agency; when the fighting ended Henry H. Sibley convened a military commission that proceeded to try 392 Dakota in trials conducted in the field; 303 men were sentenced to death; 38 of those men were executed on December 26, 1862; in 1863 the U.S. government revoked all of the Dakota's treaty rights and expelled most of the Dakota from Minnesota.

Beyond these facts, the conclusions reached will differ widely according to individual interpretations. My own conclusions are these: The vast majority of acts which can legitimately be classified as atrocities were carried out by the Dakota, but some were undeniably the work of white men; Sibley's military commission was legally convened and legally conducted up to a point, but its operation was not fair to most of the defendants and was often at odds with the due process of law; Sibley, before all was said and done, broke the law himself and did so every time he interfered with the decisions of the commission. Some of the Dakota tried by the commission were undoubtedly guilt of capital crimes specified by the Articles of War, but most of the men convicted by the commission were guilty of nothing more than fighting in open battle. There were men on the gallows at Mankato who absolutely should have been there—Tazoo, Cut Nose and others—but two men were hanged in error. Some of the worst offenders went free because the military never apprehended them; some of the perpetrators of the worst crimes were never named or identified. In the end, the Dakota people all suffered for things that not all of them had done.

There remains a wide gulf in differing interpretations, and diametrically opposing understandings of what actually happened in Minnesota that year. The extremes of perspective are sometimes so far apart as to not even sound as if they are describing the same event. So contentious is the history of the 1862 war trials that even today, as one scholar notes, "the entire subject is toxic."[2]

So again, who owes whom an apology? Perhaps before we seek an answer to that question we should ask another one. Is there anything to apologize for, more than a century after the fact when the people who fought each other, who suffered and caused each other to suffer, are all dead and gone? Not necessarily, one might say. It is hard to understand how one person can meaningfully apologize for the wrongs that another inflicted, especially when that apology is rendered to people who were not themselves directly wronged. But there is another aspect to this question.

We must acknowledge that wrongs were done. We must accept that wounds were inflicted which continue to pain the descendants of those who themselves suffered. People have long, long memories, and the healing process can continue for generations after the event. In the heat of the moment, when people are killing each other and no conciliation seems possible, it is a sad truth that we as humans too often try to deny the humanity that we share with our enemies. It is easier to kill the other person if we can convince ourselves that they are not like us, not of our kind, not really people at all. The Reverend Stephen Riggs, whose insights into the Dakota War contain more soul-searching introspection than nearly any other observer, referred to the "common erring humanity" of which we are all a part. He was absolutely right about that.

In the oral history interviews conducted by the Minnesota Historical Society, one Dakota narrator related that as she and other Native Americans walked the route of their ancestors' march to Fort Snelling, a white woman shouted at them, "Why don't you guys just forget about it?"[3] That is utterly the wrong attitude to take to this history.

Why should the Dakota people forget about it? How could they? Forgetting about it, when the "it" is our personal pasts and the histories of our people, is not something that many of us are inclined to do, and it is unrealistic to expect others to do so in their turn. For that reason we should seek to understand each other, and our different pasts, and our shared humanity. Doing so might enable us to then understand something of each other's pain, and acknowledging that is a step in the right direction. The events of the Dakota War might be a century and a half behind us, but I think it is entirely appropriate that the State of Minnesota has acknowledged, and officially apologized for, its role in the wrongs done to the Dakota in the aftermath of the war.

But if we are to honestly admit that wrongs were done, then we must also confront the fact that wrongs were done by *both* sides in this war, and that there were innocent people who suffered on both sides of the conflict. The descendants of those Dakota people who were driven from their homeland are correct to point out the considerable wrongs that their ancestors suffered at American hands, but they must also be willing to accept that some of their ancestors committed rape, murder, and the massacre of children in those dark days of 1862. I accept as historically accurate the charge that the Dakota people were cheated, abused, dispossessed and abysmally treated by the U.S.

government and many white men; however, I insist that it is also accurate that the Dakota in retaliation killed men, women and children who bore no personal responsibility for the wrongs done to the Indians. The one does not cancel out the other or balance the scale; they both just *were*.

There is a marked reluctance on the part of some commentators today to even consider the possibility that acts of wanton criminality or excessive brutality were committed by any Dakota during the war. Those who take this position on the history seem to want to argue for an all-encompassing absolution of Indian actions, suggesting that if any crimes were committed by the Dakota it was only because they were wronged by the whites, first. If we accept that sort of reasoning, then it might also be argued that any act, no matter how violent, how cruel, how heinous, is justified so long as it is committed in response to another, earlier wrong received. That is the slippery slope to an unending cycle of retaliation, hatred and revenge, and I reject it as both a philosophy and a policy.

Reading through the contemporary sources on the Dakota War, one is quickly struck by the vitriolic language and unabashed racism of many white commentators when they wrote about Indians. Reading statements such as, "the Indian races were in the wrongful possession of a continent required by the superior right of the white man," it is hard to find the views and sentiments of the writer anything but appalling.[4] Most of us today, it is to be hoped, find such attitudes and biases abhorrent, but we cannot just congratulate ourselves on our enlightened, progressive sensibilities and stop there.

If we are going to impose modern perspectives on the past and condemn the anti–Indian attitudes that were acceptable among many Americans in the 19th century, then we should also be honest enough to say that Native American traditions which condoned excessive brutality and indiscriminate killing are also deserving of modern condemnation. It may have been acceptable to 19th century Dakota to kill white children simply because they were in families that had moved onto traditional Dakota lands, but that does not mean that we must accept that infanticide today, and by accepting, condone it. We would be absolutely wrong to attempt to justify white racism and governmental policies toward Indians that in some cases amounted to acts of ethnic cleansing; why then should we accept attempts to justify murder, rape and massacre just because the perpetrators were Native Americans?

We should always remember that there are two sides to this history, and remember that perpetrators and victims are to be found on both sides of the conflict. No one has a monopoly on the pathos and suffering caused by the war. And neither side is entirely free of blame for wrongs committed during the conflict. This view was expressed very well by Daniel Buck, who was himself a veteran of the war and the author of a book about it. Buck's memories of the hanging at Mankato are worth reading:

> I rejoiced when retributive justice overtook these murderers of helpless women, children and men, and I am unable to use language sufficiently severe in denouncing their inhuman cruelties and conduct. But as I stood near the gallows, and saw thirty-eight human beings swung off at once into eternity, I wondered where the blame rested that made necessary such a taking of human life, even though it was punishing the guilty creatures. And memory of the needless cruelties of the white race warned me that they had many grievous sins of the same kind to answer for.[5]

In the final analysis, we should try to ensure that the history that we accept is as close to the historical reality as we can determine. As this book has tried to show, that is no easy process. There are no final, definitive answers to some of the most pressing questions from the conflict in 1862. In the scholarly quest for historical accuracy, however, we should not lose sight of the human side of the story. The Dakota War, as all wars do, destroyed lives, orphaned children, drove people from their homes and caused suffering that lasted far beyond the war itself. Every war is a tragedy for someone. In the Dakota War of 1862, there was tragedy enough to go around.

# Notes on Sources

I have selected the following books and articles to illustrate some of the problems with a few important sources, to highlight the strengths of some of the best sources, and to point the reader to books that can fill in details of the history which I have not covered in this text.

**Anderson, Gary Clayton.** *Little Crow: Spokesman for the Sioux,* **and** *Through Dakota Eyes: Narrative Account of the Minnesota Indian War of 1862.*

Dr. Anderson, who at the time of this writing is a history professor at the University of Oklahoma, is an authority in the field of Dakota War studies, and from the frequency with which I have taken exception to some of his statements in the course of this text, the reader might assume I hold his writings on the subject in little regard. Actually, the contrary is true. Dr. Anderson has contributed some books of lasting value to the historiography of the Dakota War, and his biography of Little Crow is particularly important. The book he co-authored with the late Allen Woolworth, *Through Dakota Eyes,* is a compilation of narratives from the Dakota side of the war and an essential source for any student studying the conflict who cannot access the original narratives, which are scattered across numerous books.

Dr. Anderson's scholarship on the history of the American West is extremely important for other reasons. He has drawn a clear line between ethnic cleansing on the one hand, which the U.S. Government certainly engaged in with regards to its Indian policies, and anti–Indian genocide, which the U.S. did not engage in, on the other. There is a distinction between the language of genocide and the act of genocide, and Dr. Anderson explicates this clearly in his work. He also is one scholar who has not shied away from unequivocally stating that what happened in Minnesota in August 1862 was, in certain cases, nothing less than massacre.

His 2012 speech at Gustavus Adolphus College, however, is highly problematic. Many of the statements Dr. Anderson made in that presentation were not simply wrong; they were outright distortions of the historical record. In particular, his claim that he is the researcher who found the trial transcripts and brought them to the Minnesota Historical Society is patently false; his assertions that Sibley himself wrote the verdict and death sentence on each trial transcript in pencil is disproved by the trial transcripts themselves, where no such notations are to be found; his statements that the military commission was in place before September 28 does not concur with any evidence; his allegation that Lincoln's decision to narrow the death list to 40 names was an arbitrary one completely disregards the compelling evidence to the contrary; his characterization of Sibley's instructions to the military commission are completely inaccurate according to both Sibley's own correspondence as well as the court records of the trial transcripts themselves; and his claim that no defendant in the course of the trials was arraigned and that there were no charges brought against them is completely false, as again shown by reading the trial transcripts.

**Bachman, Walt.** *Northern Slave, Black Dakota: The Life and Times of Joseph Godfrey.*

Bachman brings an insight to the study of the Dakota War trials that is invaluable in sorting through some of the fog surrounding the legal questions in the history. He is a retired attorney, and was for some years a prosecutor in Hennepin County, Minnesota. With that background, he is uniquely positioned to consider the trials from the standpoint of a lawyer with decades' of experience in the practice of law, and some of his insights are illuminating. He is a meticulous and thorough researcher, and his biography of Joseph Godfrey makes for compelling reading.

**Bryant, Charles S., and Abel B. Murch.** *A History of the Great Massacre by the Sioux Indians, in Minnesota: Including the Personal Narratives of Many Who Escaped.*

Published in 1863, Bryant's book was one of the first contemporary accounts of the war available to the public, after McConkey's book. As a secondary historical source it must be handled with some caution, because Bryant came to the history of the war with a clear and unapologetic agenda—he regarded the war as a criminal act on the part of the Indians, and argued for the most forceful responses possible. He was in full favor of the military commission, and felt that the majority of the condemned Indians ought to have been hung as originally sentenced. Bryant also argued against the Indians being thought of or treated as prisoners of war.

Where this source is particularly valuable, however, is in its preservation of survivor narratives. Bryant included numerous survivor narratives in his book, and made the commendable decision to reproduce most of them verbatim, as dictated or written by the survivors themselves, without paraphrasing or editing. In this way, he allowed these reports to exist in their original, first-person voices, rather than in the altered versions that Harriet McConkey used in her book *Dakota War Whoop*. Bryant included the narratives of Justina Krueger, Mary Schwandt, and Lavina Eastlick, among others. He also used the accounts of Anton Manderfeld and Valencia Reynolds, both of whom described how white settlers were saved by friendly Indians.

**Chomsky, Carol.** *United States–Dakota War Trials: A Study in Military Injustice.*

Chomsky's heavyweight article (literally; it goes 90 pages in the Stanford Law Review) is one of the most well-researched, comprehensive scholarly articles yet written on the subject of the military commission of 1862. She is not a historian as such, but a law professor at the University of Minnesota, and her research is especially relevant because of her wide-ranging and inter-disciplinary approach. She poses some insightful questions as to the legitimacy of the commission, Sibley's authority to convene it, the issue of Dakota sovereignty, and the debate over the issue of prisoner of war status for the Indians. Several of her conclusions on points of military law are, in my opinion, the wrong ones, but such is the nature of scholarly debate.

In spite of these points of contention, I recommend Chomsky's article as an example of a well-written, insightful and balanced scholarly article. In the field of secondary sources on the military commission of the Dakota War, Chomsky is the gold standard by which others should be judged. Her article is, quite simply, excellent legal writing, and her insights into the law are unparalleled in the historiography of the Dakota War. Since her article was published in 1990, nearly every subsequent study of the Dakota War that considers the trials in any depth has cited her as a foundational source, and with good reason.

**Cox, Hank H.** *Lincoln and the Sioux Uprising of 1862.*

This is one of the more recent books published on the Dakota War, coming out in 2005. It is useful for its comprehensive side-by-side consideration of what was happening in Minnesota in the summer of 1862, and at the same time what was transpiring in Washington D.C. and in the Civil War on the national level. It is not particularly scholarly in its style and suffers from a complete lack of source citation or notes, which is to its considerable detriment as a history of this war. It is a big-picture rendering of the history.

Cox's particular bias is that he is absolutely critical of Henry H. Sibley, and never misses an opportunity to denigrate him in every way possible—personally, professionally, politically and militarily. The problem, from a historical perspective, is that he offers little hard evidence to support his opinions. He does not like Sibley, that much is abundantly clear, but he fails to marshal a convincing argument to explain why his perspective should be taken as accurate and true in the face of countering evidence.

A more significant problem with Cox's text is the way in which he recycles the old, lurid stories of the most shocking atrocity allegations, and presents them as fact without attempting to distinguish between what can be supported by evidence and what is simply rumor and hearsay. Someone with no broader knowledge of the historiography of the Dakota War would likely read Cox's book and come away believing that the Indians made a common practice of nailing babies to any object close at hand. Cox repeats that particular atrocity claim at least three separate times in his book, and never makes any apparent effort to determine its validity. In this respect, he continues the exaggeration and hyperbole that began in the frenzied days of the outbreak itself.

**Derounian-Stodola, Kathryn Zabelle.** *The War in Words: Reading the Dakota Conflict Through the Captivity Literature.*

Derounian-Stodola has written or contributed to several books and articles on the Dakota War, focusing most often on the captivity narratives; her academic focus is the literature of the war, rather than the general history of it. *The War in Words* represents her most in-depth work on the subject to date.

In terms of her historical perspective, Derounian-Stodola is firmly in the camp of those who question the authenticity of most stories of Dakota atrocities; as indicated when she says, "Historically considerable doubt exists about the extent of Indian violence during the Conflict...." Her view on the aftermath of the war is clear early in her book, when she says, "the U.S. government removed or imprisoned hundreds of Dakotas, conducted hasty and illegal trials, and sent thirty-eight to the gallows...." If she has, herself, conducted a detailed study of the military commission and its legality, it is not immediately apparent from her text—she has apparently arrived at her conclusion from a reading of other secondary sources. She cites Carol Chomsky's article as a particular support for this interpretation, but I believe she has greatly over-simplified Chomsky's complex inter-disciplinary study of the legal questions.

In spite of these factors, Derounian-Stodola's book is an important contribution to the literature of the Dakota War; I would even suggest that it is essential reading for any researcher who is delving into the primary source materials. Derounian-Stodola is a first-rate researcher of literary texts and an expert on the study of contemporary narratives. She organizes her book into two parts, one for white texts on the war and another for the Dakota accounts, and then she explicates individual narrators in each section.

This is especially valuable to researchers because she does such an excellent job of examining the history of each narrator's stories. Some of these accounts went through various editions or subsequent retellings over a period of years, even decades, and Derounian-Stodola offers a comparative study of each version. There is an incredible amount of fog and contradiction in the literature of the war; Derounian-Stodola clears away some of the haze with this book.

Beyond these strengths, however, her conclusions and interpretations frequently do not hold up to scrutiny, especially when she takes a position on the political or military history of the war rather than restricting herself to its literature.

**Heard, Isaac V. D.** *History of the Sioux War and Massacres of 1862 and 1863.*

Heard's book is of particular value because he was the only member of the military commission to write at length on the war and the commission's work. As the official Recorder of the court, Heard was privy to almost all of the commission's proceedings, deliberations, and rationale. Even today, his book is considered essential reading for any historical examination of the war. At the same time, it must be acknowledged that Heard was not a careful historian, and his book contains "some factual errors," as Kenneth Carley observes, errors which I have already considered in this text.

Like Bryant, Heard reproduced some first-person survivor narratives in his book, though not as many and not to the same extant. Where Heard's account must be handled carefully is in the matter of atrocities. He cites some instances of Indian atrocities which may be accorded some degree of trustworthiness, because in these specific cases he either gives the names of victims or attributes the story to a named witness. In other instances, though, he is less dependable.

In several cases, Heard repeats the litany of atrocities that McConkey used, and does so nearly verbatim, without adding any kind of attribution that would make the alleged atrocities any more verifiable. He does the same thing with the atrocities listed in the letter written to Lincoln by Senator Wilkinson and other members of the Minnesota Congressional Delegation.

When Heard does cite his sources or gives specific corroborating details, his version of events is plausible and convincing. He is also the only source to provide deeper context into what occurred in the military commission trials, especially Godfrey's role.

**Isch, John.** *The Dakota Trials: The 1862–1864 Military Commission Trials of the Dakota.*

This is an excellent work on the functioning of the military commission, written in 2012, and it deserves a wider readership than it has yet had. Isch takes a close look at the work of the military commission, enumerates its particular flaws, and considers the secondary source perspectives. His compilation and transcription of the trial records is invaluable to any study of trials, and his efforts to identify and distinguish between the defendants are most helpful. In particular, Isch's explication of the multiple names attached to some of the defendants is a great help in clearing away some of the confusion surrounding that aspect of the trials. For researchers delving into the particulars of the military commission trials, Isch's manuscript should be required reading, and his insights into the nature of the transcripts are enlightening.

**LaBatte, John.** https://dakotawar1862.wordpress.com.

John LaBatte is a Minnesota historian with ancestors on both sides of the Dakota War, and as such he brings some unique personal insights to his examination of the conflict. Even more importantly, his approach to the history involves evaluating the various representations of the war by means of a rubric through which he evaluates the narrative by several standards. His website is an excellent source for anyone seeking a comparative analysis of both primary sources and secondary sources. Mr. LaBatte has also engaged with some of the most contentious aspects of the history, particularly on the issue of how that history is portrayed today, and his conclusions are illuminating. I do not agree with him on every single point, but his approach to the history is careful, methodical and extremely helpful for the depth of research he brings to his conclusions—he does an excellent job of not only sifting fact from fiction, but also of gauging the tone and tenor of each source he considers.

**Malmros, Oscar.** *Annual Report of the Adjutant General 1863.*

This is an important primary source, but at the same time it is a seriously flawed source. The Adjutant General's Report of 1863 covered the previous year's military operations in the state of Minnesota, and so dealt with the entire scope of the Dakota War from its outbreak all the way to the hangings at Mankato. The Adjutant General's office (a position which still exists in the U.S. today, the Adjutant General of each state being the senior military officer of that state's National Guard units) had access to all the reports and dispatches that went back and forth between the field commands and headquarters, and so could be expected to know the exact details and particulars of what was done where, and when, and by whom. One might expect this to be the case, but a careful reading of the report finds it to be inaccurate on some important points. Two examples will serve as cases in point.

In its discussion of the functioning of Sibley's military commission, the Adj. Gen. Report says that *two* commissions operated simultaneously until all the trials were complete. The error here is that while there were two commissions, the first version—the three-man commission that was intended to function as a grand jury—only operated for one day before being superseded by the five-man commission that carried on from that point forward. This misunderstanding (and misrepresenting) of the facts is important because if a grand jury body had really been functioning throughout the entire process, examining the evidence against each Indian *before* they were arraigned at trial, then some of the legitimate criticism about the lack of due process would be nullified.

The other major error that the Adj. Gen. Report makes is in its description of the movement of Indians from the Lower Agency to Fort Snelling. The report accurately describes how the prisoners under Sibley's command were attacked by the mob in New Ulm, but it then says that the large body of Dakota women, children and old men (in short, those Indians not accused of any crime) who were under Lt. Col. Marshall's charge, encountered no violence at all. "This detachment," the report reads, "received no molestation from the settlers upon the route and arrived safely at their destination on the 13th [of November]." It was Marshall's column of Indian non-combatants who were assaulted in the town of Henderson; the Indian baby who was killed by a white woman was one of the casualties in this group.

Glaring errors such as this lead the historian to approach the Adj. Gen. Report with a palpable sense of caution. In spite of these problems, though, the report is valuable for another type of information which it contains. As an official annual report, the Adj. Gen. Report is also an accounting document. When the report moves away from narrative (where it sometimes wanders rather far from the known facts) and focuses instead on the dry, unexciting monotony of lists and invoices, it becomes particularly valuable. It is in these accounting lists, after all, that we find the lists of bounties paid for killing Indians and for tanning Indian scalps, evidence that atrocities were committed by official sanction of the Minnesota government.

**Satterlee, Marion P.** *The Court Proceedings in the Trial of Dakota Indians Following the Massacre in Minnesota in August 1862.*

Satterlee was a prominent printer and publisher in Minneapolis who published several books and pamphlets on the Dakota War, including this one, published in 1927. Until his book came out, the trial transcripts of the military commission had never been published for public review; in fact, the transcripts were lost in the black hole of government bureaucracy for nearly 60 years until they were finally located in the Senate archives by the renowned Minnesota historian William Folwell.

Satterlee's book is a small one, reproducing only 109 cases of the 392 that the commission tried. This is more than just a representative sampling, though, because Satterlee included the most prominent cases and all of the cases of the men who were eventually hung at Mankato. In compiling his list, Satterlee relied heavily on William Folwell's notes. Satterlee was not a trained historian, but Folwell was, and Folwell was unabashedly critical of the commission's sloppy processes and spotty record-keeping.

Satterlee's work is useful not only for its reproduction of the trial transcripts, but also for questions about the proceedings which he posed to the reader in the form of "notes" at the beginning of the book. For example, Satterlee raises points about the function of the commission's Judge Advocate (Lt. Olin) and the reviewing officer (Brig. Gen. Sibley ), and the heavy preponderance of convictions based on no evidence other than the fact that the defendant had admitted being present at one of the four battles. Satterlee shared Folwell's critical view of the commission, a perspective which he stated in his foreword.

"A disgraceful story of passion partiality and cruelty," Satterlee wrote, "is the trial of the Dakota Indians by a Commission from the military, at the close of the outbreak in 1862." He was equally clear about his reasons for publishing the transcripts. "This Trial Record is not published to malign those concerned," he wrote, referring to the members of the military commission; "their acts can be left to the Almighty, but to show that history is far from just to the Indian people, whose lands have been taken, by force, fraud and deceit, whose demoralization and destruction as a race is due to the advent of the white man. The record is a living picture of their treatment."

**Wakefield, Sarah F.** *Six Weeks in the Sioux Tepees: A Narrative of Indian Captivity.*

Sarah Wakefield's account is important for its singular position in the canon of survivor narratives. Whereas most of these narratives are replete with the horrors experienced at the hands of the Indians, both at the moments of the attacks and during the subsequent captivities, Wakefield is unique in that she advocates most strongly for the Indians. Or, more correctly, for one Indian in particular, Chaska, who in a case of mistaken identity was hung when another man with a similar name was in fact the condemned person. Wakefield was justifiably outraged at this tragic miscarriage of justice, especially since she credited Chaska with having saved her life when she was captured and for having protected her during the six weeks she was held by the Dakota. Her account of her experience is frequently touted by revisionists who try to argue that the Indians committed no widespread atrocities and that they treated their female captives well more often than not. There are, however, several problems with this.

For one thing, Wakefield's experience was unique in that while she was captured with two small children, one an infant, none of them were harmed or killed. The man who was escorting her to Fort Ridgely, a Mr. Gleason, *was* killed by the Indians who captured her, but she does not seem to have known him very well. In the course of her captivity, she was not raped or molested in any way, almost certainly because Chaska and his family went to considerable lengths to protect her. She herself said that she was "much better treated than any other female...," which would indicate that she was aware that her experience was better than what most of the other women went through. So while she was able to speak from an eyewitness perspective to the experience of Indian captivity, she was not as directly or personally impacted by it as were most of the other female captives, almost all of whom had witnessed the murder of husbands, children, or both.

Wakefield is also a problematic witness because of her repeated statements of self-serving complicity. By her own admission, she was willing to do anything in order to survive her ordeal, and she makes some disturbing statements to that effect. Wakefield says that on one occasion, when a rumor was going around in camp that the Indians were going to kill all of their white prisoners, she told Shakopee, one of the chiefs, "if he would only spare me that I would help kill the other prisoners. I also promised never to leave his Band, and that I would sew, chop wood, and be like a squaw."[1] She explains this behavior retrospectively as a temporary state of mind brought about by desperation, but there are so many occasions of this type of collaboration in her account that her excuses are unconvincing. The single most motivating factor in her narrative is the desire to save her own life, which is completely understandable and common to most of the survivor narratives. But where other women tried to save their lives and those of their children by fighting back, or escaping (both of which were done successfully), Sarah Wakefield took the path of collaboration.

For all of that, Wakefield's defense of some Indians was legitimate, as was her objection to the contemporary impulse to indiscriminately blame all Indians for the uprising. "Suppose," she wrote, "the same number of whites were living in sight of food, purchased with their own money, and their children dying of starvation, how long do you think they would remain quiet?"[2] Her point is well made, but it should be noted that this point was also made by other survivors who had more reason than her to harbor animosity toward the Dakota, so she is not unique for this perspective. She went on to say, "I do not wish any one to think I uphold the Indians in their murderous work." Unfortunately, her actions during her captivity made it seem that she did, and that stigma followed her for the rest of her life.

# Appendix
## *The Creation of Military Commissions*

In 1862, the concept of a commission as a form of military court was not a new thing in American military law. Its antecedents were fairly recent, however, having only been given any type of official structure during the Mexican-American War in 1847. Even critics of the commission have pointed out that "although military commissions were not legislatively recognized until 1862, they were recognized in military practice and accepted as proper military tribunals long before that date, authorized to try certain types of offenders and offenses under certain conditions...."[1]

General Winfield Scott almost single-handedly created the precedent upon which all later military commissions were based, including the ones in the 21st century. Scott created military commissions to fill a judicial gap in his command during the Mexican War; his General Order 20, published in February 1847, "combined a close adherence to court-martial procedures with a flexible approach to jurisdiction and substantive law."[2] In the language of Scott's order, the commissions were to handle violations of common law crimes committed "in, by, or upon the army."[3] The military commission might have been unorthodox, but Scott's field-expedient solution was favorably regarded by the Army and retained as an option.

There is one particular feature of Scott's prototype military commission which has a direct bearing on our consideration of Sibley's use of the commission process. Similar to, but distinct from, a court-martial, Scott's commissions by dint of their purpose were "typically confined to a zone of combat operations or occupied territory."[4] Thus, they were expected to function in the field, as an expeditious alternative to judicial processes that might be more impracticable in an army's area of operations. Both of these elements—the proximity of Sibley's commission to the scene of hostilities, and the speed of its functioning—have become the focus of heavy criticism from many quarters. Some of this criticism attempts to apply the procedural requirements of formal courts-martial to the military commission, but, as Kaplan points out, "The military commission has been distinguished from the court-martial in that the former, without defined powers, and not bound by rules of procedure as are courts-martial, is able to proceed more expeditiously."[5] The fact that military commissions were not bound as strictly to the regulatory requirements placed on courts-martial was established by no less an authority than U.S. federal law, which said that commissions "will be appointed, governed, and limited, *as nearly as practicable*, as prescribed by the 65th, 66th, 67th, and 97th, of the said rules and articles of war" [italics added].[6] This provides some traction to the idea that Sibley's commission was therefore not required to conform, in every detail, to the same procedural framework as formal courts-martial.

It must be recognized that Sibley, for all of his lack of military education and lack of familiarity with military law and custom, did not simply create his commission out of whole cloth. He was standing on a firm platform of established military practice when he seated his commission. No less a figure than Major General Henry Halleck, who was recognized internationally as an expert in military law (and who in 1862 was the General in Chief of the U.S. Army), had lent some legitimacy to the idea of a military commission. Earlier in 1862, Halleck had published a paper in which he wrote:

> Many classes of people cannot be arraigned before such courts [courts-martial] for any offense whatsoever, and many crimes committed ... cannot be tried under the "Rules and Articles of War." Military commissions must be resorted to for such cases and these commissions should be ordered by the same authority....[7]

In all of his correspondence, Sibley never referred to Halleck's guidance, so it would be too much to assume that he knew of it, but in general terms the commission that he impaneled fit the criteria that Halleck had defined.

It is established, then, that within the Army of 1862 the idea was well established that a military commission was a viable option for the exercise of military law. Well established, but not well defined. Whereas there were "very specific enumeration of offenses triable by court-martial, the statutory law provided no guidance regarding the validity and proper use of military commissions."[8] In spite of this, the Army recognized the concept of military commissions even if Congress had not yet gotten around to providing a legislative framework for them. Lincoln's Judge Advocate General at the time of the Dakota War, Joseph Holt (who held the rank of Colonel in addition to his government position) stated in a letter to Secretary of War Edwin Stanton: "These 'commissions' ... have existed too long in the service, and [are] too essential to its wants and emergencies, to be now ignored. Long and uninterrupted usage has made them as it were part and parcel of the common military law."[9] The precedent and practice of military commissions, then, was in place well before Sibley convened his on September 28, 1862. Whether or not Sibley's commission adhered to the rule of law in practice, however, is an altogether different matter.

# Chapter Notes

## Introduction

1. There were 391 defendants, but actually 392 trials. One man, Charles Crawford, was tried twice (Cases No. 8 and 136) and acquitted both times.
2. These statistics are borne out by archival evidence in the Minnesota Historical Society, as well as materials held in the archives of the Brown, Nicollet, and Redwood County Historical Societies, among others.

## Chapter 1

1. These names are used in the titles of books and articles by Duane Schultz, Mary Schwandt, Helen M. Carrothers Tarble, Marion Satterlee, Michael Clodfelter, Oscar Malmros, Gary Clayton Anderson, Kathryn Zabelle Derounian-Stodola, Carol Chomsky, Charles Bryant, Curtis Dahlin, Kenneth Carley, John Koblas, Asa Daniels and David Nichols, respectively. Their works on the war were published in the span of years ranging from 1863 to 2009.
2. Kenneth Carley, *The Dakota War of 1862: Minnesota's Other Civil War* (St. Paul: Minnesota Historical Society Press, 1976), 1. In some sources, the name is rendered "Nadowe-is-iw,"
3. Royal B. Hassrick, *The Sioux: Life and Customs of a Warrior Society* (Norman, OK: University of Oklahoma Press, 1964), 6.
4. Kathryn Derounian-Stodola, *The War in Words: Reading the Dakota Conflict Through the Captivity Literature* (Lincoln, NE: University of Nebraska Press, 2009), 142.
5. In an interesting turn of phrase, the 1908 book *Minnesota in Three Centuries*, by Return I. Holcombe and Lucius F. Hubbard, the Dakota War is referred to as "the Great Holocaust of Blood and Rapine," nearly 40 years before the word "Holocaust" became associated with the Nazi genocide of the Second World War.
6. Estimates of the war's casualties vary widely, from the low hundreds to several thousand. Something more than 600 settler deaths in the first weeks of the war is a number supportable by available evidence; combat deaths among the Dakota were much lower, perhaps fewer than 50, during the six weeks of the active war.
7. Letter from Henry H. Sibley to Sarah S. Sibley, in the Sibley Papers Collection of the Minnesota Historical Society.

## Chapter 2

1. Theodore Christianson, *Minnesota: The Land of Sky-Tinted Waters: A History of the State and Its Peoples* (New York: The American Historical Society, 1935), 345.
2. It should not be assumed that these were strictly hegemonic groupings, however, as there was frequent intermarriage between men and women of the different bands.
3. Doane Robinson, *A History of the Dakota or Sioux Indians.* Reprint of the 1904 edition (Minneapolis: Ross & Haines, 1956), 213.
4. Rhoda Gilman, *Divided Heart: Henry Hastings Sibley* (St. Paul, MN: Minnesota Historical Society, 2004), 124.
5. Marion Satterlee, "Narratives of the Sioux War," *Collections of the Minnesota Historical Society*, Vol. XV (St. Paul, MN: Minnesota Historical Society, 1915), 351.
6. Henry A. Castle, *Minnesota, Its Story and Biography* (Chicago: The Lewis Publishing Co., 1915), 157.
7. Russell F. Weigley, *The American Way of War: A History of United States Military Strategy and Policy* (New York: Macmillan Publishing, 1973), 155.
8. Big Eagle, Return I. Holcombe, ed., "A Sioux History of the War: Chief Big Eagle's Story of the Sioux Outbreak of 1862," *Minnesota Historical Society Collections*, Vol. VI (St. Paul, MN: Minnesota Historical Society, 1894), 383.
9. Daniel Buck, *Indian Outbreaks*, Reprint of the 1904 edition (Minneapolis: Ross & Haines), 39.
10. Isaac V. D. Heard, *History of the Sioux War and Massacres of 1862 and 1863* (New York: Harper & Brothers, 1864), 288.
11. *Ibid.*, 33.
12. *Ibid.*, 244.
13. Antoine Freniere, *St. Paul Daily Press*, December 14, 1862 (St. Paul, MN: Minnesota Historical Society), microfilm, reel M166.
14. Moses N. Adams, "The Sioux Outbreak in the Year 1862, with Notes of Missionary Work Among the Sioux," *Collections of the Minnesota Historical Society Vol. IX* (St. Paul, MN: Minnesota Historical Society Press), 432.
15. *Ibid.*, 434.
16. Asa W. Daniels, "Reminiscences of the Little Crow Uprising," *Collections of the Minnesota Historical Society Vol. XV* (St. Paul, MN: Minnesota Historical Society Press), 336.

17. Letter from Maj. Gen. John Pope to Maj. Gen. Henry Halleck, October 7, 1862. *Minnesota in the Civil and Indian Wars 1861–1865, Vol. II: Official Reports and Correspondence* (St. Paul, MN: Minnesota Historical Society Press, 2005). Hereafter, MCIW.
18. Sec. Navy Gideon Welles, *Diary of Gideon Welles, Secretary of the Navy Under Lincoln and Johnson, Volume 1 1861–March 30, 186.* Rodney O. Davis & Douglas L. Wilson, ed. (Springfield, IL: The Knox College, Lincoln Studies Center Series, 2014), 161.
19. Christianson, *Minnesota*, 345.
20. Minnie Buce Carrigan, *Captured by the Indians: Reminiscences of Pioneer Life in Minnesota* (Forest City, SD: Forest City Press, 1907), 5.
21. F. W. Boelter, quoted in Carrigan, 31.
22. Sam Brown, quoted in Gary Clayton Anderson & Alan R. Woolworth, ed. *Through Dakota Eyes: Narrative Accounts of the Minnesota Indian War of 1862* (St. Paul, MN: Minnesota Historical Society Press, 1988), 76.
23. Letter from Bishop Henry Whipple to Gen. John Pope, File P823, Henry B. Whipple Papers, Minnesota Historical Society.
24. Bishop Henry Whipple, File 823, Henry B. Whipple Papers, Minnesota Historical Society.
25. Letter from Brig. Gen. Henry H. Sibley to Bishop Henry B. Whipple, December 7, 1862, File P823, Henry B. Whipple Papers, Minnesota Historical Society.
26. Little Crow, quoted in Clifford Allen, et al., *History of the Flandrau Santee Sioux* (Flandreau, SD: Tribal History Program, Flandreau Santee Sioux Tribe, 1971), 27. Also in Folwell, *A History of Minnesota*, Vol. II, 232.
27. Judge Martin Severance, quoted in William Folwell, *A History of Minnesota*, Vol. II (St. Paul, MN: Minnesota Historical Society Press, 1924), 222. Antoine Freniere, who was the translator for many of the trials, praised Galbraith as a dedicated man who did all he could for the Indians. Freniere was not the most reliable of witnesses, considering the frequency of his exaggerated statements in the newspapers.
28. Stephen R. Riggs, *Mary and I: Forty Years with the Sioux*, Reprint of the 1887 edition (Minneapolis. Ross & Haines, 1969), 171.
29. Christianson, *Minnesota*, 353.
30. *Ibid.*, 353.
31. Details of these events can be found in McGinnis, Gibbon, Osborn and Hassrick, to cite a few sources among many.
32. Royal B. Hassrick, *The Sioux*, 57.
33. Old Crow, quoted in William M. Osborn, *The Wild Frontier: Atrocities During the American-Indian War from Jamestown Colony to Wounded Knee* (New York: Random House, 2000), 27.
34. Big Eagle, "A Sioux History," 383.
35. Vine Deloria, Jr., *Custer Died for Your Sins: An Indian Manifesto* (Norman, OK: University of Oklahoma Press, 1969), 22.
36. Hassrick, *The Sioux*, 74.
37. Anthony McGinnis, *Counting Coup and Cutting Horses: Intertribal Warfare on the Northern Plains, 1738–1889* (Lincoln, NE: University of Nebraska Press, 1990), 108.
38. Samuel W. Pond, *The Dakota or Sioux in Minnesota as They Were in 1834*, reprint of the 1908 edition (St. Paul, MN: Minnesota Historical Society Press, 1986), 62.
39. *Ibid.*, 62.
40. *Ibid.*, 60.
41. Hassrick, *The Sioux*, 76.
42. Big Eagle, "A Sioux History," 387.
43. Darla Cordes Gebhard, and John Isch, *Eight Days in August: The Accounts of the Casualties and Survivors in Brown County During the U.S.–Dakota War of 1862* (New Ulm, MN: Brown County Historical Society, 2012).

## Chapter 3

1. For a discussion of the different versions of this story, see Chapter 24.
2. Big Eagle, Return I. Holcombe, ed., "A Sioux History of the War: Chief Big Eagle's Story of the Sioux Outbreak of 1862," *Minnesota Historical Society Collections*, Vol. VI (St. Paul, MN: Minnesota Historical Society, 1894), 386.
3. John G. Nicolay, *Lincoln's Secretary Goes West: Two Reports by John G. Nicolay on Frontier Indian Troubles 1862*, Theodore C. Blegen, ed. (Lacrosse, WI: Sumac Press, 1965), 47.
4. Robert Huhn Jones, *The Civil War in the Northwest: Nebraska, Wisconsin, Iowa, Minnesota, and the Dakotas* (Norman, OK: University of Oklahoma Press, 1960), 27.
5. Robert Wooster, *The Military and United States Indian Policy: 1865–1903* (New Haven, CT: Yale University Press, 1988), 38.
6. Big Eagle, "A Sioux History," 387.
7. John Isch makes this point very well in an unpublished monograph discussing Little Crow's apocryphal speech.
8. Wowinape, quoted in Kenneth Carley, *The Dakota War of 1862*, 11.
9. Little Crow's speech as recounted by his son, Wowinape, in Priscilla Ann Russo, "The Time to Speak Is Over," *Minnesota History* Vol. 45 (Fall, 1976), 106.
10. It would be a serious error, however, to claim as Charles Bryant does that "The manner of the execution of the infernal deed [the outbreak of war] was a deep-laid conspiracy, long cherished by Little Crow." The evidence is quite clear that the outbreak of the war was not the result of a careful conspiracy or plot by Little Crow. Charles Bryant, *History of the Sioux Massacre* (Minneapolis: North Star Publishing Company, 1882), 185.
11. Big Eagle, "A Sioux History," 390.
12. *Ibid.*, 390.
13. Big Eagle, in his narrative, also said that at this point Little Crow threatened other chiefs who were opposed to the war. "When the outbreak came," he said, "Little Crow told some of my band that if I refused to lead them to shoot me as a traitor who would not stand up for his nation, and then select another leader in my place." Big Eagle, "A Sioux History," 387.

## Chapter 4

1. John G. Nicolay, *Lincoln's Secretary Goes West: Two Reports by John G. Nicolay on Frontier Indian Troubles 1862*, Theodore C. Blegen, ed. (Lacrosse, WI: Sumac Press, 1965), 62.
2. Return I. Holcombe and Lucius F. Hubbard, *Minnesota in Three Centuries*, Vol. III (St. Paul, MN: The Publishing Society of Minnesota, 1908), 390.
3. Duane Schultz makes these points very well in his book *Over the Earth I Come: The Great Sioux Uprising of 1862*.

4. Theodore Christianson, *Minnesota: The Land of Sky-Tinted Waters: A History of the State and Its Peoples* (New York: The American Historical Society, 1935), 357.

5. Big Eagle, Return I. Holcombe, ed., "A Sioux History of the War: Chief Big Eagle's Story of the Sioux Outbreak of 1862," *Minnesota Historical Society Collections*, Vol. VI (St. Paul, MN: Minnesota Historical Society, 1894), 390.

6. Sam Brown, quoted in *Through Dakota Eyes*, 74.

7. Blue Sky Woman, quoted in *Through Dakota Eyes*, 55. One of the women that White Spider saved was Mrs. Nairn, the wife of the government carpenter at the Agency, and she later corroborated the story. She was the one who had offered White Spider her wedding ring as the only thing of value she had on her, but he would not take it. Mrs. Nairn and her family all safely reached Fort Ridgely.

8. Kenneth Carley, *The Dakota War of 1862: Minnesota's Other Civil War* (St. Paul: Minnesota Historical Society Press, 1976), 15.

9. Because of the manpower demands of the Civil War, almost all the troops on hand at the time of the outbreak were volunteer units. Some of the officers, like Captain Marsh, were veteran Regulars, but most of the rank and file were not much more than citizen militia.

10. In a sad turn of history, the ferryman's name has never been positively determined. His identity has been suggested as Hubert Miller, or Jacob Mauley. What is agreed is that he saved dozens of lives by his decision to stay at the crossing until the very end.

11. John F. Bishop, "The Encounter at Redwood Ferry—Bishop's Story of the Disaster," *Minnesota in the Civil and Indian Wars, Vol. II Official Reports and Correspondence* (St. Paul, MN: The Board of Commissioners, 1893), 166–171. Hereafter, *MCIW*.

12. Letter from Lieut. Thomas P. Gere, August 18, 1862, Minnesota Historical Society.

13. Letter from Lieut. Thomas P. Gere to Lieutenant Timothy Sheehan, August 19, 1862, reproduced in Holcombe, *Minnesota in Three Centuries Vol. 3*, 332.

14. The exact number of people killed at Milford is difficult to determine, depending upon whether one counts only residents of the village, or includes visitors, etc. The high estimate is 53—I have opted for the lower, name-specific number of 48.

15. Charles S. Bryant and Abel B. Murch, *A History of the Great Massacre by the Sioux Indians, in Minnesota: Including the Personal Narratives of Many Who Escaped* (Cincinnati, OH. Rickey & Carroll, Publishers, 1863), 328. Hereafter, *History of the Great Massacre*. This would be the same woman that another survivor, Minnie Buce Carrigan, also described seeing dead, an incident which is related later in this book.

16. Ernestina Broburg, in Bryant, *A History of the Great Massacre*, 402.

17. Lavina Eastlick, quoted in Bryant, *A History of the Great Massacre*, 348.

18. Edward D. Neill, *History of the Minnesota Valley, Including the Explorers and Pioneers of Minnesota* (Minneapolis: North Star Publishing Company, 1882), 727. Hereafter, *History of the Minnesota Valley*.

19. Charles D. Flandrau, *The History of Minnesota and Tales of the Frontier* ( St. Paul, MN: E.W. Porter, 1900), 139. Hereafter, *History of Minnesota*.

20. Dr. Damuel B. Sheardown, File P1369, Manuscripts Collection, Dakota Conflict of 1862, Minnesota Historical Society.

21. The casualties listed here are drawn from records held in the Murray County Historical Society, as well as the Minnesota Historical Society.

22. The casualties listed here can be found in the records of the Brown County Historical Society.

23. Darla Gebhard and John Isch, *Eight Days in August: The Accounts of the Casualties and Survivors in Brown County During the U.S.–Dakota War of 1862* (New Ulm, MN: Brown County Historical Society, 2012), 53.

24. Dakota advocate and academic Waziyatawin makes this claim in her 2004 article "Decolonizing the 1862 Death Marches," Waziyatawin's particular arguments will be examined in greater detail in later chapters.

25. McGinnis, *Counting Coup*, 214.

26. Folwell, *A History of Minnesota*, 142.

27. Big Eagle, "A Sioux History," 392.

28. *Ibid*.

29. In addition to the assault on Fort Ridgely, the Indians attacked Fort Abercrombie on the banks of the Red River, which separated Minnesota from present-day South Dakota. They failed to take that fort as well.

30. Depending on the source, the name of the location of this engagement appears as "Birch Coulie," "Birch Cooley," or "Birch Coulee ," I have decided to go with the spelling as it now appears on state maps. A "Coulee" is a creek.

31. The question of who was actually in command at Birch Coulee is a point of on-going controversy. The command controversy arose after the battle. For more, see Carley's *The Sioux Uprising of 1862*.

32. Letter from Col. Henry H. Sibley to Little Crow (September 3, 1982), in Oscar Malmros, *Perspective on the Sioux War: Reports of the Adjutant General to the Governor of Minnesota, September 1862 and January 1863* (St. Paul, MN: Wm. Marshall, State Printer, Press Printing Company, 1863), 34. Hereafter, *AG Report*.

33. Letter from Little Crow to Col. Henry H. Sibley (September 7, 1862), *AG Report*, 35–36.

34. Letter from Col. Henry H. Sibley to Little Crow (September 8, 1862), *AG Report*, 36.

35. Letter from Little Crow to Col. Henry H. Sibley (September 12, 1862), *AG Report*, 37.

36. Letter from Col. Henry H. Sibley to Little Crow (September 12, 1862), *AG Report*, 38.

37. Letter from Wabashaw and Taopee to Col. Henry H. Sibley (September 10, 1862), *AG Report*, 37.

38. Letter from Col. Henry H. Sibley to Wabashaw and Taopee (September 12, 1862), *AG Report*, 37–38.

39. Rdainyanka, quoted in Heard, *History of the Sioux War*, 151–52.

40. Mazzawamnuna, quoted in Duane Schultz, *Over the Earth I Come: The Great Sioux Uprising of 1862* (New York: St. Martin's Griffin, 1992), 214.

41. Paul (Little Paul) Mazakootemane, Stephen R. Riggs trans., File P1369, Manuscripts Collection, Dakota Conflict of 1862, Minnesota Historical Society. Little Paul's account has been criticized by some Dakota as being self-serving and a betrayal of his people; one of the white captives, Sarah Wakefield, alleged that Little Paul had designs on her during the captivity. Little Paul was uniquely positioned as a witness to events, but he is a figure both praised and vilified in contemporary accounts, depending on whose version one reads.

42. *Ibid*.

43. Big Eagle, "A Sioux History," 388.

44. Jones, *Civil War in the Northwest*, 37.

45. Letter from Gov. Alexander Ramsey to Pres. Abraham Lincoln (September 6 1862), *MCIW*, 225.

46. Letter from Maj. Gen. John Pope to Sec. Edwin Stanton (September 25, 1862), *MCIW*, 251.

47. Holcombe says that Sibley "In Good Time" reached the captives and friendly Indians who were waiting for him, but few of the narratives of the former captives themselves agree with that characterization of the expeditionary force's speed of march. Holcombe and Hubbard, *Minnesota in Three Centuries*, 407.

## Chapter 5

1. David Martinez, in his 2013 article, claimed that Pope ordered Sibley to form the military commission, but no such order was ever given. See Chapter 7 for more on this point.

2. Big Eagle, "A Sioux History," 393.

3. Robert Norris, "Lincoln's Dilemma," *Washington Lawyer* (May 2014), accessed June 2015.

4. "Fredrika Bremer's New Scandinavia: Minnesota in 1850," *Minnesota History* (Sept 1950), 151. Bremer was not a historian, and she wrote with the wide-eyed enthusiasm of a tourist, but she was detailed in her observations. Her impressions of Sibley are rendered without any apparent interest in his politics or reputation, and have the sense of being honest, personal impressions of the man.

5. Henry H. Sibley, "Reminiscences, Historical and Personal," *Collections of the Minnesota Historical Society*. Vol. 1, 1870, 461–462.

6. Roy Meyer, *History of the Santee Sioux: United States Indian Policy on Trial*, revised edition (Lincoln, NE: University of Nebraska Press, 1993), 124.

7. Letter from Henry H. Sibley to Sarah S. Sibley, File M164, Henry Hastings Sibley Papers, 1815–1930, Minnesota Historical Society.

8. Walt Bachman, email to author, July 30, 2014.

9. Rhoda Gilman, email to author, September 15, 2014.

10. Letter from Henry H. Sibley to Sarah Steel Sibley, File M164, Henry Hastings Sibley Papers, 1815–1930, Minnesota Historical Society, St. Paul, Minnesota.

11. Letter from Brig. Gen. Henry H. Sibley to Maj. Gen. John Pope (October 5, 1862), *MCIW*, 265.

12. Letter from Col. Henry H. Sibley to Maj. Gen John Pope (October 7, 1862), *MCIW*, 267.

## Chapter 6

1. "Article 32," in this case, refers to the modern Uniform Code of Military Justice, which is the descendant of the Articles of War extant in 1862. An Article 32 hearing is essentially similar to a grand jury proceeding in civilian law, and functions as a fact-finding process to determine whether or not the government has sufficient evidence to support its case against a defendant, and therefore whether the case ought to proceed to trial. Before a modern military court convenes, an Article 32 hearing must be held.

2. Gabriel Renville, quoted in *Through Dakota Eyes*, 232.

3. Letter from Stephen R. Riggs to Martha Riggs (September 27, 1862). File P727, Stephen Return Riggs and Family Papers, Minnesota Historical Society.

4. *Ibid.*

5. Letter from Col. Henry H. Sibley to Maj. Gen John Pope (September 28, 1862), *MCIW*, 256.

6. Letter from Maj. Gen John Pope to Col. Henry H. Sibley (September 28, 1862), *MCIW*, 257.

7. Meyer, *History of the Santee Sioux*, 125.

8. Schultz, *Over the Earth I Come*, 247.

9. Return I. Holcombe, in his history, called it a "Militia Commission," which was nothing at all what it was. Holcombe, *Minnesota in Three Centuries, Vol. III*, 409.

10. Malmros, *AG Report*, 45.

11. William Winthrop, *Military Law and Precedents*, Vol. I (Boston: Little Brown and Co., 1896), 797.

12. Letter from Col. Henry H. Sibley to Maj. Gen. John Pope (September 30, 1862), *MCIW*, 258.

13. Letter from Col. Henry H. Sibley to Maj. Gen. John Pope (October 5, 1862), *MCIW*, 265.

14. Thomas A. Robertson. File P1369, Manuscripts Collection, Dakota Conflict of 1862, Minnesota Historical Society.

15. Letter from Col. Henry H. Sibley to Maj. Gen. John Pope (October 5, 1862), *MCIW*, 265.

16. Letter from Col. Henry H. Sibley to Maj. Gen. John Pope (October 7, 1862), *MCIW*, 267.

17. Letter from Maj. Gen. John Pope to Maj. Gen. Henry Halleck (October 9, 1862), *MCIW*, 270.

18. Letter from Maj. Gen. John Pope to Maj. Gen. Henry Halleck (October 10, 1862), *MCIW*, 272.

## Chapter 7

1. Godfrey has been vilified to varying degrees by commentators from both sides of the story, but there is good reason to think that history has unfairly maligned him. Walt Bachman's book, *Northern Slave Black Dakota*, is the first in-depth biography of Godfrey and raises some important questions about the accuracy of how he has been portrayed in the historiography.

2. Malmros, *AG Report*, 42.

3. *Ibid.*

4. Dr. Elden Lawrence, the late Wahpeton Dakota scholar, stated that the Dakota gave Godfrey the nickname *after* the war, because his trial testimony was so effective and sent so many men to the gallows. I believe Dr. Lawrence confused both the sequence of events and the evidence on this question. It is also possible that Dr. Lawrence was echoing Marion Satterlee's comment in his pamphlet *The Indian Massacre in Brown County*. Godfrey, Satterlee wrote, was called "Kills Many." "They might have added 'Indians,'" Satterlee remarked, "and thus been more explicit," In this respect Satterlee was also slightly off the mark. Lawrence, *The Peace Seekers*, 135, and Satterlee, *The Indian Massacre in Brown County*, 2.

5. Royal B. Hassrick's *The Sioux: Life and Customs of a Warrior Society* details this aspect of Indian warfare very well, as does Anthony R. McGinnis' *Counting Coup and Cutting Horses: Intertribal Warfare on the Northern Plains, 1738–1889*.

6. Bachman makes a convincing argument for this understanding of Godfrey's contribution to the later trials in his biography of Godfrey, *Northern Slave Black Dakota: The Life and Times of Joseph Godfrey*.

7. Malmros, *AG Report*, 42.

8. Alexander Macomb, *The Practice of Courts Martial* (New York: Harper & Brothers, 1841), 55.

9. David Martinez, "Remembering the Thirty-Eight," *Wicaza Sa Review*, 28:2 (Fall 2013) 5–29, 15.

10. Letter from Maj. Gen. John Pope to Brig. Gen.

Henry Sibley (October 6, 1862). Records Group 393, Part 1, Department of the Northwest, 1862–65, Headquarters Records, Correspondence, E.3436, Letters Sent. National Archives, Washington, D.C.

11. Pope's letter was omitted from the official collection of military correspondence that was originally published in 1866, possibly because of the intense personal criticisms expressed in it. Until Walt Bachman discovered it, the letter's existence was largely unknown in the historiography of the war. The original document is held in Records Group 393, Part 1 of the National Archives. I am indebted to Walt for sharing his research with me.

12. Walt Bachman, email to author, July 30, 2014.

13. Letter from Maj. Gen. John Pope to Brig. Gen. Henry H. Sibley, October 7, 1862. Record Group 393, Part 1, Department of the Northwest, 1862–65, Headquarters Records, General Records, Correspondence, E.3436, Letters Sent, 3 vols., 6 in.

14. Gary Clayton Anderson, "The Dakota War Trials: Travesty of Justice or Reasonable Retribution?" (Gustavus Adolphus College, St. Peter, MN, January 10, 2012), 43:05 seq.

15. File P1423, Box 1, Trial Transcripts, Minnesota Historical Society.

16. Carol Chomsky, "The United States–Dakota Trials: A Study in Military Injustice," *Stanford Law Review*, Vol. 43, No. 1 (Nov 1990), 11–12.

17. Letter from Col. Henry H. Sibley to Maj. Gen. John Pope (October 11, 1862), *MCIW*, 273.

18. Letter from Col. Henry H. Sibley to Maj. Gen. Pope (October 15, 1862), *MCIW*, 277.

19. Letter from Col. Henry H. Sibley to Maj. Gen. Pope (October 15, 1862), *MCIW*, 278.

20. Letter from Brig. Gen. Henry H. Sibley to Maj. Gen John Pope (October 21, 1862), *MCIW*, 281.

21. Act of July 17, 1862, Ch. 201, 5, 12 Stat. 597, 598. Coincidentally, this was the same legislation that authorized the creation of the office of Judge Advocate General, "to whose office shall be returned, for revision, the records and proceedings of all courts-martial and military commissions, and where a record shall be kept of all proceedings had thereupon." The man in this position during the war was Joseph Holt, who played a substantial part in Lincoln's decision-making process with regards to the condemned Dakota prisoners. The requirement that capital sentences had to be referred to the national command authority for confirmation had already existed for some years; this legislation only reinforced that established rule.

# Chapter 8

1. Carol Chomsky, Louis Fisher, Gary Clayton Anderson, Rhoda Gilman and David Martinez are some of the commentators who have suggested or stated that Sibley did not have the legal authority to convene the military commission. Dr. Anderson has never taken such a position in print, but in his 2012 speech at Gustavus Adolphus College, Anderson said, "That's really kind of debatable, whether he [Sibley] had any kind of authority of that sort…. Until I find other evidence to the contrary, I'm going to stick with what I said," and it is on the basis of that statement that I include him in this group. See Anderson, "The Dakota War Trials," 1:14:57–1:15:20 seq.

2. *Revised United States Army Regulations of 1861, with an Appendix Containing the Changes and Laws Affecting Army Regulations and Articles of War to June 25, 1863.* Washington: Government Printing Office. 1863.

3. *Ibid*.

4. U.S. Army officers in the 19th century were exclusively male, so the male pronoun is the only term of address used in this study.

5. A misinterpretation of this Article was invoked as early as 1863, when Pope cited it as reason for not approving the military commission trial of Wowinape, Little Crow's son. Then, as now, the matter of prejudice as described in the Article was inaccurately applied to the trial of a Dakota who was not a soldier in the U.S. Army. Sibley used precisely this argument in the rebuttal he wrote after Pope's action. See Chapter Eighteen for more on this.

6. Gilman, *Divided Heart*, 185.

7. Chomsky, "The United States–Dakota War Trials," 58.

8. Letter from Maj. Gen. Halleck to Maj. Gen Pope (September 29, 1862), *MCIW,* 258.

9. Douglas Linder, "The Dakota Conflict Trials" http://www.law.umkc.edu/faculty/projects/ftrials/dakota/Dak_account.html.

10. Order No. 65, File P1423, Box 1, U.S. Army Military Commission Trials, Sioux Uprising, Minnesota Historical Society.

11. Letter from Col. Henry H. Sibley to Maj. Gen John Pope (Sept 28, 1862), *MCIW*, 256.

12. Letter from Col. Henry H. Sibley to Col. Charles Flandrau (September 28, 1862), *MCIW*, 258.

13. Letter from Maj. Gen. John Pope to Maj. Gen Henry Halleck (October 9, 1862), *MCIW*, 270.

14. Letter from Brig. Gen. Henry H. Sibley to Maj. Gen. John Pope (October 13, 1862), *MCIW*, 275.

15. Letter from Brig. Gen. Henry H. Sibley to Maj. Gen. John Pope (October 15, 1862), *MCIW*, 277.

16. Letter from Brig. Gen. Henry H. Sibley to Maj. Gen. John Pope (October 15, 1862), *MCIW*, 277.

17. Louis Fisher, *Military Tribunals and Presidential Power: American Revolution to the War on Terrorism*, Lawrence, KS: University Press of Kansas, 2005, 52.

# Chapter 9

1. Chomsky, "The United States–Dakota Trials," 15.

2. Interview with Carol Chomsky, June 30, 2014. I am grateful to Professor Chomsky for clarifying this point, as I earlier misunderstood her position on this question.

3. This perspective is implied in some recent works, such as Jerry Keenan's 2003 book *"The Great Sioux Uprising,"* Keenan subtitled his book *"Rebellion on the Plains August—September 1862,"* giving his rendition of the war a specific and unambiguous classification as an internal, domestic event.

4. Chomsky, "The United States–Dakota War Trials," 15.

5. Weigley, *The American Way of War*, 154–155.

6. William Winthrop, *A Digest of Opinions of the Judge-Advocates General of the Army, Rev. ed.* (Washington, D.C.: Government Printing Office, 1901), 411.

7. John Isch, *The Dakota Trials*.

8. Article II, Section II of the U.S. Constitution reserves to the President of the United States the power "To make treaties, provided two thirds of the Senators present concur."

9. Felix Cohen, *Handbook of Federal Indian Law*, 89.
10. Folwell, *A History of Minnesota*, 214.

## Chapter 10

1. Flandrau, *The History of Minnesota*, 177.
2. Stephen R. Riggs, in the *St. Paul Daily Press*, Dec. 17, 1863.
3. Heard, *History of the Sioux War*, 267.
4. David Glazier, "Precedents Lost: The Neglected History of the Military Commission," *Virginia Journal of International Law*, Vol. 46, No. 1 (Fall 2005), 43.
5. J.R. Poinsett of the War Department, foreword to Alexander Macomb, *The Practice of Courts Martial* (New York: Harper & Brothers, 1841), i.
6. Heard, *History of the Sioux War*, 267. It is worth pointing out that Heard was a trial lawyer of considerable experience, well versed in legal procedure. As such he almost certainly would have recognized the irregularities in much of what the commission did, especially in the later cases, so why did he not point them out and object, then or later? There is no way to know for certain. Perhaps he felt that since the trials were being conducted under military law and not civilian law that the normal requirements did not apply. Perhaps he simply did not care.
7. To be clear, the term "Judge Advocate," does not mean that the position is that of a presiding judge; it is more akin to the position of prosecutor. This terminology has confused some commentators, such as Daniel Munson, who in his book *Malice Toward None* refers to "The Acting Judge, Lieutenant Olin," Olin was in fact the Judge Advocate, and was in no way presiding over the proceedings.
8. Article 69 of the Articles of War extant 1846, from the amended 1806 Articles of War. This article remained unchanged throughout the period of the Civil War.
9. John O'Brien, *A Treatise on American Military Laws, and the Practice of Courts Martial* (Philadelphia: Lea & Blanchard, 1846), 335.
10. George Gordon Battle, "Military Tribunals," *Virginia Law Review*, Vol. 29, No. 3 (December 1942), 261.
11. Meyer, *History of the Santee Sioux*, 217.
12. Marion Satterlee, *The Court Proceedings in the Trial of Dakota Indians Following the Massacre in Minnesota in August 1862* (Minneapolis: Satterlee Printing Company, 1927) 2.
13. Thomas Watts, in the *Mankato Independent*, December 20, 1926, File M166 in the Minnesota Historical Society.
14. Heard, *History of the Sioux War*, 267.
15. *Ibid.*, 266.
16. Walt Bachman, email to author, September 6, 2014.
17. Robert Norris, "Lincoln's Dilemma," http://www.dcbar.org/bar-resources/publications, accessed October 2, 2014.
18. Anderson, "The Dakota War Trials," 29:11 seq.
19. Article 69, *Articles of War: An Act for Establishing Rules and Articles for the Government of the Armies of the United States* (Washington, D.C.: Government Printing Office, 1806).
20. Battle, "Military Tribunals," 261.
21. Walt Bachman, "Dr. Gary Clayton Anderson's Speech on the Dakota War Trials: A Critique," *Minnesota's Heritage*, No. 6 (July 2012), 13.
22. Harriet Bishop McConkey, *Dakota War Whoop, Or, Indian Massacres and War in Minnesota, of 1862–3* (Auburn: William J. Morris' Press, 1864), 184.
23. *Ibid.*
24. Chomsky, "The United States–Dakota War Trials," 55.
25. Bachman, *Northern Slave Black Dakota*, 131.
26. Heard, *History of the Sioux War*, 239.
27. *Ibid.*, 240.
28. Henry Wager Halleck, "Military Tribunals and Their Jurisdiction," *The American Journal of International Law*, Vol. 5, No. 4 (October 1911), 96.
29. Letter from Henry H. Sibley to Sarah S. Sibley, October 11, 1862. Henry Hastings Sibley Papers, File M164, Minnesota Historical Society Collection.
30. I use the phrase "relatively careful process" intentionally, but with a caveat—the early trials were careful in a comparative sense when considered in the scope of the entire list of 392 trials, but taken outside of that context they do appear incredibly precipitous.
31. Stephen R. Riggs, *Mary and I: Forty Years with the Sioux* (1885; reprint., Minneapolis: Ross & Haines, 1969), 207.
32. Heard, *History of the Sioux War*, 189.
33. Battle, "Military Tribunals," 261.
34. Edward Bates, quoted in Louis Fisher, *Military Commissions: Problems of Authority and Practice* (Boston: Boston University School of Law, 2006), 117. Italics in the original.
35. *Ibid.*, italics in the original.
36. Erling Theodore Jorstad, *The Life of Henry Hastings Sibley* (PhD diss., University of Wisconsin, 1957), 311.
37. *Ibid.*, 312.
38. Bachman, *Northern Slave Black Dakota*, 209. Bachman is, I believe, the first historian to note the crucial point that the military commission should have, and could have, called survivor witnesses from nearby communities, but never did so.
39. Letter from Stephen R. Riggs to Mary Riggs, October 17, 1862, File P727, Stephen Return Riggs and Family Papers, Minnesota Historical Society Collection.
40. John P. Williamson, letter to S. B. Treat, November 5, 1862, American Board of Commissioners for Foreign Missions Papers. Correspondence: 1 Box 1—Manuscripts and Notebooks; Boxes 2 & 7. Minnesota Historical Society.
41. Nancy McClure, "Captivity Among the Sioux," *Minnesota Historical Society Collections Vol. IX* (St. Paul, MN: Minnesota Historical Society, 1894), 463.
42. *Ibid.*, 465.
43. Anderson, "The Dakota War Trials," 49:50.
44. All quotations in this paragraph refer to Case No. 6 (Hinhanshoonkoyagmane), File 1423, Box No. 1, Trial Transcripts, Minnesota Historical Society.
45. *Ibid.*
46. Case No. 9 (Makatanajin), File P1423, Box No. 1, Trial Transcripts, Minnesota Historical Society.
47. Anderson, "The Dakota War Trials," 49:10–49:50 seq.
48. Case No. 172 (Chotankamaza), File P1423, Box No. 2, Trial Transcripts, Minnesota Historical Society.
49. Case No. 326 (Wechanhpeheyaya), File P1423, Box No. 3, Trial Transcripts, Minnesota Historical Society.
50. Case No. 316 (Wakanna), File P1423, Box No. 3, Trial Transcripts, Minnesota Historical Society.
51. Neill, *History of Minnesota*, 733.

## Chapter 11

1. Case no. 350 (Wakanhdehota), File number P1423, Box 3, Trial Transcripts, Minnesota Historical Society Collection.
2. Isch, *The Dakota War Trials*. One cannot always be certain, reading the trial transcripts, which dates correspond to which trials. This has led to some confusion in the historiography, such as the often-repeated and incorrect statement that there were 16 trials on September 28, the commission's first day of operation. Even with this caveat in mind, though, I see no reason to disagree with Isch's version of events on November 2, as it is borne out by other evidence.
3. Colette A. Hyman, "Survival at Crow Creek: 1863–1866," *Minnesota History*, Vol. 61, No. 4 (Winter, 2008/2009), 151.
4. Letter from Rev. Ezekial Gere to Bishop Henry Whipple, Dec. 19, 1862, File P823, Box 3, Henry B. Whipple Papers, Minnesota Historical Society.
5. Bachman, "Anderson's Speech on the Dakota War Trials," 10.
6. Heard, *History of the Sioux War*, 254–255.
7. Satterlee, Marion, *The Court Proceedings in the Trial of Dakota Indians*. Satterlee also knew nothing of Pope's letter of October 6, 1862. The practice of the adjutant, in this case Lieut. Col. Fowler, signing the draft of a document before or in lieu of the authorizing signature of the commanding officer, is a common protocol in the military and in no way changes Brig. Gen. Sibley's role as the convening authority of the commission and its reviewing officer.
8. Riggs. File P727, Stephen Return Riggs and Family Papers, Minnesota Historical Society.
9. Heard, *History of the Sioux War*, 257.
10. Bachman, *Northern Slave Black Dakota*, 190.
11. Stephen R. Riggs, in the December 14 1862 edition of the *St. Paul Daily Press*. File P727, Stephen R. Riggs and Family Papers, Minnesota Historical Society. Italics in the original.
12. Stephen R. Riggs, quoted by Bishop Henry Whipple in the *St. Paul Daily Press*, December 5, 1862.
13. Robinson, *A History O Fthe Dakota*, 229.
14. Letter from Brig Gen Henry H. Sibley to Assistant Secretary of the Interior J.P. Usher, December 19, 1862, File M166, Sioux Uprising Collection, Minnesota Historical Society Collection.
15. Henry H. Sibley, File M164, Henry Hastings Sibley Papers, 1815–1930, Minnesota Historical Society.
16. Kenneth Carley, "Sibley's Letters to His Wife," 110.
17. Henry H. Sibley, File M164, Henry Hastings Sibley Papers, 1815–1930, Minnesota Historical Society.

## Chapter 12

1. Meyer, *History of the Santee Sioux*, 124.
2. William Marshall, quoted in letter from Bishop Henry Whipple to Assistant Secretary of the Interior John Usher (April 21, 1863), File P823, Bishop Henry B. Whipple Papers, File P823, Minnesota Historical Society.
3. Letter from Brig. Gen. Henry H. Sibley to Asst. Sec. Interior J. P. Usher, December 19, 1862, File M166, Minnesota Historical Society.
4. Letter from Brig. Gen. Henry H. Sibley to Bishop Henry Whipple, December 7, 1862, File P823, Bishop Henry B. Whipple Papers, Minnesota Historical Society. Underlined word in the original.
5. *Ibid.*
6. Case No. 301 (Echadooza), File P1423, Box No. 3, Trial Transcripts, Minnesota Historical Society.
7. *Ibid.*
8. All quotations in this paragraph refer to Case no. 42, File P1423, Trial Transcripts, Minnesota Historical Society.
9. Case No. 42 (Winyanaketa), File 1423, Box 1, Trial Transcripts, Minnesota Historical Society.
10. Anderson, "The Dakota War Trials," 52:00–53:00 seq.
11. These points were raised by reviewers of a paper I submitted to the Minnesota Historical Society's journal, *Minnesota History*, in 2011.
12. Bachman, *Northern Slave Black Dakota*, 196.
13. Macomb, *The Practice of Courts Martial*, 67.
14. Erica Myer, "Conquering Peace: Military Commissions as a Lawfare Strategy in the Mexican War," *American Journal of Criminal Law*, Vol. 35, No. 2 (2008), 158.
15. Macomb, *The Practice of Courts Martial*, 16.
16. Walt Bachman lays this out very clearly in his book *Northern Slave Black Dakota*.

## Chapter 13

1. Telegram from Gov. Alexander Ramsey to Pres. Abraham Lincoln, *Executive Documents of the State of Minnesota for the Year 1862* (St. Paul, MN: William R. Marshall, 1863), 374.
2. Letter from President Abraham Lincoln to Gov. Alexander Ramsey, *MCIW*, 201.
3. Gideon Welles, quoted in Fisher, *Military Tribunals*, 52.
4. Joseph Holt, quoted in Fisher, *Military Tribunals*, 53.
5. Anderson, "The Dakota War Trials," 53:50.
6. Bryant, *History of the Great Massacre*, 457.
7. J. Fletcher Williams, "Memoir of Henry Hastings Sibley," *Minnesota Historical Society Collections* Vol. IX (St. Paul, MN: Minnesota Historical Society, 1894).
8. Jacob Nix, *The Sioux Uprising in Minnesota, 1862: Jacob Nix's Eyewitness History*, Don Erich Tolzmann, ed., Gretchen Steinhauser, trans. (Indianapolis: Indiana German Heritage Society, 1994), 129.
9. Bryant, *History of the Great Massacre*, 466.
10. *Mankato Independent*, November 19, 1862, File M166, Minnesota Historical Society.
11. *Saint Paul Pioneer*, November 22, 1862, File M166, Minnesota Historical Society.
12. William P. Dole, quoted in Chomsky, "The United States–Dakota War Trials," 30.
13. There is some confusion as to when Whipple met with Lincoln. Historians have suggested different dates; Halleck's note introducing Whipple to the president is undated. From Whipple's own remarks, it seems most likely that the meeting occurred sometime in October, but though both he and Lincoln later referred to the meeting, neither gave it a specific date. At least one historian, John Labatte, has questioned whether or not the meeting ever actually occurred.
14. Letter from Bishop Henry B. Whipple to editor of the *Republican Pioneer*, undated (most likely November

1862), File P823, Bishop Henry B. Whipple Papers, Minnesota Historical Society.

15. Whipple, quoted in Heard, *History of the Sioux War*, 348.

16. Letter from Reverend Ezekial Gere to Bishop Henry B. Whipple, December 1862, File P823, Bishop Henry B. Whipple Papers, Minnesota Historical Society.

17. Whipple, *Light and Shadows of a Long Episcopate*.

18. Letter from Rev. Stephen R. Riggs to Pres. Abraham Lincoln, November 17, 1862. File M166, Minnesota Historical Society. The underlined words are in the original text.

19. *Ibid.*, underlined word in the original.

20. *Ibid.*

21. *Ibid.*

22. Thomas S. Williamson, Letter in the *St. Paul Daily Press*, August 29, 1862.

23. Letter from Rev. Thomas S. Williamson to Rev. Stephen R. Riggs, November 24, 1862. Stephen Return Riggs and Family Papers, 1837–1958; File P727, Minnesota Historical Society.

24. *Ibid.*

25. Stephen R. Riggs, in the *St. Paul Daily Press*, December 14, 1862, File M166, Minnesota Historical Society. Italics in the original.

26. *Ibid.* Italics in the original.

27. Letter from Mary Riggs to Stephen R. Riggs, October 13, 1862, File F727, Stephen Return Riggs and Family Papers, Minnesota Historical Society Collection.

28. Antoine Freniere, *St. Paul Daily Press*, December 14, 1862, from a clipping in file P727, Stephen Return Riggs and Family Papers, Minnesota Historical Society.

29. John Humphrey, "Boyhood Remembrances of Life Among the Dakotas and the Massacre in 1862," *Minnesota Historical Society Collections*, Vol. XV (St. Paul, MN: Minnesota Historical Society, 1915).

30. The *Mankato Independent*, File M166, Minnesota Historical Society.

31. Sheardown, File P1369, Narratives, Minnesota Historical Society.

32. Senator Morton S. Wilkinson, "Resolution to the Senate," December 5, 1862, File M166, Sioux Uprising Collection, Minnesota Historical Society.

33. *Ibid.*

34. Sec. Navy Gideon Welles, *Diary of Gideon Welles*, 219.

35. *Ibid.*

36. Wilkinson, "Resolution to the Senate," December 5 1862, M166, Minnesota Historical Society.

37. *Ibid.*

38. Letter from Gov. Alexander Ramsey to Pres. Abraham Lincoln, November 10, 1862, *MCIW*, 289.

39. Letter from Maj. Gen. John Pope to Pres. Abraham Lincoln, November 11, 1862, *MCIW*, 289.

40. *Ibid.*

41. Letter from Maj. Gen. John Pope to Governor Alexander Ramsey, November 6, 1862, *MCIW*, 288.

42. Letter from Maj. Gen. John Pope to President Abraham Lincoln, November 11, 1862, *MCIW*, 290.

43. Letter from Maj. Gen. John Pope to President Abraham Lincoln, November 24, 1862, *MCIW*, 290.

44. Letter from Brig. Gen. Henry H. Sibley to Brig. Gen. Elliot, December 6, 1862, File M166, Minnesota Historical Society.

45. *Ibid.*

46. Letter from Brig. Gen. Henry H. Sibley to Brig. Gen. Elliot, December 8, 1862, *MCIW*, 291.

47. Letter from Sen. Morton S. Wilkinson to Gov. Alexander Ramsey, December 9, 1862, *MCIW*, 291.

48. Execution order from President Abraham Lincoln, dated December 6, 1862, Minnesota Historical Society.

49. *Ibid.*

50. The execution order in Lincoln's handwriting was actually sent to the U.S. Senate on December 11, 1862. The version that Sibley received, which was a verbatim copy, was in the handwriting of John G. Nicolay, one of Lincoln's secretaries. This was the one retained in the archives of the Minnesota Historical Society.

51. The accuracy of this detail has since been debated. William Folwell, a very thorough historian, referred to it in 1927, saying: "In a written statement, dated March 31, 1879, and subjoined to a facsimile of Lincoln's order for the execution of the Indians, in the possession of the Minnesota Historical Society, Colonel Miller gave as the reason for the postponement of the executions that he had no supply of the proper kind of rope," Folwell, *A History of Minnesota*, 210.

52. Riggs, *Mary and Me*, 210.

53. Letter from Brig. Gen. Henry H. Sibley to Reverend Stephen R. Riggs, December 15, 1862, File P727, Stephen Return Riggs and Family Papers, Minnesota Historical Society.

54. *Ibid.*

55. Riggs, *Mary and Me*, 210.

56. *Ibid.*

57. *Ibid.*

58. Telegram from President Abraham Lincoln to Brig. Gen. Henry H. Sibley, December 16, 1862, reproduced in *MCIW*, 292.

59. *Ibid.*

60. Letter from Col. Stephen Miller to Rev. Stephen R. Riggs, December 19, 1862, File P727, Stephen Return Riggs and Family Papers, Minnesota Historical Society.

61. Riggs, *Mary and Me*, 212.

62. *Ibid.*

63. *Ibid.*

64. Rdainyanka, quoted in Carley, "*The Dakota War of 1862*," 72–73.

65. Robert Norris, "Lincoln's Dilemma," *Washington Lawyer*.

66. Martinez, "Remembering the Thirty-Eight," 25.

67. *Ibid.*, 18.

68. David Martinez argues that the selection was arbitrary; Gary Clayton Anderson in his 2012 speech at Gustavus Adolphus College claimed that Lincoln's decision was both arbitrary and one of political calculation rather than judicial assessment. See notes no. 343 and no. 346.

69. Flandrau, *History of Minnesota*, 179.

70. See: Scott Barta, www.Unitednativeamerica.Com/Hanging/ and Reamus Wilson, www.Ya-Native.Com/Timeline/1862-Lincolnmass/.

71. Anderson, "The Dakota War Trials," 2012, 54:56–56:18 seq.

72. *Ibid.*, 57:08 seq.

73. President Abraham Lincoln, December 11, 1862, *Message of the President of the United States, in Answer to a Resolution of the Senate of the 5th Instant in Relation to the Indian Barbarities in Minnesota*. Message. Executive White House (Washington, D.C.: U.S. Senate, 1862).

74. Anderson, "The Dakota War Trials," 1:26:40 seq.

75. Norris, "Lincoln's Dilemma," *Washington Lawyer*.

# Chapter 14

1. Letter from Maj. Gen. John Pope to Gov. Alexander Ramsey, November 6, 1862, *MCIW*, 287.
2. *Ibid.*, 288.
3. *Ibid.* What Pope was calling for was nothing less than an official program of what would today be recognized as ethnic cleansing. For a discussion of this matter, see Chapter 16.
4. *The St. Paul Daily Press*, November 8, 1862, File M166, Minnesota Historical Society. Italics in the original.
5. Brown, quoted in *Through Dakota Eyes*, 227.
6. *Ibid.*, 228.
7. Good Star Woman, quoted in *Through Dakota Eyes*, 263.
8. Flandrau, *The History of Minnesota*, 157.
9. Malmros, *AG Report 1863*, 47.
10. John Nelson, File P1667, Sioux Uprising Collection, Minnesota Historical Society.
11. Walt Bachman, "Deaths of Dakota Indians from the New Ulm Mob Attack," *Trails of Tears: Minnesota's Dakota Indian Exile Begins*, Mary Bakeman and Antona Richardson, eds. (Roseville, MN: Prairie Echoes, 2008).
12. Gebhard and Isch, *Eight Days in August*, 138.
13. Henry S. Sibley, quoted in Carley, "Sibley's Letters to His Wife," 113.
14. *Ibid.*
15. Nix, *The Sioux Uprising*, 129.
16. *Ibid.*
17. *Mankato Semi-Weekly Record*, November 15, 1862.

# Chapter 15

1. President Abraham Lincoln, December 11, 1862, *Message of the President of the United States, in Answer to a Resolution of the Senate of the 5th Instant in Relation to the Indian Barbarities in Minnesota*, Message, Executive White House (Washington, D.C.: U.S. Senate, 1862).
2. *Ibid.*
3. Buck, *Indian Outbreaks*, 251.
4. *The New York Times*, December 26, 1862.
5. Reyff, quoted in Carrigan.
6. *The New York Times*, December 26, 1862.
7. Quoted in Hank H. Cox, *Lincoln and the Sioux Uprising of 1862* (Nashville: Cumberland House Publishing, 2005), 192.
8. A soldier of the 7th Minnesota Infantry, Amos B. Watson, described this scene in his narrative, saying that he and "two others picked him up and hung him up again." Watson did not identify the Indian; he may not have known the man's name. Watson then went on to describe placing the bodies of the executed men in army wagons, taking them down to the river, and burying them "about two feet deep in the sand." Amos B. Watson, "Reminiscences of the Sioux Outbreak," File P1369, Manuscripts Collection, Dakota Conflict of 1862, Minnesota Historical Society.
9. *The New York Times*, December 26, 1862.
10. Nix, *The Sioux Uprising*, 92.
11. *Ibid.*, 135.
12. Mark Lee Gardner gives an excellent rendition of these events in his book *Shot All to Hell: Jesse James, the Northfield Raid, and the Wild West's Greatest Escape*, published in 2013.
13. Mary Beth Faimon, "Ties That Bind: Remembering, Mourning and Healing Historical Trauma," *American Indian Quarterly*, Vol. 28, No. ½, Special Issue: Empowerment Through Literature (Winter-Spring, 2004).
14. Martinez, "Remembering the Thirty-Eight," 13.
15. Walt Bachman and I disagree on this point. Bachman believes that White Dog was in fact guilty of criminal conduct; I am not convinced of that.
16. Nix, *The Sioux Uprising*, 139.
17. Flandrau, *The History of Minnesota*, 179.
18. Bachman, *Northern Slave Black Dakota*, 261.

# Chapter 16

1. Waziyatawin is a writer, academic and Dakota activist who appears in the recent literature of the war under a variety of appellations. She has published under the name Angela Cavender and Waziyatawin Angela Wilson, and now goes by the single name of Waziyatawin.
2. I still believe this historical association holds true more often than not, but the more recent images of Serbian-run concentration camps during the Balkan wars of the 1990s are increasingly becoming a part of the history associated with concentration camps.
3. Stephan Malinowski, Lecture notes on Holocaust portrayals in recent history, Edinburgh University, Edinburgh, Scotland, November 7, 2012.
4. Waziyatawin Angela Wilson, "Decolonizing the 1862 Death Marches," *American Indian Quarterly*, Vol. 28, No. ½, Special Issue: Empowerment through Literature (Winter-Spring 2004), 191.
5. The Minnesota Historical Society estimates that between 102 and 300 Dakota died during the internment at Pine Island, "most due to outbreaks of measles and other diseases that were also sweeping through St. Peter and other communities where [white] war refugees were gathered."
6. Hyman, "Survival at Crow Creek," 151.
7. Dr. Asa Daniels, "Reminiscences of the Little Crow Uprising," *Collections of the Minnesota Historical Society*, Vol. XV (St. Paul, MN: Minnesota Historical Society), 335.
8. Letter from Steven R. Riggs to S.B. Treat, January 21, 1863. American Board of Commissioners for Foreign Missions Papers. Correspondence: 1 Box 1—Manuscripts and Notebooks; Boxes 2 & 7. Minnesota Historical Society.
9. Gabriel Renville, quoted in *Through Dakota Eyes*.
10. Raymond Owens, MNHS Oral Histories, April 20, 2011, 21.
11. E.D. Neill, *History of the Minnesota Valley, Including the Explorers and Pioneers of Minnesota, –By Rev. Edward D. Neill, and History of the Sioux Massacre, by Charles S. Bryant* (Minneapolis: North Star Publishing Company, 1882), 255.
12. Jane Grey Swisshelm, quoted in Sylvia D. Hoffert, "Gender and Vigilantism on the Minnesota Frontier: Jane Grey Swisshelm and the U.S.–Dakota Conflict of 1862," *The Western History Quarterly*, Vol. 29, No. 3 (Autumn, 1998), 357.
13. Letter from Sen. Morton S. Wilkinson to Gov. Alexander Ramsey, December 9, 1862, *MCIW*, 291.
14. Waziyatawin Angela Wilson, "Decolonizing the 1862 Death Marches," 198.
15. Gary Clayton Anderson. *Ethnic Cleansing and the Indian: The Crime That Should Haunt America*. Norman, OK: University of Oklahoma Press, 2014, 13.

16. Big Eagle, "A Sioux History of the War," 390.
17. John G. Nicolay, *Lincoln's Secretary Goes West: Two Reports by John G. Nicolay on Frontier Indian Troubles 1862*. Theodore C. Blegen, ed. (Lacrosse, WI: Sumac Press, 1965), 69.

## Chapter 17

1. Chomsky, "The United States–Dakota War Trials," 41.
2. Maj. Gen. John Pope, quoted in Chomsky, "The United States–Dakota War Trials," 42.
3. Letter from Brig. Gen. Henry H. Sibley to Judge Advocate General Joseph Holt, File P1369, Minnesota Historical Society.
4. Riggs, in the St. Paul Daily Press, December 17, 1863, clipping in File P727, Stephen Return Riggs and Family Papers Collection, File P727, Minnesota Historical Society Archives.
5. Letter from Brig. Gen. Henry H. Sibley to Pres. Abraham Lincoln, January 26, 1863, P1369, Minnesota Historical Society.
6. Ibid. Underline in the original text.
7. Henry H. Sibley, quoted in Chomsky, "The United States–Dakota War Trials," 39.
8. *St. Paul Pioneer*, November 10, 1865, File M166, Minnesota Historical Society.
9. Ibid.
10. Carley, *The Sioux Uprising of 1862*, 67.

## Chapter 18

1. Gregory Michno, and Susan Michno, *A Fate Worse than Death: Indian Captivities in the West, 1830–1885* (Caldwell, ID: Caxton Press, 2007), 458.
2. Specific examples of each of these acts are explicated in Chapter Twenty-Two, "Exaggeration, Error and Evidence,"
3. Emmerich de Vattel, *Droit Des Gens; Ou, Principes De La Loi Naturelle Appliqués À La Conduite Et–Aux Affaires Des Nations Et Des Souverains* (Philadelphia: T. & J.W. Johnson & Co., 1883), Book III, Chapter IX, § 173.
4. Chomsky, "The United States–Dakota War Trials," 466.
5. Folwell, *History of Minnesota*, 125.
6. de Vattel, *Droit Des Gens*, Book III, Chapter VIII, § 145.
7. Samuel W. Pond, "Indian Warfare in Minnesota," Vol. 3, *Collections of the Minnesota Historical Society* (St. Paul, MN: Minnesota Historical Society, 1880), 132–133.
8. Rev. Stephen Riggs, who knew Pond personally, later said that Pond "had been wanting to be an Indian, if only for half an hour, that he might know how an Indian felt and by what motives he could be moved." Riggs meant it as a compliment. *Mary and I*, 69.
9. Pond, "Indian Warfare in Minnesota," 132.
10. Chomsky, "The United States–Dakota War Trials," 88.
11. To be absolutely clear, I am *not* saying that the Dakota killed women and children indiscriminately all the time, in every case, as a matter of course. Their conduct varied from individual to individual, and situation to situation. What I am saying is that in Dakota culture, the killing of women and children was acceptable within their traditional practice of war.

12. Carol Chomsky, interview with author, June 30, 2014. I am grateful to Professor Chomsky for clarifying her position on this point for me. She is not arguing that the members of the military commission should realistically have considered Dakota warrior culture as a mitigating factor in the trials, but rather that in an ideal situation they would have. As she points out, at least one member of the commission, Lt. Col. William Marshall, did so in his personal comments.
13. *Vae Victis*: "Woe to the Vanquished," also translated as "Woe to the Conquered," a line made famous in Livy's history of the Gauls' sack of Rome in 390 BC, as recounted in *Ab Urbe Condita*.
14. Little Crow himself may have understood this. Some sources have him trying to convince his warriors to "make war after the manner of white men." If this story is true, the problem is that he only expressed such a position after the war began on August 18, and by the time he is supposed to have made this statement, many of the worst massacres and murders were already committed.
15. Bryant, *A History of the Great Massacre*, 458.
16. Herman Froetsch, *The Art of Modern War*, Theodore W. Knauth, trans (Camden, NJ: Veritas Press, Inc, 1940), 245.
17. Ibid., 246.
18. Cyrus Aldrich, and William Windom, and Morton Wilkinson, "Memorial Against the Reprieve of Any of the Murderers," *The St. Paul Pioneer Press*, December 5, 1862, File M166, Minnesota Historical Society.
19. Letter from Bishop Henry Whipple to Senator Henry M. Rice, File P823, Bishop Henry B. Whipple Papers, Minnesota Historical Society.
20. Letter from Senator Rice to Bishop Whipple, November 19, 1862, File P823, Bishop Henry B. Whipple Papers, Minnesota Historical Society.
21. Big Eagle, "A Sioux History of the War," 397.
22. Henry H. Sibley, in a letter to Acting Ass't Adj. Gen. R. Selfridge; December 22, 1862, File M166, Minnesota Historical Society .
23. Big Eagle, "A Sioux History of the War," 399–400.
24. Ibid.
25. Louis H. Roddis, *The Indian Wars of Minnesota* (Cedar Rapids, IA: The Torch Press, 1956), 152. The rest of the sentence after the ellipses, which I omitted from my text, is "and so pleaded guilty without realization that the death penalty would be given." I believe Roddis reads too much into the trial transcripts. Most of the Indian defendants in the later trials did not to enter a plea of any kind. It is more accurate to say that the Dakota did not understand that the statements they made before the commission, statements admitting to participation in or presence at battles, would be interpreted as admissions of guilt and so used against them.
26. Jorstad, *The Life of Henry Hastings Sibley*, 313. Jorstad is additionally mistaken in his assertion that the Dakota defendants "pleaded guilty." In fact, most defendants denied any guilt and proclaimed their innocence.
27. Waziyatawin Angela Wilson, "Decolonizing the 1862 Death Marches," 190.
28. Chomsky, "The United States–Dakota War Trials," 72.
29. de Vattel, Book III, Chapter VI, 137.
30. Chomsky, "The United States–Dakota War Trials," 86.
31. Article 105 of the Articles of War, edition 1861–1863.
32. John O'Brien. *A Treatise on American Military*

*Laws, and the Practice of Courts-Martial* (Philadelphia: Lea & Blanchard, 1846), 235.

33. *Ibid.*, 163.

34. de Vattel, Book III, Chapter VIII, § 149.

35. Gen. Henry W. Halleck, "Military Tribunals and Their Jurisdiction," *The American Journal of International Law*, Vol. 5, No. 4 (October, 1911), 966.

## Chapter 19

1. Waziyatawin/Wilson, "Decolonizing the 1862 Death Marches," 206.

2. Anderson, "The Dakota War Trials," 42:50–43:10 seq.

3. Thomas A. Robertson, quoted by Adrian J. Ebell in *The St. Paul Daily News*, 11 September 1862, File M166, Minnesota Historical Society.

4. Derounian-Stodola, *The War in Words*, 111.

5. *Ibid.*

6. For more on this question, see the Notes on Sources section at the end of this book. Also, Gregory Michno's book *A Fate Worse than Death* considers the question of rape in Indian captivity in much greater depth than does nearly any other single text. Michno concludes that rape, while not universal, was far from an anomaly and was inflicted on female captives more often than not.

7. Mary Schwandt quoted in Bryant, *History of the Great Massacre*, 339–40.

8. Derounian-Stodola, *The War in Words*, 110. A full reading of Mary Schwandt's narratives reveals that she did change her story over the years. In subsequent versions of her account, her accusations of violence at the hands of the Indians become more dramatic. It does not automatically follow, however, that she therefore invented the story of her rape out of thin air.

9. Letter from Stephen R. Riggs to Martha Riggs, September 27, 1862, File P727, Stephen Return Riggs and Family Papers, Minnesota Historical Society.

10. Case no. 2, File P1423, Box 1, Trial Transcripts, Minnesota Historical Society.

11. *Ibid.*

12. *Ibid.*

13. Case no. 4, File P1423, Box 1, Trial Transcripts, Minnesota Historical Society.

14. *Ibid.*

15. File P1423, Boxes 1–3.

16. *Ibid.*

## Chapter 20

1. File P1423, Trial Transcripts, Minnesota Historical Society.

2. Case no. 12, File P1423, Trial Transcripts, Minnesota Historical Society.

3. *Ibid.*

4. *Ibid.*

5. In Moses Adams' narrative of his experiences in the war, he claimed that Richardson was fatally wounded when the Indians shot him out of the saddle. Since Adams was not a witness to the incident, it is doubtful that he would have known precisely the circumstances in which Richardson was killed. According to Adams' account, Richardson was on a scouting mission when he was ambushed. There were no American eyewitnesses to the incident.

6. Case no. 12, File P1423, Trial Transcripts, Minnesota Historical Society.

7. Sibley's commission clearly did not follow the standard burden of proof requirement, as is evidenced by their expectation that the Indian defendants would make their innocence clear if they were, in fact, innocent. The commission's trials were conducted with the assumption of guilt, not innocence, in place.

8. Isch, *The Dakota Trials.*

9. Stephen R. Riggs, in *The Mankato Independent*, File M166, Minnesota Historical Society.

10. *Ibid.*

11. Holcombe, *Minnesota in Three Centuries, Vol. III*, 317–318.

12. Case no. 358, File P1423, Trial Transcripts, Minnesota Historical Society.

13. This is one of those cases where there is a frustrating certainty that more was said in the courtroom than was actually written in the transcript. The commission clearly had some reason for believing Wasoohdehayya to be innocent—they just did not feel it necessary to explain their thinking in the written record.

14. Heard, 267.

15. *Ibid.*, 270.

16. Letter from Ezekial Gere to Henry B. Whipple, December 19, 1862. Henry B. Whipple Papers, File P823, Minnesota Historical Society Collection.

17. Article 56 of the Articles of War, amended 1806 version.

18. Heard, *History of the Sioux War,* 255.

19. *Ibid.*, 256.

20. Chomsky, "The United States–Dakota War Trials," 86.

21. Some suggest this did not apply in the case of New Ulm, where the target was a civilian population center, not a military installation or an armed force in the field. I disagree.

22. John Isch raised this question during a conversation with the author at New Ulm, MN, in June 2014.

23. Bachman, *Northern Slave Black Dakota*, 260.

24. Big Eagle, "A Sioux History of the War," 400.

25. George Quinn, quoted in *Through Dakota Eyes*, 94.

26. *Ibid.*

27. *Ibid.*, 95.

28. John LaBatte offers this account in his MNHS interview. U.S.–Dakota War of 1862 Oral History Project, March 10, 2011, http://Collection.Mnhs.Org/Cms/Display, 3.

## Chapter 21

1. Holcombe, *Minnesota in Three Centuries*, 389.

2. Alan R. Woolworth, "Adrian J. Ebell, Photographer and Journalist of the Dakota War of 1862," *Minnesota History*, Vol. 54, No. 2 (Summer, 1994), 90.

3. Derounian-Stodola, *The War in Words*, 85.

4. Chomsky, "The United States–Dakota War Trials," 39. Professor Chomsky has recently said that if she was writing the article today, she would phrase it differently and say "*Some* Historians," which I think is fair. Carol Chomsky, interview with author, June 30, 2014.

5. Carley, *The Sioux Uprising of 1862*, 48.

6. Meyer, *History of the Santee*, 120.

7. Dr. Jared Daniels, "Reminiscences," File P2247, Minnesota Historical Society, 10.

8. Rev. Moses N. Adams, "The Sioux Outbreak in

the Year 1862, with Notes of Missionary Work Among the Sioux," *Collections of the Minnesota Historical Society Vol. IX* (St. Paul, MN: Minnesota Historical Society, 1901), 437.

9. Gary Clayton Anderson, in his 2012 speech at Gustavus Adolphus College, stated that Jared Daniels was his "favorite, because he's just so damned honest." For my part, I find Dr. Daniels' account to be lacking in the sort of specificity that would support the broad conclusions which later commentators have built on his testimony.

10. Dr. Jared Daniels, "Reminiscences," 11.

11. S.D. Hinman, quoted in Heard, *History of the Sioux War*, 67.

12. Gregory Michno also makes this argument, very effectively, in his book *A Fate Worse than Death*.

13. Carrigan, *Captured by the Indians*, 16 .

14. Emanual Reyff, quoted in Carrigan, *Captured by the Indians*, 25–26. The eventual fate of the Smith baby is unknown.

15. John Koblas, *Let Them Eat Grass: The 1862 Uprising in Minnesota, Vol. 1* (St. Cloud, MN: North Star Press of St. Cloud, 2006), 295.

16. Chomsky, "The United States–Dakota War Trials," 21.

17. Adams, "The Sioux Outbreak in the Year 1862," 438.

18. *Ibid.*, 440. This man was most likely William Taylor, a black barber and musician who was well known in that part of Minnesota. Satterlee came to the same conclusion in his *A Description of the Massacre by the Sioux Indians in Renville County, Minn.*

19. William S. Jones, File P1369, Manuscript Collection, Dakota Conflict of 1862, Minnesota Historical Society.

20. Justina Krueger, quoted in Buck, *Indian Outbreaks*, 205. Krueger's account is also reproduced in Bryant, *A History of the Great Massacre*.

21. C.M. Oehler, *The Great Sioux Uprising* (New York: Oxford University Press, 1959), 254.

22. McGinnis, *Counting Coup*, 81.

23. Pond, *The Dakotas in Minnesota in 1834*, 128.

24. Oehler, *The Great Sioux Uprising*, 254.

25. Michael Kammen, *Mystic Chords of Memory: The Transformation of Tradition in American Culture*.

26. Arthur M. Schlesinger, *The Disuniting of America: Reflections on a Multicultural Society* (New York: W.W. Norton & Company, 1992), 137.

27. Chomsky, "The United States–Dakota War Trials," 39.

28. Jones, *The Civil War in the Northwest*, 37.

29. Neill, *History of Minnesota*, 727.

30. McConkey, *Dakota War Whoop*, Preface. Italics in the original.

31. *Ibid.*, 28.

32. McConkey, 327.

33. Sam Brown, quoted in *Through Dakota Eyes*, 227.

34. *Ibid.*, 174.

35. Buck, *Indian Outbreaks*, 238.

36. Carrigan, *Captured by the Indians*, 13–14.

37. For several women who left narratives of their experiences, subsequent marriage or remarriage meant that the names used after the war were not the same names they used during the war. This is the case with Helen Carrothers Tarble; her last name was Carrothers during the war, and Tarble when her narrative was written later.

38. Krueger, quoted in Bryant, *A History of the Great Massacre*, 315.

39. Reyff, quoted in Carrigan, *Captured by the Indians*, 25–26. Reyff managed to make his way to New Ulm, where he told his nephew and two nieces of the murder of their parents and siblings. He enlisted in the 7th Minnesota Infantry, and was one of the nine men detailed to place the nooses around the necks of the condemned men on the gallows at Mankato on December 26, 1862.

40. Wilhelmina Ienfeldt, quoted in Carrigan, *Captured by the Indians*, 40. The wife of the man referred to as "Mr. Houf" was also a member of the party; she was killed in the wagon.

41. Sophia Ireland was killed because she refused to leave her five-year-old daughter Sarah, who had been wounded in the stomach. Laura Duley's son, who was shot in spite of her pleas, was ten-year-old William; according to witnesses, he took a very long time to die. Six of the people murdered at Lake Shetek were children between the ages of two and five years old.

42. Lavina Eastlick, quoted in Bryant, *History of the Great Massacre*, 350–351.

43. Derounian-Stodola, *The War in Words*, 82.

44. This was the same Mrs. Henderson whose corpse Dr. Jared Daniels reported seeing interred by the burial party.

45. Meyer, *History of the Santee Sioux*, 120.

46. Schultz, *Over the Earth I Come*, 257.

47. Thaddeus Williams, "Thaddeus Williams to Abraham Lincoln, Saturday, November 22, 1862," in *Abraham Lincoln Papers at the Library of Congress*, transcribed and annotated. Lincoln Studies Center, Knox College, Galesburg, Illinois. The most graphic of Dr. Williams' claims are also uncorroborated in any official record, including the trial transcripts of the military commission. There is no direct evidentiary match for most of the atrocities he recounted in his letter.

48. Heard reproduces this particular atrocity claim almost verbatim in his book *A History of the Sioux War*. Since the Wilkinson, et al., letter was written in late 1862, and Heard's book did not come out until 1863, it is likely that Heard borrowed liberally from this letter as a source.

49. The full text of this letter can be found in several readily-accessible secondary sources, including Bishop, Bryant and Cox .

50. *AG Report*, 47.

51. *Ibid.*

52. It is important to note, as Gary Clayton Anderson does, that while this offer of bounty money for killing Dakota implicates the State of Minnesota in a policy that comes dangerously to genocidal in nature, there were almost no bounties that were actually paid out.

53. Heard, *A History of the Sioux War*, 239.

54. *Ibid.*, 241.

55. *Ibid.*, 94.

56. Sylvia D. Hoffert, "Gender and Vigilantism on the Minnesota Frontier," *The Western History Quarterly*, Vol. 29, No. 3 (Autumn, 1998), 357.

57. *Ibid.*, 357.

58. *Ibid.*

59. Folwell, *A History of Minnesota*, 125.

60. Ellen Farrell and David Martinez, among others, have expressed this view. See Farrell, "The Most Terrible Stories: The 1862 Dakota Conflict in White Imagination," in *Journal of Indian Wars*, and Martinez, "Remembering the Thirty-Eight," in *Wicaza Sa Review*.

61. Welles, *Diary of Gideon Welles*, Vol. 2, 23–24.

62. *Ibid.*
63. Quoted in Bruce Tap. *Over Lincoln's Shoulder: The Committee on the Conduct of the War* (Lawrence, KS: University Press of Kansas, 1998), 203.
64. *Ibid.*, 205.
65. *Ibid.*, 207.
66. *Ibid.*

## Chapter 22

1. McConkey, *Dakota War Whoop*, 47–48.
2. Heard, *History of the Sioux War*, 261.
3. Adrian J. Ebell, "The Indian Massacres and War of 1862," *Harper's New Monthly Magazine*, No. CLVII (June, 1863, Vol. XXVII), 1–24.
4. Case No. 96 (Mahpeokenaji), File P1423, Box No. 1, Trial Transcripts, Minnesota Historical Society.
5. Buck, *Indian Outbreaks*, 272.
6. Aaron Myers, File P1369, Manuscripts Collection, Minnesota Historical Society.
7. Krueger, quoted in Bryant, *A History of the Great Massacre*, 300.
8. Gov. Alexander Ramsey, *Minnesota Executive Documents*, 1862.
9. Heard, *History of the Sioux War*, 70–71.
10. Oehler, *The Great Sioux Uprising*, 57.

## Chapter 23

1. Isch explicates the history of the misplaced trial transcripts, and their reemergence, very well in *The Dakota War Trials*.
2. Anderson, "The Dakota War Trials," 49:30–49:48 seq.
3. Riggs, *Mary and Me*, 211.
4. *Ibid.*
5. *Ibid.*
6. *Ibid.*
7. Robinson, *A History of the Dakota*, 301.
8. Letter from Henry H. Sibley to Sarah Steele Sibley, September 27, 1862, File M164, Henry Hastings Sibley Papers, 1815–1930, Minnesota Historical Society.
9. Letter from Sarah Wakefield to Rev. Stephen R. Riggs, March 22, 1863, File P727, Stephen R. Riggs and Family Papers, Minnesota Historical Society.
10. *Ibid.*
11. Letter from Sarah Wakefield to Rev. Stephen R. Riggs, April 9, 1863, File P727, Stephen R. Riggs and Family Papers, Minnesota Historical Society.
12. *Ibid.*
13. Letter from Rev. Stephen R. Riggs to Sarah Wakefield, March 22, 1863.
14. Letter from Sarah Wakefield to Rev. Stephen R. Riggs, April 25, 1863, File P727, Stephen R. Riggs and Family Papers, Minnesota Historical Society.
15. Letter from Sarah Wakefield to Rev. Stephen R. Riggs, April 9, 1863, File P727, Stephen R. Riggs and Family Papers, Minnesota Historical Society.
16. Missionary list of 1862 trial defendants, File P727, Stephen R. Riggs and Family Papers, Minnesota Historical Society.
17. The sources I refer to here are Thomas Robertson (File M582, roll 3, Minnesota Historical Society), Charles E. McColley (File M582, roll 2, Minnesota Historical Society), and John P. Williamson (MSS 101, Box 10, Hughes Papers, Southern Minnesota Historical Center).

## Chapter 24

1. Satterlee, *The Massacre by the Sioux Indians in Renville County, Minn.* (Minneapolis: The Fisher Paper Box Company, 2016).
2. Holcombe, *Minnesota in Three Centuries*, Vol. III, 303.
3. McConkey, *Dakota War Whoop*, 30.
4. Neill, *The History of Minnesota*, 725.
5. John LaBatte, https://dakotawar1862.wordpress.com/category/essays/60-causes/.
6. Nicolay, *Lincoln's Secretary Goes West*, 48.
7. Holcombe, *Minnesota in Three Centuries*, Vol. III, 331.
8. Brown, quoted in *Through Dakota Eyes*, 225.
9. Riggs, *The St. Paul Pioneer*, December 28, 1862, File P727, Stephen R. Riggs and Family Papers, Minnesota Historical Society.
10. Heard, *History of the Sioux Wars*, 73.
11. *Ibid.*, 110.
12. McConkey, *Dakota War Whoop*, 75.
13. *Ibid.*, 160.
14. *Ibid.*, 162.
15. Derounian-Stodola, *The War in Words*, 83.
16. Henry H. Sibley. File M164, Henry Hastings Sibley Papers, Minnesota Historical Society.
17. Derounian-Stodola, "Many Persons Say I Am a Mono-Maniac," 8.
18. Nix, *The Sioux Uprising in Minnesota*, 133.
19. *Ibid.*
20. Heard, *History of the Sioux Wars*, 294.
21. *Ibid.*, 272.
22. Buck, *Indian Outbreaks*, 269.
23. *Ibid.*
24. Nix, *The Sioux Uprising in Minnesota*, 135.
25. Heard, *History of the Sioux Wars*, 290.
26. Buck, *Indian Outbreaks*, 270.
27. *Ibid.*
28. Henry A. Castle, *Minnesota: Its Story and Biography* (Chicago: The Lewis Publishing Co., 1915).
29. Bryant, *History of the Sioux Massacre*, 254.
30. Jorstad, "The Life of Henry Hastings Sibley," 312.
31. Peter Maguire, *Law and War: An American Story* (New York: Columbia University Press, 2000), 30.
32. *Ibid.*
33. *Ibid.*, 32.
34. Richard Mott Jackson. "Personal Reminiscences," File P1369, Minnesota Historical Society Collections.

## Chapter 25

1. "Sympathy: Who Needs It?" *Minnesota History* (Fall, 1971), 271.
2. *Ibid.*
3. Dean Blue, MNHS Oral History Interview, April 27, 2011, 17.
4. Raymond J. DeMallie, "These Have No Ears": Narrative and the Ethnohistorical Method," *Ethnohistory*, Vol. 40, No. 4 (Autumn, 1993), 515.
5. *Ibid.*
6. David Pashe, MNHS Oral Histories, January 19 2012, 6.

7. Mary Fellegy, MNHS Oral Histories, May 31, 2011, 9.
8. Elsie Noel, MNHS Oral Histories, January 18 2012, 16.
9. John Labatte, MNHS Oral Histories, May 31, 2011, 17.
10. Dean Blue, MNHS Oral Histories, April 27, 2011, 13.
11. Sandra Geshick, MNHS Oral Histories, June 10, 2011, 6.
12. Dallas Ross, MNHS Oral Histories, May 5, 2011, 8.
13. Angela Cavender Wilson [Waziyatawin], "Grandmother to Granddaughter: Generations of Oral History in a Dakota Family," *American Indian Quarterly*, Vol. 20, No. 1 (Winter, 1996), 196.
14. Letter from John P. Williamson to S.B. Treat, November 28, 1862. ABCFM Papers, Box 7, Minnesota Historical Society.
15. Alan Woolworth and Mary H. Bakeman. "The Family Caravan," *Trails of Tears: Minnesota's Dakota Indian Exile Begins*, Mary H. Bakeman and Antona M. Richardson, editors (Roseville, MN: Prairie Echoes Press, 2008).
16. John LaBatte, MNHS Oral Histories, May 31, 2011, 17.
17. For clarification, a forced march is defined by the U.S. Army as any foot movement in excess of 36 miles in one 24-hour period, with a minimum of water and food and no more than one 10-minute rest halt every three hours. By any definition of the term, the marches in November 1862 were *not* forced marches.
18. Good Star Woman, quoted in *Through Dakota Eyes*, 263.
19. Judith L. Anywaush, MNHS Oral Histories, March 10, 2011, 18.
20. Mary Fellegy, MNHS Oral Histories, May 31, 2011, 9.
21. David Pashe, MNHS Oral Histories, January 19, 2012, 7.
22. Big Eagle, *A Sioux History of the War*, 391.
23. Dean Blue, MNHS Oral Histories, April 27, 2011, 15.
24. Dallas Ross, MNHS Oral Histories, May 5, 2011, 7.

## Chapter 26

1. Waziyatawin Angela Wilson, "Decolonizing the 1862 Death Marches," 206. Waziyatawin's statement, to which I am referring here, is: "[W]e as Dakota need to stand up most forcefully to call into question the innocence of whites in Minnesota in 1862 and to declare that the violence committed upon the whites in Minnesota during the war was not caused by the Dakota—it was caused by their own actions and the actions of their government."
2. Cecilia Campbell Stay, quoted in *Through Dakota Eyes*, 47.
3. Guy Gibbon, *The Sioux: The Dakota and Lakota Nations* (Malden: Blackwell Publishing, 2003), 167.
4. Bryant, *History of the Sioux Massacre*, 255.
5. Anton Manderfeld, quoted in Bryant, *History of the Sioux Massacre*, 386.
6. John Ames Humphrey, "Boyhood Remembrances of Life Among the Dakotas and the Massacre in 1862," *Minnesota Historical Society Collections*, Vol. XV (St. Paul: MN, Minnesota Historical Society, 1915), 341.

7. In what may have been the most justified revenge killing of the war, one of the first men killed by the Dakota at the Lower Agency on August 18 was Andrew Myrick, the trader who reportedly made the inflammatory remark, "Let them eat grass!" when told the Indians would starve without credit to buy supplies until the annuity payments arrived. Myrick, in the moral sense, might be thought of as a legitimate target, unlike most of the other victims.
8. Letter from Henry H. Sibley to Sarah S. Sibley, October 15, 1862, File M164, Henry Hastings Sibley Papers, Minnesota Historical Society.
9. It is not recorded whether this Indian baby was a boy or girl. I refer to the child as a boy without knowing if the child was male or female, because the 19th century convention of referring to a deceased child as "it" simply seems too impersonal.

## Chapter 27

1. Wowinape, quoted in Bryant, *History of the Sioux Massacre*, 501.
2. Nathan Lamson was eventually paid a reward of $500 for killing Little Crow. Chauncey Lamson received the $75 bounty for Little Crow's scalp.
3. Gary Anderson, *Little Crow, Spokesman for the Sioux* (St. Paul: MN, Minnesota Historical Society Press, 1986), 8.
4. Riggs, in the St. Paul Daily Press, December 17, 1863. Clipping in File P727, Stephen Return Riggs and Family Papers Collection, Minnesota Historical Society Archives.
5. Ibid.
6. Krueger, quoted in Bryant, *History of the Sioux Massacre*, 323.
7. John Isch has written the most detailed study of Lavina Eastlick's life to date, an excellent biography entitled *A Battle for Living: The Life and Experiences of Lavina Eastlick*, published by the Brown County Historical Society in 2012.
8. Curtis Dahlin gives a brief but compelling synopsis of Julia and Laura's experience in his book *The Dakota Uprising: A Pictorial History*.
9. Samuel Pond, quoted in S. W. Pond, Jr. *Two Volunteer Missionaries Among the Dakotas*. Congregational Sunday-School and Publishing Society, n.p., 1893, 246.

## Conclusion

1. Wowinape, son of Little Crow, quoted in Carley, *The Dakota War of 1862*, 11.
2. Walt Bachman, email to author, 20 June 2014.
3. Judith L. Anywaush, MNHS Oral Histories, March 10, 2011, 18.
4. Christianson, *The Land of Sky-Tinted Waters*, 184.
5. Buck, *Indian Outbreaks*, 274.

## Notes on Sources

1. Sarah Wakefield, *Six Weeks in the Sioux Tepees: A Narrative of Indian Captivity* (Shakopee, MN: Argus Books and Job Printing Office, 1864), 86.
2. Ibid., 64.

# Appendix

1. Harold L. Kaplan, "Constitutional Limitations on Trials by Military Commissions," *University of Pennsylvania Law Review*, Vol. 92, No 2 (December 1943).
2. Myer, "Conquering Peace," 215.
3. *Ibid.*, 216.
4. Fisher, "Military Commissions: Problems of Authority and Practice," 29.
5. Kaplan, "Constitutional Limitations on Trials by Military Commissions," 22.
6. Fisher, "Military Commissions: A Sorry History," *Presidential Studies Quarterly*, Vol. 33, No. 3 (September 2003), 486–487.
7. Halleck, quoted in Fisher, "Military Commissions: Problems of Authority and Practice," 38.
8. Chomsky, "The United States–Dakota War Trials," 62.
9. *Ibid.*, 67.

# Bibliography

## Official Publications

*Articles of War: An Act for Establishing Rules and Articles for the Government of the Armies of the United States.* Washington, D.C.: Government Printing Office, 1806.
*Executive Documents of the State of Minnesota for the Year 1862.* St. Paul: William R. Marshall, 1863.
Lincoln, Abraham. *Message of the President of the United States, in answer to a resolution of the Senate of the 5th instant in relation to the Indian barbarities in Minnesota.* Message. Executive White House. Washington, D.C.: U.S. Senate, 1862 (digital).
Malmros, Oscar. *Perspective on the Sioux War: Reports of the Adjutant General to the Governor of Minnesota, September 1862 and January 1863.* St. Paul: Wm. Marshall, State Printer, Press Printing Co.
*Minnesota in the Civil and Indian Wars 1861–1865, Vol. II Official Reports and Correspondence.* St. Paul, MN: The Board of Commissioners, 1893.
Ramsey, Alexander. *Message of Governor Ramsey to the Legislature of Minnesota Delivered at the Extra Session.* St. Paul, MN: Wm. R. Marshall, State Printer, 1862.
*Report of the Commissioner of Indian Affairs for the Year 1862.* Washington, D.C.: Government Printing Office, 1863.
*Report of the Commissioner of Indian Affairs for the Year 1863.* Washington, D.C.: Government Printing Office, 1864.
*Revised Regulations for the Army of the United States, 1861.* Philadelphia: J.B. Lippincott and Co., 1861.
*Revised United States Army Regulations of 1861: With an Appendix containing the Changes and Laws Affecting Army Regulations and Articles of War to June 25, 1863.* Washington, D.C.: Government Printing Office. 1863.
*United States Army Regulations of 1861. With an appendix containing the changes and laws affecting Army Regulations and Articles of War to June 25, 1863.* Washington, D.C.: Government Printing Office. 1863.
*United States Department of the Interior and U.S. Sioux Commissioners. Claims for Depredations by Sioux Indians.* Fairfield, WA: Galleon Press, 1974.
Winthrop, W. *A Digest of Opinions of the Judge-Advocates General of the Army, Rev. Ed.* Washington, D.C.: Government Printing Office, 1901.

## Archival Sources

**National Archives and Records Administration, Washington, D.C.**
RG 48, LS, Indian Division, Department of the Interior, M606, roll 4
RG 48, LR, Indian Division, Department of the Interior, M825, roll 20
RG 94, E173, Indian Prisoners
RG 94, M1523, "Courts-Martial and Military Commission Proceedings Against Union Soldiers, 1861–1866"
RG 153, Records of Judge Advocate General, Courts-Martial file No. KK 516
RG 393, E3436, pt. 1, Letters Sent and Received, Department of Northwest, Headquarters.
RG 393, E3449, pt. 1, Unentered Letters, Department of Northwest, 1862–65, Headquarters Records.
RG 393, E3480, pt. 1, LS, Department of Northwest, 1862 (Sibley's letters from Camp Release)

**Minnesota Historical Society, St. Paul, MN**
File P727, Stephen Return Riggs and Family Papers, 1837–1958.
File P823, Henry Benjamin Whipple Papers, 1833–1934.
File P1423, Boxes 1–3, U.S. Army; Military Commission, Sioux War Trials, Trial Transcripts.

File P1369, Manuscripts Collection, Dakota Conflict of 1862.
File P1577, Jacob Leslie Hamlin.
File P2247, Dr. Jared Daniels, "Reminiscences."
File M164, Henry Hastings Sibley Papers, 1815–1930.
File M166, Sioux Uprising Collection.

**Other Archival Repositories**
Blue Earth County Historical Society, Mankato, MN
Brown County Historical Society, New Ulm, MN
Nicollet County Historical Society, St. Peter, MN
Renville County Historical Society, Morton, MN
Southern Minnesota Historical Center, Minnesota State University, Mankato, MN

## Oral Histories

Anywaush, Judith L. Interview with Deborah Locke. U.S.–Dakota War of 1862 Oral History Project. March 10, 2011. http://collection.mnhs.org/cms/display
Fellegy, Mary. Interview with Deborah Locke. U.S.–Dakota War of 1862 Oral History Project. March 10, 2011. http://collection.mnhs.org/cms/display
Geshick, Sandra. Interview with Deborah Locke. U.S.–Dakota War of 1862 Oral History Project. March 10, 2011. http://collection.mnhs.org/cms/display
LaBatte, John. Interview with Deborah Locke. U.S.–Dakota War of 1862 Oral History Project. March 10, 2011. http://collection.mnhs.org/cms/display
Noel, Elsie. Interview with Deborah Locke. U.S.–Dakota War of 1862 Oral History Project. March 10, 2011. http://collection.mnhs.org/cms/display
Owens, Raymond. Interview with Deborah Locke. U.S.–Dakota War of 1862 Oral History Project. March 10, 2011. http://collection.mnhs.org/cms/display
Pashe, David. Interview with Deborah Locke. U.S.–Dakota War of 1862 Oral History Project. March 10, 2011. http://collection.mnhs.org/cms/display
Ross, Dallas. Interview with Deborah Locke. U.S.–Dakota War of 1862 Oral History Project. March 10, 2011. http://collection.mnhs.org/cms/display

## Primary Sources

Adams, Moses N. "The Sioux Outbreak in the Year 1862, With Notes of Missionary Work Among the Sioux." *Collections of the Minnesota Historical Society*, Vol. IX. St. Paul: Minnesota Historical Society, 1901.
Aldrich, Cyrus, William Windom, Morton Wilkinson. "Memorial Against the Reprieve of any of the Murderers." *St. Paul Pioneer Press.* 5 December 1862.
Big Eagle. Holcombe, Return I., Ed. "A Sioux History of the War: Chief Big Eagle's Story of the Sioux Outbreak of 1862." *Minnesota Historical Society Collections,* Vol. VI, St. Paul: Minnesota Historical Society, 1894.
Bryant, Charles S., and Abel B. Murch. *A History of the Great Massacre by the Sioux Indians, in Minnesota: Including the personal narratives of many who escaped.* Cincinnati, OH: Rickey & Carroll, Publishers, 1863.
_____. *History of the Sioux Massacre.* Minneapolis: North Star Publishing Co., 1882.
Carrigan, Minnie Buce. *Captured by the Indians: Reminiscences of Pioneer Life in Minnesota.* Forest City, SD: Forest City Press, 1907.
Connolly, A.P. *A Thrilling Narrative of the Minnesota Massacre and the Sioux War of 1862–3.* Chicago: A.P. Connolly, Publisher, 1896.
Daniels, Dr. Asa W. "Reminiscences of the Little Crow Uprising." *Minnesota Historical Collections*, Vol. XV. St. Paul: Minnesota Historical Society, 1915.
Eastlick, Lavina. *Thrilling Incidents of the Indian War of 1862.* Lancaster, WI: Herald Book and Job Office, 1864.
Ebell, Adrian J. "The Indian Massacres and War of 1862." *Harper's New Monthly Magazine.* No. CLVII, June, 1863, Vol. XXVII, pp. 1–24.
Flandrau, Charles E. *The History of Minnesota and Frontier Tales.* St. Paul, MN: E.W. Porter, 1900.
Heard, Isaac V.D. *History of the Sioux War and Massacres of 1862 and 1863.* New York, NY: Harper & Brothers, 1864; Millwood, NY: Kraus Reprint Co., 1975.
Humphrey, John Ames. "Boyhood Remembrances of Life Among the Dakotas and the Massacre in 1862." *Minnesota Historical Society Collections*, Vol. XV. St. Paul: Minnesota Historical Society, 1915.

Macomb, Alexander. *The Practice of Courts Martial.* New York: Harper & Brothers, 1841.
Mazakootemane, Paul. "Narrative of Paul Mazakootemane." Trans. Rev. Stephen. R. Riggs. *Collections of the Minnesota Historical Society Vol. III.* St. Paul: Minnesota Historical Society, 1880. 82–90.
McClure, Nancy. "The Story of Nancy McClure: Captivity Among the Sioux." *Minnesota Historical Society Collections Vol. VI.* St. Paul: Minnesota Historical Society, 1894.
Nix, Jacob. *The Sioux Uprising in Minnesota, 1862: Jacob Nix's Eyewitness History.* Don Erich Tolzmann, ed. Gretchen Steinhauser, Don Erich Tolzmann, and Eberhard Reichmann, trans. Indianapolis: Indiana German Heritage Society, 1994.
Pond, Samuel W. *The Dakota or Sioux in Minnesota as They Were In 1834.* St. Paul: Minnesota Historical Society Press, 1986. Reprint of the 1908 edition.
_____. Indian Warfare in Minnesota." *Collections of the Minnesota Historical Society,* Vol. III, St. Paul: Minnesota Historical Society, 1880.
Renville, Gabriel. "A Sioux Narrative of the Outbreak in 1862, and of Sibley's Expedition in 1863." *Minnesota Historical Society Collections,* Vol. X, Part 2, 595–618, St. Paul: Minnesota Historical Society, 1905.
Riggs, Stephen Return. *Mary and I: Forty Years with the Sioux.* Reprint of the 1887 edition. Minneapolis: Ross & Haines, Inc., 1969.
Robertson, Thomas. "Reminiscence of Thomas A. Robertson." *South Dakota Historical Collections.* State Historical Society, Vol. 20. Pierre, SD: 1939. 559–601.
Schwandt, Mary. "The Story of Mary Schwandt: Her Captivity During the Sioux 'Outbreak'—1862." *Minnesota Historical Society Collections,* Vol. VI. St. Paul: Minnesota Historical Society, 1894.
Sibley, Henry Hastings. "Reminiscences, Historical and Personal." *Minnesota Historical Collections,* Vol. I, St. Paul: Minnesota Historical Society, 1870.
Sweet, J.E. De Camp. "Mrs. J. E. De Camp Sweet's Narrative of Her Captivity in the Sioux Outbreak of 1862." *Minnesota Historical Collections Vol. VI,* St. Paul: Minnesota Historical Society, 1894. 354–380.
Tarble, Helen M. Carrothers. *The Story of My Capture and Escape During the Minnesota Indian Massacre of 1862.* St. Paul: Abbott Print Co., 1904.
Wakefield, Sarah F. *Six Weeks in the Sioux Tepees: A Narrative of Indian Captivity.* Shakopee, MN: Argus Books and Job Printing Office, 1864.
Whipple, Bishop Henry B. *Light and Shadows of a Long Episcopate: Being Reminiscences and Recollections of the Right Reverend Henry B. Whipple, Bishop of Minnesota.* New York: The MacMillan Company, 1899.
White, N.D. "Captivity Among the Sioux, August 18 to September 26, 1862." *Minnesota Historical Collections, Vol. IX,* St. Paul: Minnesota Historical Society, 1901.

## Secondary Sources

Allen, Clifford, ed. *History of the Flandreau Santee Sioux Tribe.* Flandreau, South Dakota: Tribal History Program, Flandreau Santee Sioux Tribe. 1971. Digital.
Anderson, Gary Clayton. *Little Crow: Spokesman for the Sioux.* St. Paul: Minnesota Historical Society Press, 1986.
_____. *Ethnic Cleansing and the Indian: The Crime That Should Haunt America.* Norman, OK: University of Oklahoma Press, 2014.
_____. "The Dakota War Trials: Travesty of Justice or Reasonable Retribution?" Gustavus Adolphus College, St. Peter, MN, January 10, 2012.
Anderson, Gary Clayton, and Alan R. Woolworth, ed. *Through Dakota Eyes: Narrative Accounts of the Minnesota Indian War of 1862.* St. Paul: Minnesota Historical Society Press, 1988.
Andrist, Ralph K. *The Long Death: The Last Days of the Plains Indians.* New York: Macmillan Publishing Co., 1964.
Babcock, Willoughby M. "Minnesota's Indian War." St. Paul: *Minnesota History.* Vol. 38, No. 3. 1962.
Bachman, Walt. "Deaths of Dakota Prisoners from the New Ulm Mob Attack." *Trails of Tears: Minnesota's Dakota Indian Exile Begins.* Mary Bakeman and Antona Richardson, editors. 179–180. Roseville, MN: Prairie Echoes, 2008.
_____. *Northern Slave Black Dakota: The Life and Times of Joseph Godfrey.* Bloomington, MN: Pond Dakota Press, 2013.
_____. "Dr. Gary Clayton Anderson's Speech on the Dakota War Trials: A Critique." *Minnesota's Heritage.* No. 6, July 2012. 5–19.
Bakeman, Mary Hawker, and Antona M. Richardson, eds. *Trails of Tears: Minnesota's Dakota Indian Exile Begins.* Roseville, MN: Prairie Echoes Press, 2008.
Bakeman, Mary Hawker, compiler. *Index to Claimants for Depredations Following the Dakota War of 1862.* Roseville, MN: Park Genealogical Books. 2001.
Battle, George Gordon. "Military Tribunals" *Virginia Law Review,* Vol. 29, No. 3 (Dec., 1942), 255–271. Digital.

Benet, S.V. *A Treatise on Military Law and the Practice of Courts-Martial*. Fifth Edition. New York: D. Van Nostrand, 1866.

Boutin, Loren Dean. *Cut Nose Who Stands on a Cloud*. St. Cloud, MN: North Star Press. 2006.

Buck, Daniel. *Indian Outbreaks*. Reprint of the 1904 edition. Minneapolis: Ross & Haines, Inc., 1965.

Carley, Kenneth. *The Dakota War of 1862: Minnesota's Other Civil War*. St. Paul: Minnesota Historical Society Press, 1976.

_____. "The Sioux Campaign of 1862: Sibley's Letters to His Wife." *Minnesota History*. Vol. 38, No. 3. St. Paul: Minnesota Historical Society, 1962.

_____. The *Sioux Uprising of 1862*. St. Paul: Minnesota Historical Society, 1961.

Castle, Henry A. *Minnesota: Its Story and Biography*. Chicago: The Lewis Publishing Co., 1915.

Chomsky, Carol. "The United States–Dakota War Trials: A Study in Military Injustice." *Stanford Law Review* Vol. 43, No. 1 (Nov, 1990), 13–98.

Christenson, Ronald. "A Political Theory of Political Trials" *The Journal of Criminal Law and Criminology* Vol. 74, No. 2 (Summer, 1983), pp. 547–577. Digital.

Christianson, Theodore. *Minnesota The Land of Sky-Tinted Waters: A History of the State and Its People, Vol. I*. New York: The American Historical Society, Inc., 1935.

Clodfelter, Michael. *The Dakota War: The United States Army Versus the Sioux, 1862–1865*. Jefferson, NC: McFarland, 2006.

Coppee, Henry. *Field Manual of Courts-Martial*. Philadelphia: Lippincott, 1863.

Cox, Hank H. *Lincoln and the Sioux Uprising of 1862*. Nashville: Cumberland House Publishing, Inc., 2005.

Cutler, Leonard. *The Rule of Law and the Law of War*. Vol. 25. Lampeter, Wales: Edwin Mellen Press, 2005.

Dahlin, Curtis L. *The Dakota Uprising: A Pictorial History*. Edina, MN: Beavers Pond Press, 2009.

Dean, Janet. "Nameless Outrages: Narrative Authority, Rape Rhetoric, and the Dakota Conflict of 1862." *American Literature*. Vol. 77, No. 1. 2005. Digital.

Derounian-Stodola, Kathryn Zabelle. "Many persons say I am a Mono Maniac: Three Letters from Dakota Conflict Captive Sarah F. Wakefield to Missionary Stephen R. Riggs" *Prospects: An Annual of American Cultural Studies* Jack Salzman, ed. Vol. 29, 2005, Cambridge University Press.

_____. *The War in Words: Reading the Dakota Conflict through the Captivity Literature*. Lincoln, NE: University of Nebraska Press, 2009.

De Vattel, Emmerich. *Droit des gens; ou, Principes de la loi naturelle appliqués à la conduite et aux affaires des nations et des souverains*. Philadelphia: T. & J.W. Johnson & Co., 1883.

Diedrich, Mark. *Little Crow and the Dakota War: The Long Historical Cover-Ups Exposed*. Rochester, MN: Coyote Books, 2006.

Farrell, Ellen. "The Most Terrible Stories: The 1862 Dakota Conflict in White Imagination." *Journal of Indian Wars* 1.2 (2000): 21–38.

Faimon, Mary Beth. "Ties that Bind: Remembering, Mourning and Healing Historical Trauma." *American Indian Quarterly*, Vol. 28, No. ½, Special Issue: Empowerment Through Literature (Winter-Spring, 2004). Digital.

Finkelman, Paul. "'I Could Not Afford to Hang Men for Votes': Lincoln the Lawyer, Humanitarian Concerns, and the Dakota Pardons." *William Mitchell Law Review*. 39:2 (405–449). Digital.

Fisher, Louis. "Military Tribunals: A Sorry History." *Presidential Studies Quarterly*. Vol. 33, No. 3, Sept 2003, 484–508. Digital.

_____. *Military Commissions: Problems of Authority and Practice*. Boston: Boston University School of Law, 2006.

_____. *Military Tribunals and Presidential Power: American Revolution to the War on Terrorism*. Lawrence, KS: University Press of Kansas, 2005.

Fitzharris, Joseph C. "Field Officer Courts and U.S. Civil War Military Justice." *The Journal of Military History*. Vol. 68, No. 1, 2004. Digital.

Folwell, William W. *A History of Minnesota, Volume II*. St. Paul: Minnesota Historical Society, 1924.

Froetsch, Herman. *The Art of Modern War*. Theodore W. Knauth, trans. Camden, NJ: Veritas Press, Inc., 1940.

Fuller, J.F.C. *The Conduct of War, 1789–1961*. London: Minerva Press, 1968.

Gardner, Mark Lee. *Shot All to Hell: Jesse James, the Northfield Raid, and the Wild West's Greatest Escape*. New York: HarperCollins, 2013.

Gebhard, Darla Cordes and John Isch. *Eight Days in August: The Accounts of the Casualties and Survivors in Brown County during the U.S.–Dakota War of 1862*. New Ulm, MN: Brown County Historical Society, 2012.

Gibbon, Guy. *The Sioux: The Dakota and Lakota Nations*. Malden: Blackwell Publishing, 2003.

Gilman, Rhoda R. "Territorial Imperative: How Minnesota Became the 32nd State." *Minnesota History*. Winter, 1998–99. 155–171.

_____. *Divided Heart: Henry Hastings Sibley*. St. Paul: Minnesota Historical Society Press, 2004.

_____. *Henry Sibley and the U.S.–Dakota War of 1862*. Saint Paul: Minnesota Historical Society Press, 2012.

Glazier, David. "Precedents Lost: The Neglected History of the Military Commission." *Virginia Journal of International Law,* Vol. 46, No. 1, Fall 2005. Digital.

Gluek, Alvin C., Jr. "The Sioux Uprising: A Problem in International Relations." *Minnesota History.* 34: 317–324 (Winter 1955).

Graves, Kathy Davis and Elizabeth Ebbott. *Indians in Minnesota.* Minneapolis: University of Minnesota Press, 2006.

Halleck, Henry Wager. "Military Tribunals and Their Jurisdiction." *The American Journal of International Law,* Vol. 5, No. 4 (Oct., 1911), 958–967. Digital.

\_\_\_\_\_. *Elements of International Law and Laws of War.* Philadelphia: Lippincott, 1874, 1866.

Hartigan, Richard Shelly. *Military Rules, Regulations and the Code of War: Francis Lieber and the Certification of Conflict.* New Brunswick, NJ: Transaction Publishers, 2011.

Hasian, Marouf. "Cultural Amnesia and Legal Rhetoric: Remembering the 1862 United States–Dakota War and the Need for Military Commissions." *American Indian Culture and Research Journal 27,* no. 1 (2003): 91–117. Digital.

Hassrick, Royal B. *The Sioux: Life and Customs of a Warrior Society.* Norman: University of Oklahoma Press, 1964.

Hatch, Thom. *The Blue, the Gray, and the Red: Indian Campaigns of the Civil War.* Mechanicsburg, PA: Stackpole Books, 2003.

Herbert, Maeve. "Explaining the Sioux Military Commission of 1862." *Columbia Human Rights Law Review.* (Columbia University) 40.3 (Spring 2009): 743–798. Digital.

Hoffert, Sylvia D. "Gender and Vigilantism on the Minnesota Frontier: Jane Grey Swisshelm and the U.S.–Dakota Conflict of 1862." *The Western Historical Quarterly,* Vol. 29, No. 3 (Autumn, 1998), 342–362. Digital.

Holcombe, Return I. and Lucius F. Hubbard. *Minnesota in Three Centuries, Vol. III.* St. Paul, MN: The Publishing Society of Minnesota, 1908.

Hyman, Colette A. "Survival at Crow Creek, 1863–1866." *Minnesota History,* Vol. 61, No. 4 (Winter 2008/2009), 148–161.

Isch, John. *A Battle For Living: The Life and Experiences of Lavina Eastlick.* New Ulm, MN: Brown County Historical Society, 2012.

\_\_\_\_\_. *The Dakota Trials: The 1862–1864 Military Commission Trials of the Dakota.* New Ulm, MN: Brown County Historical Society, 2012.

Jones, Robert Huhn. *The Civil War in the Northwest: Nebraska, Wisconsin, Iowa, Minnesota, and the Dakotas.* Norman: University of Oklahoma Press, 1960.

Jorstad, Erling Theodore. *The Life of Henry Hastings Sibley (PhD thesis, University of Wisconsin.)* Ann Arbor, MI: University Microfilms, 1957.

Kaplan, Harold L. "Constitutional Limitations on Trials by Military Commissions." *University of Pennsylvania Law Review.* Vol. 92, No. 2, December 1943. Digital.

Keenan, Jerry. *The Great Sioux Uprising: Rebellion on the Plains August—September 1862.* Cambridge: Da Capo Press, 2003.

Koblas, John. *Let Them Eat Grass: The 1862 Uprising in Minnesota, Vol. 1.* St. Cloud, MN: North Star Press of St. Cloud, Inc. 2006.

Lass, William E. "The Removal from Minnesota of the Sioux and Winnebago Indians." *Minnesota History.* Vol. 38, No. 8. 1968.

Lawrence, Elden. *Stories and Reflections: From an Indian Perspective.* Sioux Falls, SD: Pine Hill Press, 2008.

\_\_\_\_\_. *The Peace Seekers: Indian Christians and the Dakota Conflict,* Sioux Falls, SD: Pine Hill Press, 2005.

Linder, Douglas. *The Dakota Conflict Trials.* 1999. http://www.law.umkc.edu/faculty/projects/ftrials/dakota/Dak_account.html

Maguire, Peter. *Law and War: An American Story.* New York: Columbia University Press, 2000.

Martinez, David. "Remembering the Thirty-Eight." *Wicaza Sa Review.* 28:2 (Fall 2013) 5–29.

McConkey, Harriet E. Bishop. *Dakota War Whoop, or, Indian Massacres and War in Minnesota, of 1862–3.* Auburn: William J. Morris' Press, 1864.

McGinnis, Anthony R. *Counting Coup and Cutting Horses: Intertribal Warfare on the Northern Plains, 1738–1889.* Lincoln: University of Nebraska Press, 1990.

Meyer, Roy W. *History of the Santee Sioux: United States Indian Policy on Trial.* Lincoln: University of Nebraska Press, revised edition, 1993.

Michno, Gregory & Susan. *A Fate Worse than Death: Indian Captivities in the West, 1830–1885.* Caldwell, ID: Caxton Press, 2007.

\_\_\_\_\_. *Dakota Dawn.* New York: Savas Beatie, 2012.

*Minnesota History.* "Sympathy: Who Needs It?" The Editor's Page. Fall, 1971. Digital.

Monjeau-Marz, Corrine L. *The Dakota Indian Internment at Fort Snelling, 1862–1863.* St. Paul, MN: Prairie Smoke Press, 2005.

Myer, Erika. "Conquering Peace: Military Commissions as a Lawfare Strategy in the Mexican War." *American Journal of Criminal Law*. Vol. 35, No. 2. 2008. Digital.

Neill, E.D. *History of the Minnesota Valley, Including the Explorers and Pioneers of Minnesota, by Rev. Edward D. Neill, and History of the Sioux Massacre, by Charles S. Bryant*. Minneapolis: North Star Publishing Company, 1882.

Nicolay, John G. *Lincoln's Secretary Goes West: Two Reports by John G. Nicolay on Frontier Indian Troubles 1862*. Theodore C. Blegen, ed. Lacrosse, WI: Sumac Press, 1965.

Nichols, David A. *Lincoln and the Indians: Civil War Policy and Politics* Columbia, MO: University of Missouri Press, 1978.

_____. "The Other Civil War: Lincoln and the Indians." *Minnesota History*. Vol. 44, No. 1. 1974.

Niderost, Eric. "The Great Sioux Uprising of 1862." *Military Heritage*. December (2010): 59–65.

Norris, Robert B. "Lincoln's Dilemma," *Washington Lawyer*, May 2014, accessed October 2, 2014, http://www.dcbar.org/bar-resources/publications.

O'Brien, John. *A Treatise on American Military Laws, and the Practice of Courts Martial*. Philadelphia: Lea & Blanchard, 1846.

Oehler, C. M. *The Great Sioux Uprising*. New York: Oxford University Press, 1959.

Oneroad, Amos E. and Alanson B. Skinner. *Being Dakota*. Edited by Laura L. Anderson. St. Paul: Minnesota Historical Society, 2003.

Osborn, William M. *The Wild Frontier: Atrocities During the American-Indian War from Jamestown Colony to Wounded Knee*. New York: Random House, 2000.

Palmer, Jessica Dawn. *The Dakota Peoples: A History of the Dakota, Lakota and Nakota through 1863*. Jefferson, NC: McFarland & Co., 2008.

Peacock, John. "An Account of the Dakota–U.S. War of 1862 as Sacred Text: Why My Dakota Elders Value Spiritual Closure over Scholarly Balance." *American Indian Culture & Research Journal* 37:2 (2013) 185–206.

Pond, S.W., Jr. *Two Volunteer Missionaries Among the Dakota*. Congregational Sunday-School and Publishing Society, n.p., 1893.

Robinson, Doane. *A History of the Dakota or Sioux Indians*. Reprint of the 1904 edition. Minneapolis: Ross & Haines, Inc., 1956.

Roddis, Louis H. *The Indian Wars of Minnesota*. Cedar Rapids, IA: The Torch Press, 1956.

Ruckman, P.S., Jr., and David Kincaid. "Inside Lincoln's Clemency Decision Making." *Presidential Studies Quarterly*, Vol. 29, No. 1, The Human Presidency (Mar., 1999), 84–99. Digital.

Satterlee, Marion P. *The Court Proceedings in the Trial of Dakota Indians Following the Massacre in Minnesota in August 1862*. Minneapolis: Satterlee Printing Company, 1927.

_____. *A Description of the Massacre by Sioux Indians, in Renville County, Minnesota, August 18–19, 1862: A complete compilation of the names of the victims, and the circumstances of their deaths, so far as known*. Minneapolis: The Fisher Paper Box Company, 1916.

_____. *Dakota Indians Hanged at Mankato, Dec. 26, 1862*. St. Paul: Minnesota Historical Society, n.d.

_____. *The Indian Massacre in Brown County, in August 1862*. St. Paul: Minnesota Historical Society, 1922.

Schlesinger, Arthur M. *The Disuniting of America: Reflections on a Multicultural Society*. New York: W.W. Norton & Co., 1992.

Schultz, Duane. *Over the Earth I Come: The Great Sioux Uprising of 1862*. St. Martin's Griffin, 1993. Silliman, Scott. "On Military Commissions." *Case Western Reserve Journal of International Law* (Case Western Reserve University) 36 (2004): 529–540.

Stock, Catherine McNicol. *Rural Radicals: Righteous Rage in the American Grain*. Ithaca, NY: Cornell University Press, 1996.

Tap, Bruce. *Over Lincoln's Shoulder: The Committee on the Conduct of the War*. Lawrence, KS: University Press of Kansas. 1998.

Utley, Robert M. *Frontiersmen in Blue: The United States Army and the Indian, 1848–1865*. Lincoln: University of Nebraska Press. 1967.

Vogel, Virgil J. *This Country was Ours: A Documentary History of the American Indian*. New York: Harper & Row. 1972.

Weigley, Russell F. *The American Way of War: A History of United States Military Strategy and Policy*. New York: Macmillan, 1973.

Welles, Gideon. *The Diary of Gideon Welles*. John T. Morse, ed. Vol. 2. Boston: Houghton Mifflin, 1911.

Wilson, Waziyatawin Angela. "Decolonizing the 1862 Death Marches." *American Indian Quarterly*, Vol. 28, No. 1/2, Special Issue: Empowerment Through Literature (Winter—Spring, 2004), 185–215 (digital).

Williams, J. Fletcher, Ed. *Memoir of General Henry H. Sibley*. In Minnesota Historical Collections, Vol. VI. St. Paul: Minnesota Historical Society, 1894.

Wingerd, Mary Lethert. *North Country: The Making of Minnesota*. Minneapolis: University of Minnesota Press. 2010.

Winthrop, W. *Military Law and Precedents.* Vol. 1. Boston: Little, Brown & Co., 1896.
_____. *Military Law and Precedents.* Vol. 2. Boston: Little, Brown & Co., 1896.
Woolworth, Alan R. "Adrian J. Ebell, Photographer and Journalist of the Dakota War of 1862." *Minnesota History,* Vol. 54, No. 2 (Summer, 1994), 87–92.
Woolworth, Alan R., and Mary H. Bakeman, eds. *Camera and Sketchbook: Witnesses to the Sioux Uprising of 1862.* St. Paul: Prairie Smoke Press, 2004.
Wooster, Robert. *The Military and United States Indian Policy: 1865–1903.* New Haven: Yale University Press, 1988.

# Index

Acton, Minnesota murders 19, 21, 124, 198–199; skirmish 33, 160
Adams, the Rev. Moses 13, 167, 169, 249*ch*20*n*5; *see also* missionaries
Adjutant General's Report 49, 52, 64, 117, 180, 191; *see also* AG Report
AG Report 49, 52, 118, 179, 234; *see also* Adjutant General's Report
ambush 18; Battle of Wood Lake 36–37, 204; Redwood Ferry 25–26, 30, 33, 159, 164, 167, 200, 218; of Richardson 157–158, 249*ch*20*n*5
Anderson, Gary Clayton 55–56, 73, 92–93, 112–113, 130, 153, 192, 231, 239*ch*1*n*1, 243*ch*8*n*1, 246*ch*13*n*68, 250*ch*21*n*9, 250*ch*21*n*52; statements about trial transcripts 80–82
annuity payments 11, 12, 14, 15, 21, 23, 24, 30, 67, 68, 115, 199, 211, 219, 252*ch*26*n*7
arraignments 80–81, 154
Articles of War 62, 63, 68, 73, 74, 90, 143, 119, 152, 161, 237, 238; Article–56 161; Article–65 59–60, 64, 133; Article–69 70, 73; Article–105 119
atrocities 105, 142, 143, 147, 148, 152 168, 169, 179, 182; allegations 4, 171, 172, 177, 178, 184–188, 227, 250*ch*21*n*47; eyewitness testimony 169, 174–176, scholarly views 165, 166, 170, 181, 233, 236; *see also* decapitation; massacre; rape; scalping

Bachman, Walt 54, 55, 73, 75, 78, 85, 86, 94, 117, 163, 231, 242*ch*7*n*6, 243*ch*7*n*11, 244*ch*10*n*38, 247*ch*15*n*15
Bates, Atty. Gen. Edward 77
Battle of Birch Coulee 4, 33–34, 83, 91, 154, 157, 162, 163, 167, 169, 224, 241*ch*4*n*30
Battle of Fort Ridgely 4, 30, 31–32, 157, 160, 162, 241*ch*4*n*29
Battle of New Ulm 30–31, 86, 91, 116, 156, 157, 161–162, 180, 215
Battle of Wood Lake 4, 36, 38, 83, 86, 91, 154, 156, 163, 179, 204, 205
Beaver Creek *see* massacre
Big Eagle (Dakota chief) 4, 17, 18, 22, 23, 25, 32, 36, 130, 135, 147–148, 159, 163, 200, 216, 224
Bishop, Sgt. John 26
Boelter, F.W. 14
Boelter, Justina 27, 221
bounties 179–180; for scalps 180, 222, 250*ch*21*n*52
Bradley, Maj. George 62, 70
Broburg, Ernestina 27–28
Brown, Joseph E. 13, 14, 25, 33, 110, 193, 202
Brown, Sam 14, 116, 124, 172, 199, 215
Brown County, Minnesota 4, 29, 219; *see also* Milford, Minnesota; New Ulm, Minnesota
Bryant, Charles 100, 129, 146, 176, 203, 232, 239*ch*1*n*1, 240*ch*3*n*10, 250*ch*21*n*49
Buck, Daniel 11, 12, 173, 185, 189, 199, 202, 203, 229
Bureau of Indian Affairs 12, 15, 67, 191
burial party 27, 33, 166, 167, 169, 224

Camp Release 38, 50, 56, 75, 76, 78, 84, 85, 86, 87, 99, 110, 154, 195, 202, 205, 213
Cardinal, Margaret 153, 154, 155
Carley, Kenneth 7, 8, 166, 167, 198, 233
Carrigan, Minnie Buce 14, 168, 173, 193, 220, 241*ch*4*n*15
casualties 3, 32, 33, 37, 112, 152; estimates 29, 239*ch*1*n*6
Cavender, Angela *see* Waziyatawin
Chaska (Dakota man) 81, 124, 194–196, 201–202, 216, 235
Chippewa 8, 17, 144–145
Chomsky, Carol 60, 65–66, 75, 143, 145, 149, 162, 166, 169, 205, 232, 233, 239*ch*1*n*1, 243*ch*8*n*1, 243*ch*9*n*2, 248*ch*18*n*12, 249*ch*21*n*4
Cohen, Felix 67
Cox, Hank 188, 232
Crawford, Charles 56, 82, 239
Crooks, Col. William 43, 47, 70, 71, 91, 93, 205
Crow Creek Reservation 221, 226
Cut Nose (Dakota man) 71–72, 120, 124, 184–186, 203, 216, 227

Daniels, Dr. Asa 14, 128, 239*ch*1*n*1
Daniels, Dr. Jared 166–168, 249*ch*21*n*9, 249*ch*21*n*44
death march 213–215
decapitation 142, 167, 168, 170, 180; *see also* atrocities
defense counsel 71, 73, 74, 79
Deloria, Vine, Jr. 17
Derounian-Stodola, Kathryn Zabelle 153, 166, 176, 201, 202, 233, 239*ch*1*n*1
de Vattel, Emmerich 5, 142, 143, 144, 148, 149; *see also* *Law of Nations*
Dole, William P. 101, 106
Duley, Laura 153, 155, 193, 225, 250*ch*21*n*41
Duley, William 122, 193, 203

Eastlick, Lavina 28, 29, 174, 200, 220, 225; description of massacre 175–176
Eastlick, Merton 28, 200–201, 220, 225
Ebell, Adrian J. 63, 153, 185, 199
Engenhofer, Theresa 29–30
ethnic cleansing 126, 129–131, 231, 247*ch*14*n*3

Faribault, David, Jr. 134
Faribault, David, Sr. 91, 157

Flandrau, Charles E. 21, 29, 30, 63, 69, 112, 116, 125, 180
Folwell, William 31, 68, 85, 144, 181, 191–192, 235, 246ch13n51
Forfeiture Act of 1863 219
Fort Abercrombie 241ch4n29
Fort Ridgely 21, 22, 24, 25, 30, 33, 56, 164, 166, 167, 236
Fort Snelling 26, 57, 76, 88, 112, 114, 115, 126, 127, 128, 129, 135, 136, 211, 213, 214, 215, 220, 221, 235
Freniere, Antoine 13, 72, 104, 240ch2n27

Galbraith, Thomas 13, 15, 211, 241ch2n1
General Order No. 55 38, 60, 61, 82, 85
genocide 129, 130, 231
Gere, the Rev. Ezekial 84, 161
Gere, Lt. Thomas 25, 26
Gilman, Rhoda 11, 42, 243ch8n1
Godfrey, Joseph 47; trial of 52–53, 55, 72, 81, 85, 86, 95, 113, 119; atrocity allegations 173, 203, 223
Good Star Woman (Dakota woman) 116, 215
Grant, Capt. Hiram 33, 43, 47, 205

Halleck, Gen. Henry W. 37, 50, 60, 64, 75, 102, 150, 238
Hassrick, Royal 8, 17
Heard, Lt. Isaac V.D. 13, 49, 69, 70, 71, 72, 75, 76, 79, 85, 86, 92, 134, 160, 161, 162, 172, 180, 182, 184, 187, 200, 202, 203, 224, 233
Henderson, Minnesota 112, 116, 117, 181, 214, 219, 221, 235
Holcombe, Return I. 7, 160, 165, 199, 239ch1n5, 242ch4n47, 242ch6n9
Holt, Judge Adv. Gen. Joseph 99–100, 132–133, 135, 238
Humphrey, John 104, 219
Humphrey, Dr. Philander 167, 169, 219
Hurd, Alomina 28–29
Hutchinson, Minnesota 3, 34, 109

Indian Agent 13, 14, 16, 17, 20, 21, 25, 33, 193, 210, 211
Inefeldt, Wilhelmina 173, 174; description of massacre 175
Inkpaduta (Dakota chief) 21
intertribal warfare 16, 17, 144–145
Isch, John 18, 29, 67, 84, 117, 191, 234, 240ch3n7, 245ch11n2, 249ch20n22, 251ch23n1, 252ch27n7

Judge Advocate 64, 70–73, 235, 244ch10n7; see also Olin, Lt. Rollin
Judge Advocates General 66, 73, 99, 132, 133, 135, 238, 243ch8n21

Krueger, Justina 169, 187, 193, 218, 221, 224–225; description of atrocities 174

LaBatte, John 161–162, 199, 212, 214, 234, 245ch13n13
Lake Shetek, Minnesota see massacre
Law of Nations 142–145, 148, 157; see also de Vattel, Emmerich
Lincoln, Pres. Abraham 3, 16, 21, 73, 77, 95, 107, 111, 118, 146, 159, 177, 178, 194; commutation of sentences 134–135; correspondence with Gov. Ramsey 37, 99, 106; issuance of execution order 108, 110, 193; review of sentences 100–105, 112–113; and the U.S. Senate 113, 119, 191
Little Crow (Dakota chief) 4, 7, 15 38, 40, 94, 123, 124, 135, 200 226, 240ch3n10, 240ch3n13, 248ch18n14, 252ch27n2; correspondence with Sibley 34–35; death 222–223; in war counsels 20–23, 25, 30, 33
Little Paul (Dakota man) 35, 241n41
Little Six see Shakopee

Lower Agency 8, 11, 13, 15, 21, 23, 24–25, 26, 27, 30, 32, 33, 56, 62, 63, 74, 78, 86, 103, 114, 116, 166, 199, 205, 219, 235, 252ch26n7

Macomb, Gen. Alexander 53, 94
Maguire, Peter 204–205
Mahpeokanaje see Cut Nose
Malmros, Adj. Gen. Oscar 49, 234
Mankato (Dakota chief) 30, 37
Mankato, Minnesota 2, 3, 31, 107, 108, 110, 114, 116, 120, 121, 127, 137, 160, 193, 205, 214, 215, 216
Marsh, Capt. John S. 25–26, 30, 33, 159, 164, 167, 200, 218, 241ch4n9
Marshall, Lt. Col. William 43, 47, 62, 70, 90, 115, 205, 215, 223, 235
Martinez, David 54, 111–112, 124, 242ch5n1
massacre 7, 8–9, 14, 16, 43, 78, 89, 90, 107, 111, 112, 122, 144, 159, 171, 174, 176, 183, 198, 225, 226; Beaver Creek 185; Lake Shetek 8, 28, 29, 193, 200, 220, 225; Milford 27, 29
Mazakutemani (Dakota man) see Little Paul
McConkey, Harriet Bishop 74, 170, 171–173, 174, 184–185, 186, 188, 193, 199, 201, 204, 232, 234
Medicine Bottle (Dakota man) 124, 135–136
Meyer, Roy 152, 166–168, 177, 181
Michno, Gregory 249ch19n6, 250n12
Milford, Minnesota 3, 27, 29, 52, 53, 78, 105, 162, 219, 241ch4n14; see also massacre
Miller, Col. Stephen 107, 108, 109, 110, 121, 202, 223, 246ch13n51
Milord, Henry 40, 82, 120, 203, 216
Minnesota Historical Society 2, 40, 48, 93, 123, 129, 137, 144, 165, 191, 192, 209, 210, 223, 228, 231, 241ch4n21
missionaries 17, 20, 42, 102, 103, 104, 196, 210, 223; see also Adams, the Rev. Moses; Riggs, the Rev. Stephen R.; Williamson, John; Williamson, Thomas S.
Myrick, Andrew 74, 221, 252ch26n7

Neill, Edward D. 29, 171, 199
New Ulm, Minnesota 3, 24, 25, 28, 56, 69, 78, 83, 100, 154, 186, 212, 219; Battle of 30–31, 86, 91, 116, 156, 157, 161–162, 180, 215; riot at 112, 116–118, 181, 205, 214, 235
Nicolay, John G. 21, 24, 131, 187, 199
Nix, John 100, 117, 122, 124, 202, 203
Northfield Raid 122–123

O'Brien, John 71, 149
Oehler, C.M. 170, 187–188
Ojibway see Chippewa
Olin, Lieut. Rollin 71, 72, 235, 244ch10n7; see also Judge Advocate
Otakle see Godfrey, Joseph

Pond, the Rev. Samuel W. 18, 144–145, 170, 225, 248ch18n8
Pope, Gen. John 14, 37, 43, 48–64, 76, 93, 99, 100, 102, 105, 106–107, 115, 130, 133, 153, 191, 204, 242ch5n1; interference with the trials 54–55, 56, 57, 77, 85, 88, 94, 132, 242ch7n11

Quinn, George 163–164
Quinn, Peter 26, 159, 164

Ramsey, Gov. Alexander 26, 48, 108, 112, 130, 187; correspondence with Lincoln 37, 99, 106
rape 57, 79, 108, 124, 131, 142, 146, 149, 152–155, 163, 178, 181, 216, 225, 228, 229, 236, 249ch19n6; allegations 4,

141, 187; charges 47, 55–56, 83, 85, 86, 100, 119; *see also* atrocities
Rdainyanka (Dakota man) 35, 111, 122, 203, 204
Redwood Ferry, Minnesota 15, 30, 33, 163, 169; ambush 25–26, 159, 200, 218
Renville, Gabriel (Dakota man) 47, 128
Renville County 2, 26, 169, 193, 198
review of sentences 3, 57, 62, 89, 90, 92, 94, 99, 105, 108, 114, 118, 132, 135, 191, 204
Reyff, Emanuel 121, 168, 220, 250*ch*21*n*39; description of atrocities 174–175
Rice, Sen. Henry M. 101, 147
Riggs, the Rev. Stephen R. 16, 69, 71, 76, 79, 87, 90, 101, 102, 109–110, 111, 154, 160, 165, 186, 193, 194, 195–196, 200, 202, 205, 223, 224, 248*ch*18*n*8; letters 47–48, 79, 86, 103–104, 134, 154; *see also* missionaries
Roddis, Louis 148, 248*ch*18*n*25

Satterlee, Marion 45, 59, 71, 85, 191, 198, 235
scalping 167, 169, 175, 179, 180, 222
Schwandt, Mary 153–154, 187, 193, 220, 249*ch*19*n*8
Scott, Gen. Winfield 68, 237
Shakopee (Dakota man) 4, 19, 30, 123; trial and execution 135–136
Sheardown, Dr. Damuel B. 29, 105
Sheehan, Lt. Timothy 25, 26
Shoonkaska *see* White Dog
Sibley, Gen. Henry H. 10, 15, 32, 100, 106, 107, 108–110, 115, 132–134, 147, 155, 161, 171, 179, 192, 195, 201, 202, 204, 215, 221, 222–223, 225, 227, 237–238, 242*ch*5*n*1, 242*ch*5*n*4, 243*ch*8*n*1; appointment of the military commission 43, 47, 48; appointment to military command 26, 41; Battle of Wood Lake 36–37; correspondence with Indians 34–35; interference with judicial process 91–95; New Ulm riot 116–117
Soldiers' Lodge 19, 30
Spirit Lake, Iowa 21
Stanton, Secretary of War Edward 37, 38, 99, 132, 238
stereotyped charge sheet 85, 90, 91, 156, 157, 194
Strout, Capt. Richard 33–34, 160
Swisshelm, Jane Grey 129, 180–181

Taopee (Dakota man) 34, 35
Taoyateduta *see* Little Crow
Tatagaga (Dakota man) 194, 216
Tatemina (Dakota man) 119, 203
Tazoo (Dakota man) 56, 81, 119, 124, 154, 155, 216, 227
Tehehdoneche (Dakota man) 55, 81
Toonnannakinyaoahatka (Dakota man) 9, 135
Treaty of 1851 *see* Treaty of Traverse des Sioux
Treaty of Traverse des Sioux 11, 12, 42, 51
trial transcripts 9, 52, 53, 56, 79, 80, 85, 86, 92, 95, 154, 157, 178, 185, 186, 191, 196, 235, 245*ch*11*n*2, 248*ch*18*n*25; Anderson's claims about 81–82; general description 48–49; loss and rediscovery 191–192, 231, 251*ch*23*n*1; Presidential review 100, 108, 159

Upper Agency 8, 11, 35, 36, 219

vigilantism 101, 107, 110, 128, 196, 180, 181

Wabasha (Dakota chief) 4, 34–35, 111, 204
Wahehud (Dakota man) 10, 124, 157–159, 216
Wakefield, Sarah 155, 194–196, 201, 202, 220, 235, 241*ch*4*n*41
Wamditanka *see* Big Eagle
War Department, U.S. 22, 37, 60, 64, 70, 93, 94, 99, 133, 143, 191
Waziyatawin 126, 127, 130, 148, 152, 213–214, 216–217, 218, 247*ch*16*n*1
Welles, Secretary of Navy Gideon 14, 99, 106, 182
Whipple, Bishop Henry B. 15, 84, 90, 92, 102, 147, 161, 245*ch*13*n*13
White Dog 26, 119, 124, 159–160, 200, 202, 216, 247*ch*15*n*15
White Spider (Dakota man) 25, 34
Wilkinson, Sen. Morton 99, 105–106, 108, 119, 130, 146, 178, 191, 234, 250*ch*21*n*48
Williams, Mattie 153, 154, 155, 178
Williamson, John 79, 102, 136, 214; *see also* missionaries
Williamson, Thomas S. 102, 103–104, 135, 196; *see also* missionaries
Wilson, Waziyatawin Angela *see* Waziyatawin
Winthrop, William 50
Woolworth, Alan 165, 214, 231
Wowinape (Dakota man) 23, 94, 132–134, 222
Wright, Julia 153, 155, 176, 225